CREDITS

The Illuminati (Concept Team)

Cam Banks (*design lead*), Rob Donoghue, Matt Forbeck, Will Hindmarch, Philippe-Antoine Ménard, and Jesse Scoble.

Advanced Idea Mechanics (Design Support Team)

Dave Chalker, John Harper, Jeremy Keller (*art director*), Jack Norris, and Aaron Sullivan.

Damage Control (Editing Team)

Amanda Valentine (*managing editor*) with Sally Christensen, Matthew Gandy, Miranda Horner, Alex Perry, and Chad Underkoffler.

Wrecking Crew (Playtesters)

Scott Acker: Kristin Strickland, Matthew Strickland, James Buckingham, Christopher Acker; **Daniel Bacon—**Dark Sun Gang: Robert Sutton, Joseph Zabinski, Kristian Cardillo, Steven Farrell, Robert Smith, Michael Callahan; **Cam Banks—**UTC Gamers: Chris Adkins, Jeremy Keller, Adam Minnie, Michelle Nephew, Mark Reed; **Jeremy Beyer:** Ray Axmann, Seth Tiede, Risa Barrett, Dan Hemmingsen, Daniel Moenning, Tyler Wagner; **Joseph Blomquist:** Mary Blomquist, Katie Bond, Angie Espelage, Adam Lake, Jeff Lewis, Mike Walter; **T. Rob Brown—**The Midwest Avengers: Chad Denton, Jason Denton, Travis Shofler; **James Carpio—**Connecticut Crusaders: Adam Rinehart, Matt Millman, Gregory Krakovich, Mike "Best there is at what I do" Pankenier, Mary "Storm" Lindholm, Justin Schneider, Shane McCarthy; **Dave Chalker—**The Piledrivers: Fred Hicks, Kate Kirby, Dennis Twigg, Jim Henley, Josh Drobina, E Foley, Bob Bretz, Brennan Taylor, Irven Keppen, Tim Rodriguez, Brendan Conway, Matt Dukes, Danny Rupp, Dean Gilbert, Gerald Cameron, Quinn Murphy; **Jason Childs—**West Coast Wrecking Crew: Peter Childs, Kelli Turpin, Roger Bogh, John Gradilla, Ron Robinson, Robert Barry; **Joshua H. Coons:** Mark R. Crump, Keith Grace, Brandon Schipper, Richard Ignasiak II, Charles Boswell; **Jason Corley—**Vistamar College Fighting Chimeras: Kim Corley, Ryan Franklin, Golda Lloyd, Sara Kuwahara; **James Dawsey—**The Dawsey Posse: Brad Rogers, Jamal Hassan, Jeremy Dawsey, Jeremy Moore; **Matthew D. Gandy—**You Burst into Flames!: Travis Bryant, Tim Gemma, Andy Kitkowski, Joey Rodgers; **Matthew D. Gandy—**Clone Saga: Julie Baker, Mark Causey III, Darren Hennessey, Michael Kelly, Eric Provost; **Mark Garbrick:** Kelley Hightower, Jennifer Bedell, John Wright, Matthew Smith, **Roger Gray—**Blackland Gaming Group: Jim, Paul, Conner, Chris; **Jim Henley—**Scoot!: Bill Dowling, Kirt Dankmyer, Abigail Hanley; **Will Hindmarch—**Marvel Knights: Anne Petersen, Marty Gleason; **Wayne Humfleet—**The Ancient Gamers: Jeff Ayers, Tom Carpenter, Brian Kelley, Tom Kimball, George Delamater, Reg Klubeck, Chris Perrin; **Justin D. Jacobson:** Jeffrey Piroozshad, Mark Rickard, Steven Baker, Michael Ruiz; **Seth Johnson:** John Aegard, Wilhelm Fitzpatrick, Kristian Happa-Aho, Jon Leitheusser; **Rob Justice—**The Bear Swarm!: Michael Curry, Brett Zeiler, Darryl Loyd, Chad Brinkley, Jacob Evans, Jeremy Elder, Kevin Parrott; **Tim Kirk:** Larry Tull, Eve Tull, Allison Glass, Jeremy "Chu" Carroll, Chris Cox; **Christian Lindke—**The Champions of Los Angeles: Wes Kobernick, Joel Allan, James Leszuk, Jason Parker, Eric Lytle; **Paul Marcinkevage:** Harry Kaiserian, Bill White, Clark Valentine, Amanda Valentine; **Philippe-Antoine Ménard:** Yan Décarie, Alexandre David, François Jauvin, Pierre-Marc Giroux; **Joseph Meyer:** Mike Lafferty, David Goodner, Stacie Winters, Kevin Mowery, Stacey Montgomery; **Jay Miller:** Lisa Miller, Stewart Mabey, John Cheraz; **Adam Minnie—**The Other Midwest Avengers: Kelsey Speer, Aaron Speer, Stephanie Ingold, Paul Silber, Matthew Silber; **Quinn Murphy:** Gerald Cameron, Ryven Cedrylle, Matt Sheridan; **Jack Norris—**Mike Holmes, Jason Inglert, Lindsey McHenry, Matt Miller, Stephanie Miller, Danielle Reimer, Lauren Ringersma, Charles Sturgis; **Craig Payne:** Adam Berry, Chris Coates, Graham Handby, James Hunt, Mark Peyton; **Alex Perry:** Adam Perry, Marianna Csaszar; **Christopher Pierce—**Game Citadel Gamers: Merlin and Michelle Littlefield, Frank Hartnett, Logan McLaughlin, Gabriel Perro, Joshua Wilson, Zach Zoroya, Brian Barnes, Eric Knowlton; **Christopher Ruthenbeck:** Josh Acker, Ashley Adams, Brendan Flaherty, Amber Flaherty, Mark Miller, Mason Miller, Ryan Vent; **Eric Smailys—**The Wildcards:James Baize,Curtis McClain,Richard Altman,Brent Avis; **Bob Smith—**Battleground: Leonidas Argyropoulos, Dan Bacon, Jared Brown, Jason Gerstein, Alan Lucas, Sam Pearson; **David Thomas—**The Midwest Maulers: Genna Thomas, Tiffany Thomas, Eric Schroeder, Tom Holley; **Talon Waite:** Lauren Valentine; **Stacie "Glass" Winters:** Kelly "Fabien" Kiel, Justin "Savagehominid" Smith, Rausha Furgason, Erika Zofchak, Nick Wiedmaier.

Licensing

Jamie Kampel (*Marvel*), Christi Cardenas (*MWP*).

Special Thanks

D. Vincent Baker, Jessica Banks, the Bear Swarm! Podcast, Brian Michael Bendis, Dungeon Crawler Radio, Jeff Grubb, Hugh Hawkins, Fred Hicks, Steve Kenson, Paul Marcinkevage, Nearly Enough Dice Podcast, Clinton R. Nixon, Brian Overton, the Podge Cast, Mike Selinker, Source Comics & Games, Dave Thomas, Clark Valentine, Vigilance Press Podcast, Margaret Weis, and Jennifer Wong.

marvel.com

TM & © 2012 Marvel & Subs.

FOREWORD

Pick a side. It's your choice, and I'm not going to tell you what to do. But before you do, know that I'm on Captain America's side. Always have been, always will be.

I told Joe Simon that once. With Jack Kirby, he created Captain America at Timely Comics, which would soon become Marvel. Joe and I talked at San Diego Comic-Con, where I also met Stan Lee and Will Eisner in a dizzying 24 hours. I was showing off the *Marvel Super Heroes Adventure Game*, one of many in the long line of Marvel RPGs that led to this one.

I told Joe that I made Cap the most effective hero in the game—better than Thor, better than Hulk, better than Doctor Strange. Those heroes had powers, but Captain America had something better. Captain America had heart. In my game, Cap used that heart to power through more options than any other hero. When all the chips were down, you wanted to be Captain America.

But it's one thing to show what's in your heart when you're fighting the Red Skull or Doctor Doom or Adolf Hitler. It's quite another to show it when you're fighting *America*.

The Civil War presented Captain America with his greatest challenge. In the wake of a massacre that claimed dozens of children, Cap had to pick a side. He could have sided with Iron Man and Mr. Fantastic and Hank Pym—true heroes all—in their support of an act that required super heroes to register themselves. All America wanted was for its heroes to sign on the dotted line.

And then the living symbol of America thought about what that meant. He knew what it meant for Jews to sign on that line. He knew what it meant for Communists. He knew what it meant for atheists and gays and illegal immigrants. And even though it would eventually cost him his life, this is what he said in *Amazing Spider-Man #537*:

> Doesn't matter what the press says. Doesn't matter what the politicians or the mobs say. Doesn't matter if the whole country decides that something wrong is something right. This nation was founded on one principle above all else: the requirement that we stand up for what we believe, no matter the odds or the consequences. When the mob and the press and the whole world tell you to move, your job is to plant yourself like a tree beside the river of truth, and tell the whole world, "No, *you* move."

I'm on that guy's side.
Now, pick a side. Just make sure it's the right one.

Mike Selinker is the president of Lone Shark Games. He's worked on six Marvel games—seven if you count this intro—and makes it his personal goal to get the Mole Man's line "Curse you, surface dwellers!" into any such game he touches. Mission accomplished.

CONTENTS

Page numbers beginning with OM refer to the OPERATIONS MANUAL. Page numbers beginning with CW refer to the CIVIL WAR EVENT BOOK.

OPERATIONS M

Writing & Design
Cam Banks

Editing
Amanda Valentine (lead)
Matthew Gandy

Art Direction
Jeremy Keller

Cover & Interior Layout
Jeremy Keller

Graphic Design Concepts
John Harper

Cover & Interior Art
Marvel Bullpen

Before you start learning how to play **MARVEL HEROIC ROLEPLAYING**, you need an idea of what to expect. This part of the book is the OPERATIONS MANUAL, and it includes all of the game rules, divided into chapters. If you're a new player, we recommend reading the chapters in order.

01 INTRODUCTION

This chapter introduces all of the basic rules, from dice to actions to the doom pool to Plot Points.

02 PLAYING THE GAME

This chapter takes the top-down approach of how the game works, from the use of Events and Acts to the difference between an Action Scene and a Transition Scene.

03 TAKING ACTION

This chapter expands the rules to cover actions, reactions, super heroic battles, and emotionally charged conflict.

04 UNDERSTANDING DATAFILES

This chapter defines heroic characters and all of the many amazing things they can do, including Power Sets and Specialties.

05 UNDERSTANDING EVENTS

This chapter defines what Events are, how the heroes interact with them, and how to prepare them in advance.

01

INTRODUCTION

Face front, True Believers! In this game you play super heroes in the Marvel Universe, like the Avengers, Fantastic Four, or the X-Men.

As a **player**, it's your job to make decisions for your super hero, using your knowledge of his motivation and personality as a guide to how he uses his amazing powers and abilities. Players are like comic book writers and artists—they bring these super heroes to life, making the big and small choices for them, and that's what you'll do at the game table.

One player has a special job—the **Watcher**, after the enigmatic figure of the same name who observes the many timelines of the Marvel Universe and interferes from time to time at the behest of fate. This player is responsible for maintaining the coherent universe around the super heroes. The Watcher needs to know the rules well enough to determine the outcomes of the heroes' decisions, to present those consequences to the players, and to move things along at a good pace. Often this means playing the part of super villains, helpful allies, and innocent bystanders.

In a roleplaying game, your fate lies with the whims of the dice and the Watcher, but your choices lead the charge. At every decision point, the direction of the story changes. Everyone shares their ideas, describes what their heroes (or villains!) are doing, and reveals an on-going story. You might even describe what you're imagining in terms of panels and pages in a comic book—establishing shots, splash pages, extreme close ups, huge sound effects. At the heart of this game is you, working with the other players and the Watcher to be awesome. When you've had a hard day of school or work, or you're frustrated with your neighbor or the news, it's fun to get in character, ham it up a little with your friends, and play a Marvel super hero!

On your hero's **datafile** you'll find everything you need to know about your hero and the **traits**—powers, significant backgrounds, abilities, and so on—that you can use in the game. A datafile is the game equivalent of an entry in the *Official Handbook of the Marvel Universe* or the Marvel.com Wiki. We've provided Captain America's datafile here to serve as an example.

Affiliations

The three **Affiliations** reflect how well the hero acts when SOLO, with a BUDDY, or as part of a TEAM. Cap functions at his best when he's with a Team. See page OM62 for more on Affiliations.

Distinctions

Most heroes have three **Distinctions**; these are typically defining backgrounds, personality traits, or catchphrases that summarize important facets of the hero's outlook and approach to life. Whenever his ability to LEAD BY EXAMPLE, his background as a MAN OUT OF TIME, or his identity as the so-called SENTINEL OF LIBERTY may help or hinder Cap, his Distinctions can come into play. See page OM67 for more on Distinctions.

Power Sets

Most heroes have at least one **Power Set**—many have two—which is a package of amazing powers and special effects (SFX). Every Power Set has at least one Limit. Cap has two Power Sets, one for the benefits of Dr. Erskine's Super-Soldier Program and another for his iconic shield. For more on Power Sets, see page OM70.

CAPTAIN AMERICA

Affiliations	SOLO **6**	BUDDY **8**	TEAM **10**

Distinctions
LEAD BY EXAMPLE
MAN OUT OF TIME
SENTINEL OF LIBERTY

4 +1 PP or **8**

Power Sets

SUPER-SOLDIER PROGRAM

ENHANCED DURABILITY **8**	ENHANCED REFLEXES **8**
ENHANCED STAMINA **8**	ENHANCED STRENGTH **8**

SFX: *Immunity.* Spend 1 PP to ignore stress, trauma, or complications from poison, disease, or fatigue.
SFX: *Last-Ditch Effort.* Step up or double any SUPER-SOLDIER PROGRAM die on your next roll, or spend 1 PP to do both, then shutdown that power. Recover power by activating an opportunity or during a Transition Scene.
SFX: *Second Wind.* Before you make an action including a SUPER-SOLDIER PROGRAM power, you may move your physical stress die to the doom pool and step up the SUPER-SOLDIER PROGRAM power by +1 for this action.
Limit: *Patriot.* Earn 1 PP if you step up emotional stress inflicted by government forces or popular opinion by +1.

VIBRANIUM-ALLOY SHIELD

GODLIKE DURABILITY **12**	WEAPON **8**

SFX: *Area Attack.* Target multiple opponents. For every additional target, add D6 to your pool and keep +1 effect die.
SFX: *Ricochet.* Step up or double WEAPON die against a single target. Remove highest-rolling die and add an additional die to your total.
Limit: *Gear.* Shutdown VIBRANIUM-ALLOY SHIELD and gain 1 PP. Take an action vs. the doom pool to recover gear.

Specialties

ACROBATIC EXPERT **8**	COMBAT MASTER **10**
COVERT EXPERT **8**	PSYCH EXPERT **8**
VEHICLE EXPERT **8**	

[You may convert Expert D8 to 2D6, or Master D10 to 2D8 or 3D6]

Milestones

MENTOR THE HERO

1 XP when you choose to aid a specific hero for the first time.
3 XP when you aid a stressed-out hero in recovery.
10 XP when you either give leadership of the team to your chosen hero or force your chosen hero to resign or step down from the team.

AVENGERS ASSEMBLE!

1 XP when you first lead a team.
3 XP when you defeat a foe without any team member becoming stressed out.
10 XP when you either convince a hero to join a new Avengers team or disband your existing team.

PP

STRESS / TRAUMA

P
▲
6
8
10
12
M
▲
6
8
10
12
E
▲
6
8
10
12

XP

Specialties

Specialties represent the skills, contacts, knowledge, and training that each hero has beyond the level of an average person. Each Specialty is rated at either Expert or Master. Master Specialties are somewhat rare, but Expert Specialties are quite common among super heroes. Cap's an Expert at such things as acrobatic leaps, acting covertly, interacting with people, and piloting vehicles, but he's a Master at many forms of martial arts and weapons. For more on Specialties, see page OM96.

Name

This is the hero's costumed identity or heroic name—in this case, Captain America.

ID

This is the hero's real name—or at least the name he uses when he's not in costume—and whether his identity is kept secret or publicly known. Sometimes it's the same as his hero name. Cap's real name is Steve Rogers, and it's not a secret.

Steve Rogers [public]

History

Born in the early 20th Century in New York City to poor Irish parents, Steve Rogers grew up sickly. Despite his heartfelt desire to aid his country in its struggle against the Axis powers, his frailties disqualified him from active military service. However, his unyielding determination and moral character resulted in his being chosen for the top-secret Operation: Rebirth project. Dr. Abraham Erskine's Super-Soldier process transformed Rogers into a peerless physical specimen—a success that would never be reproduced thereafter, due to Erskine's subsequent murder at the hands of a Nazi spy. Trained and equipped as a spy-busting propaganda asset to counterbalance Germany's Red Skull, Rogers became Captain America. Accompanied by his partner Bucky Barnes, Captain America fought alongside the Sub-Mariner and the original Human Torch as a member of the Invaders.

While trying to stop a rocket weapon of Baron Zemo's, Barnes apparently died and Rogers was lost to the icy waters of the North Atlantic. The Super-Soldier formula put Rogers into a state of suspended animation, while the world thought him dead for decades. Eventually discovered and revived by the Avengers in more recent times, Captain America had to adapt to a world half a century different than the one that shaped him.

Personality

Captain America is the moral measure against whom most other heroes compare themselves. He is the hero's hero—fearless, selfless, noble, and unyielding. Rogers lives the ideals he represents—they aren't simply a code he espouses and works to uphold. Equality and fairness, justice and liberty for all—these are fundamental to Cap's basic character, not just words, and his every action demonstrates this.

Abilities & Resources

Operation: Rebirth transformed Rogers into the pinnacle of physical perfection. Captain America's body operates at the maximum of human physical potential, giving him levels of strength, endurance, and agility that would shame world-class athletes. His body also makes him effectively im... poison, disease, and fat... trai... ...pects of military and tactical skill, and his close-quarter combat skills combine with his physical abilities to make him one of the single best hand-to-hand fighters alive. Rogers possesses extensive battlefield experience and years working in the intelligence community, and he is a natural leader with virtually unmatched powers of inspiration.

Captain America wears a scale-mail uniform of sophisticated anti-ballistic materials and carries a circular shield. This shield is one-of-kind—... cidental alloying of steel and Vibraniu... ...ity indestructible and known to da... ...tic energy impact entirely. In additi... ...ng it defensively, Rogers has master... ...se as a throwing weapon.

Steve Ro... ...a "champion level" S.H.I.E.L.D. agent... ...ffectively unlimited security clearance ...ccess to S.H.I.E.L.D. facilities, equipment, and personnel surpassed only by Director Nick Fury. He uses customized vehicles such as a high-tech van and a heavily modified motorcycle, both gifts from the Black Panther's people. Rogers is particularly close to fellow hero the Falcon and to S.H.I.E.L.D. agent Sharon Carter. Cap's reputation, particularly among the superhuman community, is unmatched—no other figure commands the degree of respect and loyalty among heroes that he does.

History

This is a short summary of the hero's history in the Marvel Universe, in case you need a refresher.

Personality

This gives you a brief overview of the hero's hopes, dreams, quirks, and flaws.

Abilities & Resources

This goes into a little more detail about what your hero's Power Sets, Specialties, and other resources represent. Armed with this information, you're better equipped to try stunts or describe your actions to the other players.

Milestones

Every hero confronts meaningful choices, some greater than others. A hero's **Milestones** provide a guide to the sorts of decisions the hero should make or seek out during play; in return, the player gains Experience Points (XP) to unlock datafile updates, gain new traits and resources, or trigger interesting developments in the story. Cap's Milestones deal with the decision to take another hero under his wing and the question of whether or not to reassemble the Avengers. See page OM105 for more on Milestones.

HERE'S WHAT YOU NEED TO PLAY THE GAME:

- This OPERATIONS MANUAL
- A MARVEL HEROIC ROLEPLAYING Event or prepared notes for the Watcher
- Hero datafiles for all the players
- A pile of game dice: four-sided, six-sided, eight-sided, ten-sided, and twelve-sided. You'll want to have at least a set for each player and two or three sets for the Watcher, which lets you share dice around when you need to.
- Poker chips, glass beads, coins, or other tokens to represent Plot Points
- A different kind of token, playing card, action figure, or index card to show when you've taken your action
- Pencils, scratch paper, index cards, or other tools to take notes (like a tablet PC or whiteboard)
- Some place to sit or gather where you can roll the dice out in the open

IT'S A GOOD IDEA TO HAVE THE FOLLOWING:

- Cheat sheets for the Watcher and players (downloaded from www.margaretweis.com)
- Snacks and beverages
- Extra copies of the OPERATIONS MANUAL
- More sets of dice

DICE

This game uses **four-sided, six-sided, eight-sided, ten-sided,** and **twelve-sided dice**. To make things easier, these dice are abbreviated like this: D4, D6, D8, D10, D12. When there are several dice of the same type, the multiplier goes before the D so it looks like this: 2D6, 3D10. Dice are used to rate a character's **traits**: smaller sized dice represent traits that often attract trouble or complication; larger dice represent traits that usually assure success and time in the spotlight. Traits of any kind are indicated in the text with small capitals like this: TRAIT D6.

The difference in size between a D4 and D6 is called a **step**. The difference between a D4 and a D8 is two steps, and so on. **Stepping up** a die means you switch it out for a die with more sides. **Stepping back** a die is the opposite. Stepping back a D4 **removes** the die altogether. You can't step dice up beyond D12—usually the rules tell you something else happens (such as a hero being stressed out by taking more than D12 stress); otherwise you should step up the next highest die on hand (such as in a dice pool).

WHEN TO ROLL THE DICE

When you roll the dice, the Watcher or another player rolls their dice in response to see how things work out. Any time there's a meaningful choice to make, you can bring out the dice. Not every situation needs you to "roll the bones," however. Use the following lists as a guide for when dice are appropriate.

Roll the dice when...
▶ You're not sure if your hero will succeed or fail.
▶ You want to try something that's bold, challenging, or dangerous.
▶ You want to oppose, challenge, or thwart another character.
▶ You want to show off your hero's super-powers or cool abilities.

Don't roll the dice when...
▶ The outcome isn't an interesting part of the story.
▶ There's no risk, challenge, or threat involved.
▶ The only outcome of either success or failure is that nothing happens.
▶ There's nothing or nobody to stop your hero from doing something.
▶ The situation is outside your hero's ability to change.

What if the Watcher says that a situation doesn't need dice, but you want to make a big deal out of it anyway? This is your call as a player; make a case for why you want to raise the stakes and what the potential outcomes might be. If this happens, though, you have to deal with whatever consequences the dice have in store!

THE DICE POOL

Whenever you want your hero to do something for which the outcome isn't certain, the first thing you do is state clearly to the Watcher and the other players what your hero is trying to do. Then, assemble a collection of dice from various traits on your hero's datafile that support or help your hero achieve that goal. This is your **dice pool**.

Once you've added dice to the pool, it no longer matters where they came from; you don't need to keep track of which dice came from Power Sets, for instance.

ROLLING THE DICE

Roll your dice, right out there in the open, and leave them on the table for the time being. It may be helpful to arrange them in order from highest-rolling die to lowest. Set aside all of the dice that come up 1 for now. You won't use them in the next two steps.

If you don't have enough dice on hand to roll your entire pool at once, make a note on scratch paper before rerolling, or borrow from the other players. Be sure to note die type as well as the number rolled. Sometimes the dice pool can get to be a real handful. Be prepared!

I have a pool of seven dice that includes:

I roll the dice and get the following:

That's a lot of threes! I set aside the D8 and D6 that rolled 1 for now.

HERE'S A LIST OF TRAITS YOU CAN ADD TO YOUR DICE POOL:

- One Affiliation die
- One Distinction, either as a D8 or a D4
- One power from each of your Power Sets
- One Specialty
- One each of your opposition's stress or complication dice, if any
- One asset, if any
- One push die, stunt, or resource, if any

Choose any two dice that rolled higher than 1 to add together for your **total**. Your total is a measure of how much effort your hero has managed to put forward, so usually the higher the total, the better.

I'm going to take the 4 on the D10 and the 3 on one of the D8s and add them together for a total of 7.

TOTAL: **7**

You can use Plot Points to add more dice to the total. Each extra die costs 1 PP. You have to spend it now—you can't go back and add more to your total later. There are a lot of things to spend PP on, so make sure you won't want to spend it on something else later. After you set aside the dice that come up 1, if you're left with only one die, use that for your total. If you have no dice left, your total is zero.

I've got a Plot Point, so I spend that to add in the 3 from the D4, for a final total of 10.

TOTAL: **10**

Next, choose one of your remaining dice to be your **effect die**. This is a measure of how well your efforts have paid off. It might reflect the force of your blow, the helpfulness of your support, or the resistance of your defenses. You can choose any of your dice that didn't come up 1 and that you're not using for your total. You might settle for a smaller total in order to make a larger effect die available. Don't worry about the number result on the die; with effect dice it's just the type of die that matters.

Plot
Points
p. OM10

KEEPING TRACK OF DICE

In some games, the person who runs the game rolls the dice in secret—but there are no secrets in the Bullpen. Roll those bones in full view, Watchers!

Dice typically end up all over the table, so you might want to make a note on a sticky memo or scratch paper for a die that's going to hang around longer than a couple minutes of play. If you have plenty of dice, you can set them aside as a physical reminder.

FIERY EXPLOSION D8

You can use Plot Points to keep additional dice as effect dice. Each extra die costs 1 PP. Having multiple effect dice means you're able to demonstrate your effort in more than one way, such as taking out two thugs at the same time. If for some reason you have no dice left, you can always fall back to a D4 effect die. It's not great, but it's better than nothing.

I have a D8 and a D6 left, so I choose to take the D8 and use it for my effect die. If I hadn't spent my PP on including a third die in my total, I could have spent it here to keep the D6 as well.

TOTAL: **10**   EFFECT: **D8**

Any die that comes up a 1 is called an **opportunity**. It can't be used for the total or as an effect die; instead, the Watcher may use it to add dice to the **doom pool**, making the situation more challenging. If the Watcher rolls an opportunity, the players may use it to trigger certain **special effects (SFX)** on their Power Sets as well as some other things.

I rolled two ones, so that's two opportunities the Watcher may exploit. I can't add them into my total or use them as effect dice.

Doom Pool
p. OM14

SFX
p. OM88

Activating Watcher's Opportunities
p. OM12

ROLLING DICE SUMMARY

Here's a quick summary of how to roll dice.

1. Declare what your intent is before picking up dice.
2. Add dice to your pool from appropriate traits.
3. Roll dice and set aside any opportunities (dice that came up 1).
4. Add together two dice for your total. Spend PP to add more.
5. Choose one die for your effect. Spend PP to choose additional effect dice.
6. Declare total, effect die, and opportunities.
7. The Watcher or another player rolls dice in opposition. Compare totals to see which side wins.

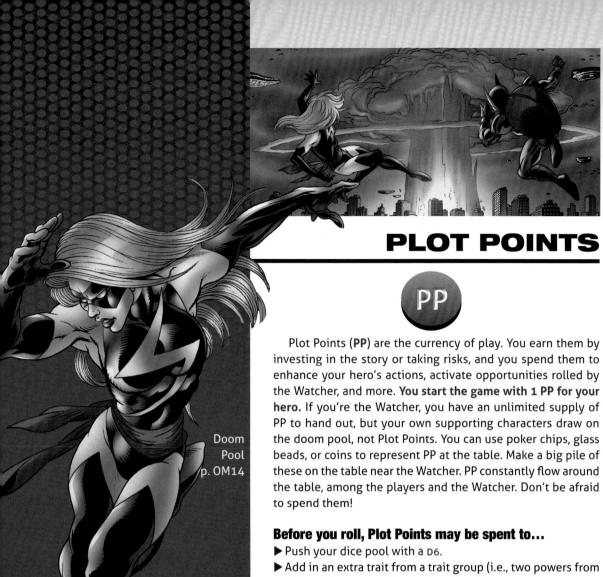

PLOT POINTS

PP

Doom
Pool
p. OM14

Plot Points (**PP**) are the currency of play. You earn them by investing in the story or taking risks, and you spend them to enhance your hero's actions, activate opportunities rolled by the Watcher, and more. **You start the game with 1 PP for your hero.** If you're the Watcher, you have an unlimited supply of PP to hand out, but your own supporting characters draw on the doom pool, not Plot Points. You can use poker chips, glass beads, or coins to represent PP at the table. Make a big pile of these on the table near the Watcher. PP constantly flow around the table, among the players and the Watcher. Don't be afraid to spend them!

Before you roll, Plot Points may be spent to...
▶ Push your dice pool with a D6.
▶ Add in an extra trait from a trait group (i.e., two powers from a Power Set, or two Distinctions).
▶ Add a stunt die for your Power Set or Specialty.
▶ Activate certain special effects (SFX) in a Power Set.

After You Roll, Plot Points may be spent to...
▶ Add an extra die from your roll to your total.
▶ Keep an extra effect die.
▶ Activate an opportunity rolled by the Watcher.
▶ Activate certain special effects (SFX) in a Power Set.
▶ Use an effect die from a reaction roll.
▶ Change stress you've taken to another type.

During a Transition Scene, Plot Points may be spent to...
▶ Add a resource die linked to a Specialty.

Plot Points may be earned when you...
▶ Use a Distinction negatively.
▶ Activate a Limit on a Power Set.
▶ Have an opportunity on your dice activated by the Watcher or another player to add to the doom pool.

SPENDING PLOT POINTS

Spending PP is always voluntary. You're never required to spend them, but the game depends on the flow of PP to keep things alive and exciting. When you spend PP, you usually drop the token that represents it—glass bead, poker chip, or coin, for instance—back into the communal pile in front of the Watcher. On some occasions, you pass the PP over to another player.

The Basic D6 Push

The least interesting—and least efficient—thing you can spend your PP on is to **push your dice pool with a D6** before you roll the dice. You can always fall back on this option if you can't think of any stunts to describe or you're out of ideas, or if your datafile doesn't have enough traits to represent the thing your hero is doing. Used in this way, the PP represents a moment of luck, some minor edge or extra effort on your hero's part to get things done. You don't have to explain it; you can just spend the PP and add the die and go.

If you create a push die when the Watcher gives you an opportunity (rolls one or more 1s), the push die is a D8, not a D6.

Add Extra Traits

Perhaps you have more than one power in a Power Set that seems appropriate, or more than one Specialty that could apply. Although you get one of these for free, **adding an extra trait to your dice pool** from each of these groups costs 1 PP. This is most useful when you have more than one rated at D10 or D12, and really not so useful when you have a D4 or D6.

Add a Stunt Die

If you can come up with a way to connect it to your Power Sets or Specialties, you can **add a D8 stunt die to your dice pool** instead of the default push D6. If you create a stunt die when the Watcher gives you an opportunity (rolls a 1 on the dice), the stunt die starts out as D10, not D8. For more on stunts, see page OM20.

Activate Special Effects

In some cases, you'll need to spend a PP to **activate SFX attached to Power Sets.**

SFX
p. OM88

Add An Extra Die To Your Total

When your dice all came up with low numbers or you're really trying to get a higher total than just two dice can offer, you can spend 1 PP to **add an extra die to your total.** You have to do this before you declare your total or choose your effect die. If you don't have extra dice to add in, this isn't an option. You can't use this to add in any dice that came up 1.

Keep An Extra Effect Die

You can spend 1 PP to **keep an additional effect die**. It doesn't combine with or add to the first one; you have to use it on something else. Do this when you describe a cool action you want your hero to take that actually ends up having multiple effects. You could compare it to those panel sequences in comics where the hero takes down one crook, then another, boom boom boom. For multiple effects you need multiple effect dice. You can use effect dice to create assets and complications as well as inflict stress, so think of it as a kind of combo—for instance, you might inflict some stress and hand an asset over to your buddy so he can follow through with his own attack.

Activate the Watcher's Opportunity

If a 1 comes up on any of the Watcher's dice, you can spend 1 PP to **activate the opportunity.**

▶ You can give yourself either a D8 push die for your dice pool or a stunt at D10. In other words, spending the PP when the Watcher rolls a 1 lets you create either the push D6 or the stunt D8 for your next roll and then immediately step it up by one. You can either use this on a reaction (if the Watcher gave you the opportunities on an action) or save it for your next action. If you're saving it, write a note as a reminder.
▶ You may use this to step up an asset you've just created with an effect die, or to create a resource during an Action Scene.
▶ Instead of creating a die, you can use the activated opportunity as a trigger for some SFX or Limits.

Use an Effect Die From a Reaction Roll

Normally, if you're making a reaction roll against the Watcher's action roll and you get a higher total than the action total, you've just stopped the opposition from doing what they wanted to (the action fails) but that's it. By spending a PP, you can also use your effect die to create an effect—stress, a complication, or an asset. See page OM49 for more on reaction rolls.

Change Stress You've Taken to Another Type

Many conflicts result in stress, which may be inflicted as physical, mental, or emotional. If you spend 1 PP, you can **change the type of stress** you've just taken into another type. This may keep you from getting stressed out, but it doesn't keep you from actually taking stress. For more on stress, see page OM23.

Add a Resource Die

During a Transition Scene, you can spend a PP to **add a resource die** connected to one of your Specialties. A resource is a temporary trait that represents a professional contact, a piece of equipment, or some kind of useful knowledge. Your resources start at D6 if you're an Expert and at D8 if you're a Master. The resource lasts until the end of the next Action Scene, which means you can use it more than once. If the Watcher gives you an opportunity (rolls 1 on the dice), you can create the resource during an Action Scene rather than waiting until after the action is over. For more on resources, see page OM20.

EARNING PLOT POINTS

If you don't earn more PP through play, you won't be nearly as astonishing, spectacular, or amazing. You start every game session with at least 1 PP, and there's no limit to how many you can earn during the game. Here's a list of where they come from.

Use a Distinction at D4

Your hero's Distinctions are defining qualities that draw from his background, personality, and famous catchphrases. When you add a Distinction to your dice pool, you get to choose whether it's a D8 (and therefore the Distinction represents something that's helpful or positive) or a D4 (and therefore it's a negative or complicating thing). Everyone at the game table may chime in and suggest one or the other, but it's your decision. **If you go with a D4, you earn 1 PP** from the communal pool in front of the Watcher. For more on Distinctions, see page OM67.

Activate a Limit on your Power Set

Most Power Sets have Limits attached to them—you can earn PP by shutting down or otherwise affecting your powers. **You may activate these yourself, or the Watcher may activate them**. If you do it yourself, you earn 1 PP. If the Watcher activates one of your Limits, it costs a die from the doom pool, but you don't get any PP. You get first refusal on this if you're the player—the Watcher may decide to spend doom pool dice, but only after giving you the chance to earn PP first.

The Watcher Activates an Opportunity

If you roll a 1 on any dice, **the Watcher may hand over a PP to activate the opportunity** and add a die to the doom pool. If you have multiple opportunities showing, the Watcher can use your extra opportunities to step up a single die going into the doom pool without giving you another PP—with two opportunities, a D6 can become a D8 and you only receive 1 PP. If the Watcher chooses to add multiple dice, you get a PP for each die that goes into the doom pool—those two opportunities could be 2D6 for the cost of two PP. We'll talk about the doom pool in the next section.

Limits
p. OM92

Doom Pool
p. OM14

THE DOOM POOL

The **doom pool** is the Watcher's resource for adding to the heroes' opposition and, at the end of an Act, populating the Event with additional threats, challenges, and situations. Dice in the doom pool are called **doom dice**. By default, the Watcher starts each Act with 2D6 in the doom pool, although some Acts may begin with larger or more dice (see Starting Doom Pool).

Acts,
Scenes,
Events
p. OM32

STARTING DOOM POOL

Act Type	Doom Pool
Standard	2D6
High Stakes	XD8
Catastrophic	XD10
Global Scale	3DX
Cosmic Scale	4DX

Note: The X in each case is the default, so if you have an Act that's both Cosmic Scale (4DX) and has Catastrophic Stakes (XD10), it's a 4D10 doom pool to start with.

I'm the Watcher and the players have chosen to play X-Men: Cyclops, Emma Frost, Beast, and Kitty Pryde. They're up against Hellfire Guards, masked thugs employed by the Inner Circle of the Hellfire Club. My doom pool starts at 2D6, as this isn't a high stakes or catastrophic Act and it won't be taking place at the global or cosmic scale.

DOOM POOL: **2D6**

BUILDING UP THE DOOM POOL

The doom pool grows as the session progresses, because a D6 is added to the doom pool whenever the Watcher activates an opportunity by handing a player a Plot Point. If multiple opportunities arise on the same roll, then the Watcher can step up the die by 1 for each additional opportunity. This doesn't cost extra PP. If the Watcher wants to instead add multiple dice to the doom pool, each additional die costs another PP.

Instead of adding a new D6 to the doom pool, the Watcher may step up the lowest die in the pool by 1. This gives the Watcher a means of making some of the doom dice larger without waiting for the players to roll multiple opportunities.

When adding dice to the doom pool, the Watcher can narrate something related to the action that was just taken—something that explains why the stakes are rising or the threat of imminent doom is increasing.

Cyclops' player rolls three 1s on his dice in a battle with the Hellfire Guards. As the Watcher, I could choose to hand over three Plot Points and add 3D6 to the doom pool, or two Plot Points for a D8 and a D6, or one Plot Point for a D10. I decide to go with the D8 and D6. Because Cyclops was using his optic blast against the Hellfire Guards, I decide that he's causing some incidental collateral damage and scaring the innocent bystanders. Now my doom pool stands at 3D6 and D8.

DOOM POOL: **3D6 + D8**

The Watcher may add to the doom pool directly by spending effect dice from a villain's action, rather than inflicting stress or creating a complication. This represents the villain causing general chaos and mayhem, threatening innocent bystanders, or grandstanding. It might not directly harm the heroes, but it makes things difficult for them later.

The doom pool also grows as a result of player actions. Some hero datafiles have Power Sets that include SFX tied to the doom pool, for example.

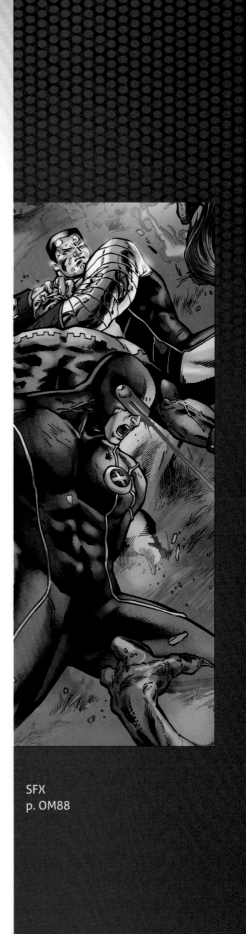

SFX
p. OM88

BEFORE THE ROLL, YOU CAN SPEND DOOM DICE TO...

- Add a doom die to a dice pool.
- Activate certain villain SFX.

AFTER THE ROLL, YOU CAN SPEND DOOM DICE TO...

- Add an extra die from the roll to the total (doom die size or smaller).
- Keep an extra effect die from your roll when attacking multiple targets (doom die size or smaller).
- Use an effect die from a reaction roll.
- Activate certain villain SFX.

DURING A SCENE, YOU CAN SPEND DOOM DICE TO...

- Create a new Scene Distinction (D8 or larger).
- Interrupt the action order with a Watcher character.
- Split a hero off from the rest of the situation (re-adjusting the SOLO/BUDDY/TEAM dynamic).
- Activate Scene or Event effects.
- Spend 2D12 to end the Scene immediately.

USING THE DOOM POOL

During the game, as the Watcher you may use dice from the doom pool in much the same way as players use their PP. Each use "costs" the die used to trigger it; remove the die from the doom pool unless otherwise specified. In some cases, the size of the dice in the doom pool limits what you can do with them.

Add a Die to a Dice Pool

You can spend a doom die and **add it directly to a dice pool** before you roll the dice. This can be for any action or reaction being performed by your Watcher characters. You're just moving the die from the doom pool to your dice pool for that action or reaction. To move it back to the doom pool after you've used it like this, you have to hand over 1 PP to the player or players the action or reaction targeted. Otherwise the die just goes away.

Activate Villain Special Effects

Many villains have Power Sets, and the SFX listed with those Power Sets often use the doom pool where a hero's SFX would use PP. Any sized doom die may be spent to **activate these SFX**, unless otherwise specified.

Add an Extra Die to the Total

You can **add more dice to the total**. To do this, you need to spend a doom die of the same size or larger than the die you want to add. Adding a D8 to the total would require spending a D8, D10, or D12 from the doom pool.

Add an Extra Effect Die

You can **keep an additional effect die** from your roll. To do this, you need to spend a doom die of the same size or larger than the die you want to keep. Keeping a D8 effect die would require spending a D8, D10, or D12 from the doom pool.

As the Watcher, it's my turn to make an attack on behalf of one of the two Hellfire Guards, but they're just a minor threat: STANDARD HELLFIRE GUARD D6 (SOLO D4, BUDDY D6, TEAM D8), ENERGY BLASTERS D6. Right now my dice pool is 3D6 (D6 from BUDDY, D6 from STANDARD HELLFIRE GUARD, and D6 from ENERGY BLASTERS). I decide to spend the D8 out of my doom pool to make the Guard's dice pool 3D6 + D8.

Once I roll the dice, I could spend one of the remaining six-siders in the doom pool to add a third die to my total, or maybe keep a second effect die, but only if the die I added or kept was a D6.

Use an Effect Die from a Reaction Total

Just as players may use PP to use an effect die from a reaction roll, you as Watcher can spend a D6 or larger out of the doom pool and do the same. Describe how the defending character capitalizes on the opening the hero made for him, either as a clever riposte or a distraction. For more on effect dice, see page OM48.

Create a New Scene Distinction

You can spend a doom die to **create a new Distinction** directly in the Scene. Scene distinctions require a D8 or larger from the doom pool. These must be entirely situation or location-based, like BURNING HALLWAY or PANICKED CROWD. These primarily exist to oppose the heroes in your opposition pool or be used by the villains as D8s, although creative players may find ways to use these Distinctions for their heroes (notably as D4s to gain Plot Points). As Watcher, if you choose to use a Scene Distinction as a D4, you may step up the smallest die in the doom pool by 1 step. See page OM69 for more on Scene Distinctions.

Interrupt the Action Order with a Watcher Character

In any Action Scene, the order in which the characters—heroes, villains, and others—act is fluid and passes from player to player, and occasionally to you as Watcher. If you want to **interrupt the action order** and have one of your characters, such as a villain or an angry mob of thugs, act before the next hero, you need to spend a doom die. The default spend is a D6, although heroes with ENHANCED, SUPERHUMAN, or GODLIKE REFLEXES (or SENSES, in some cases) require you to spend a larger die (D8, D10, or D12, respectively). If your character has REFLEXES or SENSES of his own, it can offset this greater cost. For more on action order see page OM35.

Split Up the Heroes

You can spend doom dice to **split up the heroes and separate them from each other**, or perhaps to bring them together if they're already apart.

Spend a doom die equal to or larger than the highest Affiliation die currently being used by the heroes. A hero with TEAM D8 who is currently in a team situation may be split off from that team by spending a D8, D10, or D12 from the doom pool. Similarly, a hero with SOLO D8 can be brought into a BUDDY or TEAM situation by spending a D8, D10, or D12.

This reflects some environmental shift or incident that precipitates the separation or reunion which the Watcher needs to describe, like "The floor collapses under Cyclops and he drops out of sight!" or "The wall slides away, revealing your teammates!" Then it's up to the players to steer the story toward bringing the team back together—or apart, if that's their preference.

Activate Scene or Event Effects

Sometimes, a Scene or Event has **effects that are activated** by spending from the doom pool. These are essentially additional "spend a doom die to..." options added to the generic list provided in this section. These can include bringing in more bad guys, triggering some kind of time-sensitive incident, or introducing a major villain or supporting character. The list of effects specifies the cost from the doom pool for activating these effects.

End the Scene

As the Watcher, you have the power to **end a Scene before the normal goals, requirements, or achievements have been met** by spending 2D12 from the doom pool. This is useful in a big pitched battle, which can drag out for a long time when the two sides are evenly matched or there are a lot of characters involved. This rule gives you a helpful pacing mechanic for these larger Action Scenes. Usually, the use of the doom pool to end the Scene means cutting away to a later point in the story, with the outcome being narrated by the Watcher with input from the players.

Action Scenes p. OM34

THE DOOM POOL AS OPPOSITION

The doom pool stands in as the opposition dice pool for anything the heroes want to try that's important enough to break out the dice but for which no opposing characters are present. Natural forces, sheer luck, that growing sense of dramatic tension—the doom pool acts as a generic pool of opposition when the situation demands it. The Watcher rolls the entire pool of dice and takes two dice for the total, just like any other action or reaction, with a third die as effect. If there are other traits in the Scene that might add to this pool, like inanimate objects, they can be included as well. It may be helpful to use a different colored die for these extra traits to distinguish them from doom dice.

Actions
and
Reactions
p. OM47

I'm the Watcher, and Beast is flying the X-Men Blackbird above the battle with the Hellfire Guards. His player says he'd like to launch missiles at the Guards' armored personnel carrier, hoping to destroy it. I have the Hellfire APC listed with a Reinforced Hull d8, but there's no driver right now and it's just sitting there. Right now my doom pool stands at:

DOOM POOL: 3D6 + D8

I could choose to have Beast's attack just go off without a hitch, but I like the idea that the missiles could cause some collateral damage. After Beast's player rolls his dice, I pick up the doom pool and add the Reinforced Hull die to it, for a total of 3D6 + 2D8.

Using the doom pool as the Watcher's dice pool for these situations doesn't cost any dice out of the doom pool. However, the Watcher can spend dice from the doom pool after rolling to keep more dice as effects, include more dice in the total, and so forth. If this happens, simply remove any die that is to be kept or added into the total from the doom pool after the action or reaction is resolved, rather than spending another doom die to do it. Be sure not to "spend" a die from the roll that didn't originally come from the doom pool, such as a trait in the Scene. If you use different colored dice for these extra traits, it's easier to tell them apart.

Beast's player got a total of 15 and an effect die of D8 for his missile attack on the Hellfire Guards' APC. Now it's my turn to roll the reaction, using the doom pool and the vehicle's REINFORCED HULL D8 die (which is a different color than my other doom dice). I get:

Setting aside that 1, it leaves me with a maximum possible total on two dice of 14 (the D8, and either of the two dice that rolled 6).

TOTAL: 14

I decide to spend the D6 that rolled 5 to add it into the total, giving me 19. I choose to use the D6 rather than the second D8 for my total so the D8 can stay in the doom pool.

TOTAL: 19

The APC repels the Beast's attack, but at the cost of a D6 from my doom pool.

DOOM POOL: 2D6 + D8

THE DOOM POOL AND EXPERIENCE POINTS (XP)

Players earn XP by pursuing their Milestones and engaging with the story, but they can also pick up additional XP when you use the doom pool at its fullest.

As the Watcher, every time you spend a D12 doom die from the doom pool, all affected heroes gain 1 XP. If a hero is the target of the doom die because of its use in a die roll, or if the doom die has altered or changed a Scene they're in, they get the XP. If they're not in the Scene and the doom die is spent on something that has nothing to do with them, there's no bonus.

Note that with the End the Scene function of the doom pool, which costs 2D12, that's a 2 XP award to every hero in the Scene.

STUNTS, RESOURCES, AND PUSH DICE

IS IT A STUNT OR AN ASSET?

There might be some confusion about the timing of stunts and assets and how they interact with the story. After all, quite often they're both based on powers from a Power Set and there's a fine line between, say, a huge gust of wind you create to aid you in your own dice pool, and a huge gust of wind you use your roll to create.

When thinking about your hero's intent for his next action, or even a reaction, consider whether you're showing off your powers or Specialties in a way that gives some dramatic oomph to your roll, or whether you're trying to achieve some tangible effect to either help another hero or assist you for your next roll. The former is a stunt; the latter is an asset. By using a stunt, you're spending a Plot Point to get an additional die right now. By creating an asset, you're using your effect die in a roll for something other than inflicting stress on your opponent or creating a complication.

Finally, remember that **you're the only character that may benefit from a push, stunt, or resource you create.** You can't spend PP to create those for someone else. Other heroes, on the other hand, may use assets, since they arise from the action or reaction your hero has just taken. If you give an ally an asset, it's his and goes away once he's done with it.

Super hero action is dynamic and exciting, and the game supports this through the use of **stunts, resources**, and **push dice**. These player-created traits increase the chance of success and make Action Scenes more exciting. Heroes can use them to develop spectacular fighting combos or work together as a team. They each add to a dice pool before the dice are rolled, much like any other trait, and they cost Plot Points to create.

Assets also add to a die pool, but they're created through effect dice as a result of actions. So, you might spend a PP to create a stunt to add to a dice pool in order to roll an action that creates an asset that can be added to a subsequent roll. For more on assets see page OM22.

THE PUSH

Any player can add a D6 to his dice pool just by spending a Plot Point. This is called **pushing** your dice pool; while it's the weakest way to use a Plot Point, it's often the quickest and most efficient means of adding dice to your pool. It represents the hero pushing himself, drawing on his will, or just enjoying a lucky break. The die only gets used once—in the action it's created to help out with—and then goes away. It's much more interesting to create stunts and assets, though, especially as they start out at more than D6 and have a stronger hook into the story.

PERFORMING STUNTS

A more powerful use of a Plot Point is to add a **stunt die**. Super heroes constantly use their talents in new or different ways, often just for one panel in the comic book. The game calls these thematic push dice **stunts** and they start out at D8. The catch is that you have to come up with some cool description of what your hero's doing and the stunt must be tied to either a Power Set or a Specialty your hero has. You can only create one stunt at a time for any given Power Set or Specialty; once you use it in an action or reaction, it's gone.

I'm playing Storm and I'm using my GODDESS OF THE STORM Power Set to whip up a whirlwind against a group of Hellfire Guards. Even though WEATHER SUPREMACY D12 is already listed on my datafile as a power in this Power Set, I want to call attention to the fact that Storm's picking up loose debris and dust to blind the Guards and keep them from seeing what the other X-Men are doing. I spend a Plot Point and create a BLINDING DUSTSTORM D8 stunt, and I add that into my pool together with the WEATHER SUPREMACY D12.

CALLING IN RESOURCES

A **resource** is a special kind of stunt linked to one of your Specialties and created by spending a PP during a Transition Scene, much as you would create a stunt die for a Specialty in an Action Scene. The difference is that a resource starts out as a D6 (for Expert Specialties) or D8 (for Master Specialties) and it lasts until the end of the next Action Scene. Resources represent people you may know through your circle of contacts, information provided by your connections, or locations you can make use of as a result of your background in the Specialty. You can unlock stronger and more persistent resources using Milestones.

If you activate an opportunity with a PP, you can create a resource during an Action Scene that lasts until the end of the Scene you created it in. Otherwise, resources must already exist for you to add them into a die pool during an Action Scene.

See Specialties on page OM96 for more information about resources; see page OM105 for more information on Milestones.

ACTIVATING THE WATCHER'S OPPORTUNITY FOR STUNTS, RESOURCES, AND PUSH DICE

When the Watcher gives you an opportunity by rolling one or more 1s, you can activate that opportunity with a Plot Point and create a push or stunt die that's a step up from the default die rating. Hand over the PP and add a D8 push die or a D10 stunt die to your next dice pool. You can also create a resource on the spot by activating the Watcher's opportunity, something you can otherwise only do during Transition Scenes.

EFFECTS: ASSETS, STRESS, AND COMPLICATIONS

Actions have consequences—in life, in comic books, and in this game. These repercussions direct the flow of the game and lead to heroes achieving what they want...or stumbling along the way. The game represents this with effects. An **effect** is a trait created by using an effect die. Simple enough, right? Like other traits, effects are rated with dice. They come in three flavors: **assets**, **stress**, and **complications**.

Assets are similar to stunts, resources, and push dice, because you include them in your dice pool before you roll. They're different from those traits because they're not created with Plot Points but as effects, just like stress and complications. Therefore, the assets you add to your dice pool are the effects of previous actions. Assets usually last until the end of the Scene.

Stress and complications, however, are a bit different. They're temporary traits that are inflicted on your hero during conflicts that don't go your way. Instead of including them in your own dice pool, they're available to any opposition dice pool that you roll against. In the same way, you can always build up your own dice pool by adding in the stress or complications of the characters you're up against.

It's helpful to keep a visual reminder so that everyone at the table can see when you have active stress and complications. You can mark stress on the tracks listed on your datafile with a paperclip. You might want to list complicatons on an index card to keep track. The Watcher can keep a sheet listing active stress and complications.

ESTABLISHING ASSETS

You can use an effect die from your roll to establish an **asset**. Assets are brief and situational, created to help other heroes by adding to their dice pools or as a means of giving you more dice in subsequent actions. They're also a way for you to call something out as being significant or important, like a piece of the scenery or a supporting character who previously didn't have game mechanics representing them. Like other effects, assets are rated at the same size as the effect die used to create them, although the minimum rating is a D6. If you use a D4 effect die to create an asset, it starts as a D6.

If your sole action is helping another hero out, this is called a **support action** and it almost always results in using the effect die as an asset for that other hero. In this case, the Watcher rolls the doom pool as opposition to your action. Similarly, if you're just trying to set up something significant in a Scene and it's not actually targeting a villain or other character, the Watcher uses the doom pool to oppose your hero's own dice. Success in both situations produces an asset. Failure may lead to a complication, instead (see page OM29). For more on support actions see page OM53.

I'm playing Kitty Pryde and I'm trying to decrypt a firewall so that the rest of the X-Men can break into the Hellfire Club's mansion. Putting together my dice pool from Distinctions, Specialties, and so on, I have a total pool of D10 + 2D6 + D4. I roll and get a total of 11 (7 on the D10, 4 on a D6) and my effect die is a D6. Turns out the Watcher only got an 8 total when rolling the doom pool, so Kitty breaks through the encryption. I want to use the effect die to create an asset, so I declare COMPROMISED SECURITY D6 and can either give that to one of the other players or save it for another roll against the Hellfire Club's computer system.

STRESS

Stress represents the negative consequences of conflict. When heroes and villains fight, the outcome is often determined by how much stress each side inflicts on the other. There are three types of stress: physical, mental, and emotional. Each type of stress is a trait with a die rating, and that die may be added into the opposition's dice pool when it would affect your ability to succeed in what you're trying to do. Only one type of stress may be added to the opposing dice pool. If you want to add in more, you need to spend 1 PP (as a player) or a doom die (as the Watcher).

Stress starts out with a die rating equal to the effect die that was used to inflict it, a lot like an asset. If you already have stress of a certain type and take more of it, compare the old and new stress dice—if the new die is larger than the old, replace the old rating with the new. If the new die is equal to or less than the old, step the old die up by one.

I'm playing Cyclops and I have D6 emotional stress. The Watcher says I take D10 emotional stress when I lose a furious argument with a local senator who's also a member of the Hellfire Club (I got a Plot Point out of it, but it's a lot of stress). Since the D10 is larger than my D6 emotional stress, I replace the D6 with the D10. If I had taken D4 emotional stress, which is lower than what I already have, then I would step up my existing emotional stress to D8.

Note that there's no requirement that your opponent include a stress die in his pool, and sometimes—such as when the stress is D4—it may invite opportunities instead of actually raising the level of difficulty. Having D4 stress represents being rattled, perhaps, but not noticeably hurt, shaken, or thrown off.

Stressing Out and Taking Trauma

Once any type of stress exceeds D12, your hero is **stressed out** and can't take any actions or do anything until he recovers with another hero's aid or in a Transition Scene. He also picks up a D6 of **trauma**—emotional, mental, or physical, depending on the stress that caused it—that takes longer to recover from. Like stress, trauma can be added to the opposing die pool. If you already have trauma from a previous Scene, you can take more stress of the same type, but only the highest rated die from any specific type is added to your opposition. If you have D10 physical stress and D6 physical trauma, the D10 is added, not the D10 and the D6.

If you're already stressed out in a Scene and take more stress, it translates directly to trauma. If the new stress is larger than the existing trauma of that type, replace the existing trauma with that rating. If it's equal to or smaller, step up the trauma by 1. You can spend a PP to shift the stress to a different type, as usual, which may keep your trauma from getting worse. If any kind of trauma is stepped up beyond D12, your hero is dead, in a vegetative state, or otherwise out of the story. This isn't necessarily the end for him, of course. People in the Marvel Universe have come back from far worse!

It's possible to go from having no stress at all to being stressed out and taking trauma as a result of a single action. This can happen if your opponent's effect die is stepped up beyond D12 by such things as an extraordinary success or SFX. In effect, you take more than D12 stress all at once and are stressed out by it. Spending a Plot Point to move the stress to a different type won't help you, although it's an option if you'd prefer to have a different kind of trauma.

In the Scene during which you get stressed out, you're considered to have D12 stress for the purposes of others trying to rouse you in the midst of the Action Scene. If others use a successful recovery action on you they may either bring you back into the action at D12 (if their effect die is D10 or smaller) or bring you back at D10 (if their effect die is D12 or stepped up beyond D12).

Whether or not you get help, you recover all of your stress once the Action Scene is over—but you keep any trauma you gained.

If you're the Watcher, be aware of heroes who have been stressed out. Since they can't act, they're out of the Scene and can't take part. They can make reactions, but anyone who tries to take an action against them can use the D12 stress, which weighs heavily in the attacker's favor. It's entirely within the limits of the comic book genre to have the villains leave them alone or perhaps kidnap them, rather than finish them off with more attacks.

Pulling Punches

Sometimes you don't really want to inflict that much stress on a target. That's fine; you can always **choose to inflict less stress** by choosing an effect die that's of a lower size. If you only have large effect dice to draw on, you can step back the effect die by one—sometimes you don't know your own strength!

If you **don't want to inflict trauma** on an opponent, you can make that choice when you stress him out. When he recovers from the stress, he might not have any lasting effects, but you still have what you wanted. This is an important choice to make for some heroes, who don't want to cause lasting harm but still need to deliver a knockout punch.

If you stress an opponent out but choose to pull your punch, so to speak, he recovers all but D6 of the stress at the beginning of the next Transition Scene or when an ally uses a recovery action. This represents the "Did anyone catch the license plate of that truck?" effect of some battles.

Three Types of Stress

Here's a summary of the three stress types and what trauma of each type means.

Physical stress is bodily injury, exhaustion, the effects of toxins or chemicals, and so forth. Being stressed out from physical stress means blacking out or becoming unconscious, or perhaps incapable of activity from pain or fatigue. **Physical trauma** includes serious wounds, broken limbs, system-wide infection, and worse.

Mental stress is confusion, lack of concentration, mental fatigue, and the results of telepathic assault. Being stressed out from mental stress usually leaves someone insensate, incoherent, or unconscious. **Mental trauma** includes memory lapses, identity crisis, or impaired reasoning.

Emotional stress is despair, fear, anger, or any number of negative emotional states. Being stressed out from too much emotional stress means being paralyzed with fear, lost in one's misery, or consumed with irrational anger. **Emotional trauma** includes severe phobias, crippling depression, or persistent rage.

Usually, your opposition determines the type of stress you take. If you choose to, you may spend a Plot Point immediately to turn it into a different kind of stress. When you do this, describe how the attack or conflict affected you differently—made you mad, shocked you so much you felt actual pain, staggered your senses.

I'm playing Cyclops and I've just lost a struggle with a Hellfire Guard, who opened fire with his pulse rifle. The Watcher hands over D6 physical stress. I've already taken D8 physical stress earlier in this Scene and I don't want it to step up to D10, so I spend a PP and make the stress into emotional instead at D6. I describe this as Cyclops' anger rising at the Hellfire Guard's threat to my friends.

Exploiting Your Own Stress

You may also use your own stress to your benefit when it makes some kind of narrative sense. Yes, this means you might end up rolling your stress in your own pool while your opponent rolls it against you. To do so, spend a Plot Point and roll your stress die into your dice pool as if it were a stunt or asset. This steps up your stress by one, though, so you might not want to do it too often. You can't use trauma in this manner.

Now that I'm angry, it's time to take it to the Hellfire Club. This time I roll dice for Cyclops' OPTIC BLAST D10 and spend a Plot Point to add in the D6 emotional stress. I'm counting on taking out the Guard this time, since after the roll my emotional stress is stepped up to D8.

Recovering from Stress

Stress always steps back by one at the beginning of a **Transition Scene**, i.e., after the action is over and everyone's resting up, traveling somewhere else, or talking. If you have D10 physical stress, it steps back to D8, and so forth. All D4 stress goes away. If you were stressed out in the last Scene, your stress is gone, but any trauma remains. We'll discuss recovering from trauma in the next section. If you were stressed out but your attacker chose not to inflict trauma, you start the Transition Scene with D6 stress of the type you were stressed out with and must recover that in the Transition Scene.

Pulling
Punches
p. OM24

> I'm playing Cyclops and I've survived the battle with the Hellfire Guards with D10 emotional stress, D8 physical stress, and D4 mental stress. In the Transition Scene that follows, each of these steps back by one automatically, leaving me with D8 emotional, D6 physical, and no mental stress.

Heroes can recover faster by spending a Transition Scene with a medical professional or counselor, in a quiet meditative spot, or some other situation you can justify as restorative. Roll the appropriate Affiliation die (SOLO if you're all alone, BUDDY if it's you and a friend or a single medical specialist, TEAM if it's your whole team or a staff of professionals) plus any STAMINA-based powers, appropriate Distinctions, or Specialties as desired. You may add in a trait from another player's hero, too, if it's appropriate, but you need to **hand them a Plot Point** for it, or they can roll their own support action to give an asset to you.

Cyclops can't go on his next mission carrying all of this stress, so I decide he needs to spend some time with Emma Frost, who's both Cyclops' girlfriend and a skilled counselor in her own right (and one-time White Queen of the Hellfire Club). I roll Cyclops' D8 BUDDY die, a D4 for his Distinction I DON'T HAVE TIME FOR THIS (which gives me a Plot Point), and Emma's D10 TELEPATHY power under her OMEGA-CLASS TELEPATH Power Set, which Emma's player is nice enough to throw in (after I hand her a Plot Point).

The Watcher opposes this with the doom pool and with the stress die you're trying to recover. Often, the doom pool is much lower in the Transition Scenes as it's been used up to activate Event-based effects immediately after the last Action Scene, but toward the end of an Act it might be much harder to recover this way because the doom pool is usually larger.

If you succeed on the roll, compare your effect die to the stress die. If it's equal to or greater, it's gone. If it's smaller, you step the stress back by one (in addition to the step back at the start of a Transition Scene). You can spend a Plot Point to keep an additional effect die from your roll, which you can either compare to the same stress at its new die rating or to another type of stress.

> The Watcher rolls the D8 emotional stress and the current doom pool, which is 3D8 + 2D6, for a total of 4D8 + 2D6. My total of 12 (8 on the D10 and 4 on the D4) beats the Watcher's 10 (5 on a D8 and 5 on one D6, with the other dice coming up 4s, 3s and 2s), and this leaves me with a D8 effect die. That's equal to the emotional stress die, so I can remove it. I don't have time to spend another Scene with Emma to recover the physical stress, but it's only a D6. Surely that won't come back to bite me on the mission...

You can't make a recovery action during an Action Scene unless you have a power trait or SFX that lets you do it (see Powers and Stress Recovery, later in this section) but your allies can try to treat you in the middle of the Scene. This requires your ally to use an action to roll dice against your stress die and the doom pool. If the ally's action succeeds and the effect die is equal to or greater than your stress, it's stepped back by 1. If the effect die is smaller than the stress die, nothing happens. If the action fails, your ally has made things worse and your stress is stepped up by 1. Your ally can choose to use multiple effect dice with PP, and hope to step your stress back more than once.

I'm playing Cyclops. During the next mission, Emma's player sees that my physical stress is causing problems. She attempts to recover the stress using Emma's OMEGA-CLASS TELEPATH Power Set and *Psychic Healing* SFX to induce Cyclops' body to ignore the pain and recover. She rolls her BUDDY D6, TELEPATHY D10, and ICY CONFIDENCE D8 Distinction, and gets a total of 10 (5 on D8 and 5 on D6) with a d10 effect. The Watcher announces that the doom pool total was a 14, which means Emma failed! Her psychic healing only served to hide Cyclops' pain but didn't reduce the stress, which is now stepped up to D8. Not looking good for Scott Summers.

Recovering from Trauma

Trauma is harder to recover and takes longer. Each type of trauma must be treated separately and requires some long-term narrative description. Spending a few weeks in a clinic, recuperating in the Bahamas without any interruption, or having a team of telepaths piece your shattered psyche back together again over a number of days are all good examples. Some heroes, like Wolverine, can recover from trauma in hours, but he's the best there is at what he does.

In game terms, trauma steps back by one at the start of every new Act. It works much like stress does for the purposes of recovery. If a recovery action succeeds and the effect die is equal to or larger than the trauma die, step it back by one. If the recovery action succeeds but the effect die is smaller than the trauma die, the situation remains stable. If the recovery action fails, the trauma die is stepped up by one; the situation has worsened. In other words, sometimes it's better to let nature take its course if you don't have the skill to deal with major injury or psychosis!

I'm playing Cyclops, and at the end of the last mission Emma's attempts to recover my physical stress followed by a lucky shot from a Hellfire Guard caused me to become stressed out. This gave me D6 physical trauma. During the next Transition Scene I decide to have Beast see what he can do in the medical lab. We describe a few days of recuperation and I make the roll with Beast's assistance. My dice pool is D8 (for BUDDY), D8 (I DON'T HAVE TIME FOR THIS Distinction), and a D10 that Beast's support action provided. I get a total of 12 (7 on D10, 5 on a D8) with D8 effect and the Watcher's doom pool total is 11. Comparing my D8 effect to the D6 physical trauma, I can step back the trauma by one to D4. If my effect die was a D4, I wouldn't have changed the trauma at all. If my total was 11 or less, my trauma would have stepped up to D8!

If you don't relish the idea of sitting out an entire Act or it doesn't make sense in the story for the Watcher to skip ahead several weeks in a single Transition Scene, you can opt for the spotlight route. The Watcher frames an Action Scene featuring your hero in which your trauma makes things worse for you, i.e., it's used against you in the opposition dice pools. Once you've done this, you may immediately step back the trauma by one at the beginning of the next Transition Scene and recover it like stress—eliminate the trauma die if your recovery effect die is equal to or larger, step it back by one if effect die is smaller, and no effect if you fail the recovery. If you don't get rid of all of the trauma in the Transition Scene, you can repeat the process, starting with another Action Scene. Otherwise, the trauma goes back to behaving as it usually does.

Let's say I failed my recovery action and my physical trauma was stepped up to D8. The Watcher agrees to frame a spotlight Scene for me where Cyclops goes after one of the Inner Circle of the Hellfire Club, and my D8 trauma hinders me for the whole conflict. Once that Scene ends, I can step back my D8 trauma by 1 to D6 and attempt to recover it as if it were stress rather than trauma. If I don't manage to get rid of it entirely, I'm probably going to have to play in another Action Scene to keep up this rate of recovery.

Powers and Stress Recovery

Some heroes—such as Wolverine and Luke Cage—have Power Sets with special effects that allow for recovery during Action Scenes without needing an ally's help. Usually these heroes have STAMINA as a power (ENHANCED, SUPERHUMAN, or GODLIKE). By spending a Plot Point to activate the SFX, the STAMINA is used as an effect die just as if the hero had succeeded on a recovery roll. Compare the STAMINA die to the physical stress; if it's equal or greater, the physical stress is gone. If it's less, step the physical stress back by one. Using these powers counts as an action, just as if you were making the roll itself.

I'm playing Wolverine, and I've taken D10 physical stress in a fight with the Hellfire Guards. Wolverine has GODLIKE STAMINA D12 and a *Healing Factor* SFX that lets me spend a PP to recover physical stress. Since my GODLIKE STAMINA is D12, by spending a PP I can eliminate the D10 physical stress immediately. It takes a lot to take down Wolverine.

If you want to **combine your use of recovery powers with another action**, such as healing stress at the same time as you leap into battle with the enemy, you can use one of your effect dice from the action to recover the stress. This doesn't cost a Plot Point beyond the cost of keeping the extra effect die, but the effect die you use can't be rated higher than your STAMINA die.

CREATING COMPLICATIONS

A **complication** is like stress because it's often inflicted on you as a result of an action, but it's also like an asset in reverse—you use an effect die to create a disadvantage for your opponent rather than an advantage for your hero. When a hero suffers a complication, his actions are harder to perform, much like stress. Unlike stress, complications don't lead to trauma and usually go away once the situation is resolved. Heroes may also inflict complications on their opponents, useful when you just want to impair or hinder them. You can render someone helpless with a complication that's stepped up beyond D12, which has much the same effect as being stressed out.

To create a complication, use an effect die like you do to create an asset. Give it a name and a rating equal to the size of the effect die used to create it (minimum D6). You may add it to your dice pools against the target just as you would add stress.

I'm playing Colossus and I'd rather wrap an iron bar around the Hellfire Guards than smash them. I roll my dice, including my GODLIKE STRENGTH D12, and the Watcher rolls dice for the Guard. I get the higher total, so I can now use my D8 effect die to create a complication, rather than stress. I call it BOUND IN IRON D8 and now on future rolls against the Guard I can add the D8 to my pool.

Anyone can use a complication that's been inflicted on a target, not just you. That's because the complication, like stress, is essentially a trait on the opponent's datafile rather than one on yours.

You can try to exploit a complication that's been inflicted on you, just like you can exploit stress that's been inflicted on you, but you need a good narrative reason to do it, and it steps up by one after you've used it, just like stress does when you use it this way.

PERSISTENT ASSETS AND COMPLICATIONS

You can make an asset or complication last longer than a single roll or conflict by spending a Plot Point. Write it down on an index card or sticky note and set it out in front of your datafile at the table. If you're playing online or in some other venue, make sure it's somewhere you can remember it and the other players and Watcher can see it. Persistent assets and complications exist as elements of the story and may be targeted by other characters for elimination—villains tend to try to tear free of sticky webbing, clear clouds of obscuring black smoke, or disarm your hero's makeshift club. Unless otherwise removed, persistent assets and complications last until the end of the next Action Scene.

I'm playing Kitty and I want to make sure this COMPROMISED SECURITY D6 asset of mine sticks around. I spend a PP and write it down on a sticky note. Hopefully the Hellfire Club's Inner Circle doesn't have a tech support guy on hand to restore their security.

Targeting Effects p. OM54

COMPROMISED SECURITY D6

02
PLAYING THE GAME

In the MARVEL HEROIC ROLEPLAYING game, most of the action takes place in Scenes involving the heroes being challenged by some kind of opposition. Just like in the comics, the action is broken down into moments of decision, drama, and doom. Between these **Action Scenes** are **Transition Scenes**, when the players engage in exposition, recovery, or reflection.

This game is played in game sessions, which might range from a couple of hours to a whole day, depending on the group. Because a game session can be so variable, time within the game is tracked by **Events, Acts, Scenes**, and **Panels**. This lingo comes from film, TV, and comic books, all of which are very visual media. You could even think of published **MARVEL HEROIC ROLEPLAYING** Events as the game equivalent of a comic book script.

EVENT

An Event is a **single, overarching story-line**, involving multiple story threads with many different characters. At least one super hero team is central to it, although there are usually teams, solo heroes, and other supporting characters all playing a part. The Super Hero Civil War, the Age of Apocalypse, and the Secret Invasion of the Skrulls are Events. Not every Event needs to be as far-reaching or massive in scope. Most Events could be described best as story arcs, such as the Necrosha Event that involved the X-Men.

In most **MARVEL HEROIC ROLEPLAYING** games, an Event is the length of the story. The players choose their heroes at the beginning of the Event, unlock cool powers, locations, and story hooks along the way, and then retire the hero at the end. When the next Event starts, they might take the same hero (maybe with a new datafile) and move them forward, or choose a new one, based on the Event in question.

ACT

Each Event is made up of at least two Acts, like the acts in a play or movie script. An Act represents a chunk of time with multiple Scenes, all **leading up to some pivotal point or moment**. In a typical Event, the final Act ends in the climactic battle with the villainous threat as the heroes overcome whatever mighty challenge presented itself earlier in the story. The number of Acts it takes to get to that point can vary, but three is the standard.

In every Act, the doom pool grows, gets used, and grows some more. Each Act begins with the doom pool reset to a starting number of dice, which means that at the end of an Act the doom dice are spent by the Watcher on unlocking certain triggered conditions, introducing new threats, and so on. In fact, the size of the doom pool or the dice in it might trigger the point at which the final Scene of an Act takes place. Acts may also be connected strongly to a hero's Milestones. See page OM105 for more information on Milestones.

SCENE

A Scene is a period of time centered on a **single conflict or situation**. It might not involve all of the heroes—sometimes it only involves one or two of them. A Scene should focus on answering a question, resolving a problem, or settling a dispute or exchange. The game considers two types of Scenes. **Action Scenes** involve the characters doing something to drive the story along and move it forward. **Transition Scenes** connect Action Scenes together and are usually used to recover, gather information, or plan the next Scene.

As the Watcher, framing every Scene is your responsibility—we'll talk more about that in just a moment—although the players might suggest what comes next in the story. A Scene ends when the central conflict or situation is resolved; this means you need to have a sense of what the Scene is about as you frame it. It's often as simple as saying "Okay, so the next day you're at the site of the last Purifier attack, and you find a wounded Purifier being dragged away by some Morlocks. He's sure to have the security codes you need to shut down the Purifier's orbital platform. Are you going to stop the Morlocks?" The implication here is that this Scene is about this wounded Purifier, the information he has, and the Morlocks that want to finish him off. The Scene ends when that's been resolved somehow.

PANEL

A Panel is a moment in the Scene, usually encompassing a **single character's action or effort to do something**. It's a helpful visual reference when you're describing what a character does, because if it can fit into a panel in a comic book, it's doable with a character's action. Even if there are other characters involved in a Panel, the spotlight is on one of them, the one whose turn it is in the action order. Everyone else is supporting you, opposing you, or off in the background.

There are as many Panels in a Scene as there need to be to resolve the Scene's problem or conflict. Even if the Watcher and players are just sitting around acting out their characters without rolling dice, we can assume this is taking place in Panels. For practical purposes, a Panel starts when a player picks up the dice and declares his intent, and it ends when the action he's taking is resolved.

Action Order p. OM35

As the Watcher you can also prematurely end a Scene before it's resolved using the doom pool, usually to move things along. If this happens, you should consider whether the player heroes were close to resolving it successfully or not. If they were, let them summarize the outcome and establish those truths in the story. If they weren't, you do the honors, and move on to the next Scene, where they deal with the fallout.

ACTION SCENES

Some Scenes are more investigatory in nature or revolve around more social or personal activity, but they are Action Scenes in their own right. A pitched battle across the frozen wastes of Jotunheim and a tense diplomatic meeting between agents of the Shi'ar and Kree empires are both examples of Action Scenes. An Action Scene might begin *in medias res*, in the middle of the action—Thor and his Warriors Three are already in the midst of a titanic battle with Frost Giants, or Cyclops and the X-Men are already three hours into the middle of the diplomatic encounter. What's important is that this is where the real action starts.

FRAMING ACTION SCENES

If you're the Watcher, you get things started by establishing who is present in a Scene and where. This is called **framing the Scene**, and it's your chief responsibility in the game—other than playing the bad guys, keeping the doom pool, and rolling opposition dice. You should ask directed questions of the players, encouraging them to describe what their hero is doing or how they plan to respond to something. Rather than asking, "Where are you?" try something like, "Are you in the middle of the rank-and-file, or are you with the officers near the rear?" You might even establish a particular fact at the same time: "You're with the officers of the Imperial Force. How did you agree to this position?"

If you're a player, you should allow for some relaxation of control over your hero for this purpose, because after this point everything you do and say is up to you and the roll of the dice. If the Watcher asks you, "How did you agree to this position?" use that as an opportunity to build on the story. You might say, "Cyclops wants to see the big picture, so he's staying back to be sure his tactical genius is put to good use." Or, "Cyclops doesn't trust the Shi'ar officers, so he's staying near them in case they decide to pull a fast one on his team."

PRESENTING THE CHALLENGE

Once you frame a Scene as the Watcher, it's time to present the challenge to the players. Sometimes, this is a villain or mob of bad guys. Other times, it's a family of four trapped in a burning building. You're encouraging the players to think about how they're going to respond to something immediate and exciting. Action Scenes are no place for slow deliberation. Get right to it and present the problem! You can frame this as a question, as well: "Ronan the Accuser steps in front of his Kree soldiers and demands your head! How do you react to his threat?" Or, "Ronan hurls a blast of cosmic energy from his Universal Weapon at you, signaling the end of peaceful negotiations! How do you defend yourself?"

As a player, you now have the core situation—or at least the implication of one—laid out in front of you for this Scene. It's time to drop into character, think about what your hero would do in this situation, and perhaps talk it over with the other players. Some groups of players are hardcore and won't allow "table talk"—players giving suggestions to each other even when their own heroes aren't present in the same Scene—but others are more relaxed. What matters is that you're engaged with the new challenge and ready to go.

WHO GOES FIRST?

Imagine a page in a comic book, with multiple panels in it where each hero pulls off his amazing stunt or swings into action against the villain. A series of actions in the game is like this, with each hero getting a Panel—a moment when all of the attention is on him. The same is usually true of the villains, although often the villains' thugs and supporting characters tend to just act all at once—a menacing mob of mooks swarming over the heroes.

Once the Scene has been introduced to the players and the challenges are made clear, it's time to swing the spotlight around. One of the players gets to go first, chosen by the Watcher based on the description of the Scene or by the consensus of the group. Quite often, this is the central leader hero, or the fastest one, or the one played by the player who speaks up first! If you're the Watcher, you might decide this when you frame the Scene. Otherwise, go with who makes the most sense.

I'm playing Captain America. Spider-Man, Black Widow, and Cap have arrived at a Texas-style steak house that's apparently a cover for a crime syndicate in New York. The Watcher frames a Scene in which a scuffle is breaking out between some restaurant guests, one of whom looks like a seedy character we've already heard about. I announce that I'm going to do something, which means I'm first up in the action order. It could be that Black Widow's player or Spidey's player wants to go before me; if that's the case, we'll have a quick chat about it. The Watcher will settle the score if we can't.

If you're the Watcher and you want one of your own characters to go first, you need to spend doom to do it. It costs at least a D6 doom die—if there's a hero at the table with ENHANCED, SUPERHUMAN, or GODLIKE SENSES or REFLEXES and you don't have a character with SENSES or REFLEXES of that die rating, you need to match either their SENSES or REFLEXES die with a doom die of the same size. Whether it's SENSES or REFLEXES depends on the framing of the Scene; typically, surprise attacks, ambushes, and sudden arrivals hinge on SENSES, while a sudden attack from a foe that's already present and engaged with the heroes would be REFLEXES.

I'm the Watcher and I've decided that Spider-Man, Black Widow, and Captain America are going to be ambushed at the steak house by a group of Hydra agents. Rather than let one of the players go first, I'm spending from the doom pool to give Hydra the jump on the heroes. First I need to check with the players to see who has the highest SENSES power trait, since this is an ambush. Looks like that's Spider-Man with ENHANCED SENSES D8. I need to spend a D8 or larger from the doom pool to have the Hydra agents go first. Hail Hydra!

WHO GOES NEXT?

Everyone gets a Panel of their own to act, and this string of Panels is called the action order. Once the first character has acted—whether it's a player hero or a Watcher character—the action order has begun. **It's the player of the character who just acted that determines who goes next.** As the Watcher, your job is to wrangle all of this, but don't worry—it's not as difficult as you might think. All you need to do is pose the question to the player, "Who's next?"

As a player, you have a choice between another hero or one of the Watcher's characters. It might work to your advantage to choose the opposition next. Why? Well, apart from making the story flow better, or seeing what the villain has planned and then being able to let somebody else respond to it, **the person in control of the last character to act in any action order chooses who goes first at the top of the next action order**. So if you'd like that to be a player's responsibility, have a player hero go last.

I'm playing Captain America and the Watcher ambushed the team with a group of Hydra agents. After they take their action, the Watcher picks me to go next. After my action, which I used to knock away a bunch of the goons with my shield, I turn to the other two players. We agree that Black Widow's going next, and she's going to pick the seedy character we saw when we arrived to go next, since it's obvious he's a Watcher character. That leaves Spidey, assuming the Watcher has no more surprises in store for us. Once Spidey takes his action, he can choose who starts the next action order.

INTERRUPTING THE ACTION ORDER

As the Watcher, you can interrupt the action order at any point using doom dice. If a player chooses another player to go, you can spend a die out of the doom pool to have one of your characters act before that next player. Just like the use of doom dice to seize the control of the first Panel in the action order, you have to spend at least a D6 to do this. If the interrupted player has a hero with ENHANCED or greater REFLEXES or SENSES, you have to match that with your Watcher character's own powers or spend a larger die.

You can also interrupt the action order with doom dice to introduce threats that weren't there before (like another group of Hydra agents smashing through the steak house windows), to split the group up with some kind of explosive effect or twist, or anything else that may potentially cause a break in the action. In each case, the same restrictions apply—you have to match the REFLEXES or SENSES, or spend a larger doom die.

I'm the Watcher. Black Widow's about to go next as Captain America's player has chosen her. If I decide that I'm going to make the seedy crime syndicate guy go next, now would be a good time to do it, but Black Widow has ENHANCED REFLEXES D8, and the seedy guy's already in the Scene. If I wanted to throw in more Hydra agents, or even the Hydra leader Baron Strucker, then that would be against SENSES, and Black Widow's Power Sets don't give her any edge in that department. In the end, I decide I'm just going to wait and see which character Black Widow's player picks next. I'll save the Baron for later...

KEEPING TRACK OF THE ACTION ORDER

If a lot of characters are involved in an Action Scene, it can be easy to lose track of who's gone and who hasn't. There are a lot of ways we've found to keep track of this, but one of the easiest is to have each player keep a two-sided token—a coin, a playing card, or something like that—in front of them during the Scene. As the Watcher, you need something for each of your characters or groups of characters (in the case of mobs of Hydra agents, Hand ninjas, and so on). If you want to be really flavorful, use cards with the character's image on one side and nothing on the other side. You might even use action figures, miniatures, or folded cardboard standees.

When the action order starts, everyone puts their token in front of them facing up. After your character acts and it's time to pick the next character to act, turn your token over (or lay it on its side, or whatever seems appropriate) so that it's clear you've acted. It should be possible for everyone at the table to glance at you and see whether you've acted in the action order or not.

Once everyone has taken an action and it's time for a new action order, flip all the tokens or cards up and go again!

If you interrupt a hero with doom dice, make sure that you flip over the action order marker for the character you interrupted with before the interrupted hero takes an action. An interrupting character doesn't get to go later in the action order; you've basically just cut in line.

WHEN ARE WE DONE?

You can run through multiple action orders in a Scene—usually you'll have to in order for everyone to achieve what they're trying to do. Most Scenes run through the action order three or four times, especially in a big battle or a tense confrontation. Just have the last active player (or you, as the Watcher) call out the first active player in the next action order. If you're using flipcards or some other kind of indicator to show whether characters have acted in the action order, reset them.

Sometimes, you can set aside the action order for a few minutes while there's a break in the action. Maybe the players want to roleplay their heroes for a bit as they're crouched behind the remains of a water tower, planning their next move. Maybe the villains broke away and are hiding, ready to spring at the heroes. Or maybe you just want to play out some banter between the team leader and the villain while the others take a breather. As soon as the action picks up again, go the top of the action order and carry on!

Typically, the Scene itself ends in one of two ways. Either the heroes stop the villains, avert disaster, and claim victory over the challenge, or the alternative happens. In either case, the situation is resolved, even if it's not how the players might like! The Watcher summarizes the action so far, touches base with each player to note where his or her hero ended up, and then frames the next Scene.

The Scene with the seedy character in the steak house and the Hydra agents has a pretty simple conflict: Cap, Spidey, and Black Widow have to take care of the Hydra agents so they can find out what's going on from the seedy crime syndicate guy. The Scene's over once the agents are all knocked out or chased off, so we can play through a few Action Scenes until that's done. Given the level of opposition, that's not going to take too long!

Most Action Scenes are followed by a Transition Scene, linking one period of activity to another. This isn't always the case, of course. Sometimes an Action Scene leads directly to another one, with the stakes raised even higher.

Transition
Scenes
p. OM40

Using the Doom Pool to End the Scene

As the Watcher, you can always cut the Scene early—before the problem or conflict has been resolved—by spending 2D12 out of the doom pool and handing out 2 XP to each affected player. If you do this when the heroes are looking good and the villains are on the ropes, ask the players how they want to wrap it up. Ask questions just like you do at the beginning of a Scene. If a major villain's involved, present a tough choice to the heroes, though make it clear that they've won something even if the villain's presence colors it somewhat.

> "So the Hydra agents are running scared. How long does it take you to round them up? How many of them escape?"

> "Baron Strucker's clutching his side and hurling insults at you as his forces disperse. You can capture him, or you can stop his troops from getting away with the crime syndicate leader. What do you do?"

If, on the other hand, you spend the 2D12 when the Scene is going against the heroes, or they're struggling against insurmountable odds, you can bring the Scene to a close and invite the players to describe how they lost or what they had to sacrifice.

> "The Hydra forces have you surrounded and you're at Baron Strucker's mercy. Which one of you escapes their clutches?"

> "The crime syndicate leader has escaped and the Hydra forces have all scattered. The steak house is on fire and collapsing all around you. How did you get out of there, and what else did it cost you?"

Bringing the players in on this underscores how important they are as the writer/artist of their heroes, while still making it clear that the doom pool brought this about.

Doom Pool and XP p. OM19

TRANSITION SCENES

Action and adventure is what most of us think of when we imagine a super hero story set in the Marvel Universe, but these stories are more than just big brawls and conflict. Between these Scenes, linking them together are Scenes of reflection, recovery, and regrouping. We call these **Transition Scenes**, and they allow the characters involved to do something with what they've learned before the next conflict is met head-on.

As well as being used for recovery actions, a Transition Scene's purpose is to determine what the next Action Scene is. If this is already settled, then the Transition Scene helps to put that into context.

FRAMING TRANSITION SCENES

As the Watcher, it's your responsibility to frame Transition Scenes just like you would any Action Scene. Start out by asking directed questions of the players. You want them to decide what their heroes are doing and how they're using their resources before they start into the next dramatic Action Scene, so put them in a situation that's not as charged with conflict; instead, open up options to roleplay and talk with each other or with support characters.

You might lead with something like:

> "It's the next morning on the S.H.I.E.L.D. Helicarrier. You've got the leader of the crime syndicate in lockup, but now you know Hydra's involved. What's Captain America doing to track down the Hydra agents? What's Black Widow going to do with the crime syndicate leader? And does Spidey check in with Mary Jane to let her know he might have to skip her play this evening?"

As a player, Transition Scenes are where your hero recovers stress, follows up any information collected in the last Scene, and reaches out to new heroes and support characters. When the Watcher leads off with a question, make it clear what you want your hero to do.

RECOVERY ACTIONS

They're called actions because they're one of the things you can try to do in the middle of an Action Scene, but Transition Scenes tend to be the most effective time to use recovery actions. First, all of your hero's stress steps back by one at the start of a Transition Scene, which makes it easier to recover the rest of it. Second, you don't have villains and thugs and other threats complicating things. And third, you can make use of your allies with recovery-based powers by spending Plot Points, which has the added benefit of giving your allies more PP.

You can't attempt to recover a specific type of stress more than once in any Transition Scene. It's assumed that this action represents all of your efforts at getting better before the next Scene starts. You can, however, try to recover different types of stress, and you can make the best use of your Plot Points and assistance from others if you use multiple effect dice to recover more than one type of stress in a single action. For more information on stress and recovery actions, see page OM53.

If you've taken trauma after being stressed out in the previous Action Scene, you can't recover all of it in the space of time a Transition Scene generally covers. Recovery actions used for trauma can only step back the die by one, and carry a risk of stepping up the trauma as well. There are exceptions, of course, such as heroes with amazing recuperative powers like Wolverine or Deadpool. Trauma recovery can be taken care of with a specific Milestone, during which your hero can also earn XP. See page OM27 for more on trauma, and page OM105 for more information on Milestones.

You can use a recovery action to get rid of a lingering complication, too, if you can justify it. Instead of stepping back or eliminating a stress die, you're stepping back or eliminating a complication die. The Watcher may also just declare that the complication no longer exists, especially if it was entirely dependent on a situation that's ended.

RECRUITMENT

You can use the downtime of a Transition Scene to play out the **recruitment of a new hero** to the story, which is great if a new player shows up to the game and wants to play. While there's nothing keeping a hero from just showing up in the middle of an Action Scene, that requires something like SPEED, FLIGHT, TELEPORTATION, or some other super-power to explain why they've just arrived. Also, if your group likes to have multiple heroes in the control of each player (also known as troupe style play) the Transition Scene is a good place to switch out your hero datafile with another one.

Your hero may also spend PP to **recruit resources** connected to a Specialty during a Transition Scene. This represents the hero calling in favors, reaching out to connections, doing research on something related to the Specialty, or identifying important details about a location you're expecting to go to. Any resource created must fall under the Specialty in question.

REGROUPING

Some Scenes involve the team splitting up to more than one location. While that can continue during the Transition Scene as heroes go off by themselves to get better or hang out with one or two others, the Transition Scene is a good time to play out the gathering together of the team and have them all touch base with each other.

It can give the Watcher a better sense of which heroes may be together at the beginning of the next Action Scene, too, if you establish within the story that your heroes are planning on being in one or more groups to face whatever challenges next arise.

Resources and Specialties p.OM97

RELOCATION

One use of Transition Scenes is to describe what the heroes are doing in transit to a new location. It's easy to skip ahead and just describe the next Action Scene as being in Los Angeles or Cuba or the Blue Area of the Moon, but as the Watcher you have an opportunity to bring this to the players' attention and have them make choices.

Sometimes the next Action Scene's location isn't settled until there's a Transition Scene that centers on that decision. As a player, how does your hero plan to pursue the team's foes? Where does the team expect to find the hidden base? Who do you want to take with you on the trip, and what will that involve? Have you been there before (and if so, are you going to spend PP on getting an information-based resource die for it) or are you going in blind?

ROLEPLAYING

Finally, the Transition Scene is a great excuse to really get into those sorts of purely roleplayed conversations with other characters that don't have much to do with powers, battles, investigation, or adventure, but give context to your hero and the world around him. Whether it's time spent in your hero's secret identity, reassuring loved ones that you're still alive, or enjoying a pizza with heroes who aren't even in the story (special guest stars?), Transition Scenes give you a moment to put those subplots in the spotlight.

From a gameplay perspective, many of a hero's Milestones hook into the activity that takes place outside of Action Scenes, so Transition Scenes are ideal for earning XP and moving toward your Milestone. For more on Milestones, see page OM105.

03
TAKING ACTION

Let's assume you're reading this book in order—since you read the *Introduction*, you already know how to roll dice, add dice together for a total, and choose an effect die. In *Playing the Game* you read about how Action Scenes and Transition Scenes work and flow together. This section expands on the basic rules and tells you how the game rules interact with each other in those action and Transition Scenes.

Remember, one of the core rules of the game is that you don't need to use the dice unless there's some kind of interesting outcome for both success and failure. During the game, your heroes face plenty of challenges, engage in innumerable conflicts, and both succeed and fail repeatedly. It's the nature of comic book adventure, right? But if nothing's at stake, there's no real risk, and failure would be boring, the Watcher should just say, "Yep, that works," and move on.

By default, the person who picks up the dice is the active side of any conflict. Picking up the dice means, "I want to do this thing." If a player's describing something he wants to do and hasn't picked up dice, the Watcher can nudge this along with a question, like, "What traits are you going to use to do that?" or "What are the ways this can go?" The Watcher may also be the one to pick up the dice, which is another way of saying, "What have you got? What are you going to do about this?"

IT'S CLOBBERIN' TIME!

Open any Marvel comic book or graphic novel and you're likely to see action spread across multiple pages and panels, with the heroes at odds with the villains while innocent bystanders dive out of the way. The tension finally snaps; the optic blasts, adamantium claws, and big rocky fists come out; buildings shake, the sidewalk shudders, and you know that it's definitely time for a super hero battle.

This section is primarily weighted toward classic comic book battles, but that's only one side of comic book conflict. Your heroes may also get involved in tense emotional or mental confrontations using these same rules.

Non-combat Actions p. OM56

MAKE YOUR INTENT CLEAR

As a player, when it's time for your **action**, you need to make your intent as clear as possible to the Watcher and other players before you even pick up the dice. If you've said what you want to do, make sure you're suggesting what you want out of the action. The Watcher might suggest the alternative outcome—i.e., what happens if you don't succeed at your action—but you can also define this from the outset. Knowing what you want if you succeed and what you think will happen if you don't is key to the next step.

If you're the Watcher, you need to do the same thing. Be shamelessly transparent. There's no sense in hiding from the players what the outcomes might be; they're partners in telling the story, too. It helps knowing how high the stakes are before the dice are rolled!

Let's go back to Cyclops and Emma, who have arrived at their next mission zone and are confronting a pair of Sentinels. I'm playing Cyclops, so I want to use my FORCE BLAST power to take out a Sentinel. That's a nice, clear intent. What's the alternative outcome? Well, the Sentinel will probably close in on me and that won't be great. Either way, things are going to heat up.

GATHER YOUR DICE

Pick up all the dice that are appropriate for the action. If you're a player, always start with an Affiliation die based on your hero's current situation—SOLO, BUDDY, or TEAM. Next, check to see if there's a Distinction that fits the occasion and whether it's going to help or hinder your hero. For each action, you may choose one power from each Power Set and one Specialty without paying PP to add them to your pool. By choosing these traits you're saying, "These things have an impact on what I do!"

You can spend Plot Points to add in stunt dice as desired. If there are SFX that might be useful, like Captain America's *Ricochet*, this is where it's used. Once you've settled the dice pool, roll the dice.

My opening move as Cyclops is to blast at one of the Sentinels with a touch of my ruby-quartz visor. Now I need to gather my dice pool. I'm with Emma, so I pick up my D8 BUDDY die. I've got the TACTICAL GENIUS Distinction, which is a D8, and COMBAT EXPERT, which I'm using as 2D6. Finally, I have my FORCE BLAST D10. So my dice pool is:

I've also got 2 PP on hand:

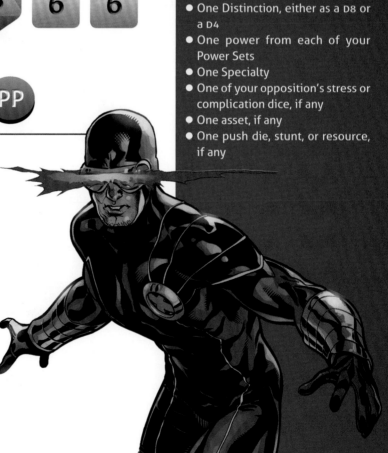

Affilations
p. OM62

Distinctions
p. OM67

Power Sets
p. OM70

Specialties
p. OM96

Plot Points
p. OM10

SFX
p. OM88

TRAITS YOU CAN ADD TO YOUR DICE POOL:

- One Affiliation die
- One Distinction, either as a D8 or a D4
- One power from each of your Power Sets
- One Specialty
- One of your opposition's stress or complication dice, if any
- One asset, if any
- One push die, stunt, or resource, if any

FIND THE TOTAL AND EFFECT DIE

Roll the dice. Choose two dice and add them together as your total. Any dice that come up 1 are opportunities and they're set aside. At this point, you can spend a Plot Point to include a third die from the remaining dice on the table—you can add as many dice to the total as you have Plot Points you want to spend. Then announce the total. If there are dice remaining, choose one to use as the effect die. If there are no more dice, the effect die is a D4.

I roll the dice and get:

I set aside the D6 with the 1; that's an opportunity. The Watcher activates it, adding a D6 to the doom pool and handing me a PP, bringing my total up to 3 PP.

Taking two dice and adding them together, my total is 12.

TOTAL: **12**

I could spend a PP to kick that up to 14 by using either the D10 or the D6. It's my choice, and I'd rather leave the D10 out as my effect die, so I choose to add in the D6. My total is 14, my effect die is a D10, and I have 2 PP remaining.

TOTAL: **14**   EFFECT: **D10**

THE REACTION ROLL

After you've rolled the dice for the action and there's a total and an effect die, your opponent gets to roll a reaction. The opposition gathers dice and makes a dice pool, same as the side that's taking action. The choice of traits to draw on here should reflect that it's a reaction to the acting player's attempt to do something. The reacting side describes what this response is, like "Cap's raising his shield and deflecting the blow!" or "Storm's whipping up a whirlwind to push the Purifier back!" It's important to know the nature of the reaction, because this not only determines what traits to use but what happens next.

As Watcher, I state that the Sentinel is just going to advance on Cyclops, soaking up the damage on account of it having advanced shielding and armored plate. That's EXPERT SENTINEL D8, BUDDY D8 (the Sentinel is one of two in the Scene) and SUPERHUMAN DURABILITY D10, plus a D6 doom die that I pull from the doom pool.

With a roll of:

...that's a total of 17—greater than Cyclops' total—and a D6 effect die (I can't choose the D8 because it rolled a 1).

TOTAL: **17**   EFFECT: **D6**

WATCHER ACTIONS

If you're the Watcher and you're taking action with one of your characters—a villain launching a surprise attack or trying to strike terror into the heroes—the dice might be different. A major villain has a datafile that's pretty similar to the hero datafiles. But other Watcher datafiles are usually shorter and don't have the same level of detail as the player heroes. Usually it's a broad Specialty that sums up the character's profession, role, or primary talent, followed by Affiliation dice and any super-powers, weapons, or specialized traits. The doom pool is always available as a source of additional dice. Once your pool is settled, pick up all the dice and roll them.

Data File

EXPERT SENTINEL ⑧
SOLO ⑥	BUDDY ⑧	TEAM ⑩

SUPERHUMAN STRENGTH ⑩   SUPERHUMAN DURABILITY ⑩

ENERGY BEAM PROJECTOR ⑩   ENHANCED SENSES ⑧

SFX: *Adaptive Learning.* Add D6 to dice pool for each failed action against a superhuman opponent.

Limit: *Robotic Systems.* On electromagnetic attack, shutdown a trait and gain D6 doom.

NARRATING FAILURE

Don't let failure bring you down. This game is all about action, sure, but it's also about making tough choices and accepting the consequences. If you're a player and the Watcher's reaction total beats yours, the story doesn't remain static. How does the Watcher describe the villain's defense against your mighty attack? Where did the villain end up? Where is your hero after the action?

As the Watcher, make sure to keep the description of the action going. Ask the players what happens when their hero fails to blast the Sentinels or if their reaction to the Sentinel's energy beams isn't enough to stop them. Ask those questions, and keep things moving at a good clip.

RESOLVING ACTION

Once you have the two totals (action and reaction) you can compare them to each other. You're looking to see if your opponent's reaction total is greater than your action total. If this is the case, your action fails. Don't worry about your effect die, because it won't be used.

I'm playing Cyclops, and the Watcher rolled a higher total than I did as a reaction. This means Cyclops' optic beam had no luck against the Sentinel's armor. I don't get to use my effect die to do anything, so it's time to choose who goes next in the action order.

If the reaction total is equal to or lower than your action total, your action succeeds. You can use your effect die to **create an effect**: stress, an asset, or a complication. If you have more than one effect die (you spend PP to keep more, or you have SFX in one of your Power Sets that give you more), you can create multiple effects. If you're trying to inflict stress or a complication, you have to first compare the effect die against the effect die of the reacting side. **If the reaction effect die is larger than yours, you have to step back your effect die by one.** In other words, they have at least a little defense up against you. This isn't an issue if you're only creating an asset.

If the Watcher hadn't rolled a higher total for the Sentinel than my action total for Cyclops, I'd be able to use my effect die for stress. My effect die is D10, which is higher than the Sentinel's D6 effect die, so I wouldn't have had to step back the effect. Inflicting D10 of physical stress on the Sentinel would have been a big plus.

If your action fails, your opponent may spend a Plot Point (if a player) or a D6 or larger from the doom pool (if the Watcher) to create an effect, just as you would have had you succeeded on your action.

As the Watcher, I could decide to use my doom pool to jump on that failed action. For the cost of a D6 out of the pool, I can use the Sentinel's D6 effect die to create some kind of asset, inflict stress on Cyclops, or introduce some kind of complication. Luckily for Cyclops' player, I decide not to worry about it.

EXTRAORDINARY SUCCESS

If your action total is 5 or more points higher than your opponent's reaction total, you've gained an **extraordinary success**. This lets you step up your effect die by one and describe just how amazing your efforts were. For every additional 5-point increment, you can step your effect die up again. By this method, it's possible to step an effect die up past D12, in which case you can either declare that you've automatically stressed out your opponent (if you were trying to inflict stress) or you can use a second remaining die from your roll as an effect die.

As Cyclops' player, what if I'd succeeded against the Sentinel by 5 points in the last action? I could have delivered a D12 effect on the Sentinel and would be that much closer to stressing it out. If my total were 10 points higher, that would be a single hit takedown.

Note that there's no such thing as an extraordinary failure, but if your opponent does have a reaction total of 5 or more greater than yours, he can consider it an extraordinary success on his part. What does this mean? If he's spent a PP (or doom die) to use his own effect die, he can step it up just as you could, had you rolled an extraordinary success of your own.

As the Watcher, I could have spent a D6 out of the pool to use the Sentinel's D6 effect die to create some kind of asset, stress, or complication against Cyclops. If my reaction total had been 5 points higher than his action, the D6 would be stepped up to a D8. If it had been 10 points higher, that'd be a D10.

DIVIDING YOUR ATTENTION

Let's say you want to take out more than one target at once or do more than one thing at a time. Generally in a comic book panel, a super hero can be assumed to be moving into position, calling out something, or any number of other minor actions. Those are free and shouldn't be a big deal. What does matter is when you want to actively do two or more things with the same roll. The key here is broadcasting your intent and then using effect dice.

If you spend a Plot Point, you may keep another of your remaining dice—after adding up the total—as a second effect die. Your targets each get a reaction roll as usual. Your single total applies to each target. It's possible that one target may roll higher than your total while a second loses to you. You can choose to use each effect die for a different kind of effect, so long as it's in line with your original intent. Thus you can create assets for yourself, or inflict stress of different types or multiple complications. You can't inflict the same type of stress with two or more effect dice.

As Cyclops, I could have decided to widen the beam of my optic blast to attack both Sentinels. While they would both have been able to roll reactions against me, possibly increasing the likelihood of my getting stress, there's a chance I could have taken them both out. Looking at my roll from earlier, my only option would have been to not increase my total from 12 to 14, instead keeping the D6 as one of my two effect dice (a D10 and a D6).

Some **special effects** (SFX) allow area attacks without spending Plot Points; these allow you to add a D6 to your pool and keep an additional effect die after the roll, one for each target. The downside to this is that it increases the likelihood of complications.

Cyclops has the *Area Attack* SFX for his OPTIC BEAM Power Set, meaning I could have added a bonus D6 to my pool and kept an extra effect die at no cost. I could also have spent a Plot Point to give Cyclops a stunt at D8 (such as "banked shot off the wall and into both Sentinels") and started out with a dice pool of D10 + 3D8 + 3D6. Maybe I should have thought this through earlier...

SUPPORTING AND RECOVERY ACTIONS

Not every hero is right in the thick of things every time. If you're playing a hero who's more of a supporter than a fighter, or more of a fighter than a talker (depending on the action), there's still always something you can do. You might want to help a stressed out teammate recover, or provide covering fire for someone.

Support Actions

If you want to use your action to support another hero or supporting character, assemble your dice pool and roll it just as you would normally. This is called a **support action**. The Watcher rolls the doom pool against you. If the Watcher doesn't generate a higher total than yours, you succeed in helping the other character and may use your effect die to create an asset. If you don't succeed, because the Watcher's doom pool generates a higher total than yours, the Watcher might decide to spend the effect die from the doom roll and create a complication for the character you were trying to support.

Recovery Actions

A **recovery action** counts as a support action, too. You're rolling to reduce an ally's stress with your effect die, but it's the same process—gather appropriate dice for your dice pool, roll the dice, choose a total and an effect die, and compare the total to the Watcher's doom pool total. Just like any other support action, if you fail to help another character recover stress, the Watcher may spend the effect die from the doom roll and inflict stress or a complication on you or your ally. For more on recovery actions, see page OM41.

Let's say Emma Frost's player went before me in the action order, and she wants to help me against the Sentinel. In her Diamond Form, she's blessed with ENHANCED STRENGTH D8 and SUPERHUMAN DURABILITY D10. If she picks up her ENHANCED STRENGTH D8, BUDDY D6, and ONE STEP AHEAD OF YOU Distinction at D8, she can roll them all and try to get a better action total than the Watcher's roll on the doom pool. Emma's player describes this as Emma charging forward and bashing at the earth in front of the Sentinel, trying to unbalance it so

I get a better shot. The dice come up 8 (D10), 5 (D8), and 5 (D6). Emma's player risks going with a 10 total (from the D8 and the D6) in order to get a D10 effect die. Luckily, the Watcher's total on the doom pool comes up 9. Emma's player announces that I'm next in the action order and hands me the D10 to add to my dice pool.

Support and Recovery Actions by Watcher Characters

As the Watcher, your characters don't roll against the doom pool. If you want to have one Watcher character aid another, just take a die from an appropriate helping trait and add it to the supported character's next dice pool. This counts as an action for the Watcher character who's doing the supporting, so he can't do anything else in that action order. Recovery actions work the same way.

There are two Sentinels in this battle, even though only one is pressing the attack. As Watcher, I could decide to have the passive Sentinel hand over a helpful trait like SUPERHUMAN STRENGTH to the acting Sentinel's dice pool, giving it another D10.

Remember, as the Watcher you can always spend (and thus remove) dice out of the doom pool to improve a Watcher character's chances, to add more dice to the total, or to keep effect dice. All of this can be described in the story as support, too, if it makes sense to you. The key thing to be aware of is that Watcher characters represent something different in any Scene; they're primarily the obstacles, not the protagonists. This is why you as the Watcher spend doom dice and not Plot Points, and why supporting actions are much simpler. Keep the spotlight on the heroes, not your own characters, whenever possible.

TARGETING ASSETS, COMPLICATIONS, AND OTHER TRAITS

Not everything you want to affect in a big Action Scene is a character. You'll often want to use your powers or natural talents to destroy, eliminate, overcome, or repair something in play that's either causing trouble for you and your allies or helping your opponents. You can target significant objects and conditions with your actions when they're represented in the game by traits.

Do You Need to Roll?

First of all, make sure it's actually a trait to begin with. A lot of things in the story don't have dice associated with them because they're a part of the fiction that everyone at the table just agrees on. Lampposts, sidewalks, plate windows, random passersby, bouquets of flowers, newspapers, and other items that aren't immediately important are just context and color. You can make them important by using your effect dice to make them assets, or use them as part of your description for stunts, but so long as you have the power to smash a glass window (most people) or rip a lamppost out of the street (anyone with SUPERHUMAN STRENGTH) it shouldn't even require dice.

You also need to check whether the item or condition can even be targeted. You can probably disarm a thug with a BIG GUN D6, but you can't disarm them of being an EXPERT THUG D8. Some Power Sets have a Gear Limit that not only has a specific way to be shutdown by the player or the Watcher, but also may be targeted by opponents. The Watcher has final say on this matter, but present your case to the table and see what happens.

I'm playing Colossus, and I want to disable the Sentinel's energy beam projector. I ask the Watcher if that's possible, and he says sure—the Sentinel's datafile has ENERGY BEAM PROJECTOR D10 listed on it. No sweat!

Take the Shot!

Now that you're sure something's an asset, complication, or some other trait, you can target it with an action. This works much like a recovery action. You gather together a dice pool that's appropriate, roll against the doom pool plus a die for the trait you're targeting. If you win, use your effect die against the trait. If your effect die is equal to or larger than the trait you're targeting, it's eliminated. If it's smaller, you step back the trait by one.

If the condition, asset, or another trait is somehow connected to a character who would understandably resist you seizing, destroying, or disabling it, that character becomes the opposition, not the doom pool. You're taking action against him and using your effect die, but it's to shutdown his trait rather than inflict a complication or stress.

Since the Sentinel's ENERGY BEAM PROJECTOR is a component of the Sentinel itself, the Sentinel, not the doom pool, is my opposition. The Watcher might still use doom dice to add to the Sentinel's dice pool, of course. Since the ENERGY BEAM PROJECTOR is being targeted, that die is included in the Sentinel's dice pool even if it's not going to use it as part of its reaction. If I succeed and get a D10 or higher effect die, that blaster's history. If I end up with only a D8 or less, I step back the ENERGY BLASTER to a D8.

Everyone Has Limits

You might have ENHANCED STRENGTH D8, but that doesn't mean you can destroy a car with a mighty punch to the radiator. Your energy powers might give you an ENERGY BLAST D10, but it's not going to bring down a skyscraper (maybe just trash the ground floor lobby). The action you take against an asset, complication, or trait must **fall within the realm of possibility** for you, given your Power Sets and Specialties. Even before you roll the dice, check to see whether the targeted trait is too strong (dice rating) or just untouchable (situation).

The Watcher may rule that you can target an asset, complication, or trait, but that your effect die can only step back the trait's die rating by one if it's equal to or larger, and have no effect at all if it's smaller. This is most often the case when you're targeting something that's just really huge, or it's kind of a toss-up whether your abilities and powers could affect it. A good rule of thumb here is that if your own power is equal to the trait die you're targeting, it falls into this category. This continues even if you've stepped the trait back from its original rating; stepping back something from D10 to D8 doesn't mean your D10 power is now more capable of eliminating the trait, even though the trait's die rating is smaller for the purposes of rolling against it.

Colossus has GODLIKE STRENGTH D12, which means he's one of the strongest heroes around. He can rip down small buildings, toss cars clear across town, and punch all the way through a bank vault door. But against something really large or rated with a GODLIKE DURABILITY D12, chances are he can only step it back by one—and only if he has at least a D12 effect die. Plus, while I might step it back by one with a success, I still only get to step it back by one next time, even though it's now a D10.

Automatic Success

If you have a power that might be useful in eliminating an asset, complication, or some other trait, you might be able to forego the roll entirely and just **spend 1 PP to succeed automatically**. This works the same way heroes with a STAMINA power trait can spend 1 PP to eliminate stress. Most of the time, this only works when your hero has either the time or the freedom to do this without interference, and the Watcher should already have established that you'd need to roll the dice as opposed to simply letting you get what you want.

I tell the Watcher that I'd like Colossus to bust through a REINFORCED DOOR D10. The Watcher might just let me do this, since he knows I've got GODLIKE STRENGTH D12. Or he might ask me to roll against the doom pool and apply an effect die against the door's D10 die rating. If that's the case, I can just spend 1 PP and smash through it.

If you're the Watcher, remember that having amazing powers is a lot of the fun of playing in the Marvel Universe. Unless you've got a good reason, you shouldn't worry too much about having the heroes roll to bust through walls or smash cars. The automatic success rule lets you move quickly through the action and get to the real showdowns between the heroes and villains; it offers them a way out of frustrating situations and lets them show off their powers!

Also, the Watcher's characters can do the same thing by spending dice from the doom pool (the doom die must equal or exceed the value of the targeted power or trait). As a player, that's something to keep in mind when you're webbing up Juggernaut's limbs or creating ice structures around a Sentinel...

HEROISM, HEADACHES, AND HEARTBREAK

Not every Action Scene is a fight between the heroes and an opposing force made up of villains and thugs. In fact, some of the best Action Scenes don't involve physical stress at all, but focus on what you might call **mental** or **emotional conflict**. For these Scenes, there are still clear lines of opposition. One side wants something that the other side doesn't, or one side wants to do something that the other side opposes. The difference in these Scenes is that intimidation, seduction, manipulation, and diplomacy may each be brought to bear, with or without super-powers to back them up.

Non-physical conflict actions use many of the same rules as combat or physical actions, so everything we've introduced so far is fair game. Actions, reactions, effects, extraordinary successes, and dividing your attention are all just as valid in tense Scenes between Spider-Man and Mary Jane or Tony Stark and Steve Rogers. And any emotionally charged Scene can escalate to a knockdown drag-out fight, depending on who's involved. So keep this in mind as you read on—an Action Scene can be physical, mental, emotional, or any combination of the three.

MENTAL CONFLICT

Whether it's a duel of wits or a psychic struggle for control, mental conflict has **mental stress as the primary consequence**. Heroes who engage in mental conflict are attempting to outwit their opponents, distracting them from seeing the truth, or trying to bring them around to a new way of seeing things. Mental conflict doesn't even need to be particularly antagonistic. Every good collegiate debate is a mental conflict.

Even more than for a brawl or firefight, mental conflict requires that the intent of the participants is clear. Are you trying to fool someone into thinking you're someone else? Are you trying to upstage another person on a topic that you're sure you're more of an expert in? You have to put forward what your desired outcome is, and then pick up your dice.

I'm playing Kitty Pryde and I'm trying to poke holes in an anti-mutant protestor's logic. After talking with the Watcher, we decide that if I win, the protestor won't change his mind right away but will at least realize he was harboring mistaken and hateful ideas. If I lose, I probably reinforce his prejudices and should get out of there!

In a mental conflict, the most common effect is **mental stress**. This can represent anything from wearing down your opponent's ability to resist, confusing your opponent, or making a stronger case for what you want. Once you stress out your opponent, you have them where you want them. Don't forget, you can pull your punches when it comes to stressing someone out. This is a wise choice to make if you don't want to inflict mental trauma. See page OM24 for more on pulling your punches when inflicting stress.

As Kitty Pryde, the mental stress I inflict on the anti-mutant protester represents conflicting arguments, confusing him, and keeping him from pushing his own agenda. If I stress him out, I'll pull my punches and so I don't give him trauma, but I think it will be an epiphany of sorts.

Complications are also potential effects, especially when, instead of stress, you want to inflict something like Distracted, Outwitted, Scientific Fallacy, or Too Much Information on them. Complications, like stress, can make life difficult for your opponent but won't actually get you what you want unless the player or the Watcher decides to throw in the towel.

I could choose to inflict a complication on the anti-mutant protester, something like He's a Raving Lunatic! or Unpopular Opinion. Those would be interesting, but I'm trying to change his way of thinking, not just saddle him with annoying perceptions.

EMOTIONAL CONFLICT

Anything from intimidation to taunting to seductive manipulation can be chalked up to an emotional conflict where **emotional stress is the primary consequence**. If you're using emotional conflict, you want to change your opponents' emotional state, getting them angry, afraid, insecure, or flustered. If they don't object to having their emotional state changed, then there's not really any conflict. Emotional conflict only happens when emotions are at the heart of a divide.

Before you launch into an action with emotional consequences, you need to figure out what those consequences are. If you're trying to scare your opponent, what happens if his reaction gets a higher total than yours? What's the thing you want to get out of scaring him? If you're trying to seduce the business executive, is failure going to end up with you being embarrassed, the executive getting mad, or worse?

> I'm playing Wolverine and I'm The Best There Is At What I Do. When I'm trying to scare the living daylights out of one of these anti-mutant protesters bothering Kitty, I need to be careful not to make things worse for mutants, so I decide to be subtle and just use my body language and a couple of grunts to give the guy reason to leave.

Emotional stress is irrational and heavy with melodrama, but what it really means is that your opponent's emotions are clouding his judgment or getting in the way of rational thinking. This is different from just being outwitted or tricked, which is mental stress. No, this is crazy gut reaction material, the kind of stress that brings dark clouds or fiery moods. If you stress out your opponent with emotional stress, chances are he's reduced to an angry, insecure, frustrated, or terrified mess. Or, if you've been pulling your punches and were clear in your goals, he's unable to stand in your way.

> So, as Wolverine, I rolled so well in my emotional conflict action that I stressed the anti-mutant protester out in one go (having SFX that step up emotional stress I inflict also helps). The Watcher agrees that this means he's taken off at a brisk run, convinced that he shouldn't be attending rallies like this when scary people with claws are present. If I had only inflicted emotional stress but not stressed him out, he might have stayed around, but his rattled nerves would have hindered his activity.

Some good examples of complications in an emotional conflict are Really Bad News, Romantic Overtures, Sibling Rivalry, and Embarrassing Revelations. Each of these gets in the way of your opponents' activity but won't stress them out by themselves.

> I could have chosen to inflict both emotional stress and a complication on the protester if I'd spent a PP to keep another effect die. As it happened, stressing him out did the trick.

USING TRAITS IN NON-COMBAT CONFLICT

Powers and Specialties can be added into the dice pool when attempting to win a mental or emotional conflict. Psychic powers like TELEPATHY or MIND CONTROL are great. PSYCHIC BLAST is more of a traditional combat power, but it can be a great last resort. If it's psychic or emotion-based as a rule, it can be brought into any non-combat conflict as a means of pushing your hero's agenda or fighting off the ambitions of your opponents. See page OM70 for more on Power Sets.

Specialties that work best in mental and emotional conflicts include MENACE, MYSTIC, PSYCH, and SCIENCE. If it's a conflict over knowledge or understanding, any Specialty that covers that area of knowledge is perfect. MENACE is specifically aggressive and PSYCH is a little more passive or indirect. For more on using Specialties see page OM96.

Don't forget that many heroic Milestones are dependent on non-combat interaction with others; they pose interesting choices that can be worked into these kinds of Scenes. For more on Milestones see page OM105.

LOSING CONTROL AND PLAYER AGENCY

It's easier to understand being knocked out in a pitched battle with the forces of Hydra than it is to wrap your head around losing control of your character's emotions or mental state. Roleplaying games are about getting into character and making decisions for a heroic persona, right? When the rules tell you that you have to make decisions you didn't want to make, or when the rules make those decisions for you, it can seem worse than having your hero get clobbered.

In this game, the big decisions are yours to make. There are two ways to handle it when your hero is stressed out mentally, emotionally, or both. The first is that you can just let the Watcher describe what happens, and trust that the situation's going to change again soon. Since a stressed out character can't actually do anything like rolling dice or taking action, your character might temporarily take a bit of a back seat to the story. Alternately, the Watcher might skip to a new Scene, where you've recovered your stress and now you're back in control but dealing with trauma.

The other option is to play it up! If you know what your opponent wanted you to do, you can take direction from that and make decisions for your hero that have that in mind. You can even do this when you haven't been stressed out yet, but you're wrestling with high levels of mental or emotional stress. Describe how your hero paces back and forth, angry and frustrated. Or have your hero lost in despair, opening up his heart to the manipulative villain. It's still an interesting story, and this way you're still in charge. And if you do choose to play it out, the Watcher might reward an exceptional performance with a Plot Point, especially if it lines up with one of your Distinctions or Milestones.

If you're being mind controlled or possessed, the same applies. Mind control starts out as influence (a complication) that can lead to full-on domination ("stressed out" by complication). Villains with mind control powers, like the Purple Man, usually try to have heroes do things that they otherwise wouldn't do, or keep them from doing things they want or need to do. Fighting this kind of influence is equivalent to making a recovery action, but you're not rolling against the doom pool. Instead, the character with mind control powers opposes, keeping you from stepping back or eliminating that mental stress.

If you're the Watcher, keep all of the above in mind when you're playing villains with the power to control minds or make heroes their unwilling slaves. It's perfectly reasonable for a player to get upset at losing control, so remind them that it's temporary and that it's a great way to earn Plot Points via Distinctions or Limits. The good thing about mental and emotional conflict is that the players have an opportunity to resist it, so it's never just a sudden off switch. Like any other situation, make it a good story, drop the heroes in danger and conflict, and give them a way out.

Mind Control p. OM79

UNDERSTANDING DATAFILES

A hero's datafile is like an entry from the *Official Handbook of the Marvel Universe* or one of Nick Fury's S.H.I.E.L.D. files, presented in terms of game stats. All of your hero's Power Sets, Specialties, Distinctions, and other traits are provided, along with biographical details and key information, ready to play.

This chapter goes into detail about all areas of your hero's datafile. From Affiliations and Distinctions to Power Sets and Specialties, consider this your primary reference.

AFFILIATION OPTIONS

Can you be a SOLO while you're in a crowd of other heroes? Can you be my BUDDY over a commlink while I'm in a TEAM? All of these are potential issues relating to Affiliations. Our rule of thumb is this: if the situation demands it, that's what it is. Keep in mind that what matters most rules-wise is whether you can give support or accept it, using those extra dice and benefits on your own actions and reactions. That doesn't mean it should be your only consideration. Is Wolverine using his SOLO D10 when he slashes away at the Sentinel, even though the other X-Men are fighting their own hunter-killer robots? Maybe. But he's not going to be including Storm's WHIRLWIND asset, or Colossus' FASTBALL SPECIAL asset, if he is.

AFFILIATIONS

There's a long-standing tradition in the Marvel Universe that some heroes just do their best work when they're working with others, while others have a reputation of being loners. Many heroes are well known for fighting crime with a part-ner—whether it's Luke Cage and Iron Fist, or Spider-Man and... well, pretty much the rest of the Marvel Universe, one hero at a time. This game represents these varying situations with **Affiliations**—traits that embody a hero's comfort level, capabil-ity, and confidence with others or alone.

Affiliations are the core of your action in any situation. When you're putting together your dice pool, Affiliations are the first step. Each hero has the three Affiliations prioritized by dice: D6, D8, and D10. Which die goes where reflects how the hero performs in those situations. You may choose to use your D8 or even D6 Affiliation on a regular basis; this increases your chances of earning Plot Points from opportunities. However, this isn't the only reason to use a lower-rated trait—at the heart of the Affiliations traits is the question of how the story changes when you step outside of your comfort zone.

▶ If your hero runs into more trouble or doesn't take up as much of the spotlight in a type of situation, it's probably a D6.
▶ If your hero functions just fine but not necessarily at his peak in a specific type of situation, it's a D8.
▶ If your hero is most at home and at his best in a specific type of situation, it's a D10.

Some heroes recover better by themselves, and others prefer hanging out in the Avengers Mansion eating dinner with their teammates. For this reason, **Affiliation dice apply even when you're not in a big battle or heroic Scene**. Your current situa-tion—whether alone, with a friend, or as part of a group—de-termines which Affiliation die you use in recovery actions and other rolls.

SOLO

This is the hero acting alone, scouting around, and taking down the bad guys single-handedly when the rest of the team is unconscious or lost.

Game Rules for Being Solo

When you're solo, you may use the SOLO die for all of your actions and reactions. When you use the SOLO die, you can't accept help or support from any other hero, and you can't give support to any other hero, until your next action or reaction lets you change the Affiliation you're using.

I'm playing Wolverine and I've been hunting down Hellfire Guards through an underground tunnel complex. When I burst in on a few of them, I go to town using my SOLO D10. Cyclops and Emma Frost show up after I've made my first action, but they can't help me out with support assets until I take another action or reaction. I'll be using TEAM on my next action because my situation has changed.

Notable Solo Heroes

Black Panther, Black Widow, Daredevil, Iron Man, the Sentry, and Wolverine all have a SOLO D10.

▶ Even though Wolverine and Iron Man work on teams all the time, they're at their best when alone.
▶ Daredevil avoids being on a team because it's not his comfort zone.
▶ Black Panther and Black Widow have also been frequent team members, but their approach is definitely more solitary.
▶ The Sentry brings complications more frequently when he's with anyone else, making him a more appropriate SOLO.

YOU'RE SOLO IF:

● You're in a location or situation where there are no allies with you or helping you.
● You were with a team but were split off from them by some force or barrier which prevents you from working with them.
● You've moved your activity to a different level of conflict—such as to the astral plane or through a computer system.

YOU STOP BEING SOLO IF:

● Other heroes show up to fight alongside you against the same opponent or group of opponents.
● You partner up with someone over telepathic link or comms network in a way that lets you help or support that partner and vice versa.
● You have Watcher characters like cops or S.H.I.E.L.D. agents helping you out.

YOU HAVE A BUDDY IF:

- There is one other hero or supporting character working with you against the opposition or in pursuit of a goal.
- You're by yourself in the field but you have another hero actively assisting you over a comms network or via telepathy.
- You and another member of a team split off to do something without the rest of the team present.

YOU STOP HAVING A BUDDY IF:

- You pick up a third hero or supporting character who helps you pursue a goal or oppose a villain or threat.
- You lose or deliberately part company with your companion, or your companion is knocked out in a battle.
- You turn upon or are forced to engage in a conflict with your partner or companion.

BUDDY

This is the hero with a single companion or partner. It's a classic Marvel arrangement, and includes a lot more than a hero and his sidekick. When two heroes team up to take down a foe neither of them could handle alone, or when a hero feels he needs a complementary set of skills or abilities, BUDDY is the solution.

Game Rules for Having a Buddy

When you have a partner, sidekick, or single ally, you may use the BUDDY die for all of your actions and reactions. When you use the BUDDY die, you can only accept help or support from your chosen buddy, and you can't give support to any other hero until your next action or reaction.

Notable Buddy Heroes

Armor, Iron Fist, the Human Torch, Luke Cage, Shadowcat, Spider-Man, and the Thing all have a BUDDY D10.

▶ Iron Fist and Luke Cage are famous for their partnership.
▶ Spider-Man has a lot more luck when he has another hero with him to play off his wisecracks.
▶ Armor, Shadowcat, the Human Torch, and the Thing operate on a team most of the time, but their strongest moments are when they're teamed up with one other team member—even if that other team member's strong suit isn't BUDDY.

TEAM

This is your hero as part of a group of three or more heroes or allied characters. Often, heroes unite as a single response to a common threat, like the Avengers. Other times, the heroes are part of a family, like the Fantastic Four. Being on a team isn't always the ideal Affiliation for a hero, but it never hurts to have backup and support.

Game Rules for Being on a Team

When you're with a team, you may use the TEAM die for all of your actions and reactions. When you use the TEAM die, you can give and accept support dice from any ally. You can't give support assets to or otherwise help another character if they used a SOLO die for their last action or reaction or if they used their BUDDY die and have already had help from another character.

Notable Team Heroes

Beast, Captain America, Cyclops, Emma Frost, Invisible Woman, Mr. Fantastic, Ms. Marvel, Spider-Woman, and Storm all have a TEAM D10.

▶ Sue, Reed, and Ben have all spent a great deal of time together in the Fantastic Four.
▶ Beast, Storm, Cyclops, Colossus, and Emma Frost are likewise at their best in the X-Men.
▶ Captain America, Ms. Marvel, and Spider-Woman all have a history of being part of large covert or military organizations, working with other agents.

YOU'RE ON A TEAM IF:

● You're one of at least three heroes or supporting characters working together in pursuit of a goal or against an opposing force.
● You're by yourself in the field but you have at least two other heroes actively assisting you over a comms network or via telepathy.
● You have a squad or group of Watcher characters assigned to you, such as S.H.I.E.L.D. agents or first responders.

YOU STOP BEING ON A TEAM IF:

● You lose contact with or are separated from your teammates, leaving you either alone or with a single partner.
● You intentionally leave a group and don't maintain voice, telepathy, or other contact with the group.
● You turn upon or are forced to engage in a conflict with the other heroes on your team, with or without another character aiding you against them.

AFFILIATIONS AND WATCHER CHARACTERS

If you're the Watcher, your characters also use Affiliations as the basis for their dice pools. Villains of any significance use the same three dice as heroes do: D6, D8, and D10, arranged as appropriate among the three Affiliation traits. You use these the same way players use the Affiliations on their hero datafiles.

Minor characters, including most "normal" people the heroes may run into and various guards, minions, and animals, have a different set of dice: D4, D6, D8. Even in their best situations, these characters are only as good as heroes and villains are at their middle Affiliation trait.

Mobs of Characters

Sometimes, characters appear in organized—or occasionally unorganized—groups, called **mobs**. A mob is anywhere from two to a dozen or more individuals that act and behave as a unit. Mobs are represented with multiple dice in their TEAM Affiliation, such as 3D6 or 5D8. A highly trained squad of professionals usually has a TEAM D8, while a mad, chaotic rabble would have a TEAM D4. The mob's other traits are shared among the mob. Instead of each die representing a single individual, you use 2D for a handful of minor characters, 3D for a dozen, 4D for a room full of people, and 5D for a large crowd. See page OM115 for more on mobs as Watcher characters.

Large-Scale Threats

Occasionally, a particularly large, dangerous, or powerful character has multiple dice in SOLO or BUDDY. These **large-scale threats** have a stronger chance of standing up to multiple heroes at once, but they can be brought low if attacked as if they were a mob (with the *Area Attack* SFX and so forth). See page OM115 for more on large-scale threats.

DISTINCTIONS

What's the essence of a super hero? You might think it's her super-powers or her astonishing skills and training. But those things can change or come and go. If you want to take a snapshot of a hero's personality, background, and attitude, you need to look at her **Distinctions**.

Distinctions are traits with two sides. They're catchphrases, significant personality types, and interesting backgrounds that can both help and hinder your hero in her efforts. For this game, we use Distinctions to capture the essence of a Marvel super hero—they also give you as a player a way to earn Plot Points.

HELP OR HINDER?

When you're picking up dice, you can add in one or more Distinctions if they would be appropriate. Pick up a D8 if the Distinction describes some part of your hero that would help the action you're taking. Pick up a D4 and gain a Plot Point if the Distinction is something that would likely complicate a situation or attract trouble.

You can always **add at least one Distinction to your dice pool**. It costs you a PP for every extra Distinction you want to add. Because you earn 1 PP for using a Distinction as a D4 and it costs 1 PP to add a second Distinction, you can always choose to have a D8 Distinction and a D4 Distinction in the same dice pool. It just won't earn you any extra PP.

I'm playing Wolverine. He has the following Distinctions: I'M THE BEST THERE IS AT WHAT I DO, MASTERLESS SAMURAI, and MYSTERIOUS PAST. The first one's his classic catchphrase, and it usually comes into play when Logan's carrying out some violence. But it could also be used for the D4 in a situation requiring civility. The second one's appropriate when rolling something to do with his past in Japan, or his honorable nature, or a duel. But it's also great when interacting with old foes from that period in his life or rejecting authority. And finally, the third Distinction is an easy bonus D8 if Logan's checkered and half-remembered history conjures up something useful and a great D4 when it just brings him grief.

At a formal dinner party hosted by the Hellfire Club, Wolverine's learned that the Black King, Shinobi Shaw, is planning to seize the X-Men's newest recruit, Hisako Ichiki, also known as Armor. I don't really want to pop the claws right away, so I figure it's a good time to use my own style of negotiation. I decide to approach Shaw and challenge him to a duel—in front of a lot of wealthy donors and Hellfire Club members who don't know he's also a psychopathic mutant killer. When picking up my dice, I'm going to use the MASTERLESS SAMURAI at D8 and I'M THE BEST THERE IS AT WHAT I DO at D4 (normally I'm not this polite). That's D8 and D4 added to my dice pool, but I don't get the extra PP because it cost 1 PP to bring the second Distinction in.

Don't worry if you have a Distinction on your datafile that seems as if it would be appropriate as a D8 in a lot more situations than the others. Some heroes are designed that way to encourage a certain kind of approach to action. Others seem loaded down with problematic-sounding Distinctions—this ensures that your heroes' flaws are supported by rewards like Plot Points.

DISTINCTIONS AND WATCHER CHARACTERS

The Watcher's characters, including the villains and ordinary people who interact with the heroes, don't use Distinctions in the same way as the players. As the Watcher, when you use a Distinction to add a D4 to the villain's dice pool, instead of earning Plot Points you can choose to **add a D6 to the doom pool or step up the smallest die in the doom pool**. This is true for any character with Distinctions. Many Watcher characters don't have them, in which case this won't apply.

Villains, especially, often have one or two Distinctions that seem deliberately weighted toward the negative. You might find it challenging to use them positively. This is fine, because it encourages you to use the Distinctions as D4s, provide the players with more opportunities, and grow the doom pool. More importantly, it encourages you to play the villain as the flawed or offbeat character that he is.

I'm the Watcher, and I've just set up the Scene where Wolverine and Shinobi Shaw are facing off for a duel in a courtyard. My datafile for Shinobi gives him the Distinctions ILLEGITIMATE UPSTART, BLACK KING OF HELLFIRE, and VENGEFUL PSYCHOPATH. I think VENGEFUL PSYCHOPATH is definitely appropriate, so I decide to add it as a D4; this allows me to step up a D6 that's already in the doom pool.

Your characters should rarely use more than one Distinction. With each action or reaction, make a decision to go with a D4 (and add a doom die) or a D8. If you decide to use a Distinction as a D4 and another at D8, don't add any dice to the doom pool. If you decide to use two Distinctions at D8, the extra Distinction costs a D8 or larger from the doom pool.

Shinobi is not only agreeing to this duel out of vengeance at Wolverine for calling him out in public, but because it's his duty as the Black King of the Hellfire Club. I might decide that, instead of growing the doom pool, I'm going to add BLACK KING OF HELLFIRE to Shinobi's dice pool at D8. It doesn't really do much for Shinobi's chances, though. Another option would be to spend a D8 out of the doom pool in order to have both VENGEFUL PSYCHOPATH and BLACK KING OF HELLFIRE Distinctions added in at D8.

SCENE DISTINCTIONS

Heroes and villains aren't alone in having Distinctions. The Scene (or the location the Scene takes place in) may also be described using Distinctions. These are defining qualities of the Scene that could help or hinder the characters in it. Examples of Scene Distinctions include CLUTTERED, FLOODED, NOISY, PITCH BLACK, QUIET, and UNSTABLE.

As the Watcher, you decide whether to give a Scene any Distinctions at all, or perhaps just one or two. Each Scene may have no more than three Distinctions to start, and the Watcher may add more during the Scene. Players can't create Scene Distinctions, although as the Watcher you might want to add them based on the players' suggestion—it helps involve the players as well as making your life easier! Make sure, however, that the players know about any Scene Distinctions when you frame the Scene.

A Scene Distinction is often a sensory condition, like NOISY or PITCH BLACK. Other times, it suggests physical or environmental color, such as CLUTTERED or FLOODED. Not all Scene Distinctions need to be so precise or direct; you could toy with TRANQUIL MOOD, STACKS AND STACKS OF CRATES, or CREEPY ATMOSPHERE.

As a player, it's your choice whether or not to include a Scene Distinction in your dice pool, and whether you're going to use it for a D4 (and get a PP) or a D8. Scene Distinctions count as Distinctions when putting together your dice pool—if you're already using one from your datafile, adding in one from the Scene costs you PP. On the other hand, if you're having trouble finding an applicable Distinction from your datafile, you can use a Scene Distinction instead.

I'm playing Wolverine, about to duel Shinobi Shaw before a whole courtyard full of invited party guests. The Watcher has established CROWD OF ONLOOKERS, SLICK COBBLESTONES, and EXPERTLY-TRIMMED HEDGES as Scene Distinctions. I like the first two, not sure about how to use the third one yet...

You might want to write each Scene Distinction on an index card and place it in the middle of the table—this way, they're easily visible to you and the players, and you can note any changes that occur during the Scene. You can also hang on to the ones that seem to come up time and time again, so you can quickly add ON FIRE or CRUMBLING BUILDINGS or STUNNED ONLOOKERS to any Scene.

As the Watcher, you can similarly add a D4 to a villain or supporting character's dice pool (and add or step up a doom die) or a D8. Scene Distinctions are great for supporting characters that don't have Distinctions of their own, like groups of thugs or minor villains. You can also spend a D8 or larger die from the doom pool to create a new Scene Distinction after the Scene has started.

I'm the Watcher, and even if I didn't already have a compelling reason to use Shinobi Shaw's own Distinctions as a D4 to grow the doom pool, I could pull in the CROWD OF ONLOOKERS Scene Distinction here to do so. Part of being the Watcher means coming up with interesting and flavorful ways for both my characters and the players' heroes to interact with the scenery, so to speak. In fact, the EXPERTLY-TRIMMED HEDGES Distinction is like a challenge to a creative player.

Scene Distinctions are similar to complications because they often seem to represent negative or hindering conditions in the environment. You can even target a Scene Distinction in the same way you target a complication (it counts as a D8 for these purposes) if it makes sense. The key difference is that a Distinction should always offer some way to use it positively, even if it's not an equal balance between help and hindrance.

Targeting
Effects
p. OM54

In the duel Scene, Wolverine or Shinobi Shaw could target the CROWD OF ONLOOKERS, with the explanation that the two of them are using their intimidating powers or presence to drive the crowd off. Simply moving to the grassy lawn might ignore SLICK COBBLESTONES. EXPERTLY-TRIMMED HEDGES, of course, are a natural target for someone with razor-sharp claws.

POWER SETS

A Power Set is a collection of super-powers, special effects (SFX), and Limits on those powers. Power Sets are always grouped around a common theme, source, or manifestation. A Power Set might represent innate super-powers, special gear, or any other extraordinary group of effects that can't be represented by a Specialty or Distinction. A Power Set might even be a pet or sidekick, like Lockheed the Dragon is to Kitty Pryde. Most super heroes have one or two Power Sets, with a rare few who have more and some who don't have any Power Sets at all.

Power Sets follow a standard format, as follows:

POWER SET NAME

POWER TRAIT DX   POWER TRAIT DX

SFX: Name of SFX. How SFX works.
Limit: Name of Limit. How Limit works.

Here's the BESTIAL MUTANT Power Set for the X-Men's **Hank McCoy** AKA **Beast**, which you can refer to as you read over this section. Beast's single Power Set is aptly named—it describes his animalistic abilities. If you're creating a new Power Set for a hero or villain, try to summarize what the Power Set represents in the title so it's easy to distinguish from, say, OMEGA-CLASS TELEPATH or POWERED ARMOR.

BESTIAL MUTANT

ENHANCED DURABILITY D8   ENHANCED SENSES D8
ENHANCED STAMINA D8   SUPERHUMAN REFLEXES D10
SUPERHUMAN STRENGTH D10

SFX: *Claws & Fangs.* Add a D6 to your dice pool for an attack action and step back the highest die in your pool by −1. Step up physical stress inflicted by +1.
SFX: *Oh My Stars and Garters!* Spend 1 PP to borrow the highest die in the doom pool as an asset for your next action, then step back and return the doom die.
Limit: Mutant. Earn 1 PP when affected by mutant-specific Milestones and tech.

POWER TRAITS

Each Power Set includes a number of traits that represent super-powers, called **power traits**. Power traits can be added to a dice pool when they benefit or support the action that's being taken. Whether they're appropriate is usually up to you as the player, but the Watcher and other players will let you know if you're being really weak with the justification. Many powers can be used without even making a roll, if there's nothing riding on the outcome.

I'm playing Beast and my BESTIAL MUTANT Power Set includes the ENHANCED SENSES D8 power trait. I can add this die into my dice pool whenever having senses that extend beyond the normal human range would be especially useful. I can also use it without rolling dice, such as when I describe Beast sniffing at a wine rack in the Hellfire Club's wine cellar and picking out the most expensive bottle based on the vintage.

POWER RATINGS

Powers are usually rated from D6 to D12, based on the following rough guidelines. Some powers start at D8.

- **D6:** Powers of this rating aren't the hero's signature power or don't get much of a spotlight when they're used. D6 powers are often utility-type effects, or only of **Minor** effect. Having a D6 power is useful because it gives you justification for doing something that ordinary people can't do, or it may come in handy when other powers are shut-down or unavailable.

- **D8:** Powers of this rating include all of the **Enhanced** rank of ability; these are levels of performance beyond that of ordinary human beings. A D8 power is one that sees a lot of use and is roughly equivalent to being an Expert in a Specialty in terms of how effective it is, such as Spider-Man's SENSES or Captain America's DURABILITY.

- **D10:** This rating of power includes all of the **Superhuman** degrees of ability; these are significantly beyond those possessed by normal humans. Few super heroes have powers rated higher than this. It's a power that's roughly equivalent in effectiveness to a Master in a Specialty, i.e., world-class in scope, like Luke Cage's STRENGTH or Emma Frost's TELEPATHY.

- **D12:** This rating is reserved for **Godlike** levels of ability and the topmost level of performance possible. Very few super heroes have D12 powers, and usually they're limited to single, specific powers or effects such as Wolverine's STAMINA or Colossus' STRENGTH.

POWER TRAIT EXAMPLES

Some power traits are common across many Power Sets, because they are archetypal super hero abilities. This section goes into more detail about each of these and how to use them.

Beast's five power traits are rated either D8 or D10. His ENHANCED DURABILITY, ENHANCED SENSES, and ENHANCED STAMINA mean that he's tougher and can push himself longer than any hero without these powers, at or above peak human ranges. His SUPERHUMAN REFLEXES and SUPERHUMAN STRENGTH indicate that his hand-eye coordination and reaction time are amazing, and he's able to snap a lamppost from a city street or crash through a brick wall.

Attack Powers (Blasts, Weapons)

Attack powers are almost always used in action dice pools.

Powers that represent attacks—whether it's an energy blast or razor-sharp claws—are included in this category. Most mundane weapons are represented by D6 or possibly D8 die ratings in a Power Set. Use the following as a guideline for other types.

▶ At D6, the power is roughly equivalent to small arms fire or dangerous close combat weapons.
▶ At D8, the power is capable of greater injury or harm, roughly equivalent to automatic weapons or small explosives.
▶ At D10, the power is equivalent to heavy explosives or lightning bolts.
▶ At D12, the power is truly devastating, even if the area of effect isn't widespread.

An Attack power's name gives you more suggestions about when it works. Often, the Attack uses a specific type of energy, such as fire, electricity, cold, or darkforce. This may affect how you describe the effects of stress caused by the Attack and by other powers or SFX that provide resistance to those types. A generic ENERGY BLAST is usually explosive plasma or cosmic energy with few side effects, unlike FLAME BLASTS or LIGHTNING BOLTS that set things on fire, or COLD BLASTS that freeze. PSYCHIC BLASTS can target heavily armored foes but they're useless against opponents without minds.

Some Attacks may be used at range, while others are only effective in close quarters. Whether this is an advantage or a drawback varies on the situation. It's easier to hit a flying target with a FORCE BLAST than ELBOW SPIKES, but in a confined space the FORCE BLAST poses problems the ELBOW SPIKES do not.

Durability

DURABILITY is usually included in reaction dice pools.

The hero is more resistant to injury and harmful effects than the average human.

▶ ENHANCED DURABILITY D8 confers toughened skin and muscle, as well as the ability to withstand most minor blunt trauma or pain and low-level extremes of heat or cold.

▶ SUPERHUMAN DURABILITY D10 is bulletproof skin and resistance to extreme temperatures or hazards.

▶ GODLIKE DURABILITY D12 indicates invulnerability to almost all conventional forms of injury and harmful effects.

DURABILITY is also used in Power Sets that represent **force fields or hardened objects**. Use common sense and the descriptions in the Power Set as your guide for when you can factor in DURABILITY. Invisible Woman's GODLIKE DURABILITY in her FORCE PROJECTION Power Set is a good example. Because her force fields are transparent, light-based attacks could ignore them. Similarly, Luke Cage's SUPERHUMAN DURABILITY doesn't protect him from gas attacks or some kinds of mystic blasts.

DURABILITY usually, but not always, comes with an associated level of life support or protection from the environment. Whether this life support is continuous or only when the hero is using the power may depend on SFX or how the DURABILITY is described.

Energy powers are typically resisted by DURABILITY. Some SFX protects against other, more specific types of harm—such as disease or toxins—over and above any protection DURABILITY might give. For protection against magic or psychic powers, use MYSTIC RESISTANCE or PSYCHIC RESISTANCE.

Resistance
p. OM80

COMMON ELEMENTS IN THE MARVEL UNIVERSE

- **Air:** Moving air masses around, increasing or decreasing air pressure, creating whirlwinds
- **Cosmic:** Channeling and redirecting the quantum power of the universe, altering or destroying the bonds between energy and matter, and connecting with the cosmos
- **Darkforce:** Summoning and manipulating the extradimensional energy known as darkforce
- **Earth:** Moving soil, dirt, and rock; shaping it or altering its consistency
- **Electric:** Strengthening, weakening, redirecting, and otherwise altering the properties of electrical current
- **Fire/Heat:** Rapidly increasing the thermal properties of the environment, shaping existing flame, combusting materials
- **Gravity:** Intensifying or diminishing the hold the Earth's gravimetric field has on objects, shifting centers of gravity
- **Ice/Cold:** Rapidly decreasing the thermal properties of the environment, producing ice, freezing things

Elemental Control Powers (including Influence, Mastery, and Supremacy)

Elemental Control powers may be used in either action or reaction dice pools.

The ability to control the elements is a common power trait for super heroes. What exactly is meant by "elements" can vary from hero to hero. They aren't necessarily elements in the periodic table sense, or the classical elements of air, fire, earth, and water—in many cases they're more properly categorized as energy types or compounds.

For the purposes of the game, a material, energy, or substance being controlled is called an **element**. Each Elemental Control power trait must be specified, i.e., FIRE, LIGHT, MAGNETIC.

▶ ELEMENTAL INFLUENCE D6 gives minor or basic control: extinguishing all the candle flames in a room; cooling the air in a room; shorting out household appliances.

▶ ELEMENTAL CONTROL D8 gives significant local control: extinguishing a burning room; snap-freezing the air in a room; shorting out a building's electrical system.

▶ ELEMENTAL MASTERY D10 provides citywide control: extinguishing a burning skyscraper; freezing over a city street; bringing down a city's power grid.

▶ ELEMENTAL SUPREMACY D12 provides regional control: extinguishing a forest fire; freezing over Lake Michigan; rerouting the national power grid.

COMMON ELEMENTS (CONTINUED)

- **Kinetic/Telekinetic:** Intensifying or diminishing the stored kinetic potential of objects, moving things around, holding them in place
- **Light:** Intensifying or diminishing the ambient light in the environment, creating bright flashes, forming holograms
- **Magnetic:** Strengthening, weakening, redirecting, or otherwise manipulating magnetic fields, affecting ferrous metals
- **Sonic:** Intensifying or diminishing the ambient sound in the environment, altering sound waves, mimicking noises
- **Technology:** Activating, shutting down, assembling, and manipulating technology or machinery from a distance; merging several existing machines together or creating hybrid technology
- **Weather:** Anticipating, directing, and manipulating local and regional weather patterns to create meteorological effects from rain and snow to wind and drought
- **Water:** Moving aqueous masses around, increasing or decreasing water volume and pressure, dehydrating a living target

Elemental Control powers offer many opportunities for stunts; when tied together with SFX, they may be applied in dozens of ways. The basic rule of thumb is that the larger the die rating, the greater the scope of the power's control effect. ELEMENTAL INFLUENCE D6 usually only extends to one or two types of effect, while ELEMENTAL SUPREMACY indicates unsurpassed manipulation of the controlled element.

Note that MIND CONTROL and other psychic powers aren't considered Elemental Control. The same is true for SORCERY, which is its own power trait type. Psychics or sorcerers often possess some of these elemental powers, of course; KINETIC/TELEKINETIC CONTROL, FIRE CONTROL, and WEATHER CONTROL are frequently psychic in nature.

Some Elemental Control powers might overlap with each other; it's possible to create frosty conditions using both ICE CONTROL and WEATHER CONTROL, though the former has more accuracy and depth than the latter. Similarly, Magneto's MAGNETIC SUPREMACY has been used before to alter electrical currents and other types of energy, though these are likely stunts rather than SFX. This sort of overlap is more likely at the MASTERY and SUPREMACY levels; INFLUENCE and CONTROL rarely allow the character to step outside the standard boundaries of those elements.

Elemental Control doesn't usually exist by itself in a Power Set. In order to properly represent the kinds of abilities that are associated with heroes with Elemental Control, these Power Sets also include powers like ENERGY BLAST, FLIGHT, or SENSES, and SFX like *Area Attack*, *Energy Absorption*, and *Multipower*.

Intangibility

INTANGIBILITY is usually used in reaction dice pools.

The hero is able to become less solid, either through reduced molecular density, shifting phase, or becoming fluid. The primary effect of this power trait is that passing through obstacles becomes much easier, and physical objects pass through the body.

▶ At D6, the power lets you mildly disperse your molecules, reducing the impact of some physical attacks and allowing you to slowly move through highly porous or permeable obstacles, such as chicken wire fences or barred gates.

▶ At D8, the power represents substantial fluidity or dispersal, giving you the power to seep through tiny holes in obstacles and reduce the impact of most physical attacks.

▶ At D10, the power makes you ghostlike or out of phase—you can walk through almost any physical obstacle other than super-high density substances, and your movements make very little noise. Physical attacks rarely affect you.

▶ At D12, the power makes you completely out of phase with reality, including even energy waveforms. You're essentially not even there.

INTAGIBILITY is a power trait often associated with Power Sets that describe transforming into liquids or, at low ratings, the ability to deform or compress your body. It's a close cousin to STRETCHING and is often included in the same Power Set. If the hero's Power Set represents molecular or dimensional phasing, powers like FLIGHT or AIRWALKING are common.

SFX that accompany Power Sets with INTANGIBILITY include being able to disrupt people or things by phasing or passing through them, and sharing your INTANGIBILITY with others.

Invisibility

INVISIBILITY is usually used in reaction dice pools.

The hero is able to make herself unable to be seen, whether through the bending of light waves, high-tech chameleon technology, or shifting out of phase with this dimension.

- ▶ At D6, the power blurs or obscures your visual image; it's often limited to obscuring your image in mirrors or electronic surveillance, or in situations where vision is already impaired, such as at night. It may also be a psychic field that makes others pay less attention to you, even though you're still visible.
- ▶ At D8, you are concealed to a greater degree, such as with chameleon-like blending, ghost-like transparency, or psychic misdirection. While still visible to others if they focus, you've got the equivalent of a stealth field.
- ▶ At D10, the power renders you completely invisible to standard visual means. You can move around without being noticed, and you don't leave a shadow or other signs of being there. Certain spectrums of visual detection may spot you, such as infrared or dimensional locators.
- ▶ At D12, you are impossible to detect with any visual-based sense. You never show up on any device, and likely don't even give off energy signatures of any kind.

Depending on how this is defined within a Power Set, INVISIBILITY may be psychic- or physics-based. If it's psychic-based, that affects how others might detect the hero. If it's physics-based, sometimes all you need to do is to turn up the sound detection to realize an invisible hero is nearby. This power trait when combined with others like INTANGIBILITY or FLIGHT can essentially make the hero a phantom or apparition.

Mimic

MIMIC may be used in both action and reaction dice pools.

This isn't the ability to change shape into other forms or look like other people—that's SHAPESHIFTING. MIMIC is the ability to copy or even steal powers from others. It may also be used to represent a hero who has no fixed powers but instead spontaneously creates them as the need arises.

In order to manifest a power, the hero must create an asset with an action using this power's die. Sometimes, the hero must physically touch or cause stress to the target; in other cases, the hero can just develop a power. The description and SFX usually define how this works. The asset created serves as the power trait in the short term.

MIMIC's die rating directly corresponds to the ability of the hero to effectively copy or mimic another power. Regardless of which power the hero attempts to mimic or the effect die chosen, the scope and extent of the copied power is limited by MIMIC's die rating. If you want to copy or steal FLIGHT as a power and only have MIMIC D8, you won't be capable of supersonic speed. You might have a D12 asset being used to represent FLIGHT and roll that die into any actions or reactions, but the actual speed won't be GODLIKE.

Heroes with MIMIC usually have a number of SFX and Limits that refine the power. They may also have other powers in their Power Set, such as SHAPESHIFTING, that extend the ability of the hero to copy others.

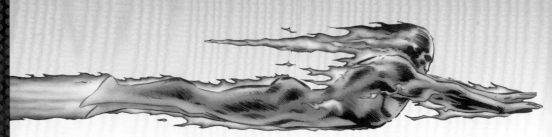

Movement Powers (Speed/Flight/Swingline/Airwalking/Burrowing/Leaping/Swimming)

Movement power traits are usually used in action dice pools.

Movement powers confer the ability to move at greater than human speed. SPEED is ground or surface travel, while FLIGHT is air or space travel. The actual speed each die rating represents differs between SPEED and FLIGHT.

▶ At SPEED D6, you can run as fast as the world's fastest humans; FLIGHT D6 is the speed of a hawk or news chopper.

▶ At ENHANCED SPEED D8, you can run at the speed of a horse; with SUBSONIC FLIGHT D8, you can fly as fast as a missile or passenger airliner.

▶ At SUPERHUMAN SPEED D10, you're faster than a bullet train; with SUPERSONIC FLIGHT D10, you can fly as fast as a jet fighter.

▶ At GODLIKE SPEED D12, you can travel around the world in moments; SPACE FLIGHT D12 permits swift interplanetary travel.

Other Movement powers appear in Power Sets, too. SWINGLINE, AIRWALKING, BURROWING, SWIMMING, and so forth are all Movement powers. They generally operate at the same speed as the SPEED power trait, but how and when they might be used differs. SWINGLINES let Spider-Man and Daredevil swing through city streets above the traffic, giving them access to areas others don't have; BURROWING is something Moloids can do that surface-dwellers can't. LEAPING describes traveling large distances with mighty bounds or spring-like steps. SWIMMING is being able to move through water as fast as—or faster than—an Olympic medalist.

One Movement power, TELEPORT, gets its own entry—it doesn't actually represent traveling but rather crossing distances without Movement at all.

Movement powers are often included in Power Sets together with REFLEXES or STAMINA, but not always. Similarly, STRENGTH and LEAPING are often found in the same Power Set. They're most often used to guide how quickly and in what ways someone can get to places. Creating stunts with Movement powers factor in the velocity and speed of the power more than, say, the reaction time or endurance of the hero.

Movement powers that explicitly allow travel in specific environments are assumed to include the ability to survive in those environments at or beyond the D8 level. So, ENHANCED SWIMMING D8 affords an air supply or the ability to breathe underwater, while SUBSONIC FLIGHT D8 means you don't suffer the negative effects of high velocity. If you have SPACE FLIGHT, you're not worried about the vacuum of space.

Psychic Powers (Mind Control/Telepathy/Animal Control/Plant Control)

Psychic power traits are usually used in action dice pools.

Psychic powers are powers that affect or influence other minds, although most people don't include plants as minds. The two most common are MIND CONTROL and TELEPATHY. **Psychic powers are used to create complications on their targets**. If the complication is stepped up beyond D12 and the target is "stressed out" then your effect is total. Until then, the target gets a chance to resist it or fight it off, with the complication making things tough for them. To cause mental or emotional stress, use PSYCHIC BLAST instead.

MIND CONTROL relies on planting suggestions, influencing perceptions, and altering behavior—it's **getting people to do what you want**, especially when they wouldn't otherwise. A complication you create with MIND CONTROL (such as FIGHT YOUR FRIENDS! Or LET US IN!) hinders your target if he resists or tries to oppose what you want him to do. If he goes along with it, even if you haven't stepped the complication past D12, the complication doesn't pose any problem for him.

▶ At D6, you can push the target to do something he was inclined to do already, such as buy something he likes or make advances on someone he's attracted to. You can also intensify his senses to a degree—making the room seem colder, a smell seem stronger, or other mild effects.

▶ At D8, you can override the target's impulse control, remove inhibitions, or provoke irrational behavior. You can make him see, smell, or hear things that aren't there for short periods, enough to distract him.

▶ At D10, you can take over the target's motor control and movements, create vivid and believable hallucinations that last for hours, or cause him to go against his core beliefs for a short time.

▶ At D12, you can completely possess the target, create entire fictional universes within his mind, and permanently alter his beliefs or perceptions.

TELEPATHY is **making contact with other minds** for the purposes of communication, although it also allows reading surface or deeper thoughts, anticipating actions, and sharing or altering memories. A complication you create with TELEPATHY might hinder your target if he's trying to block you out, screen his thoughts, or remember something you've made him forget. Much of the time you won't need to roll this power, especially if it's used on willing targets. If the target isn't willing, you need to "stress out" your target with the complication before you can pull out the information you want.

▶ At D6, you can maintain a link with another mind with some effort, using the link to talk or share thoughts.

▶ At D8, you can read surface thoughts, emotions, and share one or two senses (like sight and hearing), as well as link a half-dozen minds together for communication.

▶ At D10, you can probe minds for memories, thoughts, and instincts, create persistent mental links among large groups of people across great distances, and even block or influence a specific target's memories.

▶ At D12, you can remain in constant communication with vast numbers of people, skim the surface thoughts of everyone on the planet, and implant entirely new life histories within specific minds.

ANIMAL CONTROL is used to make animals do what you want, though how this happens can vary. PLANT CONTROL is the same, only with vegetable matter. These powers, while psychic in nature, are really a kind of Elemental Control, with the die rating representing the scope and power of the control. At D6, your influence and ability to connect with animals or plants is limited to nudges or suggestions; at D12, you have supremacy over all animal or plant life, and you may even be connected directly to the living web of life on the planet.

Elemental
Control
p. OM74

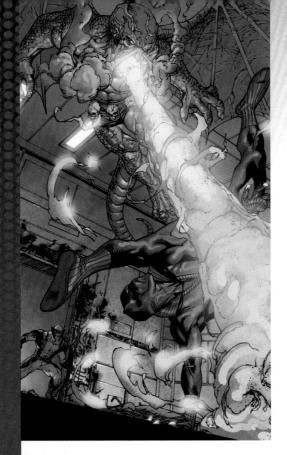

Resistance Powers

Resistance power traits are almost always used in reaction dice pools.

The hero is resistant to types of harm or attack that most people have no defense against. It could be innate or provided by equipment or gear. The most common types are MYSTIC RESISTANCE and PSYCHIC RESISTANCE. Other Resistance powers are provided by DURABILITY or show up as SFX for a Power Set (such as being immune to toxins or disease).

▶ A RESISTANCE D6 is slight, but still more than any normal person would have.
▶ A RESISTANCE D8 is enough to turn aside most standard attacks of this type.
▶ A RESISTANCE D10 gives substantial defense against most attacks of this type.
▶ A RESISTANCE D12 represents near-invulnerability to attacks of this type.

Reflexes

REFLEXES may be used in either action or reaction dice pools.

The hero has a greater response time, physical agility, and aim than an average human.

▶ ENHANCED REFLEXES D8 represents two to three times the normal human response time and hand-eye coordination.
▶ SUPERHUMAN REFLEXES D10 indicates as much as ten times the response time and coordination of an ordinary human.
▶ GODLIKE REFLEXES D12 confers the ability to react as if the world around you had slowed to a crawl; you have lightning-fast hand-eye coordination.

Many heroes with a REFLEXES power also have Movement powers, although they are not synonymous. Quicksilver has GODLIKE REFLEXES and GODLIKE SPEED, while Daredevil has ENHANCED REFLEXES and no Movement power trait. It's more common to have both when the REFLEXES power trait is rated at SUPERHUMAN or GODLIKE.

These power traits are similar to Durability in that they provide resistance or protection from harmful or damaging attacks. SFX may also provide protection against specific types of attack, on top of whatever protection is given by a Resistance or Durability. Most heroes with mystic or psychic powers also possess a Resistance of that type in their Power Set.

Senses

SENSES may be used in either action or re-action dice pools.

The hero's senses are more acute, keen, or developed than a normal human.

▶ SENSES at a D6 rating are usually additional senses that might be brought in, like CYBERNETIC SENSE or MYSTIC SENSE, mostly to give you other ways to pick up on information.
▶ ENHANCED SENSES D8 represent extraordinary levels of awareness, closer to those of predatory animals.
▶ SUPERHUMAN SENSES D10 reach beyond nature, offering incredible levels of awareness.
▶ GODLIKE SENSES D12 touch upon cosmic threads of information and perception.

It's more or less assumed that most people have SENSES at the D6 level, and that if you ever need to roll it, you'd just use a Push die. For this reason, SENSES D6 is primarily descriptive. In some Power Sets, extraordinary senses outside of the normal human types are actually SFX, such as Spider-Man's *Spider-Senses* and Daredevil's *Radar Sense*. This is because those abilities build on those heroes' SENSES power traits to give them a means of rerolling dice in their pool. Iron Man's CYBERNETIC SENSES on the other hand give his player a means of including computer network access in a dice pool even when Tony Stark doesn't have normal access.

These power traits don't specify which senses are heightened. In the game, this is left up to individual character description. For the most part, Marvel characters with a SENSES power enjoy heightened awareness across the spectrum, at least in terms of acquiring information from their immediate environment.

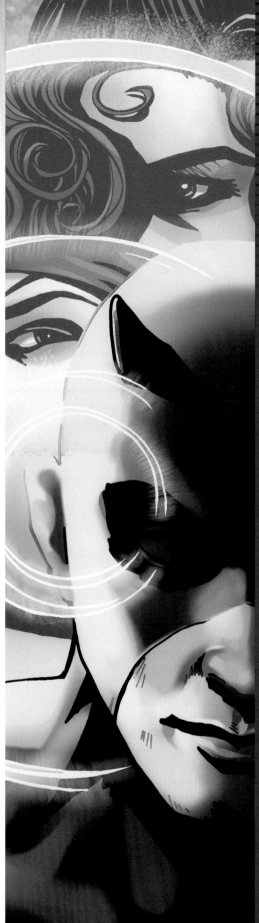

Push Dice
p. OM20

- ▶ At D6, you can make minor changes to your facial features or aspects of your appearance, but not enough to closely mimic anyone in particular.
- ▶ At D8, you can take on the external form of someone else, fooling most onlookers and passing as the person you're imitating. You may also be able to take on the external form of an animal or other living creature.
- ▶ At D10, you may fully shift into another living physical form or shape, even down to the cellular level, fooling scientific instruments, extraordinary senses, and so on. Non-living shapes will still register as being organic.
- ▶ At D12, you may shapeshift into anything— living and non-living forms—fooling even cosmic senses. For all intents and purposes, you become that other thing.

SHAPESHIFTING can be used to acquire things a hero doesn't normally have access to, such as claws or wings. These can either be represented by stunts, thus having limited use, or by assets, which might be extended with PP. If the hero regularly creates wings or claws, they're probably represented by other power traits in the Power Set. Hulkling, for instance, shapeshifts wings all the time, but he has FLIGHT as a power trait to avoid having to create them as a stunt or asset. A hero might also have the MIMIC power, giving him the ability to copy other powers, instead of or together with SHAPESHIFTING.

SHAPESHIFTING is often in a Power Set with STRETCHING, with size-changing powers like GROWTH or SHRINKING, and with physical enhancement powers like DURABILITY, STAMINA, or STRENGTH.

If a hero only ever shapeshifts into one form, he probably doesn't have this power. Instead, his Power Set would include powers that describe his other form (such as DURABILITY or REFLEXES), and a Limit that shuts down these powers when he's not in the alternate form.

Shapeshifting

SHAPESHIFTING may be used in either action or reaction dice pools.

Being able to alter the way you look or to take on the form of something else is a great stealth power; the best example in the Marvel Universe is the race of Skrulls. It can also represent the use of magic to disguise one's appearance, as Loki does, or the power to transform into non-human shapes, like certain transforming robots or battle suits.

Size-Changing Powers
(Growth, Shrinking)

Size-changing powers may be used in either action or reaction dice pools.

With these powers, the hero may grow or shrink in size. This is often through the use of the so-called Pym Particles that shunt mass into and out of the Kosmos dimension, but there are other ways of changing size in the Marvel Universe, such as mystic spells or gathering more mass from your environment.

▶ At D6, you can bulk up considerably (GROWTH) or compress your mass tightly (SHRINKING). This doesn't change your overall height or weight so much as it represents being able to snap out of or slip from restraints, fit into cramped spaces, or look somewhat more menacing.

▶ With GROWTH D8, you can grow to at least fifteen feet, more than doubling in size. With SHRINKING D8, you can reduce your size to that of a doll or small animal.

▶ With GROWTH D10 , you can grow to the size of a building, upwards of a hundred feet, dwarfing all around you. With SHRINKING D10, you can become insect-sized.

▶ With GROWTH D12 , you can become truly massive, perhaps without limit, almost a geographic formation of your own. With SHRINKING D12, you can become microscopic, able to pierce through the barrier into the Microverse.

Size-changing powers are used when you think that being really big or really small could be helpful in a dice pool or let you change the situation in a Scene. They are almost always included in a Power Set with other power traits—GROWTH with STRENGTH, DURABILITY, or STAMINA; SHRINKING with REFLEXES, FLIGHT, and SENSES. You can't use both Size-changing powers at the same time—it makes no sense to roll both GROWTH and SHRINKING. Most Power Sets with these powers have a shutdown Limit that makes the associated power traits shutdown at the same time as the GROWTH or SHRINKING. In other words, if you have SUPERHUMAN STRENGTH and SUPERHUMAN DURABILITY while you're a giant, shutting down GROWTH will shut those down also.

Is it easier for opponents to hit you when you're fifty feet tall? Are you less of a target when you're the size of an ant? With these powers, ensure that there's a Limit in your Power Set to handle the former (*Huge*: Earn 1 PP when your GROWTH becomes a complication for you) and just use your die in a reaction to handle the latter (that SHRINKING D10 sure helps avoid danger!).

Sorcery

SORCERY may be used in either action or reaction dice pools.

The hero can alter or change magical fields or channel power from other dimensions to affect change in this one.

▶ With SORCERY NOVICE D6, you can achieve the equivalent of parlor tricks, prestidigitation, and conjuring without having the stage magic equipment to do it. Nothing more than pulling out long scarves, lighting a candle with a snap of the fingers, or concealing doves in a cage.

▶ With SORCERY ADEPT D8, you have genuine powers of summoning and controlling mystic forces—usually to create constructs and illusions, commune with other dimensions, and invoke changes in the laws of physics.

▶ With SORCERY MASTERY D10, you have great mystical powers, channeling power into longer lasting constructs or objects, bending the laws of physics, and dispelling the magical works of others.

▶ With SORCERY SUPREMECY D12, you can draw on world-shattering mystic power to affect far-reaching changes, bring things to and from other dimensions, and empower mystical objects or creatures of frightening strength.

SORCERY is a trait that may seem confusing or too powerful, but it's really just another form of Elemental Control. The descriptive nature of Sorcery makes for flashy effects and interesting stunts, assets, and complications, but the power itself should not be any more potent than others. It's included in Power Sets with many other power traits that represent specific magical effects, from MYSTIC BLAST and FLIGHT to STRENGTH and TELEPORT. **SORCERY can't usually inflict stress on its own** but it can create assets and complications.

In the Marvel Universe, magic is often defined as coming from three sources: the invocation of beings of great power, tapping the ambient mystical forces in the world, and the magician's own psychic resources. This power trait, combined with others in a Power Set, usually takes care of the first two. Note that the MYSTIC Specialty allows for other avenues into occult lore, including rituals, items of power, and knowledge. Heroes with SORCERY usually have this Specialty.

Stamina

STAMINA is almost always used in recovery dice pools.

The hero has increased endurance and staying power, as well as recuperative ability and resistance to fatigue or toxins.

▶ ENHANCED STAMINA D8 indicates faster than normal healing and recovery, resistance to minor diseases, and the ability to perform at maximum effort for an hour or more.

▶ SUPERHUMAN STAMINA D10 allows for rapid recovery from injury, resistance to most terrestrial diseases or toxins, and the ability to operate at maximum effort for several hours.

▶ GODLIKE STAMINA D12 indicates extremely rapid recovery from even near-fatal wounds or trauma, resistance to even extraterrestrial diseases, and almost limitless ability to operate at maximum effort.

Although STAMINA finds the most use in recovery, it can also be used in reaction dice pools against attacks that target a hero's endurance or staying power, or that try to induce paralysis, sleep, or fatigue. If a hero is trying to hold his breath or some other more active effort, you might use STAMINA in the action dice pool.

STAMINA extends the hero's lifespan, too, if that ever comes into question, though it won't necessarily prevent aging so much as keep the effects of aging from slowing the hero down. Heroes with a STAMINA power are more resistant to chemical substances like drugs, alcohol, and caffeine; no matter how much Wolverine drinks, he never actually gets drunk.

Strength

STRENGTH is almost always used in action dice pools.

The hero has strength and muscular power beyond that of a normal human.

▶ ENHANCED STRENGTH D8 allows you to turn over cars, break through solid barriers, and bend ordinary iron bars.

▶ SUPERHUMAN STRENGTH D10 allows you to lift and throw vehicles, smash through stone and metal, and tear apart most barriers.

▶ GODLIKE STRENGTH D12 confers the power to hurl objects into orbit, push over tall buildings, and demolish most structures.

This is one of the most common superpowers, and represents everything from mutant-enhanced musculature to high-tech powered armor. As with many power traits, it's often assumed to just work if there's nothing challenging the hero, or if using STRENGTH is part of the description of an action (like ripping a telephone pole out of the ground to smash a tank). It's usually, though not always, included in a Power Set with DURABILITY, often at a different die rating. It may also be used with LEAPING, representing the use of STRENGTH to leap great distances.

If the STRENGTH is only in one limb or otherwise limited to specific conditions, this is just part of the Power Set's definition. There's usually no reason to worry about Misty Knight only having SUPERHUMAN STRENGTH D10 in her bionic right arm unless the situation specifically talks about needing strength in the legs or the left arm.

Stretching

STRETCHING is usually used in action dice pools.

The hero is able to elongate or increase the length of his limbs or other body parts, often to great distances. In some cases this is through prosthetic devices like Doctor Octopus' robotic tentacles, although in other cases it's a metamorphic ability like Mr. Fantastic's elastic body.

▶ At D6, you can reach across a normal room or access high places. It's the equivalent of having double the usual reach with arms or legs.
▶ At D8, you can reach across a street, up the side of a building, or down an elevator shaft.
▶ At D10, you can stretch to considerable distances, several city blocks away. You can clear buildings, rivers, or wide ravines with your elongated legs and arms.
▶ At D12, you can reach ridiculous distances, perhaps without limit—across lakes, oceans, and even into orbit—although the further you stretch the less you're able to make use of your limbs.

STRETCHING can be used much like a Movement power (long legs make travel easier), defensively (an elastic body can mitigate a lot of damage), or an offensively (a punch hurled across a street can hurt). While the way the Power Set is defined should inform how it's used, STRETCHING is primarily a means of extending reach and access. Stretching is often coupled with powers like Durability, Intangibility (at low ratings), Growth, Strength, Reflexes, Shapeshifting, and even Elemental Control.

SFX included in a Power Set with Stretching include *Area Attack, Grapple*, and *Versatility*.

Teleport

TELEPORT may be used in action or reaction dice pools.

The hero may travel from one point to another instantaneously. Usually, no actual distance is traveled; the hero just vanishes from one place and appears in another. The power rating informs the distance that's possible.

▶ At D6, you can blink in and out of place in a single location, crossing a room or a gap between buildings, effectively eliminating the need to walk. Line of sight is usually required.
▶ At D8, you can teleport across several miles, such as from place to place in a metropolitan area or, by taking multiple jumps, from one city to another.
▶ At D10, you can travel around the world in single or multiple jumps, and perhaps as far as the moon.
▶ At D12, you can travel across vast distances, even to other planets or galaxies.

Depending on the nature of the power (sorcery, technology, mutant, etc.), the way TELEPORT works can vary greatly. If the teleportation is through manifested portals or wormholes, this might affect the SFX used in the Power Set. In some cases, the teleportation is limited to the extreme ranges of the die rating; the mutant Lila Cheney has TELEPORT D12 but can only use it to travel intergalactic distances.

At the D10 and D12 rating, you can choose to have the power *only* allow travel to other dimensions or other worlds; travel between locations on Earth in such instances would be a stunt.

Some heroes with this power may use it to grab people and teleport them, either going along with you as a passenger or by making portals to send them away. This is represented best with SFX or by using the power with a stunt as part of an attack. Nightcrawler of the X-Men frequently uses this kind of stunt.

Transmutation

TRANSMUTATION is usually used in action dice pools.

The hero has the power to transmute one substance to another. This is known to mystics as alchemy and to scientists as matter alteration; the specific details may vary.

▶ At D6, you can affect the integrity or cohesion of a target, causing it to soften or harden, perhaps degrade or take on other qualities, but not actually change into another substance.
▶ At D8, you can alter the properties of a non-living target to make it solid, liquid, or gas, or change it from one kind of solid, liquid, or gas to another.
▶ At D10, you can operate on the chemical or elemental level and can change one substance, living or nonliving, into another. Stone can be made flesh, water can be transmuted into oil, and so on.
▶ At D12, you can change any object or item into another, regardless of its original substance, shape, or qualities.

TRANSMUTATION is very powerful and, as such, typically doesn't confer long-lasting effects. Most TRANSMUTATION actions create assets or complications that represent the change in quality. The power can be used to inflict stress, too—such as a disintegrator ray—but unless the target is stressed out, the effect isn't complete or permanent. Usually, the die rating of the power also informs how well it can alter a target with Durability or Resistance.

TRANSMUTATION is often found in Power Sets with Elemental Control, SHAPESHIFTING, STRETCHING, or some kind of Attack power. If the hero is able to transmute or change himself into different forms of matter, this is best represented by SHAPESHIFTING or physical powers like DURABILITY or STRENGTH, with the actual elemental change being descriptive.

POSSIBLE TRIGGERS INCLUDE THE FOLLOWING:

- Spend 1 PP
- Shutdown a power trait
- Add a die to the doom pool
- Step back a die
- Take a specific action
- Do some other thing

THE BENEFITS FROM SFX INCLUDE ONE OR MORE OF THE FOLLOWING:

- Step up a die
- Double a die (add another die of the same size)
- Add a die (usually a D6)
- Keep an effect die
- Recover (i.e., eliminate) stress
- Reroll your dice

SPECIAL EFFECTS

Power Sets are more than just power traits, because even two heroes with the same basic set of powers may use them differently. To represent these cool personalized tricks, every Power Set includes one or more **special effects (SFX)**. Spider-Man and Luke Cage both have SUPERHUMAN STRENGTH D10 in their Power Sets, but Luke's also got the *Area Attack* SFX while Spider-Man does not. SFX differ from stunts in that they allow you to do something you otherwise wouldn't be able to do with an action or reaction, or they give you some kind of narrative benefit coupled to a trigger.

SFX are presented as **do A to get B** or, to get technical, **use trigger to get benefit**. The trigger is the part of the SFX description that tells you what you need to do in order to enjoy the benefit of the SFX.

SFX always have a cost of some kind, represented by the trigger. Some SFX may seem as if they're more or less "expensive" than others, but usually there's an additional narrative restriction that keeps things fair and square.

I'm playing Beast and my BESTIAL MUTANT Power Set has two SFX: *Claws & Fangs* and *Oh My Stars and Garters!* The latter one reads: "Spend 1 PP to borrow the highest die in the doom pool as an asset for your next action, then step back and return the doom die." The trigger for this SFX is the PP cost, and the benefit is being able to use a doom die as an asset and then put it back in the doom pool as a smaller die. Wolverine has a similar SFX in his WEAPON X PROGRAM Power Set called *Berserk*, which lets him use a doom die in his actions, but instead of spending PP he has to step up the doom die before returning it.

Unless otherwise stated, SFX aren't tied to specific power traits. They are connected primarily to the Power Set itself and therefore represent expressions of that Power Set's theme. You don't necessarily need to use a power trait from the SFX's Power Set in order to benefit from the SFX, but you should always include that Power Set as part of the description of your action or reaction. And, of course, if the SFX says it's connected to the use of a power trait, you should be using that power trait.

I'm playing Beast and my *Oh My Stars and Garters!* SFX lets me borrow doom dice to use as an asset. There's no specific power trait connected to this—it's just part of being able to briefly turn a bad situation around to Beast's advantage due to his bestial talents and smart thinking. On the other hand, Cyclops' *Versatile* SFX is directly connected to his FORCE BLAST power trait, representing his ability to be resourceful with his optic blasts.

Shutdown

One trigger that's also used in Limits is the **shutdown**. This is almost always connected to either a power trait or, occasionally, a Power Set. When you shutdown a power trait or Power Set, you can't use it until the recovery condition is met. Sometimes this requires you to **activate an opportunity** (spend a PP when the Watcher rolls a 1) or **take an action** (using up your turn in the action order).

Shutdown traits may also be recovered during Transition Scenes, just like stress. Add the power trait's die rating (or the highest power trait in the Power Set, if the Power Set is shutdown) to the hero's dice pool, together with appropriate Distinctions, Affiliation, and powers from other Power Sets if applicable. The Watcher opposes with the doom pool and any other kinds of stress or complication. If the effect die is equal to or greater than the power trait's die rating, the power is recovered and no longer shutdown. If the effect die is smaller than the power trait's die rating, the power is recovered but stepped back by one until another recovery effort during a Transition Scene or until the Limit's usual recovery condition is met.

Iron Man's POWERED ARMOR Power Set has the following SFX: "*Boost.* Shutdown highest rated WEAPONS PLATFORM or POWERED ARMOR power to step up another POWERED ARMOR power by +1. Activate an opportunity to recover power." This means that if I'm playing Iron Man I can choose to shutdown one of my WEAPONS PLATFORM powers (like FLIGHT D10) and step up another power trait, like SUPERHUMAN STRENGTH D10. This gives me SUPERHUMAN STRENGTH D12 for the rest of the Scene or until the Watcher rolls an opportunity and I activate it with a Plot Point , thus regaining use of the shutdown power. I can also attempt to recover the power during a Transition Scene. If I go with the latter, I add the D10 for the power I shutdown to my dice pool, but the Watcher also uses it in the dice pool opposing me.

EXAMPLES OF SPECIAL EFFECTS

There are a number of SFX that frequently show up in hero datafiles. These are listed below, with some general guidelines for when they might be included and why. Substitute the words in ALL CAPS for actual traits or types when used in a Power Set. You'll find more SFX examples in the hero datafiles included in any Event book. SFX may be renamed (or "reskinned") where necessary, to inject a little individual flavor into the Power Set.

Absorption

On a successful reaction against a TYPE OF ATTACK action, convert your opponent's effect die into a POWER SET stunt or step up a POWER SET power by +1 for your next action. Spend 1 PP to use this stunt if your opponent's action succeeds.

▶ This is an example of something that might otherwise be represented with a power trait but that works best as SFX, e.g., *Energy Absorption* or *Kinetic Absorption*.

▶ Usually included in a Power Set with Elemental Control powers, Attack powers, STRENGTH, or REFLEXES.

Afflict

Add a D6 and step up your effect die by +1 when inflicting TYPE complication on a target.

▶ Usually appears in Power Sets that represent gear, grappling, entangling, etc.

▶ The type of complication is usually connected to the Power Set. Spider-Man's *Grapple* is web-based, for example.

Area Attack

Add a D6 and keep an additional effect die for each additional target.

▶ Frequently included in Power Sets with STRENGTH, Attack powers, or Elemental Control powers.

▶ Useful against mobs (similar opponents grouped together as a single threat).

▶ Rolling opportunities on an *Area Attack* action generally causes collateral damage, represented by the doom pool getting bigger.

Berserk

Add a die from the doom pool to one or more attack actions. Step up the doom pool die by +1 for each action; return it to the doom pool when you're done.

▶ Variations include a PP cost, but the doom die is stepped back by −1 when it's returned. This is a good SFX for rage-based characters.

Boost

Shutdown your highest rated POWER SET power to step up another POWER SET power by +1. Recover power by activating an opportunity or during a Transition Scene.

▶ Great for Power Sets that represent powered armor, cybernetics, or robotic systems.

Burst

Step up or double a POWER TRAIT die against a single target. Remove the highest rolling die and add 3 dice for your total.

▶ Usually appears in Power Sets that represent gear. For heroes with a lot of Specialties, this supports the extra dice Specialties often add.

▶ Represents a wide spread of attack, or ricocheting the attack from one or more surfaces and thus around corners, obstacles, and so on.

Constructs

Add a D6 and step up your effect die by +1 when using POWER SET to create assets.

▶ Usually included in Power Sets that represent control over substances, the ability to summon things, etc. Compare with *Grapple*, which is used to create complications.

Counterattack

On a reaction against a STRESS TYPE attack action, inflict STRESS TYPE with your effect die at no PP cost or spend a PP to step it up by +1.

▶ Used in Power Sets that represent being able to surround yourself with or transform yourself into an energy form. Also works for spiked armor, acidic skin, etc. (physical stress); psychic booby traps (mental stress); or empathic fields (emotional stress).

Dangerous

Add a D6 to your dice pool for an attack action and step back highest die in pool by −1. Step up STRESS TYPE inflicted by +1.

▶ Included in Power Sets as *Claws & Fangs* or *Belt of Strength* or when representing some dangerous use of the character's abilities.

Focus

If a pool includes a POWER SET power, you may replace two dice of equal size with one die +1 step larger.

▶ Great for heroes who have a lot of Specialties or whose Power Sets represent skill, training, or conditioning.

Healing

Add POWER TRAIT to your dice pool when helping others recover stress. Spend 1 PP to recover your own or another's STRESS TYPE or step back your own or another's TRAUMA TYPE by −1.

▶ Depending on the stress type that it recovers, this might represent psychic healing, chi healing, empathic healing, or spiritual aura.

Immunity

Spend 1 PP to ignore stress, trauma, or complications from SPECIFIC ATTACK TYPE(S).

▶ Attack types include poisons, disease, psychic attack, magical attack, electricity, radiation, and so forth.

Invulnerable

Spend 1 PP to ignore STRESS TYPE or TRAUMA TYPE unless caused by SPECIFIC ATTACK TYPE.

▶ Similar to *Immunity* but restricted to a specific type of stress or trauma and with an exception for a specific attack type.

Multipower

Use two or more POWER SET powers in a single dice pool at -1 step for each additional power.

▶ Usually appears in Power Sets with several power traits and when the hero has no other Power Sets.

▶ Step back only the power dice that you include, not all of the dice in the dice pool.

Second Chance

Spend 1 PP to reroll when using any POWER SET power.

▶ Good for Power Sets that represent luck, fortitude, or chance.

Second Wind

Before you make an action including a POWER SET power, you may move your STRESS TYPE die to the doom pool and step up the POWER SET power by +1 for this action.

▶ Almost always appears in a Power Set with the STAMINA power trait. Variations might work with emotional or mental stress and be tied instead to another power trait.

Unleashed

Step up or double any POWER SET power for one action. If the action fails, add a die to doom pool equal to the normal rating of your power die.

▶ Pairs well with power traits that are at the D8 or D10 rating.

▶ Represents a hero or villain who typically maintains strict control over his own powers and sometimes cuts loose.

Versatile

Split POWER TRAIT into 2d at −1 step, or 3d at −2 steps.

▶ Usually appears in Power Sets with power traits rated D10 or D12 and when the hero has no other Power Sets.

▶ Dice that result from *Versatile* are each considered separate power trait dice for the purposes of other SFX that step up or step back the power.

LIMITS

Every Power Set has at least one **Limit**. Some have more than one. Limits exist for two reasons. One is because a hero is nothing without his flaws and weaknesses, and most Marvel super heroes have an Achilles' Heel, even if it's just that their powers wear them out! The other reason is that Limits provide the player with a way to quickly gain more Plot Points or affect the story in an interesting way.

Players aren't the only people at the table who can activate a Limit. The Watcher may also spend doom dice from the doom pool to activate them, under certain circumstances. This doesn't earn the player a PP, so **the option to activate a Limit is always given to the player first.** If the player decides not to, the option then goes to the Watcher.

Limits are much like SFX except their effects are usually negative. Limits should make life difficult for the hero. Sometimes a power trait or even an entire Power Set is shutdown (see page OM89). Other Limits create a situation similar to a complication or stress.

Limits might also represent occasions or conditions that affect the hero more than they otherwise would. Power Sets with Limits like this usually have some other Limit to make up for the rare or unusual situations the Limit operates under.

I'm playing Cyclops, a mutant member of the X-Men. All mutants have the *Mutant* Limit: "Earn 1 PP when affected by mutant-specific Milestones and tech." This doesn't come up too often, but when it does, Cyclops is subject to increased stress or other problems, though I get a PP as a bonus. I also have the *Ruby Quartz Visor* Limit which works on the idea that my special visor keeps my power from going out of control.

EXAMPLES OF LIMITS

Some Limits, like *Mutant* or *Conscious Activation*, are fairly common, while others are quite specific to the Power Set they're part of. Here are a few of the standard Limits that appear on datafiles. For more Limit examples, review the hero datafiles published with Events. Just like SFX, you can rename Limits to suit the Power Set they're attached to.

Conscious Activation

If stressed out, asleep, or unconscious, shutdown POWER SET. Recover POWER SET when stress is recovered or you awake. If TRAUMA TYPE is taken, shutdown POWER SET until trauma is recovered.

▶ This Limit is common when the hero's powers stop working if the hero is unconscious, incoherent, or otherwise stressed out. It usually only applies to a specific type of trauma, such as physical or emotional.

Exhausted

Shutdown any POWER SET power to gain 1 PP. Recover power by activating an opportunity or during a Transition Scene.

▶ This Limit is straightforward and to the point. The hero gets tired, and one of his powers stops working. Note that it isn't the whole Power Set but only specific power traits.

▶ Alternatives to this include Daredevil's *Overstim*, Iron Man's *Power Surge*, and Ms. Marvel's *Overload*. Each presents a situation where the power trait just shuts down and takes time to recover.

Gear

Shutdown POWER SET and gain 1 PP. Take an action vs. doom pool to recover.

▶ This Limit represents a piece of equipment or other powered item that, if lost or stolen or knocked away, shuts down the hero's use of it. Good examples are Captain America's shield, Daredevil's billy club, and Thor's hammer.

▶ Recovery is by taking some kind of action to get the gear back, reset it, fix it, or otherwise recover it. The Watcher rolls the doom pool in opposition.

Growing Dread

Both 1 and 2 on your dice count as opportunities when using a POWER SET power, but only 1s are excluded from being used for totals or effect dice.

▶ This is a good Limit for mystical or very powerful heroes whose use of their fantastic abilities typically makes things worse. If the Power Set represents a pact with a demon, a dangerous power source, or similar, this Limit makes it clear that using those powers comes at a greater cost.

Mutant

Earn 1 PP when affected by mutant-specific Milestones and tech.

▶ This can be modified to work with other significant power sources, such as being a robot, synthezoid, mystical being, or alien. What a mutant-specific Milestone or tech is depends on the situation, but it refers most of the time to anti-mutant technology that suppresses mutant powers, or pivotal mutant-related storylines represented by Milestones. It doesn't include each time your mutant hero gets hit by a Sentinel.

Mutually Exclusive

Shutdown POWER SET A to activate POWER SET B. Shutdown POWER SET B to recover POWER SET A.

▶ This Limit represents someone whose use of one set of powers depends on their other set of powers being inactive. For example, Emma Frost's ability to turn into living diamond keeps her from using her telepathic powers.

Uncontrollable

Change any POWER SET power into a complication and gain 1 PP. Activate an opportunity or remove the complication to recover the power.

▶ This Limit represents powers that aren't necessarily dangerous or don't increase the level of doom, but they're unreliable or prone to causing immediate problems.

▶ Powers turned into complications with Limits like this one can also be targeted like any other complication. Eliminating the complication recovers the power.

POWER SETS AND WATCHER CHARACTERS

Heroes aren't the only characters with amazing powers; in fact, the super villain is often the core of any threat to New York, Earth, or the entire Marvel Universe. Watcher characters may have Power Sets of their own, or they may possess power traits individually without SFX. The latter usually only applies to minor characters, such as guards, thugs, creatures, and alien attack robots. For the majority of villains, however, Power Sets provide the means by which mayhem manifests.

As the Watcher, you don't spend or earn Plot Points for your characters, so SFX and Limits work a little differently. Anything that costs a PP for players requires you to spend a doom die, though any size die is enough. Similarly, any Limit that would earn a player a PP instead adds a D6 to the doom pool or steps up an existing doom die by one (just like using Distinctions as a D4). Any SFX or Limits that involve the doom pool work exactly the same—the doom pool represents the general threat as opposed to a particular villain's power, so villains whose powers complicate the situation aren't really very different from heroes that do.

I'm the Watcher and I've got a corrupted Wolverine from an alternate future acting against the X-Men. I decide to use Wolverine's datafile almost as-is, though some of his SFX and Limits work differently as a Watcher character. His *Healing Factor* SFX lets him recover physical stress and step back physical trauma by −1 for only 1 PP. As a Watcher character, I spend a doom die to use this SFX. His *Berserk* SFX lets him borrow a doom die and use it in his actions, but every action he uses it in steps it up by +1. There's no change for this SFX, which makes a corrupted Wolverine a really nasty piece of work.

Limits on villains are a great way for players to use teamwork and resourcefulness to take down their opponents. Much as the Watcher may spend a doom die to activate a hero's Limits after the player passes up the option to earn 1 PP from the Limit, **players may spend PP to activate a similar Limit on a villain**. Of course, before this happens, the Watcher has the option of activating the Limit himself—adding a D6 to the doom pool or stepping up an existing doom die. Just as with Limits on heroes, the story has to allow for the Limit being triggered. If the triggering conditions aren't met, players can't spend the PP.

Wolverine has the *Heavy Metal* Limit that turns one of his WEAPON X PROGRAM powers into a complication until he activates an opportunity to recover it. If a corrupt Wolverine is a Watcher character, the players could trigger this by spending a PP, making him sink like a stone (using his ADAMANTIUM CLAWS as a D10 complication, for instance) or subject to magnetic powers. I could trigger it first, of course, and add to the doom pool. In either case, my corrupt Wolverine would actually have to be in the water or the heroes would have to be using magnetic powers for this to work.

Some SFX and Limits have "activate an opportunity to recover" as a way to recover from shutdowns. When this is part of a Watcher character's Power Set, it means **the Watcher needs to hand over a PP to a player who rolls an opportunity**. If this happens, no doom die is added to the doom pool—you can think of that die being used to recover the power trait or Power Set for the Watcher character.

CREATING NEW POWERS

All of the traits that go into a single Power Set are flexible enough that you should be able to represent any super-powered individual, high-tech gadget, or fantastic creature with these rules. You may have noticed that, in some cases, a traditional super-power from the comics is represented by a single power trait, but in others, it's a whole Power Set.

New Trait, SFX, Limit, or Power Set?

Your guide to creating your own Power Sets, power traits, SFX, and Limits is figuring out where the concept meets the game mechanics, and where a simple collection of traits can do the trick.

▶ Does the power or ability fit into a single die that you would roll into a dice pool and affect the outcome? Is it something you can measure on the scale of D6 to D12? Is it different enough from the other power traits in this section? Then it might be a good candidate for a new power trait.
▶ Does the power or ability have multiple aspects to it, many of which are already described by one or more power traits, SFX, or Limits? Does the hero lose all of his powers at once when things go wrong? Are there others out there who have been given these same sets of abilities? Then it might be a Power Set.
▶ Does the ability enhance, boost, or otherwise affect another part of the game? Is it a refinement or special trick of the hero that lets her do something cool, like reroll her dice, or affect more targets? Then it's probably SFX, not a power trait.
▶ Does the ability hinder or restrict the hero? Is it a side effect or common drawback of having powers in the first place? Then it's either just a descriptive part of the Power Set (especially if it's not that significant) or it's a Limit (especially if it forces the hero to make a tough choice).

FILING OFF THE SERIAL NUMBERS

When it comes to creating new powers, whether they're entire Power Sets or just the elements of one, look at existing hero and villain datafiles for ideas and places where a simple change of color and description can make the work much easier. If you strip away some of the color and description—the "serial numbers" that make it specific to a character—you end up with a functional baseline for something new.

Many characters have similar Power Sets, sometimes because they're related to one another, or because they share a common origin or power source. In these cases, it's easiest to just lift the Power Set whole cloth from one character and use it for another. You can sometimes adjust the die ratings, add an SFX here and remove one there, and you're good to go.

Remember, this game doesn't sweat a lot of the finer details in the rules. This is intentional; we want you to fill the gaps between the traits and the dice with your own vision of your hero, and allow you to follow your imagination. This is always the case for Power Sets. If you come up with something that works, and you know the rules for stunts, assets, complications, and stress, and everyone at the table is rocking that Marvel action, those finer details will emerge on their own—or else they won't matter as much as you thought!

SPECIALTIES

Advanced training and skill often define a super hero more than super-powers. **Specialties** cover a variety of broad skill sets commonly used by super heroes in the comics, and they represent a degree of training that exceeds the standard amount that's otherwise expected. A Specialty is rated at either Expert or Master level.

▶ EXPERTS are a cut above the rest, having had extensive experience and practice using skills in this field. If you're an Expert, you know the theory and application of the skill set, probably have contacts in the field of study, and can recognize others with this level of training just by observation. Any time you roll dice to do something for which your training might help, you may choose to add *either* a D8 *or* 2D6 to the dice pool.

▶ MASTERS are world-class specialists in their field. If you're a Master, your experience and training extends beyond that of Experts, and definitely includes a thorough understanding of both the field itself and those who practice it. When you want to use your training to help in an action, you may choose to add *either* a D10 *or* 2D8 *or* 3D6 to your dice pool.

Each time you use your Specialty, the decision to use one, two, or—in the case of Master—three dice is up to you. Using fewer dice of a larger size means a higher total or larger effect die is possible, but more dice may help support your action and provide you with more dice to include in your total or as effect dice by spending PP. Adding more dice also increases the chance of rolling an opportunity—but if you're low on PP that might be a good thing.

STUNTS AND RESOURCE DICE

You can use PP to create stunts with your Specialties (see page OM20 for more on stunts). Stunts are single-use tricks or callouts to your specialized training and expertise. If you're an Expert or a Master in that Specialty, stunts provide a D8 bonus to your dice pool, and they don't stick around.

You may also spend a Plot Point during a Transition Scene to invoke some kind of **beneficial contact or helpful association** with a Watcher character—including dirty secrets about their past or some observation about their fighting style—by spending a Plot Point to create a **resource die**. These work just like the assets you create using effect dice. For Experts, resource dice start at D6. For Masters, resource dice start at D8. In both cases, they last until the beginning of the next Transition Scene. You can also introduce a resource during an Action Scene if you activate an opportunity from the Watcher, but it still only lasts until the beginning of the next Transition Scene.

Similarly, if you want **some kind of gadget, gear, tool, or other trapping** that belongs to your field of Specialty, you can spend a PP to access it as a stunt or as a resource die, as long as the situation makes that reasonable. The key is knowing how long you want to use it (once if it's a stunt, or until the beginning of the next Transition Scene with a resource). Obviously, there are limits to this, but you can assume those with Master level in a Specialty have significantly greater resources than Experts, who in turn have more than ordinary people.

I'm playing Shadowcat, who is a TECH EXPERT. If I want to perform a clever stunt with my hacking skills, I could spend a PP and add a D8 stunt die to my dice pool to represent using shadow servers to hide my tracks when hacking a security firm. In a Transition Scene earlier, I might also have declared that I have friends in the hacker community, spending a PP and adding a D6 resource die, HACKER SUPPORT. I can keep using my HACKER SUPPORT until the beginning of the next Transition Scene. If I had forgotten to do this, but the Watcher just rolled a 1 on his dice, I could spend the PP to activate that opportunity and get a resource in the middle of the Scene.

As Shadowcat, it's reasonable for me to declare that I've got some state-of-the-art hacking equipment, all the latest software, and those cables with gold connectors, thanks to my TECH EXPERT. They would all be D6 resource dice if I wanted to use them over and over, or D8 stunts if I just wanted to use them once for an action. If I were playing Beast, who is a TECH MASTER, I'd be able to declare tech-based resource assets that are decades in advance of most gadgets, and they'd start out as D8 resource assets or D8 stunts.

THE SPECIALTY LIST

Not everyone has all of these Specialties. In fact, most ordinary people won't have more than one. Heroes and villains demonstrate a level of training and ability beyond ordinary people, of course, so expect to have several Expert Specialties and even some Master Specialties on your hero datafile. It's also important to note that you don't need a Specialty at Expert level to know something about it. You can assume that if you don't have Tech Expert, you still know how to operate a smart phone, a GPS device, or a high-tech coffee maker.

Each Specialty description gives you basic information about what the Specialty includes under its umbrella, what sorts of stunts you could expect to make with it, resources associated with it, and the difference between Expert and Master.

Acrobatic

You've had training in leaping, jumping, contorting, and dodging out of the way. You've got a great sense of balance and you're not afraid of heights.

▶ An **ACROBATIC EXPERT** is the equivalent of a competitive gymnast, circus performer, or dancer.
▶ An **ACROBATIC MASTER** is world-class, at the level of the greatest Olympic gymnasts and performers.
▶ **ACROBATIC stunts** include amazing handsprings, back flips, running along tightropes or beams, or squeezing into tight spaces.
▶ **ACROBATIC resources** include contacts in the circus, gymnastics, or dancing communities, knowledge of fitness and dance routines, tightrope and harness equipment, and great spots to practice or compete.

Business

You've got business acumen and know your way around economics, finances, small businesses, corporations, and sales. You can talk statistics and spreadsheets, forecasts and futures.

▶ A **BUSINESS EXPERT** is the equivalent of a college graduate in business or someone who has spent considerable years selling, buying, or trading.
▶ A **BUSINESS MASTER** has the keen experience and understanding of the world of finance that comes of doctoral study and being one of the world's most successful business leaders.
▶ **BUSINESS stunts** include intuitive analyses of business deals, running off lists of important figures, sizing up a salesperson, predicting stock market trends, and obscuring the truth with spin and jargon.
▶ **BUSINESS resources** include contacts in the world of high finance or corporate culture, industry analysts, archives of sales figures, top-level financial software, insiders on Wall Street, and friends in grass roots businesses.

Combat

You're good in a fight and have the training and talent required to act on the offensive or, if you like, the defensive. Your experience may involve anything from hand-to-hand conflict with fists and swords to fire-fights with modern weapons.

- ▶ A **COMBAT EXPERT** is experienced in at least one martial art or style of combat, and probably others, including the use of weapons.
- ▶ A **COMBAT MASTER** knows many, if not all, fighting styles and weapons, and is on par with the world's greatest fighters.
- ▶ **COMBAT stunts** include tricks, martial arts moves, clever parries, tactical maneuvers, and reloading guns really fast or one-handed.
- ▶ **COMBAT resources** include contacts in the martial arts or military communities, secrets of Kung Fu, historical warfare, specialized guns, knives, swords, or ammo, and some insight into the fighting styles of people like Shang-Chi, Captain America, and Iron Fist.

Cosmic

You've got knowledge and even experience with other worlds and other races beyond the stars. You have some sense of what alien cultures exist and the sheer scope of the Marvel Universe.

- ▶ A **COSMIC EXPERT** can list all of the known alien races and which of them have been to Earth, as well as identify cosmic phenomena at the level of a college graduate in astrophysics.
- ▶ A **COSMIC MASTER** knows more about other planetary systems, galaxies—even alternate dimensions—than most professors and astrophysicists, and has probably ventured into space, the Negative Zone, or beyond the temporal barrier more times than he can count.
- ▶ **COSMIC stunts** are almost always info-based—useful bits of knowledge about other planets, alien diets, space vessels, or dimensional constructs.
- ▶ **COSMIC resources** include fellow researchers into the cosmos, representatives of alien species on Earth, the occasional piece of alien technology, classified government documents about alien visitors or invaders, and perhaps somebody with a space ship, rocket, or teleporter.

Covert

Whether you're a spy or a private eye, you've got the training and the skills to sneak into, infiltrate, investigate, and even overthrow other organizations or locations. You could have been trained by S.H.I.E.L.D., Hydra, the Secret Empire, or whatever agency you like, even your own government. Or you could just be a really good police detective.

▶ A **COVERT EXPERT** is the equivalent of a trained covert operative, secret agent, or detective, familiar with espionage techniques, stealth, disguise, and infiltration.
▶ A **COVERT MASTER** is a highly trained professional with years of experience in black ops, deep cover, and rendition, even if no agency on Earth would admit to using her services.
▶ **COVERT stunts** include stealthy techniques, single-use spy gear, fake IDs, a temporary disguise, or a great hiding place.
▶ **COVERT resources** range from espionage contacts, unnamed sources, and classified government records to robust spy gadgets, safe houses, and friends in high places.

Crime

You have a professional understanding of the criminal mind, either because you are a criminal yourself, or you hunt them down. You know how crooks think, you know the law, and you know all the tricks of the trade.

▶ A **CRIME EXPERT** has a working knowledge of the justice system and how crime is carried out. She can plan or foil a criminal operation, defend or prosecute a criminal case, and pick a criminal out of a lineup just by his eyes.
▶ A **CRIME MASTER** is a genius at criminal organization, from either side of the justice system. She can plan out or foil a global crime ring, defend or prosecute major cases of theft, terrorism, or conspiracy, and sense the underlying motives and trends in criminal society day by day.
▶ **CRIME stunts** cover classic cons, police techniques, sleight-of-hand, safecracking tricks, and prison lingo.
▶ **CRIME resources** include snitches, ex-cons, contacts in the police force or criminal organizations, safecracking gear, and criminal case files.

Medical

You've had medical training. You might be an EMT, a nurse, a pharmacist, or an endocrinologist. Maybe you specialized, or perhaps you focus on general practice. You might even study ancient or tribal medicine. You know your Rx from your IV.

▶ A **MEDICAL EXPERT** is the equivalent of a graduate from medical school with enough knowledge of medicine to diagnose, treat, and perform many surgical procedures on a patient. An Expert is comfortable working in one or two fields in which he's devoted his efforts.
▶ A **MEDICAL MASTER** is a world-class surgeon, specialist, or medical researcher, who's most likely published in medical journals or a leading advocate for a narrow field in medical science.
▶ **MEDICAL stunts** include specific surgical techniques, life-saving procedures, shortcuts for first aid, and beneficial drug interactions.
▶ **MEDICAL resources** include leading medical journal articles, medical equipment, contacts within the medical community, or mysterious Tibetan or Wakandan herbal remedies.

Menace

You know what scares people. You're familiar with how to get others to do what you want through force, threats, intimidation, and fear. You're also better able to resist these things yourself. This is the kind of thing Wolverine is the best there is at doing. Contrast it with PSYCH, which is more insightful and better for recovery.

▶ A **MENACE EXPERT** is the equivalent of a drill sergeant at basic training or an experienced interrogator.
▶ A **MENACE MASTER** has either a lifetime of threats behind him and the muscle to back it up, or the kind of fearful presence that makes world leaders recoil in terror.
▶ **MENACE stunts** include insightful threats, tried-and-tested scare tactics, or improvised intimidation.
▶ **MENACE resources** include fear-inducing equipment, associates in the horror film industry, questionable research, or a band of dangerous thugs.

Mystic

You have seen the world in the shadows, beyond the veil of the mundane. Or you're at least blessed with a library of occult books and a passport stamped with a lot of strange places. Note: While you can create fun magical stunts with this Specialty, actual mystic blasts and arcane summonings should be described with Power Sets.

▶ A **MYSTIC EXPERT** has an understanding—beyond simple folklore or myth—of magic, sorceries, mystical dimensions, and the beings that reside there. He may know a few cleansing spells, rituals to contact benign beings, and the good sense not to try anything dangerous.
▶ A **MYSTIC MASTER** has a much greater knowledge of the mystic arts, from many years of study and interaction with magical creatures or patrons. He has committed dozens of rituals and wards against evil to memory; he's the world's foremost expert in one of many obscure fields.
▶ **MYSTIC stunts** include focusing mantras, healing charms, gestures against darkness, and quotes from arcane texts.
▶ **MYSTIC resources** include rare volumes of mystic knowledge, magical tools of invocation or divination, experts in other mystic arts, and helpful acolytes.

Psych

You have a gift for understanding human behavior. You've been a counselor, therapist, researcher, or confidante. You might even be a stand-up comedian or actor. This Specialty is the opposite of MENACE, which draws on fear and negative persuasion.

▶ A **PSYCH EXPERT** is the equivalent of a post-graduate in psychology, communication, or sociology. She's a skilled negotiator, interviewer, or orator.
▶ A **PSYCH MASTER** understands the human mind and emotions better than most; she can reliably assess and correct many psychological or behavioral problems...or make them worse.
▶ **PSYCH stunts** include hypnotic suggestion, reflective listening, calming words, or inspirational quotes.
▶ **PSYCH resources** include therapeutic locations, professional counselors, videotaped sessions, psych profiles, or specialist equipment.

Science

You know how the world works, and how scientific laws answer life's problems. You've studied biology, physics, chemistry, or any of the other natural or physical sciences. For astrophysics and the mysteries of the cosmos, use the Cosmic Specialty. For alchemy and occult sciences, use Mystic.

▶ A **Science Expert** is the equivalent of a college graduate, someone who's devoted her time to scientific study. Most scientists have further concentration in a specific field of science.
▶ A **Science Master** has achieved repute and renown among her peers in the global scientific community and delved into advanced areas of scientific knowledge and practice. She's likely the world's expert in her chosen field of research.
▶ **Science stunts** include intuitive leaps, careful planning, improvised equipment, and experiments on the fly.
▶ **Science resources** include other experts in the scientific community, specialized research notes, experimental equipment, and laboratory space.

Tech

You can use, repair, and invent electronic, digital, or mechanical gear. You're an inventor, mechanic, beta tester, or hacker. Tech covers a broad range of equipment, from hand-held computers to deep space rockets. You probably have a specific area of expertise, though if anything breaks, you can probably fix it.

▶ A **Tech Expert** is able to use, build, and repair technology using readily available parts and tools; he's the equivalent of a college graduate engineer, technician, or systems designer.
▶ A **Tech Master** is at the bleeding edge of technology and design, among the world's most inventive talents.
▶ **Tech stunts** include jury-rigging, retrofitting, kit bashing, and rerouting tech or tech systems.
▶ **Tech resources** include specific technology, new advances in applied tech, theoretical knowledge, or experts in any of hundreds of tech communities.

Vehicle

You don't just know how to drive a car; you were born behind that wheel. You're an aircraft pilot, skilled driver, or a talented vehicle operator. It might just be a hobby for you, but you make it look easy.

▶ A **Vehicle Expert** is a professionally trained operator of more than one type of vehicle, able to maneuver and handle them in dangerous conditions or under stress.
▶ A **Vehicle Master** is among the best in the world, able to sit down at the controls of even the most advanced transportation and pull off amazing feats with it.
▶ **Vehicle stunts** include fancy maneuvers of all kinds, from controlled slides to barrel rolls.
▶ **Vehicle resources** include knowing how to acquire any sort of vehicle, someone who can build one, or the schematics and history of particular vehicles.

SPECIALTIES AND WATCHER CHARACTERS

Because they don't rely on superhuman powers and abilities, Specialties are more common in Watcher characters than Power Sets. Most Watcher characters have at least one Specialty; in fact, some of them are defined by it, which is why we call them **specialty characters**. These are distinct from **major and minor characters**, who also have Distinctions, Power Sets, and so forth. For more on the differences among these three types of Watcher characters, see Creating Watcher Characters on page OM114.

You can create a specialty character on the fly by choosing one of the Specialties, deciding if it's Expert or Master, and then assigning Affiliation ratings of D4, D6, and D8. You can even define specialty characters with narrow variations of the listed Specialties that standard heroes have on their datafiles, which is helpful when describing specific professions. If the character's not quite to Expert level, you can write him up by using a third level of Specialty, Rookie. A Rookie Specialty starts as a D6 and can't be split into smaller dice.

You can activate stunts and resources for any Watcher character if you want, though they cost doom dice instead of PP. See page OM14 for more on spending doom dice. Rookies can't use stunts or resources.

When players introduce characters into the game as resources, once the resource expires you have the option of treating those characters as specialty characters with a Specialty connected to the one used to create them. If you do, the die rating of the resource is your guide to the rating of the character's Specialty.

I'm the Watcher and I'm describing a Scene where Shadowcat stumbles on a Hellfire Club security team. I can quickly describe each team member as a specialty character—Combat Expert D8, (Solo D4, Buddy D8, Team D6) Pistol D6, Kevlar Armor D6—and know right away what dice to put together for a dice pool. I could just as easily write up Security Expert D8, or Guard Expert D8, or—if I wanted to make things a little easier—Combat Rookie D6.

I'm the Watcher, and Shadowcat's player spent PP to create a helpful Tech resource during the last Transition Scene, which she describes as Ronnie, a fellow hacker. This gives her a D6 to add into appropriate dice pools. I could decide to make Ronnie stick around longer as a specialty character after the beginning of the next Transition Scene. If I did, he'd be a Tech Rookie, since he was a D6 resource to start with.

MILESTONES

Heroes don't exist in a story vacuum. They're tied to the Events that unfold around them, to other heroes, to villains, and to the important supporting characters in their lives. This game tracks these story threads with **Milestones**. Each Milestone represents a significant decision point in your hero's life—one that's a culmination of choices you make as a player.

At the beginning of an Event, **you may choose to pursue one or two Milestones**. You can use one or both Milestones provided with your datafile, or you can ask the Watcher if there are Event Milestones available—these connect you to the ongoing story of the Event, which can be a lot of fun. If you only have one Milestone, you may add a second during any Transition Scene. Once you have two Milestones, you must reach at least one before you pursue others.

I'm playing Beast, and the datafile I'm given has two Milestones included with it: Mutants Sans Frontières and Workplace Ethics. These both sound interesting, but I'm going to stick to just one for the time being. I like Mutants Sans Frontières because it deals with helping other mutants, which is where I want to take Beast's story. If it turns out that the Event we're in offers Milestones that line up with the one I've chosen, I might decide to add a second Milestone.

Milestones follow a standard format, as follows:

MILESTONE NAME
Short description of the Milestone
- **1 XP** when...
- **3 XP** when...
- **10 XP** when...

Here's one of Beast's Milestones, as described in the example.

MUTANTS SANS FRONTIÈRES
Created by Warren Worthington III, this international relief agency offers mutants support they can't get anywhere else. Will it inspire Beast?
- **1 XP** when you use your Medical Expert to help a mutant recover stress.
- **3 XP** when you choose not to engage in a confrontation in order to rescue or support noncombatant mutants.
- **10 XP** when you either allow a mutant to die or give up your status or reputation to save them.

MILESTONES IN PLAY

Using Milestones in play might not feel as intuitive as traits, such as Affiliations, Distinctions, Power Sets, or Specialties. You don't include Milestones in dice pools, for example, and they don't modify the game rules directly. Instead, you use them as a guide for playing the role of your hero, to give him something to aim for. Even relatively new or inexperienced heroes are connected to the story and have important decisions to make of their own. Milestones are an incentive for you to make interesting choices that suit your hero's personality and background.

As the Watcher, you don't have Milestones to keep track of for your Watcher characters. Instead, you can help the players by framing Scenes and establishing situations that encourage them to pursue their Milestones. Keep a list of which Milestones are in play, and use them as a guide for the various subplots and Transition Scenes that give shape and substance to the Event.

Event Milestones

Every Event has at least two Milestones available to the heroes. In some cases, these Event Milestones represent links in a chain of story that progresses from Act to Act. Once players complete one Event Milestone, they can choose a new one that continues that story. Of course the heroes can still fully interact with the story if they're only pursuing personal Milestones, but pursuing an Event Milestone offers them a way to earn XP for being a part of the story.

In addition to the standard list of 1 XP, 3 XP, and 10 XP rewards, Event Milestones may be attached to specific upgrades or unlockable resources which require the hero to pursue that Milestone in order to unlock them with XP. As the Watcher, you should make it clear that these special upgrades exist, even if you don't give many specifics. For instance, if an Event Milestone deals with an experimental technology and the potential side effects of that tech, the Milestone could offer a new Power Set to unlock or a set of unique resources connected to the technology.

CREATING NEW MILESTONES

There are occasions where you might need to create a new Milestone for your hero. Or, as the Watcher, you may want to create a new Event Milestone. In either case, you need to begin where the Milestone ends—thinking about the big decision the hero needs to make in order to hit that 10 XP trigger. For inspiration, take a look at the Milestones that come pre-loaded on the hero datafiles.

Every Milestone follows a loose formula that's reflected in how frequently you can hit the triggers—many times during a Scene, once per Scene, and once per Act. The 1 XP trigger puts the hero on the road toward the big decision. The 3 XP trigger might be a Scene-defining moment, depending on how it plays out. It all follows along a path, but the outcome—the 10 XP trigger—should be a tough decision point.

With this as a guide, think about how the Milestone might encourage interaction with other heroes or Watcher characters. Milestones should be player-driven in almost every case. Don't create a Milestone that relies on other players or the Watcher doing things for you—the triggers should follow from choices you make as a player. In some cases they might be triggered by reactions from other player heroes, but make your hero the center of that drama, and make your hero the one provoking the reactions!

Event Milestones are the province of the Watcher and are part of the Event itself. If you're interested, take a look at any Event and the Milestones that come with it. They tie directly into themes and plotlines that are important to shaping the Event's outcomes, while still giving the players the choice to act as they please. They can apply to multiple heroes, not just one or two. For more on how to prepare and manage Events, see page OM120.

EXPERIENCE POINTS (XP)

Decisions that you make as a player that are connected to your hero's Milestones earn you small amounts of **Experience Points (XP)**. XP are used to unlock or upgrade traits on your hero's datafile, or introduce new story elements and characters to the Event. Every Milestone has a 1 XP, 3 XP, and 10 XP trigger—the last of which is earned when you're in a position to make the central choice of the Milestone. Completing the requirements to get the XP award is called **hitting the trigger**.

In addition to rewarding different amounts of XP, each trigger is also limited in the number of times it can be hit during the game.

You may hit the 1 XP trigger as many times as you like in a Scene, assuming the triggering action or situation takes place, but no more than 1 XP may be rewarded for any single action or reaction you take.

I'm playing Beast, and during the game I get an opportunity to help another mutant recover stress. Since I use my MEDICAL EXPERT Specialty to do this, I can hit my 1 XP trigger. I could even use it again to help another mutant recover stress in the same Scene. I wouldn't get 2 XP for using a single action to help multiple mutants recover stress (such as if I used extra effect dice by spending Plot Points or something).

You may hit the 3 XP trigger no more than once per Scene for any given Milestone. If you've got two Milestones and come up with a way to hit the 3 XP trigger of both of them, that's 6 XP for the Scene.

My 3 XP trigger for MUTANTS SANS FRONTIÈRES is when I choose not to engage in a confrontation in order to help rescue noncombatant mutants. If Sentinels attack the mutant island of Utopia and I'm given the option, I could choose to whisk the children away to the mainland rather than fight the Sentinels. This would let me hit the 3 XP trigger. However, if the Sentinels follow us and attack us again, I won't get the 3 XP a second time for moving the kids unless the Watcher has framed this as a new Scene. Likewise, I wouldn't hit the trigger once for each kid I end up rescuing.

You may hit the 10 XP trigger only once per Act and once you hit this trigger you've **reached your Milestone.** You may now close out the Milestone and choose a new one. If it makes sense within the story, you can choose the same Milestone again, ready to pursue it in the next Act.

Beast's 10 XP trigger is a really tough one—allowing a mutant to die or giving up my status or reputation to save him. Neither outcome is favorable, but that's what makes this storyline so compelling to me! Thank goodness it can only be hit once an Act, and then counts as reaching the Milestone. Since it all comes down to this decision, I'm sure the Watcher is going to frame a Scene where I'm forced to make this tough choice. Once it happens and I get the 10 XP, I can explore the consequences of my choice and pick up a new Milestone.

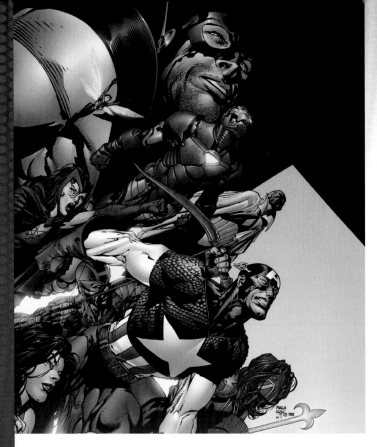

Earning XP

As a player, it's up to you to keep track of your Milestones. Alert the Watcher to them when there's a lot going on and things get chaotic—the Watcher can't keep track of them for you, although it's generally a good idea for the Watcher to have each hero's Milestones written down in a list in the Event notes. When something happens that lets you hit a trigger for XP, speak up and announce it to the table. Then, assuming you're not way off your mark, make a note of the XP you just earned.

Everyone at the table earns 1 XP when the Watcher spends a D12 out of the doom pool for any reason. Closing a Scene early with 2D12 earns 2 XP for everyone. It helps ease the pain when things are going rapidly downhill; we call it the **School of Hard Knocks** rule.

Keep a running tally of XP on your datafile or on a sheet of paper specifically for managing your Milestones, upgrades, and XP. **You don't need to keep separate tallies for each Milestone.** Just add in all XP you gain from Milestones or from the Watcher's doom dice.

Doom
Pool
p. OM14

MENTOR THE HERO

1 XP when you choose to aid a specific hero for the first time.

3 XP when you aid a stressed-out hero in recovery.

10 XP when you either give leadership of the team to your chosen hero or force your chosen hero to resign or step down from the team.

AVENGERS ASSEMBLE!

1 XP when you first lead a team.

3 XP when you defeat a foe without any team member becoming stressed out.

10 XP when you either convince a hero to join a new Avengers team or disband your existing team.

Spending XP

As a player, you can spend XP on unlockable upgrades to your hero datafile or robust resources that help you out during the Event (see page OM122 for more on Unlockables). Once you've earned XP, you can spend it during a Transition Scene.

As the Watcher, you should be framing these Scenes around the kind of upgrade or resource the player has just unlocked, at least on the surface. If the player unlocks a resource like the *Daily Bugle*, make the Transition Scene about the *Daily Bugle*. If he's upgraded his hero's Distinctions, make the Transition Scene about this change in his hero's personality or identity.

Events provide a number of things that players can spend XP on, but there are some standard upgrades. Here's a list for starters.

You can spend 5 XP to do the following...

▶ Replace an existing Distinction with a new one.
▶ Add or replace a Limit in a Power Set.
▶ Switch two Affiliation traits.
▶ Unlock a minor Event resource.

You can spend 10 XP to do the following...

▶ Add a new SFX to a Power Set.
▶ Step up a D6 or D8 power trait by one step.
▶ Add a new D6 power trait to a Power Set.
▶ Remove a Limit from a Power Set that has two or more Limits.
▶ Unlock a major Event resource.

You can spend 15 XP to do the following...

▶ Step up a D10 power trait by one step.
▶ Replace an existing Power Set with a new one.
▶ Add a new Expert Specialty or upgrade an existing Expert to Master.

As a player, you always have the option to **spend 1 XP to add a Plot Point** to your current pool of PP. This also increases the minimum PP you start each session with by +1 to a maximum of 5 PP (with 4 XP spent). It's not the most efficient use of your XP, but maybe you really want to get ahead of the game! This increased minimum starting amount resets to 1 at the beginning of a new Act, though—make use of 'em while you've got 'em.

PERMANENT OR TEMPORARY?

An Event is a **broad story arc featuring our cast of Marvel heroes**, who grow and respond as the story unfolds. After the close of the Event, something new comes along. You might exchange hero datafiles with another player, grab a new one, or play the same hero next time. Likely, your hero starts over, with a brand new datafile prepared for the new Event.

But this is a roleplaying game, and many players like to keep their heroes from one big Event to the next. Our suggestion is to sit down with the Watcher and discuss the various changes you made to the datafile during the Event that's just ended. Are all the Distinctions and Affiliations where they need to be? How about the Power Sets or Specialties? Were any new SFX or Limits just temporary storyline benefits, perhaps never to be seen again? Or are they changes you and the Watcher agree on?

Whatever your decision, most if not all of the Event resources should fade into the background, ready to be brought out again in the next Event where necessary. In some cases, the resources simply aren't part of the new storyline. In others, they're popular Marvel Universe mainstays! Either way, your hero should begin the new Event with fresh goals and some new Milestones, ready for more adventure.

CREATING NEW DATAFILES

The Marvel Universe has over eight thousand characters; while many of them are dreadful villains or supporting characters or planet-sized gods, a considerable number of them are heroes. It goes without saying that you may find yourself without a hero datafile for a character that you've always wanted to play, whether it's an obscure favorite like Killraven or a version of a hero connected to an as-yet unpublished Event, like the Joe Fixit Gray Hulk. With these guidelines, we hope you'll be able to create your own hero datafiles in under half an hour.

FIRST THINGS FIRST

To create your hero the way you want, you need to know as much about him or her as you can. If you're already a big fan of the character from the comics, that's the best source. Maybe you've read about someone in the *Official Handbook of the Marvel Universe*, or on the Characters archive at Marvel.com. These are all great resources.

For many characters, you might have Marvel's own official rankings in areas like Strength, Energy Projection, and Speed. Take a note of those, but remember that this game doesn't completely line up with the Power Grid's system of measurement. You may even disagree with how they ranked your favorite character, so just go with your gut. The game is quite forgiving! And you can always change your hero datafile later if you and the Watcher agree that it's not quite right.

From this information, write up a short summary of the hero. Write down his name, his origin story or background, some notes about his powers and skills, notable catchphrases, that sort of thing. You should be able to hand this to someone who has never heard of your hero before and they should get a sense of who he is and what he can do.

Now you're ready for the checklist.

THE CHECKLIST

To put together a new datafile, you need to do the following:

▶ Assign Affiliations
▶ Choose Distinctions
▶ Create Power Sets
▶ Assign Specialties
▶ Create Milestones

You can do these in any order you like. Take a look back at page OM04, where we showed you what Captain America's hero datafile looks like and what all of the traits and categories mean. In the following section, Cap serves as our example of how we create a new datafile.

Assign Affiliations

This is the easiest part. Every hero has a D6, a D8, and a D10 to assign to SOLO, BUDDY, and TEAM. Using the information and guidelines on page OM62, assign each die rating to an Affiliation. It doesn't have to be perfect. Sometimes you can't decide. If you're totally stuck, assign the D6 to the Affiliation you think might be most fun for your hero to get into trouble with. Then assign the D10 to the Affiliation you think it would be most fun for your hero to excel at. Then assign the D8 to the remaining Affiliation. Done!

Captain America is the quintessential Marvel leader and team player. He's no slouch alone or with a partner, but being on a team is where he's at his best. I assign the D10 to TEAM, and figure that he's probably most beset with problems when he's alone, so SOLO gets the D6. The D8 goes to his BUDDY Affiliation.

SOLO 6   BUDDY 8   TEAM 10

Choose Distinctions

Every hero has three of these. You can use your short writeup as a guide to which Distinctions make the most sense for your hero. If your hero has a catchphrase or favorite battle cry, *and* it's something you can see helping or hindering her during the game, make it a Distinction. If your hero has an interesting background or profession, *and* it could bring good times as well as bad, make it a Distinction. If she has a significant personality, quirk, or theme, *and* it's a double-edged sword, make it a Distinction.

Distinctions don't need to cover everything. You can use a clever catchphrase as the name for an SFX, like Beast does for *Oh My Stars and Garters!* It might be the name for a Milestone, instead, like Wolverine's ...AND WHAT I DO ISN'T VERY NICE. You might decide that Specialties cover a profession or skillset better, and not worry about it here. All you're trying to do is shine the spotlight on three facets of your hero's identity.

Don't make them dull or boring. SOLDIER isn't much of a Distinction; SOLDIER OF FORTUNE is better. ADVENTURER could be any hero; TOMB ROBBER is more interesting and ripe for conflict! If you're stuck, look at a few existing hero datafiles, especially those of characters who are similar to yours. You can borrow or steal ones you like, and change them later if you're not happy with them.

Cap's got a few catchphrases or nicknames that might be useful, but I want to really get to the heart of who the man is behind the shield. So I choose SENTINEL OF LIBERTY, which might cause him trouble as well as inspire him; MAN OUT OF TIME, since I like the issues he faces being born in the early 20th century and frozen for many years after WWII; and LEAD BY EXAMPLE, because he really does take charge in any situation.

LEAD BY EXAMPLE
MAN OUT OF TIME   4   or   8
SENTINEL OF LIBERTY   +1 PP

Create Power Sets

This is probably the most time-consuming part of creating a new datafile. You have to summarize the important aspects of your hero's super hero abilities in one or two bundles of tricks—in some cases, there are hundreds of ways to look at this.

We've found it's best to think about it like this:

▶ Does the hero have a singular thematic set of powers?
▶ Does he have a special or unique item, weapon, or gadget?
▶ If some power-stealing tech were used on the hero, which abilities would go?
▶ If the hero is a member of an alien race, super-powered organization, or shared heroic origin, what characteristics does that group have in common?

Become familiar with the Power Sets section of *Understanding Datafiles*, beginning on page OM70. Look over a number of existing hero datafiles, or even some of the villains in an Event. Figure out what's best served with a power trait and die rating, and what's probably SFX. Some things may be stunts you bring into the game, especially if the hero only uses them once or twice in her own comic book. Give every Power Set you create at least one Limit, tied into the Power Set's theme.

Don't be afraid to just copy a Power Set from an existing hero datafile. Rename the SFX, or the entire Power Set. Step a die up or down. Don't worry about whether or not the hero is balanced; just assign die ratings and powers that best fit the description of the hero you want to play. The game is designed to make sure everyone gets their fair share of fun. Remember that it's also a group activity. If you create a hero with D12 in every power, your friends are going to give you that look. You know the one.

Finally, you know the saying, "It's an art and not a science?" That applies here. Power Sets are descriptive, narrative, and flexible. If it looks right to you, and the Watcher and everyone else at the table says, "Yeah, looks about right," then it's probably right!

Captain America's powers can be grouped into two categories—his enhancements via the Super-Soldier Serum, and his invulnerable shield. This makes me think they'd work as two Power Sets. I go with SUPER-SOLDIER PROGRAM because it's more than just the serum and Vita-Rays—it's the whole expectation of being the first of a new breed of hero, too. Based on what I know Cap can do, I assign his power traits, all at ENHANCED D8 rating. For SFX, I pick somewhat defensive tricks—*Last Ditch Effort*, *Immunity*, and *Second Wind*. They're all designed to help keep him going. His *Patriot* Limit lets me earn PP when he's ordered into situations he may not like or he comes into conflict with the government.

For his VIBRANIUM-ALLOY SHIELD, I note that it's perfect for defense while he has it, and it's unbreakable, so GODLIKE DURABILITY D12 is perfect. It's not an unbeatable weapon, though, so I assign D8 to WEAPON and figure he can find ways to step it up. To that end, I want to represent his ability to clear the room of henchmen and thugs (*Area Attack*) and bounce the shield off walls and into the bad guy (*Ricochet*). And of course, *Gear* is the Limit in this case.

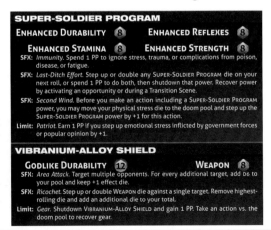

SUPER-SOLDIER PROGRAM

| ENHANCED DURABILITY (8) | ENHANCED REFLEXES (8) |
| ENHANCED STAMINA (8) | ENHANCED STRENGTH (8) |

SFX: *Immunity.* Spend 1 PP to ignore stress, trauma, or complications from poison, disease, or fatigue.

SFX: *Last-Ditch Effort.* Step up or double any SUPER-SOLDIER PROGRAM die on your next roll, or spend 1 PP to do both, then shutdown that power. Recover power by activating an opportunity or during a Transition Scene.

SFX: *Second Wind.* Before you make an action including a SUPER-SOLDIER PROGRAM power, you may move your physical stress die to the doom pool and step up the SUPER-SOLDIER PROGRAM power by +1 for this action.

Limit: *Patriot.* Earn 1 PP if you step up emotional stress inflicted by government forces or popular opinion by +1.

VIBRANIUM-ALLOY SHIELD

| GODLIKE DURABILITY (12) | WEAPON (8) |

SFX: *Area Attack.* Target multiple opponents. For every additional target, add D6 to your pool and keep +1 effect die.

SFX: *Ricochet.* Step up or double WEAPON die against a single target. Remove highest-rolling die and add an additional die to your total.

Limit: *Gear.* Shutdown VIBRANIUM-ALLOY SHIELD and gain 1 PP. Take an action vs. the doom pool to recover gear.

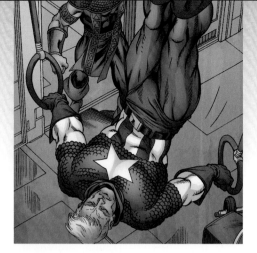

Assign Specialties

Some heroes have only one or two Specialties, while others have a lot. You have two things to think about here: does my hero display above average talent or ability in one of these areas? And, if so, is she world-renowned and at the top of her game? That's really all there is to it.

Using the guidelines on page OM96 for Specialties, pick those that you want to showcase in the Event, and write them down as Expert. Next, compare your hero to those heroes and villains known throughout the Marvel Universe for being the best there is in each Specialty. Is your hero in the same weight class? Could they stand toe-to-toe? If so, upgrade the Specialty to Master.

You should rarely, if ever, have a hero datafile that has all of the Specialties listed on page OM98. Leave some of them, at least, for other heroes to show off!

Based on his military background, training, and S.H.I.E.L.D. connections, Cap seems suited to five Specialties: ACROBATIC, COMBAT, COVERT, PSYCH, and VEHICLES. I chose PSYCH because Cap isn't only an inspiration to others; he's also great at influencing behavior positively. Seemed like a good fit. I wouldn't say he's world-class at any of these except COMBAT—he's one of the top five fighting men in the world. So it's Master for that one, and Expert for all the others.

ACROBATIC EXPERT	8	COMBAT MASTER	10
COVERT EXPERT	8	PSYCH EXPERT	8
VEHICLE EXPERT	8		
[You may convert Expert D8 to 2D6, or Master D10 to 2D8 or 3D6]			

Create Milestones

You may want to bring the Watcher in on this one, or you may not. You need to define at least one Milestone for your hero, preferably two. Even if you don't plan on using both to start with, it's good to have a secondary personal Milestone for when you've reached your primary one. Milestones are great places to load your hero up with personal relationship problems, long-term ambitions, short-term dramatic conflicts, and interesting subplots.

Stealing ideas from other hero datafiles is always a good plan—you can lift some Milestones almost whole cloth from other characters and use them for your own. You may tweak the triggers a little, change some wording, but there are common threads connecting many of the Milestones published in hero datafiles. After a little examination, you may get a better sense of the patterns— common triggers, iconic situations, that kind of thing.

This version of Captain America is based on his appearance in *New Avengers* #1-6. It's prior to the Civil War and follows the attack on the Avengers Mansion by the Scarlet Witch. He's trying to get the gang back together and maybe introduce some new blood. So for Milestones I go with MENTOR THE HERO and AVENGERS ASSEMBLE! I'm really keen on exploring what Cap does to reunite the Avengers, and whether or not he succeeds. These two Milestones push me to interact with the other heroes on the team, and that seems right up Cap's alley.

MENTOR THE HERO
1 XP when you choose to aid a specific hero for the first time.
3 XP when you aid a stressed-out hero in recovery.
10 XP when you either give leadership of the team to your chosen hero or force your chosen hero to resign or step down from the team.

AVENGERS ASSEMBLE!
1 XP when you first lead a team.
3 XP when you defeat a foe without any team member becoming stressed out.
10 XP when you either convince a hero to join a new Avengers team or disband your existing team.

CUSTOMIZING DATAFILES

The standard method described here works for most hero concepts, but sometimes a hero datafile already exists. You may have one from an Event that you really like, but the Watcher's running another Event entirely. If this happens to you, or if you're a fan of Marvel's "What If?" stories, you can customize an existing datafile and make it suit your own preferences.

In much the same way as you would when creating a datafile from scratch, you should go down the checklist. See if there's something you want to alter, tweak, or rename. With many Event-specific versions of popular characters, their core Power Sets are mostly unchanged, but some of the SFX or die ratings could be different. Raise or lower those as you need to.

More than Power Sets, die ratings, and numbers, perhaps the most important area to customize are Distinctions and Milestones. You'd be surprised how different a hero can feel in play when those are what distinguish him from another hero with the same powers.

I could take my Captain America hero datafile and, with a little tweaking, use the same datafile for Cap's replacement back in the '90s, John Walker (later U.S.Agent). Walker was notably stronger than Cap, so I could nudge his ENHANCED STRENGTH D8 up to SUPERHUMAN STRENGTH D10. His Distinctions are different: ARROGANT, GOOD OL' BOY, IN CAP'S SHADOW. And he's definitely not a COMBAT MASTER like Steve Rogers, just an EXPERT. Rename the SUPER-SOLDIER PROGRAM to POWER BROKER TREATMENT, maybe change the Limit to *Easily Angered* and make it apply to insults... simple as that!

CREATING WATCHER CHARACTERS

There are three types of characters controlled by the Watcher. Use the following guidelines for creating new Watcher characters for when you want to expand an existing Event or create a new one of your own.

The first is a **major character**, usually an antagonist of the player heroes and created using the same rules as hero datafiles are created with. Major characters have the following:

▶ Affiliations of D6, D8, and D10
▶ Three Distinctions
▶ One or two Power Sets
▶ Two or more Specialties

The second type is a **minor character**, usually a secondary villain or hero. Minor characters may be important and significant to the Marvel Universe in general but are not a significant part of the current Event being run. Captain America or Spider-Man could well be demoted to a minor character in an X-Men story, for instance. Minor characters are the most common characters in Events. They have the following:

▶ Affiliations of D4, D6, and D8
▶ Two Distinctions
▶ May have one or two Power Sets
▶ May have one or more Specialties

The third type is a **specialty character**, also referred to sometimes as a mook, thug, or minion. Specialty characters are the rank and file, very often nameless or without much more than a handful of traits. When heroes burst into a room filled with hired heavies, or call on a squad of S.H.I.E.L.D. agents to help take down Hydra, these are all specialty characters. Specialty characters have the following:

▶ Affiliations of D4, D6, and D8
▶ One Specialty at Rookie D6, Expert D8, or Master D10
▶ May have one or more power traits, but not Power Sets

Watcher characters do not pursue Milestones and do not earn XP.

The Watcher controls the major and minor characters in a Scene and they each act individually. Specialty characters may be grouped together or act individually, but usually go at the same time in the action order.

Major and minor characters take stress and are affected by assets and complications in the same way that heroes are. Specialty characters are easier to stress out. Their Specialty level (ROOKIE, EXPERT or MASTER) tells you the amount of stress of any type they can take before being stressed out. ROOKIES whose stress reaches D8, EXPERTS whose stress reaches D10, and MASTERS whose stress reaches D12 are each stressed out. Think of heroes and minor and major characters as having an unstated D12 tolerance for stress (and thus, only stressed out when their stress goes over D12), and you'll see the logic here. Similarly, the amount of trauma specialty characters can take is reduced; more trauma than their Specialty die means a tragic ending.

A Hellfire Guard takes a shot at Ronnie, Shadowcat's Tech support friend. Since he's a TECH ROOKIE, physical stress of D8 or greater is going to stress him out. That gives him D6 physical trauma, too, so if he gets shot again he's history. It's a good thing she's not depending on him to fight with her!

Mobs and Large-Scale Threats

A mob is a **group of characters that act as one minor character**. Mobs have multiple dice in their TEAM Affiliation. This slightly improves their odds at engaging with the heroes. Mobs are usually written up as a minor character, complete with Distinctions and even Power Sets. They might have a special SFX that allows them to make concerted attacks on single heroes (i.e., *Focus* SFX), swarm over many heroes at once (i.e., *Area Attack* SFX), or grapple their enemies (i.e., *Afflict* SFX).

Mobs can be targeted by the *Area Attack* SFX or by multiple effect dice. Mobs can be reduced in size by targeting their TEAM Affiliation in the same way that specialty characters may be stressed out by inflicting more stress than their Specialty die rating or that effects may be targeted by heroes. A Mob with TEAM 3D8 would need the heroes to deal D10 or greater stress to it in order to reduce it to TEAM 2D8. Once a die is eliminated, the stress goes away and the heroes must deal more. This is why using *Area Attack* is helpful; you can stress out entire mobs with multiple effect dice.

A large-scale threat is a **single character that acts like a mob**. Large-scale threats have multiple dice in SOLO and possibly even in BUDDY. Like mobs, they are written up as a minor character and can be targeted with *Area Attack* and multiple effect dice. A rampaging subterranean monster summoned to the surface world by the Mole Man is a good example of a large-scale threat. Reducing the dice on a large-scale threat can be described as disabling a limb, weakening its resolve, or some other debilitating effect; the only way to take out a large-scale threat completely is by stressing out all of its dice. This makes them great opponents for entire teams of heroes.

SFX
p. OM88

UPGRADING WATCHER CHARACTERS TO HEROES

Events often include a number of Watcher characters that are not written up specifically as hero datafiles. These may be minor heroes, antagonists, or even villains. If you want to explore those characters as heroes for play, all you need to do is upgrade their datafiles to meet the standard format for existing heroes. You can't apply these rules to single-line specialty characters like S.H.I.E.L.D. agents or random non-combatants; it's best for characters who already have Distinctions, Power Sets, and Specialties.

Use the checklist just as you would if you were creating a new datafile or customizing an existing one. In some cases, you need to step up the Affiliations for Watcher characters, as they might use the weaker assortment of D4, D6, and D8. Simply step each die rating up by one, or if you choose to tweak it, assign the D6, D8, and D10 ratings where you prefer them to be. Distinctions, Power Sets, and Specialties should be fine as-is, but may also be modified.

The biggest upgrade is adding Milestones. You should read over the section on creating new Milestones on page OM105 in order to create at least one for your new upgraded hero datafile. You might skip this step and just pursue an Event Milestone, but at some point you probably want to get XP for playing in character and making decisions for your specific hero.

With these simple guidelines, almost any character in the Marvel Universe is open to you. Playing a published Event can be even more interesting when you're in the role of a sideline character suddenly promoted to the major leagues. Just as comic book writers take obscure heroes from Marvel's history and shine the spotlight on them, you can do the same for your favorite second-stringer!

05
UNDERSTANDING EVENTS

As exciting as it is to play a Marvel hero, every story needs a plot, somewhere for it to take place, and a lot of things to do in it. That's what the Event is all about. In other games, the Event would be called the adventure, or the scenario, or the situation. In **MARVEL HEROIC ROLEPLAYING**, an Event is all of those things, combined with the sort of script outline you'd expect a comic book writer to work from. The key difference is that the Event is full of branching opportunities, ready for the players to make the big choices and deal with the consequences.

You should already be familiar with the Event/Act/Scene structure that this game uses to break out the action and timing. Don't remember? See page OM32 for more on these terms. Then come right on back here.

You're back? Good! Events incorporate all of those terms and add guidelines and direction for play. As the Watcher, it's your job to frame the Scenes and manage the doom pool, but with an Event you're also keeping track of things like playing Watcher characters, managing the story's pace and speed, describing locations for Scenes, and making sure the players are getting enough opportunities to have a good time and hit their Milestone triggers.

Civil War, Annihilation, and the *Age of Apocalypse* are all Events tied to points in Marvel history, and each includes its own set of hero datafiles, Watcher characters, Event Milestones, key Scenes, and background. Not all Events are so large and world-shaking. Some, like *Shadowland*, take place almost entirely within a section of New York. Others, like the *Fall of the Mutants*, are actually multiple Events taking place at the same time, reflecting an overall dark point in mutant history.

FINCH · MIKI 04 fgd

EVENT FORMAT

An Event is presented to you with a specific format. It's an outline with notes, more or less. This section introduces you to the elements of this format and, with any luck, inspires you to prepare Events of your own. The best way to learn how Events work is to take a look at a published Event, then follow along.

PREPARING FOR THE EVENT

Hero
Datafiles
p. CW156

Milestones
p. OM105

This section runs down the important things you need to do as Watcher before you kick things off, such as having the players choose their hero datafiles, choose one or two Milestones, get their dice and Plot Point tokens, that sort of thing. Since this is the same for most Events, it's mainly included as a reminder to Watchers who haven't prepared an Event before.

STRUCTURE OF THE EVENT

This section summarizes how many Acts are in the Event and what happens in them. Most Events have at least two Acts; they might have as many as five or as few as one.

MILESTONES FOR THIS EVENT

Event
Milestones
p. OM106

Event Milestones provide the heroes with a connection to the storyline presented in the Event. This section lists the specific Event Milestones and their triggers, as well as additional information you might need to keep in mind when presenting them. An Event's Milestones are designed to link into the main plot or perhaps suggest interesting subplots that crop up alongside the main plot.

Players don't need to choose an Event Milestone to pursue when they play through an Event, but it's strongly encouraged. The Event itself works with these Milestones, giving players more opportunity to hit their Milestone triggers and become a part of the story.

ACT

Each Act begins with a simple overview statement of what happens in this Act. All of the following sections are contained within the Act. If there are multiple Acts in the Event, the following sections are repeated.

SETTING

Where does the Act take place? What's the overall backdrop? The Setting describes this for you and also includes a list of **Prominent Locations** with suggested Scene Distinctions (see page OM67). If your first Act takes place in New York City, the list might include the *Daily Bugle*, or Central Park, or any other place that an Action Scene (see page OM34) could be set. The Setting could be as large as the Andromeda Galaxy or as small as the Baxter Building, depending on the needs of the Act.

HOOK

The Hook section introduces ways to get the heroes into the story. It helps you determine where they've been before the Act starts, gives you suggestions for where to place them, and so on. Hooks also suggest motivation for why the heroes should get involved, which makes the Act more about appealing to the players' sense of their characters and less about "I guess we're super heroes. Let's fight the bad guys!"

In published Events, the Hook is tailored to the hero datafiles provided with the Event. If it's an X-Men Event, there won't be many suggestions for Avengers or the Fantastic Four, so if your players decide to play those heroes you need to adapt the Hook for them. In most cases, simply knowing the heroes' personality or history with the default hero lineup is enough to get you started. Beast is one of the X-Men but also an Avenger, and Wolverine was briefly a member of a Fantastic Four lineup, so that's enough shared history to work with.

DOOM POOL

Every Act suggests how many dice to start out with in the doom pool. The default, if this isn't listed, is 2D6, but in some Acts the tension is already high. See page OM14 for more on the starting doom pool.

BUILDUP

This section helps you frame your first Scenes, the ones that establish the heroes' place in the story. It follows on from the Hook, which is "where are things when we start?" and moves toward the main action of the story. The Buildup often describes how to get to the locations, so you can decide whether your first Scene is an Action Scene (just drop the heroes right into a confrontation!) or a Transition Scene (let them investigate or get resources). Your first Scenes often serve as the gateway into the story, not necessarily the meat of the story.

Sometimes the Buildup is what's known as a **cold open** or **tease**, which means the heroes are involved in something interesting right away, but it isn't necessarily connected to the first Act. This might be an Action Scene where they're thwarting a B-list villain's crime—perhaps even opening this Scene midway through the conflict (a technique called *in medias res*, or "in the middle of things")—and the Hook comes about as a result of this Scene's resolution. You can frame a cold open with a few short descriptive sentences and then move on to questions, like "Cyclops, how much collateral damage is already around you?" or "Colossus, you're using all of your strength to keep something from falling. What is it?" Once the immediate action is over, the heroes are informed of something else, something bigger. Or, they find a clue on the villain's unconscious body or left behind when he escapes.

Your Buildup isn't a Scene written out like the later Scenes are, but guidelines for getting the story started. If you're creating your own Event, use this section to get the Watcher thinking of how to get the heroes to the main Event, either by dropping them into the action or establishing the themes and ideas up front as transition.

Action Scenes p. OM34

Transition Scenes p. OM40

ACTION

Events provide a few core Action Scenes for you to use to move things along, but they're not the only Action Scenes you have available. Typically, an Action Scene write-up gives you the information on the bad guy, threat, dire situation, or other obstacle that the heroes must confront or deal with. If you're preparing an Event of your own, use this as a place to make all of your notes about the villains and dangers you're keen to make center stage. But don't be afraid to tweak things later.

These sections also include **Options for Action** that suggest ways you can introduce more bad guys, switch things up, modify the Action Scene for specific heroes, and more. It's just a reminder that once the Event meets your players, anything can happen.

A few Action Scenes are tied to a specific order or sequence. You can't have an Action Scene in the ruins of the fallen Asteroid M if you haven't already played the Scene where Asteroid M crashes to Earth. Otherwise, most Action Scene writeups give you suggestions for when the Scene is best used and what potential consequences may arise from it, to give you an idea of when you should bring them into the story.

TRANSITION

Transition Scenes don't always need to be spelled out with their own section, but in some Events there are great moments of recovery, reflection, or recruitment and they're written up with more detail. A Transition Scene should be a break from the action, a moment to gather your wits about you and then move on. You can—and usually will—string several Action Scenes together, but you need the Transition Scene to keep your players from using up all of their energy.

UNLOCKABLES

Events should provide a few additional things to spend XP on, beyond the standard list of upgrades (see page OM109). Each Event offers unique and interesting subplots and characters, so give the players more ways to buy into it. Even if it's something as specific as a short term boost in their status with an organization like S.H.I.E.L.D. or access to some area or location they wouldn't have had otherwise, it gives the Event its own identity.

Unlockables are priced at 5, 10, or rarely 15. Often, an unlockable item has two or more versions at different costs. You might have a minor resource at 5 XP and a major resource at 10 XP (see page OM21 for more on resources). This gives the players some options and makes the more expensive version appealing, without completely ruling it out.

CONCLUSION

Most Events have a section that runs down the outcomes of the Event. Because Events have many possible endings, the Conclusion is like the bookend to the Buildup section and gives you some ideas for how to wrap things up. It's a good idea to look at each player's progress with Milestones, especially Event Milestones, and then compare this to the basic plot. Have all villains been taken care of? Have the goals of the Act been reached? Are there loose ends to tie up? Make use of this part of the game to frame Scenes that bring this to a close. A Transition Scene, especially, gives the heroes a chance to regroup and recover.

The Scenes at the very end of a story are often called the dénouement. It's a good idea to frame these with an eye toward getting the heroes back together, giving them a chance to address the public, reveal the identity of the mystery super villain to the news media, or slip away unnoticed. And if there's a romantic subplot or a tense dramatic moment you want to spotlight, bring it in here.

MODIFYING EVENTS

Events are a codified, standard template for comic book stories in the Marvel Universe. They're not supposed to be straitjackets or constraints upon your freedom. If you pick up a published Event and want to use it as the basis for some entirely different storyline, go ahead and do that! Stories only come about once characters meet situations head on, and in a roleplaying game there's so much that can happen, so many creative minds working at the same time, that you are almost guaranteed to go off the tracks. This is why Events are presented more as toolboxes and outlines for your own stories, and why we encourage you to inject your own personality as Watcher into the game.

Here are just a few ideas for how to expand and twist a published Event for new and different adventures.

▶ **Change out the hero datafiles**. It's not like you're ever required to use the ones in the Event, but sometimes you want to limit the choices to suit the story. What would happen if the story used the Fantastic Four instead of the X-Men? What if it were an entirely new cast of heroes that hadn't worked together before?

▶ **Add or change existing Milestones**. Milestones are the vertical thread of plot in the Event. They're like the muscles, with the Event outline as skeleton. So what if you switched them out with new ones? What if the focus was on a different kind of theme, or if the players were interacting with the story from a different direction? Change the Milestones and you'll change the story.

▶ **Replace the villains**. Do your players have history with a certain bad guy? Would they prefer to go up against Magneto than Loki? See what happens when the mastermind behind the whole operation is a hero turned bad! Or an alien race! Or Ultron! Changing the villain makes a big difference.

CREATING NEW EVENTS

It's no shocker to discover that there are many more stories in the Marvel Universe than you could ever see published as Event Books for **MARVEL HEROIC ROLEPLAYING**. That's where you come in. An Event that you create yourself has all the benefits of a published Event, with the added knowledge that you're designing it to suit your players. You don't need to spend hours and hours writing things up exactly as they're presented in published Events, however. You just need to have an outline and some notes.

▶ First, **sketch up the premise or the idea**, and see if you can do it in one sentence. "Villains break out of a supermax prison" is an example, as is "Aliens attack Los Angeles."
▶ Next, **determine how many Acts** you want this to play out across. It doesn't need to have more than one, especially if your premise is limited to a single dramatic situation. If you have multiple Acts, you can chain together interesting situations and think of ways that one leads to another, but don't get too ambitious. If you want to play out the sequel, you can always write that up later. "Villains break out" could just be two Acts. "Aliens attack" may be three or more.
▶ Draw up a flowchart, or bullet point list, or a rough timeline— something that helps you **organize the flow of each Act** and when things happen in your Event. This is an important step, because even if you only have the barest skeleton of a plot ("Supermax prison loses all power, villains make their escape" or "Aliens arrive in saucers, attack downtown LA, seize captives, and take them to their orbital base") that's enough to flesh out.
▶ **Each Act needs a Setting, Hook, and Buildup.** You know your players and what heroes they like, so you can write the Hook directly to those preferences. The Setting and Buildup come out of the plot you've got in mind for the Event, so make a few notes about those. Remember, if this is just for your own group and not intended for anyone else to play, you don't need too much here. A breakout story uses the prison facility as the Setting for the first Act, word of villains breaking out as the Hook, and getting to the prison as the Buildup. An alien attack story uses a city like Los Angeles as the setting for the first Act, sightings of saucers and news footage of aliens as the Hook, and showing up in the city as the Buildup.

▶ Next, **sketch out a few Action Scenes**, usually two to four for each Act. Give any villains or threats some kind of motivation. Why are they a threat? What do they want to do? What stands in their way? When you're framing this Scene for your players, knowing why someone wants to break out a whole prison full of villains or why the aliens are attacking West Coast cities is central to understanding what they do next. The heroes are going to get involved, which means some kind of confrontation, but how the confrontation plays out depends on motivation. If escape is the motivation, the villain only fights when his route is blocked. However, if revenge is the motive, he'll do what's necessary to hurt the hero.

▶ **Transition Scenes are optional**; you don't really need to prep these in advance unless you have a specific situation in mind to use as a Transition Scene, such as a meeting with an informant or a mysterious chamber filled with alien tech. They often develop as suggested by the players. However, if you don't build in any time in your Act for a Transition Scene—even if it's just at the end of the Act—you need to go back and figure how to do that. Gathering together at the heroes' base of operations to review inmate files or traveling in the heroes' supersonic jet into Earth orbit are good examples.

▶ Once you have all of your notes together, **consider creating some Event Milestones or unlockables** for your players to interact with. You don't need many of these. You can link them together thematically (spend XP from a Milestone to unlock this thing related to it) or not. You could run an entire Event for your players without anything but their own personal Milestones and standard datafile upgrades, but it adds a little touch of creativity and choice for them if you come up with some connected to the Event. If your story is a

prison breakout, a Milestone connected to bringing them all back in is good. If it's an alien attack, a Milestone surrounding the discovery of alien technology and weaknesses rewards the players who go after this sort of investigation. Even better, offering an unlockable Power Set of alien tech (a battlesuit, nanobyte packets, really big blasters) gives them a "turn the tables" twist.

▶ Finally, **sketch out a Conclusion**. Settle on what your end goals are and what the winning and losing conditions might be for specific plot threads. More interesting than winning or losing, however, are outcomes. What happens when the villains are all captured, or if there are still some at large? If the alien attack was devastating, how does the city recover? Will the California government do something about defending their cities from future alien attack? Your Conclusion should also suggest further stories that build on the consequences of the one that just finished. A teaser for some bigger threat lets you get your players excited for the next Event. Perhaps the prison breakout was part of a much larger conspiracy, and the alien attack on Los Angeles was just the first exploratory mission on the part of the alien empire.

We suggest using a published Event as a guide for your first attempts at preparing an Event from scratch. You may want to start by modifying one first, and then once you're comfortable with the way Events work you can use the list of suggested steps to strike out on your own.

Creating new Events is a fun and exciting way to show off your own Marvel knowledge and gives your players something unique to your group. Don't be intimidated, read comics for ideas, and take notes during the middle of your existing Events. In the Marvel Universe, nothing is ever static!

APPENDIX
RANDOM DATAFILE GENERATOR

Everyone loves dice. We love them because they push the action along into often unexpected places, inspiring us to create more exciting stories. So why aren't the dice a part of creating hero datafiles in **MARVEL HEROIC ROLEPLAYING**? Surely there's a way to let the dice shake things up before the game even starts. Great news, True Believers! With this bonus content, there is.

The original *Marvel Super Heroes RPG* from TSR had three ways to choose a character: pick one of the character cards included in the game, model an existing character idea or concept by assigning stats and powers, or break out the dice. The **MARVEL HEROIC ROLEPLAYING** OPERATIONS MANUAL includes the first two. But we know how much fun random generators can be, so we decided to make that third option a reality.

You'll still need the OPERATIONS MANUAL for this Random Datafile Generator to work, but using these tables and charts with a blank datafile or scratch paper, you'll be whipping up crazy super heroes in no time!

As an added bonus, the Random Datafile Generator can serve as a guide for assigning Power Sets, power traits, Specialties, and other variable traits, even if you don't use dice to roll up new heroes.

We've done our best to emulate the source material, but feel free to adjust or tweak the tables as you and your friends like for your **MARVEL HEROIC ROLEPLAYING** games.

Design
Dave Chalker

**Additional Design and
Development**
Cam Banks
Jeremy Keller
Adam Minnie

Editing
Amanda Valentine

Playtesting
Piledrivers:
Fred Hicks
Adam Minnie
Quinn Murphy
Danny Rupp

ORIGIN: ALTERED HUMAN

5

One Power Set
Add one D8 power trait
Add one Expert Specialty

ORIGIN EXPLANATIONS

Mutants are those who have an activated mutant gene granting them some kind of ability or abilities. Example: Wolverine and the X-Men.

Altered Humans were once ordinary people; they were changed by another force to possess innate powers. Example: Spider-Man and the Fantastic Four.

Non-Humans are those who are not human, including aliens, robots, and Asgardians. Often, their abilities aren't that unusual to others where they come from. Example: Thor and the Vision.

Trained Humans are those whose super powers are the results of fantastic technology or intense personal training. Example: Iron Man and Hawkeye.

Rolling a 12 on the Origins table can turn up some strange results. Come up with the most appropriate story you can without worrying too much about the contradiction. A Trained Human + Non-Human could be someone who started human but had their body replaced by a robot body, or perhaps an alien who somehow acquired all the memories of a Trained Human. An Altered Human + Mutant might have been involved in an accident that grants powers, but also triggered a latent mutant gene at the same time.

OVERVIEW

▶ Roll your Origin (or Origins), which determines the number of Power Sets you have, as well as additional benefits for that Origin.
▶ Roll your Affiliations.
▶ Roll to determine the makeup of your Power Sets; this gives you a spread of dice for your power traits within those Power Sets.
▶ For each Power Set, roll the theme of that Power Set.
▶ For each power trait in a Power Set, roll on that theme's table. Repeat until all power traits are assigned.
▶ Assign SFX and Limits to your Power Set(s).
▶ Name your Power Sets.
▶ Assign and roll your Specialties.
▶ Roll and create your Distinctions and Milestones.
▶ Name your new hero.

ORIGINS

Roll 1D12:

1-2: Mutant: One Power Set. Add an additional SFX. After rolling them all, step up one of the traits in your Power Set. You automatically have the Mutant Limit.

3: Mutant: Two Power Sets. After rolling them all, step up one of the traits in your primary Power Set. You automatically have the Mutant Limit on at least one Power Set.

4-5: Altered Human: One Power Set. Add an additional SFX. Add an additional power trait at D8 to your primary Power Set and an additional Expert Specialty.

6: Altered Human: Two Power Sets. Add an additional power trait at D8 to your primary Power Set and an additional Expert Specialty.

7: Non-Human: One Power Set. Add two additional SFX and an additional Limit.

8: Non-Human: Two Power Sets. Add an additional SFX and an additional Limit to the primary Power Set.

9-10: Trained Human: One Power Set. Gain two more Specialties, one at Expert, and one at Master.

11: Trained Human: Two Power Sets. At least one must represent equipment, and have the Gear or other Limit representing its status. Gain one more Specialty at Master.

12: Roll twice. Take the higher number of Power Sets offered, re-rolling any duplicate Origins. Take all other benefits or Limits.

AFFILIATIONS

Roll 1D6:

- **1:** Solo D10, Buddy D8, Team D6
- **2:** Solo D10, Team D8, Buddy D6
- **3:** Buddy D10, Solo D8, Team D6
- **4:** Buddy D10, Team D8, Solo D6
- **5:** Team D10, Buddy D8, Solo D6
- **6:** Team D10, Solo D8, Buddy D6

Affilliations
p. OM62

1

Affiliations	Solo D10	Buddy D8	Team D6

PRIMARY POWER SET

Roll 1D12:

- **1:** One power trait at D10. Add an additional SFX.
- **2:** Two power traits at D8.
- **3:** One power trait at D10, another at D8.
- **4:** Three power traits at D8.
- **5-6:** One power trait at D10, two at D8.
- **7-8:** Two power traits at D10, one at D8.
- **9:** Two power traits at D10, and two at D8.
- **10:** Two power traits at D10, and three at D8.
- **11:** Three power traits at D10, and two at D8.
- **12:** Roll twice, gaining the benefits of both.

Power Sets
p. OM70

SECONDARY POWER SET (IF TWO)

Roll 1D10:

- **1-3:** Two power traits at D8.
- **4-5:** One power trait at D10.
- **6-7:** One power trait at D10, another at D8.
- **8-9:** Two power traits at D10.
- **10:** Roll twice, gaining the benefits of both.

11

PRIMARY POWER SET
Three D10 power traits
Two D8 Power Traits
(Add one D8 Power Trait
from Origin)

POWER TRAITS

For each Power Set, roll 1D10 on the appropriate table for the Origin of the hero (in the case of multiple Origins, pick between them) to determine the general thematic group of the powers in that Power Set.

Mutant:
- 1-4: Common Powers
- 5-6: Uncommon Powers
- 7-9: Psychic Powers
- 10: Mystic Powers

Altered Human:
- 1-4: Common Powers
- 5-7: Uncommon Powers
- 8: Technological Powers
- 9: Mystic Powers
- 10: Psychic Powers

Non-Human:
- 1-5: Common Powers
- 6-7: Uncommon Powers
- 8: Technological Powers
- 9: Mystic Powers
- 10: Psychic Powers

Trained Human:
- 1-4: Common Powers
- 5-7: Technological Powers
- 8-9: Mystic Powers
- 10: Uncommon Powers

Then for each power trait (start with the largest die size first), roll on the corresponding table. If you roll a power trait you already possess within the same Power Set—and it's not an option with multiple choices—roll again on that table.

Roll 1D10 on the corresponding table:

COMMON POWERS TABLE

- 1: Attack Power (Step back the power trait's die. Choose between Weapon or type of Energy Blast. This option can be rolled multiple times.)
- 2: DURABILITY
- 3: Movement-Based Power (Step back the power trait's die. Choose between: AIRWALKING, BURROWING, FLIGHT, LEAPING, SPEED, SWIMMING, or SWINGLINE. This option can be rolled multiple times.)
- 4: REFLEXES
- 5: Resistance (Choose an Energy type. If you have Elemental Control, you must choose that same Energy. This option can be rolled multiple times.)
- 6: SENSES
- 7: STAMINA
- 8: STRENGTH
- 9: Roll on Uncommon Powers for this power trait only.
- 10: Re-roll on your Origin's table to the left, re-rolling any Common Powers result, for this power trait only.

ALTERED HUMAN THEMATIC GROUP:
Common Powers

POWER TRAITS:
HEAT RESISTANCE D10
COLD RESISTANCE D10
(+ 9) STRETCHING D10
ENHANCED DURABILITY D8
ENHANCED STRENGTH D8
WEAPON D6

UNCOMMON POWERS TABLE

1: Elemental Control Power (Step back the power trait's die. Choose from one of the following: AIR, COSMIC, DARKFORCE, EARTH, ELECTRIC, FIRE/HEAT, GRAVITY, ICE/COLD, KINETIC, LIGHT, MAGNETIC, SONIC, TECHNOLOGY, WEATHER, or WATER. This option can be rolled multiple times.)

2: INTANGIBILITY

3: INVISIBILITY

4: MIMIC

5: ANIMAL CONTROL

6: PLANT CONTROL

7: SHAPESHIFTING

8: SIZE-CHANGING

9: STRETCHING

10: TELEPORT

MYSTIC POWERS TABLE

1-2: SORCERY

3: Blast (Choose Energy or another specific elemental type. This option can be rolled multiple times.)

4: Elemental Control Power (Choose from one of the following: AIR, COSMIC, DARKFORCE, EARTH, ELECTRIC, FIRE/HEAT, GRAVITY, ICE/COLD, KINETIC, LIGHT, MAGNETIC, SONIC, WEATHER, or WATER. This option can be rolled multiple times.)

5: Movement-Based Power (Choose from one of the following: AIRWALKING, FLIGHT, or SPEED. This option can be rolled multiple times.)

6: SENSES

7: TELEPORT

8: TRANSMUTATION

9-10: Roll on Uncommon Powers for this power trait only.

PSYCHIC POWERS TABLE

1-2: TELEPATHY

3: PSYCHIC BLAST

4: Elemental Control Power (Choose from one of the following: COSMIC, ELECTRIC, FIRE, GRAVITY, ICE, KINETIC, LIGHT, MAGNETIC, or WATER. This option can be rolled multiple times.)

5: INVISIBILITY

6: MIND CONTROL

7: ANIMAL CONTROL

8: PSYCHIC RESISTANCE (Or if you have Elemental Control, choose the same kind of Resistance as the type controlled.)

9: SENSES

10: TELEPORT

TECHNOLOGICAL POWERS TABLE

1: Attack Power (Choose between Weapon or Blast. If Blast, choose specific type. This option can be rolled multiple times.)

2: DURABILITY

3: INVISIBILITY

4: Movement-Based Power (Choose from BURROWING, FLIGHT, LEAPING, SPEED, SWIMMING, or SWINGLINE. This option can be rolled multiple times.)

5: REFLEXES

6: SENSES

7: STAMINA

8: STRENGTH

9-10: Roll on Uncommon Powers for this power trait only.

SFX AND LIMITS

Each Power Set automatically comes with one SFX and one Limit. These numbers might be modified by your Origin, Power Set, or other factors.

These are not rolled, since various combinations of power traits may make certain SFX and Limits unworkable. The following are some suggested SFX by character type:

SFX:
Multipower

▶ Single Power Set: *Unleashed, Versatile*
▶ Many power traits: *Focus, Multipower*
▶ Few power traits: *Affliction, Constructs, Counterattack*
▶ Mutant: *Dangerous, Unleashed*
▶ Altered Human: *Absorption, Counterattack*
▶ Trained Human: *Focus, Second Wind*
▶ Technological Power Set: *Afflict, Area Attack, Boost, Burst*
▶ Psychic Power Set: *Constructs, Unleashed*
▶ Mystic Power Set: *Constructs, Healing*

Limits are also chosen similarly, though some Limits may be required (usually *Mutant* or *Gear*.)

Some good Limits by character type:

LIMIT:
Exhausted

▶ Mutant: In addition to the required *Mutant* Limit, *Conscious Activation* is common.
▶ Altered Human: *Exhausted*.
▶ Technological Power Set: *Gear, Exhausted* (as *Power Surge*)
▶ Mystic Power Set: *Growing Dread, Uncontrollable*
▶ Psychic Power Set: *Conscious Activation, Uncontrollable*
▶ Two Power Sets: *Mutually Exclusive*
▶ Powerful heroes: *Growing Dread, Uncontrollable*

After this, name each of your Power Sets.

Power Sets	MOLTEN SKIN			
	ENHANCED DURABILITY	D8	ENHANCED STRENGTH	D8
	COLD RESISTANCE	D10	HEAT RESISTANCE	D10
	STRETCHING	D10	WEAPON	D6

SFX/Limits:
  SFX: *Multipower.* Use two or more MOLTEN SKIN powers in your dice pool, at −1 step for each additional power.
  Limit: *Exhausted.* Shutdown any MOLTEN SKIN power and gain 1 PP. Recover power by activating an opportunity or during a Transition Scene.

SPECIALTIES

Roll 1D10:
- **1-2:** Two Expert Specialties
- **3-4:** One Expert Specialty and One Master Specialty
- **5-6:** Two Expert Specialties and One Master Specialty
- **7-8:** Three Expert Specialties
- **9-10:** Three Expert Specialties and One Master Specialty

Plus any bonuses granted for Origins.

Before rolling to determine what your Specialties are, you may assign some Specialties automatically:

▶ If you have Mystic Powers, you must take the MYSTIC, COSMIC, or both Specialties.
▶ If you have Psychic Powers, you must take the PSYCH, MENACE, or both Specialties.
▶ If you have Technological Powers, you must take the SCIENCE, TECH, or both Specialties.
▶ If you have any Uncommon Powers, you may take the COSMIC Specialty.
▶ You may take the COMBAT Specialty regardless of Powers.

You choose if the above assigned Specialties are Expert or Master (if available.) Then for each other Specialty available, roll on the following table. Choose whether it's going to be for your Expert or Master Specialty before rolling. Re-roll any duplicates.

Roll 1D10:
- **1:** ACROBATIC
- **2:** BUSINESS
- **3:** COVERT
- **4:** CRIME
- **5:** MEDICAL
- **6:** MENACE
- **7:** PSYCH
- **8:** SCIENCE
- **9:** TECH
- **10:** VEHICLE

SPECIALTIES:
One Expert Specialty
One Master Specialty
Add one Expert Specialty
(from Origin)

Specialties
p. OM96

8
2
5

SPECIALTIES:
SCIENCE EXPERT
BUSINESS EXPERT
MEDICAL MASTER

Specialties	BUSINESS EXPERT	D8	MEDICAL MASTER	D10
	SCIENCE EXPERT	D8		
	[You may convert Expert D8 to 2D6, or Master D10 to 2D8 or 3D6]			

DISTINCTIONS, MILESTONES, AND FINISHING TOUCHES

By this point, you should have an idea of who your character is. The last two steps are to drive home that concept; therefore they are less random.

DISTINCTIONS

Distinctions
p. OM67

Round out your character by choosing three Distinctions. Roll on the following table to get a category for each Distinction. It's OK to have multiple of the same category.

Roll 1D6:

1: **Personality Trait:** NATURAL LEADER, QUICK TO ANGER, UNCOMPROMISING, etc.
2: **Outlook or Reputation:** HARDHEADED FUTURIST, MISUNDERSTOOD MENACE, NEVER GROWS UP, etc.
3: **History/Backstory:** CRIMINAL PAST, MYSTERIOUS DESTINY, TEXAS FARMBOY, etc.
4: **Catchphrase or Title:** DEFENDER OF JUSTICE, "I DON'T BELIEVE IN NO WIN SCENARIOS", "SMASH!", etc.
5: **Notable Feature:** ALLURING, CUTTING EDGE TECH, WORLD-CLASS INTELLECT, etc.
6: **Profession:** ACE REPORTER, BILLIONAIRE PLAYBOY, RUSSIAN SUPERSPY, etc.

2

6

4

DISTINCTIONS:

MISUNDERSTOOD MENACE

MEDICAL GENIUS

THINGS ARE ABOUT TO ERUPT!

You'll want to customize the Distinction to your hero. See OM111 for examples of how to make good Distinctions.

DOCTOR VOLCANO

Name:			
Affiliations	SOLO D10	BUDDY D8	TEAM D6

Distinctions	MISUNDERSTOOD MENACE	④ or ⑧
	MEDICAL GENIUS	+1 PP
	THINGS ARE ABOUT TO ERUPT!	

Power Sets	**MOLTEN SKIN**		
	ENHANCED DURABILITY	D8	ENHANCED STRENGTH D8
	COLD RESISTANCE	D10	HEAT RESISTANCE D10
	STRETCHING	D10	WEAPON D6

SFX/Limits:
SFX: *Versatile.* Replace STRETCHING die with 2D8 or 3D6 on your next roll.
SFX: *Shutdown* any MOLTEN SKIN power and gain 1 PP. Recover power

FINDING PATIENT ZERO

1 XP when...you follow a lead pertaining to the origin of the Volcan Virus.

3 XP when...you confront one of the infected people who caused you to contract the Virus.

10 XP when...you find Patient Zero and turn him in to government officials or let him go.

FREAK OF MEDICAL SCIENCE

1 XP when...you use your MISUNDERSTOOD MENACE distinction for a d4 and a PP.

3 XP when...use of your powers results in stress to an ally or an innocent.

10 XP when...you find a cure for your Volcan Virus and regain your normal life or refuse a cure and embrace your new identity as a hero or villain.

MILESTONES

Your hero starts with two Milestones. To determine what kind they are, roll on the table below. It's OK to have multiple of the same category.

Milestones
p. OM105

Roll 1D10:

1-2: Affiliation Milestone: Choose your highest or lowest Affiliation die and create a Milestone based on that. For example, someone with a TEAM D10 might take a Milestone about keeping his team together. Someone with a TEAM D6 might take a Milestone about resisting joining a team.

3-4: Origin Milestone: Create a Milestone based on your Origin. For example, a Mutant Origin could involve being a self-hating mutant. A Trained Human might make a Milestone based on keeping up with mutants and gods in a team.

5-6: Power Milestone: Create a Milestone that relates to one of your Power Sets. A hero with a Mystical Power Set might make a Milestone around mastering the arcane arts. A hero with Uncontrollable Powers might make a Milestone about keeping those powers under control.

7-8: Distinction Milestone: Create a Milestone that relates to one of your Distinctions. These include personal Milestones like succumbing to an addiction, or having the past come back to haunt your hero.

9-10: Specialty Milestone: Create a Milestone that relates to one of your Specialties, particularly if you have a Master-level Specialty. A dedicated doctor with MEDICAL MASTER who is attempting to cure a dangerous disease might make this kind of Milestone.

See OM113 for guidelines on creating Milestones and triggers for each step of 1 XP/3 XP/10 XP.

Finally, decide if your hero has a public or private identity, and give your super hero a name.

3
5

MILESTONES:
Origin Milestone
Power Milestone

EVENT

Based on Marvel's Civil War by
Mark Millar, Brian Michael Bendis,
Marc Guggenheim, Paul Jenkins,
and J. Michael Straczynski
with Ramon Bachs,
Leandro Fernandez, Ron Garney,
Kano, Steve Lieber, John Lucas,
Mike McKone, Steve McNiven,
Humberto Ramos, Dexter Vines,
and Lee Weeks

Writing & Design
Cam Banks, Logan Bonner,
Maurice Broaddus, T. Rob Brown,
David A. Hill Jr., Judd Karlman,
Philippe-Antoine Ménard,
Jack Norris, Travis Stout,
Aaron Sullivan,
and Filamena Young

Editing
Amanda Valentine with
John Adamus, Sally Christensen,
Matthew Gandy, and Alex Perry

Art Direction & Layout
Jeremy Keller

Graphic Design Concepts
John Harper

Interior Art
Marvel Bullpen

Welcome to
Dade Ian Hill, b. 5/25/12

CIVIL WAR

This full-featured Event for **MARVEL HEROIC ROLEPLAYING** is based on the Marvel *Civil War* crossover by Mark Millar, with additional material inspired by J. Michael Straczynski's *Civil War: Amazing Spider-Man* and *Fantastic Four*, Paul Jenkins' *Civil War: Front Line*, and Marc Guggenheim's *Civil War: Wolverine*, as well as Brian Michael Bendis' *New Avengers*. Upcoming Event Supplements feature material based on other Civil War tie-in storylines and content, including the *Fifty State Initiative*, *Young Avengers/Runaways*, and *X-Men*.

CIVIL WAR works best as an Event for 4 to 6 players and may take as long as six months to play through in its entirety, with each of the three Acts including many Scenes playable over one or two sessions each. The many hero and Watcher character datafiles and Event Milestones included may inspire you to continue the story beyond these three Acts. Supplements will build on this content and provide additional hero datafiles, Scenes, Milestones, and setting material.

Everything in this Event is intended for the Watcher, although much of the material in the Sourcebook section may be distributed either before the game begins or throughout play as resource material for heroes interested in certain aspects of the Marvel Universe during the Civil War.

PREPARING FOR THE EVENT

CIVIL WAR requires some preparation before you run it for the first time. Here's what you need:

▶ Read over the entire Event provided here and become familiar with the three Acts and the flow of Scenes within each Act. Become acquainted with the Sourcebook section; you might want to make copies of some of the entries for easy access during play.

▶ When your group meets to play the first session, have each player choose a hero from the datafiles provided. The Sub-Mariner and Black Panther are unlockable heroes, starting out as rulers in their respective nations. Review the rules options for Troupe Play if your group would like to try playing multiple heroes throughout the Event.

▶ Each player should choose two Milestones to pursue for this Event. They may choose from the Milestones in their hero datafile and from the Event Milestones included in the Sourcebook.

▶ If your players want to choose heroes outside of the ones provided, be aware that you need to determine how best to tie them into the story. It might be a good idea to ensure that such a hero has at least one Event Milestone to pursue, linking them to the CIVIL WAR Event.

▶ Make sure you have enough dice, plenty of Plot Point tokens, and some kind of action order token for each player. You may also benefit from taking note of each hero's Affiliations and what Milestones the players have chosen. Keep this list near you for reference during the game.

▶ If this is your group's first session of **MARVEL HEROIC ROLEPLAYING**, you should introduce them to the basic rules from the **OPERATIONS MANUAL** and go over their datafiles with them. Hand out copies of the cheat sheet for their reference.

Troupe Play
p. CW04

Event Milestones
p. CW15

STRUCTURE OF THE EVENT

CIVIL WAR is an Event in three Acts. Each Act gives the players plenty of opportunities to bust out their heroes' super powers and amazing talents, and allows the Watcher to mix up the action a little with a large selection of bad guys and heroes on the other side of the Civil War.

▶ **Civil War Sourcebook** includes extensive background information on many of the important organizations, nations, and factions with an interest in the Super Hero Civil War. This chapter also includes a full list of Event Milestones and many Unlockables tied to specific groups.

▶ **Act One** is the lead-up to the Superhuman Registration Act becoming law.

▶ **Act Two** covers the nation's new status quo as the SHRA requires every superhuman individual to register or be locked up. Some heroes join the SHRA, others choose to resist.

▶ **Act Three** follows what happens when the government reveals its two new programs: the Thunderbolts, villains recruited to hunt down fugitive heroes; and Prison 42, the maximum security installation built within the Negative Zone.

Each Act follows the Event structure described in *Understanding Events* in the OPERATIONS MANUAL. We've provided the **Hook** and **Buildup** for each Act, as well as **Key Scenes** that help to set the stage properly for your group to play through the story. We've also included ideas, inspiration, and suggestions for throwing in optional Action Scenes, Transition Scenes, and your choice of opposing characters.

There are many datafiles included in this book, including some in various Action Scenes and others collected at the end of Act Three. The latter are available for use in any Act, some of them best served as Anti-Registration heroes and others as Pro-Registration. It's up to you and your group to use them however you want. A full index of all datafiles is provided at the end of this Event Book.

Understanding Events p. OM118

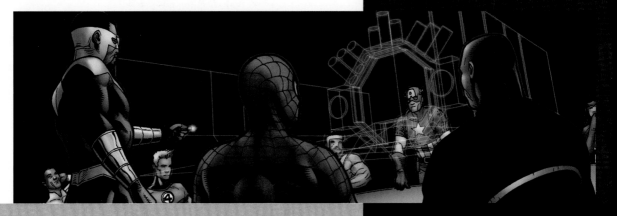

RULES OPTION: TROUPE PLAY

With its impressive roster of playable heroes and many potential Key Scenes to play out, the Civil War presents your group with interesting challenges: you can pick a side in the conflict; choose the one hero you want to play; decide what Scenes to play through; engage in hero vs. hero battles if everybody wants to, and so on. Choosing a single character limits the breadth of such a powerful and story-rich Event. If, as a group, you want to explore as much of the Civil War as you can, consider adopting **troupe play**.

Troupe play is a gaming style where each player choses several characters and plays one, or in some cases more, at a time. When you start the Event, have everyone pick two or more characters they're interested in playing. Then decide the level of flexibility you want. Do you want to allow switching heroes between play sessions, between Acts, or between Scenes? Whatever approach you take, you should consider allowing switching whenever a hero takes too much stress or trauma to be of much use in an upcoming Scene. As the Watcher, knowing which heroes are in play at any given time helps you frame Scenes for the enjoyment of everyone at the table.

POOLING XP

XP
p. OM107

When you adopt troupe play, **all XP are granted to the player, not the individual heroes being played.** Thus a player manages his XP as a pool and can spend them on any allowed unlockables, including those linked to any of the heroes he plays.

> I've got both the Wasp and Ms. Marvel in my roster, so I gain XP by hitting the Milestones triggers of whatever hero I'm currently playing. I can then spend my accumulated XP on either of my heroes or any other unlockable the Watcher has made available from the Event.

ADVANCED TROUPE PLAY

Once your group is comfortable with the concept of troupe play, you can make it more dynamic by allowing players to add new heroes to their roster during play, especially those unlocked through XP. The group might even want to pool their heroes and switch to other characters as they see fit. Another way to go is for you as the Watcher to set some Key Scenes with the heroes of your choice, giving you more control over the story when necessary.

If you take this further, your group may want to explore play from both sides of the conflict, picking up both Pro- and Anti-SHRA heroes. If this happens, discuss if everyone should play heroes of the same side in a given Scene, or whether half the group wants to play on one side with the other half in opposition. You can also frame Scenes where undecided or wavering heroes interact with those who've picked a side. For groups who want to recreate impassioned hero vs. hero Scenes (see page CW08), the second and third options are the best, though the third might be a lot less intense. Troupe play means that getting a character captured or stressed out beyond playability doesn't deprive anyone of the possibility of being active in the next Scene, and it lessens the emotional "gotcha!" when another player's hero takes down your hero.

Regardless of the style you choose to adopt, the decision to play a Scene (or longer) with heroes from opposing sides should be agreed upon by everyone in the group. It's not easy for some players to engage in what amounts to player vs. player actions; if this bothers anyone, don't include it in the game.

USING SCENE & CHARACTER DISTINCTIONS

The standard rules in the **OPERATIONS MANUAL** say that you can add either a Distinction from your datafile *or* a Scene Distinction. If you want to use both, you have to spend a PP. This may make Scene Distinctions be used less often by players who still want to engage their own hero Distinctions. The following optional rule encourages using both:

You can add a Scene Distinction and a character Distinction to your dice pool for free, so long as you use each in a different way i.e., one at D4 to gain a PP and the other for a D8.

Using the
Doom Pool
p. OM17

RULES OPTION: SCENE DISTINCTIONS & COMPLICATIONS

The events unfolding in the Super Hero Civil War are fraught with heart-wrenching situations, polarized issues, and violent conflicts. As the Watcher, it's your job to stage catastrophic conflicts often in Scenes that were never part of the published storyline. It's also your job to add whatever you can to each Scene to make it stand out, to make it about something more than heroes and the occasional villain throwing each other through walls.

Fortunately, as the Watcher you have many tools at your disposal to turn the most mundane conflict into a mind-bending fiasco of exploding cars, screaming civilians, and collapsing buildings. Scene Distinctions and complications are key to making the lives of heroes more challenging, if not downright miserable, for a few Panels' worth of action.

Throughout this book, you'll find locations, organizations, and Action Scenes that include several suggested Scene Distinctions (for example ANGRY CITIZENS or FLAMING BUILDING). When you frame a Scene, you have the choice of using those as Scene Distinctions without having to spend any doom dice. You can also decide to introduce them later by spending a D8 or greater doom die.

With these rules, you can make your Scene even more dynamic by taking dice from the doom pool to turn existing Scene Distinctions into complications, bigger and more serious than any Distinction.

I'm the Watcher and I'm framing an Action Scene where heroes face off in the streets of Manhattan. I add a PRO-REGISTRATION PROTESTORS Scene Distinction right off the bat. If I framed the Scene without this, I could spend a D8 to add it later, no problem. Then, as the fight escalates, I decide to indicate that the protestors are getting restless, violent, or just too close to remain safe. To represent this change into an actual obstacle for the heroes, I spend a D10 from the doom pool and change the Scene Distinction into an ENDANGERED PRO-REGISTRATION PROTESTORS D10 complication.

Take into account things like locations, witnesses, and other Scene Distinctions when your Watcher characters create complications with their actions. Remember that you don't have to target the heroes themselves with effect dice granted by successful actions. As long as you described your Watcher character's actions accordingly, they can put BUILDINGS ON FIRE, be responsible for COLLAPSING BRIDGES, and create all kinds of devious diversions that force difficult choices on heroes. This doesn't cost doom dice, either—it's a normal use of an effect die.

In all cases, remind heroes that Scene Distinctions and complications, like most traits, can be targeted with an action to be stepped down or removed.

One way to make Scene Distinctions stand out is to make them more interactive by adding abilities that the players or your Watcher characters can tap into by spending PP. This allows you to create objects or scene elements that grant a special power trait or even give characters access to a SFX-like mechanic.

Targeting
Traits
p. OM54

I'm playing Ms. Marvel in a Scene where, along with a squad of S.H.I.E.L.D. agents, I bust into what I thought was a secret Anti-Registration headquarters. However, the Watcher gleefully reveals that it's a Hydra hideout and sets a CRATE OF STUN GRENADES Scene Distinction as well as a huge mob of Hydra agents. He then explains that anyone using a grenade can spend a PP or D6 doom to make an area attack with the grenades. Hail Hydra!

RESOLVING HERO VS. HERO CONFLICTS

Troupe Play
p. CW04

If there's one key story opportunity in the Super Hero Civil War it's how allies, friends, and family members turn on each other as their belief in their side of the conflict becomes so much stronger than the bonds of their relationships. This Event features multiple Scenes where players might find their heroes battling one another. This is especially true if your group engages in troupe play using characters from both sides of the registration issue.

While the current conflict rules are perfectly suited to handle hero vs. hero action, the Watcher's role as an arbiter becomes particularly important. With mechanics that give a lot of leniency in how actions can affect the story, it can be easy to play the system and force the narrative to your advantage. As Watcher, you—and the other players at the table—want to make sure that the assets and complications created are fair, fun, and within the spirit of believability.

> I'm the Watcher. Emma Frost's player picks her D8 effect die and calls it PSYCHIC COMA D8. It's my responsibility to suggest something less drastic, like PSYCHIC DIZZINESS D8. Later, the Thing's player describes kicking Luke Cage into New Jersey where he lands in a RUSH HOUR D12 complication. That's probably not nearly as fun or exciting as having the Thing's player describe how he punches Luke Cage through the windows of Avengers Tower.

Maintaining a believable fiction and acting as a neutral arbiter of the rules are the two most important roles of the Watcher in hero vs. hero conflicts. That's not to say that they can't be immensely fun, though. Such conflicts are grounds for great moments of awesome action.

Heroes should consider taking out their opponents through complications rather than stress. Pushing a complication past D12 takes a hero out of the Scene, much like stress. Complications, however, don't linger between Scenes. This allows a defeated hero to start the next Scene without any trauma. Also, having complications pile up on a hero forces him and his allies to act on the complications instead of the opposition.

▶ If a hero is stressed out during such a Scene, the losing player should not be penalized. A Transition Scene should be played to allow recuperation and explore the consequences of the recent battle. If the hero still has too much trauma to be effective in an upcoming Action Scene, you can suggest that the player play a new hero, much like described in troupe play (page CW04). If a hero gets captured, the team can set up a rescue much like the **Transport/Rescue a Captured Superhuman** Scene in Act Two (page CW84).

▶ Finally, remember that hero vs. hero conflict doesn't have to be limited to slugging it out—it can also be a clash of ideas around issues like registration or an intense mindgame between heroes who aren't above manipulation and lies to protect a loved one.

WATCHER-CONTROLLED SUPPORT CHARACTERS

Beyond framing Scenes and playing the significant opposition, the Watcher gets to play a large cast of minor and Specialty characters that are key to permeating the Event with the cataclysmic issues of the Civil War. The Event is rife with inquisitive reporters, loyal S.H.I.E.L.D. agents, fanatical Hydra spies, opportunistic A.I.M. scientists, and Atlantean sleeper cell agents. Sometimes, in the heat of things, playing more than a few characters can make Scene management feel burdensome. Here are a few things you can do to keep things manageable.

Conflict Scenes usually involve one Watcher character per hero and sometimes a few more minor characters. If you find there are too many Watcher characters to handle easily, don't hesitate to use doom dice to separate the heroes and the opposition they face to create smaller, more manageable conflict Scenes.

I'm playing Ms. Marvel and my friend is playing Iron Man. A mob of Anti-Registration protesters has engaged us just as we were about to face off against Luke Cage, Spider-Man, and Captain America. To make the fight easier to manage, the Watcher decides to spend a doom die to describe how the mob has surrounded me and Luke Cage and forced Iron Man into the air where Spidey and Cap use the occasion to set an ambush.

When you have Specialty characters in a Scene—whether brought by the heroes' resources, unlocked by the players, or part of the Scene's framing—you must first decide who controls them. You can usually let heroes control Specialty characters that are naturally allied to them.

I'm playing Ms. Marvel, who has been drafted as a S.H.I.E.L.D. Super Agent and assigned a squad of 4 Cape-Killers (Superhuman Response Unit officers). The Watcher tells me they're under my control but suggests I make the Scene more manageable by using them as a Mob by pooling their TEAM and BUDDY Affiliation dice.

Minor and Specialty characters might start a Scene either neutral or engaged in the conflict. As the Watcher, you can choose to skip neutral characters' actions until a hero or Watcher character pulls them in. In fact, you could decide to give a neutral hero a cost, either in PP or in doom dice, to activate him as a temporary ally. Give the players the option first, before spending doom, just like activating certain Limits.

I'm playing Ms. Marvel and I've partnered with the Wasp to track down a mysterious unregistered hero, possibly the Winter Soldier. A cell of Anti-Registration heroes who hope to recruit the fugitive interrupts us. The hiding fugitive, who's undecided about the registration issue, might be brought into the conflict as a temporary ally if Wasp's player or I spend 1 PP or if the Watcher spends a D6 from the doom pool.

Once engaged in a Scene, a minor or Specialty character acts like any other character. Instead of having them roll dice, you may wish to use these characters as support characters, lending a trait die to their allies during their turn in the action sequence (much like a persistent asset).

Mobs
p. OM115

CIVIL WAR
SOURCEBOOK

Marvel's Superhuman Civil War drives a staggering number of characters, nations, organizations, and landmarks into the midst of heart-wrenching conflicts. This chapter provides the Watcher with a plethora of setting elements for running the Event. It includes all the details you need about the Superhuman Registration Act, various factions and nations potentially involved in the Event, and a list of New York City locations—as well as some notes on Washington, DC—that can be used as settings for your Scenes. This chapter also contains Milestones and unlockables that your characters can use throughout the Event.

THE SUPERHUMAN REGISTRATION ACT (SHRA)

6 U.S.C. S. 558—also known as the Superhuman Registration Act, or SHRA—proposes that all those with superhuman abilities who are active within the United States of America register with the United States federal government as "living weapons of mass destruction." This applies to all such cases, including those naturally occurring, those endowed with magic, or those subject to the effects of extreme sciences. It even includes gods and those using remarkable and unique technology, such as Iron Man.

▶ While an American law, its introduction inspires other nations to propose similar legislation, such as the Canadian Super-Powers Registration Act.
▶ Individual states respond with their own legislation to complement the law on a state level. These are usually more specific or restrictive.
▶ The proposed Act was stuck in committee for months before the Stamford tragedy.
▶ The Commission on Superhuman Activities (CSA) drafted the legislation. They're a government intelligence group responsible for its enforcement.
▶ The SHRA is a modification and extension of the Mutant Registration Act. The SHRA extends the MRA's provisions to those not born with their abilities.

IN SUPPORT OF THE SHRA

Superhumans have damaged their reputation with the public. Many people view even the most heroic super heroes as dangerous vigilantes who have no regard for collateral damage in their pursuits of justice. In the original comic series, Iron Man leads the movement for the Superhuman Registration Act. He believes that the SHRA might restore some faith in the super heroes of the United States, affording them greater public support. Iron Man fears that, without the legislation, a future catastrophe will cause the government to seek even more restrictive legislation.

IN OPPOSITION TO THE SHRA

Their stance is that superhumans should enjoy the same civil rights as other American citizens. Opponents believe that the Superhuman Registration database infringes on their fundamental rights to privacy and it paints them as guilty without trial. In the original comic series, Captain America leads the voices against the Superhuman Registration Act. Detractors believe that the SHRA is an unnecessary measure, and that excessive government interference and scrutiny will prevent those heroes from defending the people. Others realize that, once their identities are no longer secret, their loved ones' safety will be in question.

WHAT'S AT STAKE WITH THE SUPER HERO CIVIL WAR?

Collateral damage is always a threat during superhuman conflicts, and villains seek to benefit any time a conflict removes heroes. But what's at stake for the heroes you're playing?

FOR THOSE SUPPORTING THE SHRA

If the Registration Act passes, opponents of the bill won't take the loss lightly. Even if Captain America—or whoever is leading the protests—backs down, there will always be dissent. No amount of legislation can crush a philosophy, and there will always be bad blood between those who feel their rights were violated and those who are responsible for the bill.

FOR THOSE OPPOSING THE SHRA

Those against the Registration Act seem like they have the most to lose. Their very rights are on the line, and possibly their lives. Protesting publicly is putting your name out there. Those who support the bill may view a superhuman opposing it as just another confirmation of their fears and apprehensions.

WHAT IF? HEROES CHOOSING DIFFERENT SIDES

In the Earth-616 continuity, the SHRA divided the superhuman community down the middle as some heroes sided with the SHRA and others opposed it. When playing out the CIVIL WAR Event, players are encouraged to choose whatever sides they want for their heroes, regardless of the one chosen in the official storyline. For instance, maybe you'd like Mr. Fantastic to become the voice of reason against registration. Alternatively, you might want to play out how Captain America might start as a staunch defender of registration and see how his loyalty evolves as play progresses. Any such choices will have significant consequences on the overall story, but that's what's so appealing about playing through an Event with **MARVEL HEROIC ROLEPLAYING**.

IF THE ACT PASSES

If the SHRA passes, these things happen:
▶ Superhumans must register with government officials.
▶ Government agencies regulate, approve, or deny professional use of superhuman abilities.
▶ Those not in compliance are declared in contempt of the law.

In extreme circumstances, other consequences might arise:
▶ The database is hacked and sold to those interested in hurting the families of superhumans.
▶ Precedent is set for internment camps or technological branding.
▶ Some teams stop fighting, for fear of government intervention. Chaos ensues in their absence.

IF THE ACT FAILS

If the SHRA fails, these things happen:
▶ Proponents for the bill promote other, more extremist bills to encourage harsher restrictions.
▶ Superhumans supporting the SHRA are seen as traitors to the cause.
▶ Villains use this to justify superhuman supremacy agendas.

In extreme circumstances, other consequences might arise:
▶ Riots in the streets due to an uneasy populace.
▶ Enemies target the families of Anti-Registration voices.
▶ Extremists propose a seceded union, with a state for "abominations."

A player can choose to pursue one or two of these Milestones in place of Milestones in the hero's datafile. More than one hero can have the same Milestone, and one like MY ALLY, MY ENEMY might even be taken by two players to refer to each other's characters. Multiple Milestones may lead you to switch sides in the conflict, but you gain 10 XP for this action only once. Switching sides has a big impact—flip-flopping doesn't.

XP
p. OM107

CAPTURE OUTLAW HEROES (PRO-REGISTRATION)

Vigilantes have long skirted the law, but breaking this law brings on serious consequences. You're one of the heroes tasked with apprehending those who refuse to register.

1 XP when you capture an Anti-Registration super hero.

3 XP when you let an Anti-Registration hero escape for personal reasons.

10 XP when your attempt to capture another hero leads to their death, or your leniency gets you declared a fugitive yourself.

COMPROMISE SHRA INFRASTRUCTURE (ANTI-REGISTRATION)

S.H.I.E.L.D. and their SHRA allies possess much greater resources and equipment than the underground. If you're going to stand a chance, you'll need to even the playing field.

1 XP when you stress out a Cape-Killer team or wreck a piece of S.H.I.E.L.D. hardware.

3 XP when your destruction of infrastructure results in collateral damage to innocent bystanders or heroes on your side.

10 XP when you destroy or commandeer a major S.H.I.E.L.D. resource or an irreplaceable piece of technology created by the Pro-Registration forces.

CONVERT THE ENEMY

You're sure you've chosen the right side. You just know that you can convince your opponents they've made a mistake, if they'll just listen to reason! So many heroes could go either way that your persuasive efforts could make a massive difference in the war.

1 XP when you make a specific plea to another hero, in a forum that exposes you to the other side (like a live TV interview or open Avengers frequency).

3 XP when your efforts to recruit someone cause that hero to quarrel with his allies or oppose your side even more strongly.

10 XP when you directly convince an opposing hero to switch to your side, causing emotional stress or you fight a hero you've tried to convert and one of you stresses out the other.

FREE THE PRISONERS (ANTI-REGISTRATION)

The SHRA heroes and Cape-Killers are rounding up anyone who refuses to register and making them disappear. You need to find out where they're being held and give them back their freedom!

1 XP when one of your allies is captured.

3 XP when you successfully raid a prisoner convoy or uncover important information about Prison 42 in the Negative Zone.

10 XP when you free the heroes imprisoned in Prison 42 or become captured and put into Prison 42.

LEAD THE CHARGE!

Before the fight against the SHRA, it might have been easy to be a lone wolf or maintain a carefree attitude. Now heroes need to band together with the others on their side of the fight, and someone needs to step up and lead. Maybe that someone is you.

1 XP when you accept leadership or act as the leader in the midst of a conflict.

3 XP when you discuss the difficulties of leading your allies against other heroes with an ally.

10 XP when you lead your side to a significant victory, or your actions as leader result in the death of one of your teammates.

MY ALLY, MY ENEMY

You were never as close to anyone as you were with one old teammate, lover, or best friend. But now that the battle lines are drawn, you find yourselves on opposite sides. Can you reconcile, or will this strain break your relationship for good?

1 XP when you visit a place the two of you frequented, encounter an enemy you fought together, or meet up with a mutual friend.

3 XP when you use your powers against your old ally.

10 XP when one of you switches sides, or one of you removes the other from the conflict.

REDEEM HEROES IN THE PUBLIC EYE

Many of the "heroes" in this conflict have turned a blind eye to the very people they're supposed to protect. You haven't. Reestablishing the public's trust in super heroes won't be easy, but you're committed to the task.

1 XP when you protect an innocent bystander or layperson instead of fighting an opposing hero.

3 XP when you prevent injury or death to an uninvolved person present in an Action Scene.

10 XP when you curtail your super hero life to join public service or create a lasting program to foster goodwill with the public. If you're Anti-Registration, you can instead register to fit the new mold of hero the public wants or create a program that attempts to heal the public perception of super heroes in a different way.

SACRIFICE FOR THE CAUSE

You're committed to your side no matter what. Even as your life falls apart around you, and you face off against your best friends, you'll fight the good fight. Sticking to your convictions could cost you dearly.

1 XP when you're assaulted because of the side you've chosen.

3 XP when you sacrifice your career, your finances, or a part of your personal life in order to help your side.

10 XP when you make it impossible to return to your former life, must adopt a new identity, or take trauma in order to protect your side.

SPY ON YOUR FOES

Both sides try to place moles within the other's ranks to gather good intel on their plans. With so many alliances, it can be easy to plant yourself among your foes—either as yourself or in disguise.

- **1 XP** when you feed information to the side you're secretly working for.
- **3 XP** when you provide intel to gain trust as a mole and the information leads to the capture of one of your secret allies on the other side.
- **10 XP** when you get exposed as a mole and either fight against your false allies or switch sides to truly join them.

TEST YOUR ALLEGIANCE

There are a few heroes who know they've chosen the right side, but you're not one of them. You have friends on both sides, and you see them acting in ways you don't consider exactly "heroic." The side you've chosen might not be the right one after all.

- **1 XP** when you confront another hero about the ethics of actions they've taken to help your side, or another hero confronts you about yours.
- **3 XP** when you confess to another hero you're not certain you've chosen the right side.
- **10 XP** when you either cause enough emotional stress on another hero to force them to switch sides or react to emotional stress or trauma by switching sides yourself.

UNMASK (PRO-REGISTRATION)

If heroes are going to register, one of the strongest gestures you can make is to reveal your secret identity. It's not a decision made lightly, but it could make a major difference for the Pro-Registration argument.

- **1 XP** when you discuss the ramifications of taking off your mask with your loved ones and family.
- **3 XP** when you reveal your identity to someone who didn't know it before.
- **10 XP** when you reveal your secret identity in a public forum, or you publicly refuse a direct order to unmask and are declared a fugitive.

EVIL FOR JUSTICE

Can super-villains be used to turn the tide to your side as potent tools to use against your super heroic enemies? The enemies of your enemies are still thieves and murderers.

- **1 XP** when you talk to a super villain about fighting on your side.
- **3 XP** when you take precautions to keep the villains in check so they will not go out of control.
- **10 XP** when you either decide that this is folly or see the true potential of this approach, gather villains as a team and lead them.

FACTIONS

The Marvel Universe is filled with factions that struggle against one another for influence or control over resources, people, or each other. Some of the most significant factions involved with or affected by the Civil War are discussed here. Heroes will likely interact with them and may need to gain their support or interrupt their plans in order to achieve victory for their side of the war.

NATIONS

The Civil War is mostly focused on the United States, but it has repercussions on other nations as well. While America has its attention drawn upon itself because superhumans are fighting each other in the streets of its cities, other nations brace for the outcome or maneuver to gain long-sought-after advantages. If the heroes can't gain support within their own country, it might be worth fishing for allies outside of the U.S.A.'s boundaries.

ATLANTIS

Deep beneath the waves lies an ancient land, nearly forgotten for many lifetimes, populated by *homo mermanus*, or Atlanteans. These blue-skinned, humanoid dwellers of the deep possess powerful physiques and aquatic abilities such as gills and an affinity with other aquatic creatures.

Key locations in Atlantis include: City of Atlantis, Hydrobase, City of Kamuu, Cave of Shadows, Namor's Solitary Place, Realm of the Faceless One, Tomb of Princess Fen, and the Ruins of Tha-Korr.

Once a small continent estimated to be about the size of Australia, the kingdom of Atlantis suffered a Great Cataclysm about 21,000 years ago and was lost to the world of humans. The fabled kingdom was re-discovered in 1920 in the North Atlantic, purely by accident. Nazi attacks during World War II and earthquake shocks by Paul Destine's use of the Helmet of Power destroyed much of the legendary city of Atlantis, killing Emperor Thakorr, grandfather of **Prince Namor**.

After a time away, Namor returned home to the Atlantean survivors who, in turn, welcomed him as their rightful king. Despite a history of conflicts with the surface-dwellers, Namor has tried to maintain peace with those above. Namor represented Atlantis as part of the **Illuminati** (see page CW32), a group of elite super heroes.

PLAYING THE CIVIL WAR FROM AN ATLANTEAN PERSPECTIVE

If you choose to play an Atlantean ally or hero, keep in mind that Prince Namor's cousin **Namorita** dies in the Stamford tragedy; your hero likely desires vengeance for this atrocity. Like Namor, patriotic Atlantean characters probably oppose the Superhuman Registration Act. On the other hand, some Atlanteans have no dealings or love of surface-dwellers and may have no opinion about the Civil War on either side.

ATLANTEAN AGENTS

EXPERT ATLANTEAN SPY 8

SOLO 8	BUDDY 4	TEAM 6
ATLANTEAN WEAPONS 8	ENHANCED STRENGTH 8	
ENHANCED SWIMMING 8	ENHANCED DURABILITY 8	

Limit: *Gills.* Step back traits when not immersed in water. When dehydrated, shutdown all traits other than ATLANTEAN WEAPONS and step up lowest doom die or add D6 to the doom pool. Recover all traits when returned to water.

These deep-cover Atlantean agents—such as the one simply called "Joe"—have been living among the surface-dwellers for many years. They have built lives, married, made friends, opened businesses, and blended in well enough that nearly anyone could be an Atlantean Sleeper Agent. Oblivious of their true nature, they spend their lives as humans until a predetermined signal triggers them. A quick dose of a green serum and they're back to Atlantean form.

EXPERT ATLANTEAN WARRIOR 8

SOLO 4	BUDDY 6	TEAM 8
ATLANTEAN WEAPONS 8	ENHANCED STRENGTH 8	
ENHANCED SWIMMING 8	ENHANCED DURABILITY 8	

Limit: *Gills.* Step back traits when not immersed in water. When dehydrated, shutdown all traits other than ATLANTEAN WEAPONS and step up lowest doom die or add D6 to the doom pool. Recover all traits when returned to water.

The military backbone of the Atlantean people, these highly-trained and proficient warriors guard Atlantis from the surface-dwellers or are the front lines for an invasion. Their weapons of choice include Atlantean ray weapons, power tridents, or spears.

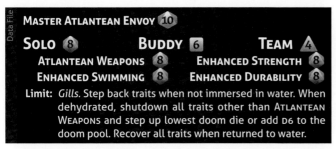

MASTER ATLANTEAN ENVOY 10

SOLO 8	BUDDY 6	TEAM 4
ATLANTEAN WEAPONS 8	ENHANCED STRENGTH 8	
ENHANCED SWIMMING 8	ENHANCED DURABILITY 8	

Limit: *Gills.* Step back traits when not immersed in water. When dehydrated, shutdown all traits other than ATLANTEAN WEAPONS and step up lowest doom die or add D6 to the doom pool. Recover all traits when returned to water.

Representatives of the Atlantean Monarchy who work to keep the peace between surface-dwellers and Atlantis. The key Atlantean Envoy during the Civil War is Ambassador Govan.

SIGNIFICANT ATLANTEANS

Sub-Mariner
Datafile
p. CW208

Namor McKenzie

Commonly called Prince Namor, and sometimes known as the Sub-Mariner, Namor the First is cousin to one of the heroes who died during the Stamford incident. Namor is a half-breed and mutant born to Fen, an Atlantean princess, and human sea captain Leonard McKenzie. Prince Namor may be unlocked as a player hero after Act One.

ANDROMEDA ATTUMASEN

Affiliations
SOLO 6
BUDDY 4
TEAM 8

Distinctions
OXYGEN SERUM
PEACEKEEPER

A peacekeeper and former warlord, Andromeda is the daughter of the barbarian warlord Attuma and Lady Gelva. She spent time on the surface with the Defenders, taking a serum to appear human and not suffer the effects of water deprivation. She is now an important leader of Namor's military forces.

Power Sets

ATLANTEAN TRAITS
ENHANCED DURABILITY 8   ENHANCED STAMINA 8
SUPERHUMAN STRENGTH 10   SUPERHUMAN SWIMMING 10

Limit: *Gills.* Step back ATLANTEAN TRAITS power traits when not immersed in water. When dehydrated, shutdown ATLANTEAN TRAITS and step up lowest doom die or add D6 to the doom pool. Recover the Power Set when returned to water.

ATLANTEAN WEAPONRY
ATLANTEAN TRIDENT 10

Specs
COMBAT MASTER 10   SCIENCE EXPERT 8
VEHICLES EXPERT 8

JANUS

Affiliations
SOLO 10
BUDDY 8
TEAM 6

Distinctions
DOUSE THE FIRE
SLEEPER AGENT

Janus is an Atlantean sleeper agent ordered to capture Nitro and return him to Atlantis. He is notably stronger than most Atlanteans.

Power Sets

ATLANTEAN TRAITS
ENHANCED DURABILITY 8   ENHANCED SWIMMING 8
SUPERHUMAN STRENGTH 10

Limit: *Gills.* Step back ATLANTEAN TRAITS power traits when not immersed in water. When dehydrated, shutdown ATLANTEAN TRAITS and step up lowest doom die or add D6 to the doom pool. Recover the Power Set when returned to water.

ATLANTEAN WEAPONRY
ATLANTEAN RIFLE 8   ATLANTEAN SPEAR 10
ATLANTEAN TRIDENT 10

Specs
COMBAT EXPERT 8   COVERT EXPERT 8
MENACE EXPERT 8

ATLANTEAN TECHNOLOGY

Through interaction with the non-human Deviant race that live in Earth's isolated reaches, the Atlanteans have achieved an advanced level of aquatic and amphibious technology. Their sleeper agent system requires sophisticated technology to convert an Atlantean into a human for lengthy—even extreme—periods of time.

Another scientific innovation includes a serum that allows an Atlantean to absorb oxygen through her skin for extended surface trips. Their weapons technology includes developments in spears, power tridents, and ray weapons. Many of the physical sciences, though, still remain a mystery to the Atlantean people.

ATLANTIS UNLOCKABLES

These unlockables are available to any hero connected to Atlantis.

▶ **[10 XP/15 XP] Unlock Prince Namor:** Although he isn't always friendly to surface-dwellers, Namor looks out for those he considers allies. For 10 XP, you receive a personal favor from Prince Namor, such as: aid in an investigation, a peaceful intervention, or his help as backup on a mission. Alternately, you may unlock Prince Namor as a player hero for Act Two. For 15 XP, Namor leads a TEAM 3D8 squad of Atlantean forces, shares secret information only he can provide regarding the Event, or provides some other significant aid within his powers.

▶ **[5 XP/10 XP] Atlantean Assistance:** While not openly Pro- or Anti-Registration, Atlantean forces could affect the outcome of the Civil War. For 5 XP, a small insurgence can be averted or you may gain favor with Atlantis. For 10 XP, the Atlanteans consider you an ally and will offer troops, weapons, vital information, or other forms of assistance to aid you.

▶ **[5 XP/10 XP] Atlantean Heritage:** Not everyone knows their true bloodlines. For 5 XP, you learn you might have some family connection to Atlantis and you find favor among the Atlanteans. For 10 XP, you learn you are part of an Atlantean bloodline and gain this HYBRID ATLANTEAN TRAITS Power Set– ENHANCED DURABILITY D8, ENHANCED STRENGTH D8, ENHANCED SWIMMING D8, **Limit:** *Mutant.*

WAKANDA

Located in equatorial Africa, Wakanda is one of the wealthiest and most advanced nations on the planet. Its population of about 6 million people includes the 18 marsh tribes surrounding the capital city of Central Wakanda. Three languages are spoken within its borders: Wakandan, Yoruba, and Hausa. An independent, spiritually based warrior culture, the country has largely chosen to conceal itself from the outside world. Despite its membership in the United Nations, Wakanda has no formal alliances with anyone; a non-aggression policy is a cornerstone of Wakanda's political and military history. The Wakandan people have never been defeated.

RESOURCES AND TECHNOLOGY OF WAKANDA

In its distant past, a meteorite containing a huge store of the element Vibranium crashed in Wakanda. Vibranium's properties include the ability to absorb vibrations and any kinetic energy directed at it. It can magnify mystical energies and mutate those exposed to it into creatures resembling demons. Protecting the Vibranium mound led, not only to worship, but also to the formation of the Cult of the Panther.

Maintaining its edge as the most technologically advanced nation on Earth, Wakanda's focus on science and learning has led to countless medical discoveries, such as cures for cancer and AIDS, and the development of eco-friendly power sources such as solar and hydrogen use, which has allowed Wakanda to leave its huge oil deposits untouched. The Wakanda Design Group serves as the corporate arm of the nation. One of its main exports is security and technology that was first developed to protect the Vibranium mound. Due to Wakanda's rich and diverse natural resources, there is almost no trade, not even for food. What little trade does occur revolves around its deposit of Vibranium.

WAKANDAN AGENTS

Data File

EXPERT WAKANDAN SOLDIER 8

SOLO 4   **BUDDY** 6   **TEAM** 8

BODY ARMOR 8   **HI-TECH WEAPONS** 8

This is a standard enlisted Wakandan army trooper, loyal to the King and nation of Wakanda. The same datafile may also be used for Navy personnel.

EXPERT WAKANDAN AIR GUARD 8

SOLO 6   **BUDDY** 4   **TEAM** 8

ENHANCED SENSES 8   **HI-TECH WEAPONS** 8

Wakanda's Air Guard consists of highly trained pilots equipped with cutting-edge equipment and aircraft.

MASTER PANTHER GUARD 10

SOLO 4   **BUDDY** 8   **TEAM** 6

BODY ARMOR 8   **ENHANCED SENSES** 8

HI-TECH WEAPONS 8

The so-called "Panther Posse" is a specialized elite unit serving to protect and defend Wakanda from external threats.

THE DORA MILAJE

Affiliations

SOLO 6
BUDDY 10
TEAM 8

Distinctions

DAUGHTER OF THE TRIBES
PROTECT THE KING!

Power Sets

ADORED ONE

ENHANCED REFLEXES 8   **ENHANCED STAMINA** 8

WEAPON 8

SFX: *Deadly Focus.* In a pool including an ADORED ONE die, replace two dice of equal steps with one stepped-up die.

SFX: *Take the Hit.* Spend a die from the doom pool to take physical stress intended for a nearby ally or friend.

Limit: *Rage.* Step up emotional stress and step up the lowest doom die or add D6 to doom.

Specs

COMBAT MASTER 10   **MENACE EXPERT** 8

As a means of keeping the peace, one woman from each of the eighteen tribes in Wakanda is sent to serve as one of the King's elite bodyguard, the Dora Milaje. Traditionally, the King chooses one of these women to be his Queen. Even a single Dora Milaje is a deadly opponent, with formidable weapons and combat training and skill. As a group, they can face down whole armies.

Black Panther
Datafile
p. CW160

SIGNIFICANT WAKANDANS

The Black Panther

The Black Panther is the head of Wakandan religion, politics, and military. The Black Panther is the embodiment of the warrior cult as well as the nation's ideals. It's a hereditary title, and the royal line of the Chieftain of the Wakanda Panther Cult began with Bashenga, the first king of unified Wakanda and the first Black Panther, 10,000 years ago. The Black Panther ingests a heart-shaped herb that connects him to the Panther God and enhances his senses and increases his strength. The current Black Panther is T'Challa, son of T'Chaka.

MAN-APE

M'baku

Affiliations
SOLO 6
BUDDY 4
TEAM 8

Distinctions
CHIEFTAIN OF THE JABARI
CRIMINAL MERCENARY
PANTHER'S RIVAL

Power Sets

WHITE GORILLA TOTEM

ENHANCED REFLEXES 8   ENHANCED STAMINA 8
SUPERHUMAN DURABILITY 10   SUPERHUMAN STRENGTH 10

SFX: *Chest Thumping.* When inflicting emotional stress, add a D6 and step up your effect die.

SFX: *Gorilla Slam.* Step up or double SUPERHUMAN STRENGTH for your next action, then step back SUPERHUMAN STRENGTH to 2D8. Activate an opportunity to recover.

Limit: *You Dare!* Step up emotional stress when taunted, mocked, or insulted to add a D6 to the doom pool.

Specs
COMBAT MASTER 10   CRIME EXPERT 8
MENACE MASTER 10   MYSTIC EXPERT 8

M'baku, leader of the antagonistic Jabari tribe in Wakanda, is more commonly known as the Man-Ape. As the representative of the White Gorilla Cult and a mercenary, Man-Ape has clashed many times with the Black Panther in an effort to seize control of the nation for his own people. He has allied with the so-called Lethal Legion and Masters of Evil on several occasions. The Jabari—and Man-Ape—currently maintain a civil if strained relationship with the King and the other Wakandan tribes.

UNLOCKABLES FOR WAKANDA

These unlockables are available to any hero connected to Wakanda.

▶ **[5 XP/10 XP] Ear of the King:** For 5 XP you may choose to either unlock the Black Panther as a player hero, or use him as a resource in the next Act. For 10 XP, you gain the previous benefits and the Black Panther shows up personally to aid you in a single Action Scene.

▶ **[10 XP] Panther-Blessed:** For 5 XP, any player can gain the blessing of Wakanda's Panther God, gained by making a pilgrimage to the Wakandan holy sites or from the blessing of a techno-priest or the king himself. The blessing lasts until the end of the Act. The Panther God's blessings only come out of Wakanda during troubled times; for a hero to be able to gain these powers, the situation must be dire indeed or the hero's deeds must have amazing nobility and grace to have gained the Panther God's eye.

BLESSINGS OF THE PANTHER GOD

ENHANCED REFLEXES	8	ENHANCED SENSES	8

——OR——

ENHANCED STAMINA	8	ENHANCED STRENGTH	8

SFX: *Ferocious Hunter.* Step back the highest die in your attack action pool to add a D6 and step up physical stress inflicted.

SFX: *Panther's Wrath.* Against a single target, step up or double a BLESSINGS OF THE PANTHER GOD die. Remove the highest rolling die and use three dice for your total.

Limit: *Dangerous Totem.* If your pool includes a BLESSINGS OF THE PANTHER GOD power, both 1 and 2 on your dice count as opportunities, but only 1s are excluded from being used for totals or effect dice.

▶ **[5 XP/10 XP] Wakandan Arsenal:** For 5 XP, any player can gain a Wakandan arsenal, gaining a new Power Set. If the Limit is ever put into play, the arsenal is broken or stolen and must be fixed by a Wakandan scientist. For 10 XP, the player is also trained in the repair and upkeep of his arsenal and it is a new Power Set on the datafile, like any other.

WAKANDAN ARSENAL

CYBERNETIC SENSES	6	ENHANCED DURABILITY	8
WALL-CRAWLING	6	WEAPON	6

SFX: *State of the Art Weapon Systems.* Shutdown your highest rated WAKANDAN ARSENAL power to step up another WAKANDAN ARSENAL power. Activate an opportunity to recover or during a Transition Scene.

Limit: *Gear.* Shutdown a WAKANDAN ARSENAL power and gain 1 PP. If 10 XP was spent, may take an action vs. the doom pool to recover.

ORGANIZATIONS

In the Marvel Universe, there are several organizations that oppose or support world governments. They serve their own agendas first, only allying with others so long as their goals overlap. Groups like Hydra, A.I.M., and S.H.I.E.L.D. are notoriously secretive. Each organization is only as successful as its leadership and resources allow, and as those are prone to changing without warning, an organization's reliability is often questionable.

ADVANCED IDEA MECHANICS (A.I.M.)

Born of Hydra's ambitions near the close of World War II, Advanced Idea Mechanics is devoted to the overthrow of all world governments in favor of a technological utopia—with itself running the show, of course. A.I.M. supplies advanced weaponry and technological support to super villains and terrorist groups alike; it's been directly responsible for the creation of more than a few super villains in its own right.

Although it began as Hydra's weapons-development arm, A.I.M. split off from its parent organization years ago. The two groups have had a tempestuous relationship ever since. Under the leadership of **M.O.D.O.K.**, A.I.M. has alternately clashed and allied with Hydra, but its primary opponent has always been S.H.I.E.L.D. Nick Fury devoted considerable resources to shutting down A.I.M. over the years, and it appears that Maria Hill is continuing that trend as Director.

A.I.M. PERSONNEL

Data File		
EXPERT A.I.M. SCIENTIST 8		
SOLO 6	**BUDDY** 8	**TEAM** 4
	BLASTER 6	BODY ARMOR 6
	HAZMAT SUIT 6	

SFX: *Immunity.* Spend D6 from the doom pool to ignore stress, trauma, or complications from airborne poisons or diseases, radiation, or chemicals.

This is a standard A.I.M. scientist, assigned to one project or another and generally willing to fight and die to protect it.

Data File		
EXPERT A.I.M. TROOPER 8		
SOLO 4	**BUDDY** 6	**TEAM** 8
	BLASTER RIFLE 8	BODY ARMOR 6
	HAZMAT SUIT 6	

SFX: *Immunity.* Spend D6 from the doom pool to ignore stress, trauma, or complications from airborne poisons or diseases, radiation, or chemicals.

A.I.M. troopers serve as lab assistants and physical labor as well as performing guard duties or entering into combat situations.

M.O.D.O.K.

Affiliations
- SOLO ⑧
- BUDDY ⑥
- TEAM ⑩

Distinctions
- DESIGNED ONLY FOR KILLING
- EVOLUTIONARILY ADVANCED
- TO ME, MY MINIONS!

George Tarleton

A.I.M. Scientist George Tarleton was an unimaginative cretin, until he volunteered to undergo an evolutionary advancement to finish A.I.M.'s Cosmic Cube project. The process warped Tarleton's body, advanced his mind immensely, gave him astounding mental powers, and also drove him to conclude that life is an unpredictable variable that should be eliminated. Thus, he became the Mobile Organism Designed Only for Killing. Now, M.O.D.O.K. wants to take back control of A.I.M. from Scientist Supreme Monica Rappacinni, who spurned his advances just prior to his transformation.

EVOLVED ORGANISM

Power Sets

ENHANCED DURABILITY ⑧	MENTAL BLAST ⑩
MIND CONTROL ⑩	PSYCHIC RESISTANCE ⑩
SUPERHUMAN SENSES ⑩	TELEPATHY ⑩

SFX: *Area Attack.* Against multiple targets, for each additional target add D6 and keep an additional effect die.

SFX: *Mental Illusions.* When creating illusion-based assets, add a D6 to your dice pool and step up your effect die.

SFX: *Mental Taxation:* Step up or double an EVOLVED ORGANISM power for your next action then shutdown that power afterward. Spend a doom die to do both.

SFX: *Probability Prediction.* When you add a die from the doom pool to M.O.D.O.K.'s pool including an EVOLVED ORGANISM power, double that die. You may keep an extra effect die as a probability-related asset.

Limit: *Exhausted.* Shutdown any EVOLVED ORGANISM power and step up lowest doom die or add D6 to the doom pool. Recover power by activating an opportunity.

MOBILE PLATFORM

ENHANCED DURABILITY ⑧	FLIGHT ⑧
LASERS ⑧	MISSILES ⑩

SFX: *Technological Genius.* Step up any technology-related asset created with a pool including TECH MASTER.

Limit: *Charged System.* Shutdown highest-rated MOBILE PLATFORM power to add that power die to the doom pool. Activate an opportunity to recover the power.

Limit: *Massive Head.* Shutdown MOBILE PLATFORM powers when suffering from any complication involving M.O.D.O.K.'s body. Remove complication to recover powers.

Specs

COSMIC MASTER ⑩	CRIME EXPERT ⑧
MENACE EXPERT ⑧	PSYCH EXPERT ⑧
SCIENCE MASTER ⑩	TECH MASTER ⑩

A.I.M. LABORATORIES

A.I.M. has secret laboratories all over the world, sometimes masquerading as R&D facilities belonging to its various front companies and sometimes operating below the radar altogether. A.I.M. laboratories are protected by squads of yellow-clad A.I.M. troopers, and usually have a variety of High-Tech Booby Traps. The projects being developed in A.I.M. laboratories range from advanced weapons to superhuman-nullification devices to sophisticated cybernetic systems. Just about all of them are highly volatile and Prone to Explode.

A.I.M. MILESTONES

Any hero who wishes to have a closer connection to A.I.M. can choose to follow one or both of these Milestones.

I Was an Advanced Idea

You know you owe some or all of your superpowers to A.I.M. technology. While you may not share the organization's objectives or agenda, you remain grateful to them and seek to know more about your origins in order to fully exploit your powers.

1 XP when you mention the A.I.M. origin of one of your powers while using it.

3 XP when you learn a new piece of information about how you were created.

10 XP when you discover the truth about the project that created you or you destroy an A.I.M. facility even though it means you'll lose that information forever.

Hunted by M.O.D.O.K.

For some reason, A.I.M. and its insane giant-headed leader want to get their hands on you. They won't stop until they get to study you or the technology that powers you, and they're not asking nicely.

1 XP when you confront A.I.M.-affiliated villains bent on capturing you (or your technology) for study.

3 XP when you shutdown one of your powers to prevent A.I.M. from gaining access to it.

10 XP when you defeat M.O.D.O.K. himself or give A.I.M. the opportunity to study you in exchange for the safety of innocents.

A.I.M. UNLOCKABLES

Any character following one of the A.I.M. Milestones can access these unlockables during the game.

▶**[5 XP] Shutdown Codes:** For 5 XP, you acquire remote shutdown codes for A.I.M. weapons technology. Once during the Act, you can declare that a villain with a technology-based Power Set is using A.I.M. tech; your codes act as a new Limit that shuts down one of the villain's Power Sets and adds a d6 to the Doom Pool or steps up the lowest die. This Limit only lasts for one Action Scene.

▶**[5 XP/10 XP] Shady Dealings:** A.I.M. will sell their tech to anyone who can pay. By buying this unlockable during a Transition Scene, you can create a resource as though you had one of the following Specialties: Cosmic, Science, Tech, or Vehicle. For 5 XP, treat the resource as though you had an Expert Specialty. For 10 XP, treat it as a Master Specialty.

HYDRA

For over fifty years, Hydra has been the most insidious, far-reaching, and powerful terrorist organization in the Marvel Universe. Founded in the waning days of World War II by renegade Nazi leaders and Japanese ultranationalists, Hydra's goal is nothing less than complete world domination. Its agents are everywhere, its leaders are ruthless, and for every cell that falls, two more rise to take its place. *Hail Hydra!*

HYDRA BASES

Since the near-total destruction of Hydra Island years ago, Hydra cells have operated out of a variety of secret bases in major cities throughout the world. Some, like the Hydra Terror-Carrier or Hydra's flying island, are technological marvels; others are just ordinary warehouses purchased by shell companies. Hydra bases are REGULARLY PATROLLED by FACELESS GOONS, and with a rare few exceptions are manned by ISOLATED CELLS with no knowledge of Hydra's activities anywhere else.

HYDRA PERSONNEL

EXPERT HYDRA TROOPER 8

SOLO 6	BUDDY 4	TEAM 8
HYDRA ARMOR 6		SMALL ARMS 6

SFX: *Two More Rise To Take Its Place.* A mob of Hydra Troopers is SOLO D6, BUDDY 2D4, TEAM 3D8. When a die is knocked out from the TEAM Affiliation, the Watcher may spend a D8 or greater out of the doom pool to add two additional dice to the mob, to a maximum of 6D8.

MASTER HYDRA AGENT 10

SOLO 8	BUDDY 6	TEAM 4
DISGUISES 6		HOLDOUT PISTOL 6

BARON WOLFGANG VON STRUCKER

Affiliations
- SOLO **8**
- BUDDY **6**
- TEAM **10**

Distinctions
- FORMER NAZI
- HAIL HYDRA!
- SCHEMER

DEATH SPORE VIRUS

DEATH SPORE TOUCH **10**   **SUPERHUMAN STAMINA** **10**

SFX: *Area Attack.* Against multiple targets, for each additional target add D6 and keep an additional effect die.

SFX: *Healing Factor.* Spend a die from the doom pool to recover your physical stress and step back your physical trauma.

Limit: *Exhausted.* Shutdown a DEATH SPORE VIRUS power to add a D6 to the doom pool or step up the smallest doom die.

SATAN CLAW

ELECTRIC BLAST **10**   **SUPERHUMAN STRENGTH** **10**

SFX: *Death Blow.* Step up or double a SATAN CLAW power for one action. If that action fails, shutdown SATAN CLAW.

Limit: *Technological.* Shutdown SATAN CLAW versus EMP-based attacks to add a D6 to the doom pool or step up the smallest doom die and.

Specs

COSMIC MASTER **10**	COVERT MASTER **10**
CRIME MASTER **10**	MENACE MASTER **10**

Wolfgang von Strucker was a Nazi officer in World War II and one of the founders of Hydra. He has battled Captain America, Nick Fury, and even Spider-Man, but his primary foes have always been agents of S.H.I.E.L.D. The Death Spore Virus that grants him his superhuman regenerative abilities also makes killing him a non-option—if Strucker ever dies, the spores will be released from his body, ending nearly all life on the planet.

MADAME HYDRA

Ophelia Sarkissian

Affiliations
- SOLO **6**
- BUDDY **4**
- TEAM **8**

Distinctions
- FEMME FATALE
- RUTHLESS AND SUBTLE
- SCARRED

ARSENAL

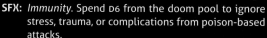

SWINGLINE **6**   **WEAPON** **8**

SFX: *Immunity.* Spend D6 from the doom pool to ignore stress, trauma, or complications from poison-based attacks.

SFX: *Toxins.* When creating poison-related complications, add D6 and step up effect die.

Limit: *Gear.* Shutdown an ARSENAL power to add a D6 to the doom pool or step up the smallest doom die. Spend D6 from the doom pool to recover.

Specs

ACROBATICS EXPERT **8**	COMBAT EXPERT **8**
COVERT MASTER **10**	CRIME MASTER **10**
SCIENCE EXPERT **8**	

Ophelia Sarkissian was granted a vastly-extended lifespan by the Elder God Chthon. She used this long life to pursue a career as an assassin, terrorist, and master criminal. She has served Hydra loyally for years, and she's responsible for restoring Spider-Woman's powers in exchange for the hero's service as a double agent and for renewing ties between Hydra and the Hand.

HYDRA MILESTONES

Characters associated with Hydra may choose from one or both of these Milestones.

Deep Cover Agent

You have either infiltrated or allied yourself with one or more organizations in order to report on their activities to Hydra, or you're reporting to one of those organizations by joining Hydra. You may also be a sleeper agent waiting to receive specific instructions to execute one of Hydra's glorious secret plans. Hail Hydra!

1 XP when you make a choice or perform an action that could put your true allegiance in question.

3 XP when you allow the organization you're infiltrating to accomplish one of its goals to maintain your cover identity.

10 XP when you either blow your cover to protect someone or allow innocents to suffer to maintain your secret.

Child of Hydra

Hydra's influence transcends generations and filial loyalties. An older relative has been involved with Hydra, making you and your family a potential target of the organization itself or some of its many enemies.

1 XP when you mention that a parent, older sibling, or other relative is or was a Hydra agent.

3 XP when you suffer mental or emotional stress related to your family's affiliation.

10 XP when you stress out a Hydra-affiliated family member or forsake your allies to join your family.

HYDRA UNLOCKABLES

These unlockables are available to any hero following one of the Hydra Milestones presented above.

▶ **[5 XP/10 XP] Mysterious Agenda:** Hydra's plans are both subtle and far-reaching; sometimes that means offering aid (or at least appearing to offer aid) to heroes. For 5 XP, a group of four Hydra troopers or a single Hydra agent shows up to help you out during a single Action Scene, then departs. For 10 XP, Madame Hydra herself appears. Naturally, this will have repercussions down the line.

THE ILLUMINATI

Made up of the great leaders and minds of the superhuman community, the Illuminati was formed to share information so threats could be recognized and prevented before they happened. Shortly after the Kree-Skrull war, **Tony Stark** (Iron Man) assembled the group to ensure that heroes would be prepared for similar perils. While Tony wanted a large, official public delegation of super heroes, they finally agreed that just the few of them would secretly meet to deal with matters of great importance.

MEMBERS OF THE ILLUMINATI

Only the most influential and powerful leaders among the superhuman community join the Illuminati. Each of them speaks on behalf of some portion of the superhuman community, such as mutants, magicians, or Inhumans.

Iron Man
Datafile
p. CW188

Mister
Fantastic
Datafile
p. CW192

Doctor
Strange
Datafile
p. CW176

Black Bolt
Datafile
See
ANNIHILATION:
WAR OF KINGS
SUPPLEMENT

Sub-Marinor
Datafile
p. CW208

Professor X
Datafile
See CIVIL
WAR: X-MEN
SUPPLEMENT

Tony Stark

Besides being Iron Man, a wealthy industrialist, and an inventor, Anthony Stark considers himself a futurist. He gathered the Illuminati with the intention of predicting and preventing danger. Tony's conscience tells him that the heroes can and should do more to protect people, and that the superhumans need to find a place in the world rather than constantly finding themselves at odds with it.

Dr. Stephen Strange

The Master of the Mystic Arts brings his magical expertise to the group. Even scientists as skilled as Stark and Richards can't uncover the secrets that Strange can divine through spells and on his travels to the Astral Plane. Strange generally sides with independence and freedom from despotism; occasionally he abstains from voting on either side of a conflict, perhaps because he is so removed from the actions of those bound to the Earth dimension.

Prof. Charles Xavier

The group's representative from mutantkind, Professor X uses his telepathic powers to ensure the members of the Illuminati keep their actions secret and don't betray one another. By the time the Civil War begins, Xavier has gone missing, and the others presume he's dead. In actuality, he's in space.

Dr. Reed Richards

In many ways, Mr. Fantastic has stronger bonds to Stark than anyone else in the Illuminati. The two are both prominent leaders among the superhuman community in New York, and their scientific contributions are unmatched. The two see eye to eye on most issues the Illuminati have dealt with.

Black Bolt

The King of the Inhumans became a silent participant in the Illuminati, communicating via Professor X's telepathy. He joined the Illuminati as a way to give his isolated people a connection to the larger world without opening them to the interference of foreign governments.

Namor

The king of Atlantis proves he's as headstrong as ever as a part of the Illuminati. Though he doesn't object to the purpose of the group—he is, after all, accustomed to rulership—Namor disagrees with many of the decisions of Stark and the others. And he's not one to keep his thoughts to himself.

THE BIG PICTURE

Playing one of the Illuminati means looking farther down the road than the other heroes—seeing the bigger picture. Stopping the current threat matters, but shaping the world matters more. That might mean stepping on the toes of other heroes, or taking actions they wouldn't approve of. So be it. You can't make the world a better place by punching people anymore.

Focus on the greater good your work will accomplish, even if it means some of your actions right now might not make sense to those outside the Illuminati. If you have more than one Illuminati member in the same group, you might talk about your larger plans apart from the rest of the group, particularly in Transition Scenes. You might even share your secret plans with other characters. Just remember that the Watcher sees all!

ILLUMINATI MILESTONES

Shortly before the Civil War began, Tony revealed an early copy of the Superhuman Registration Act to the Illuminati. He outlined a scenario very similar to the events that eventually triggered the Civil War, and suggested that they go along with the efforts to register and legitimize super heroes. This split the group, seemingly for good, with only Reed siding with Tony. Still, the "greater good" can continue to influence these heroes' goals.

Shape the Future

You have the solution to the problems of today, but you need some time to put all the pieces into place. Friends, family, and allies might not understand, or might wonder why you're distant. You know it will all be worth it.

1 XP when actions you take in service of your future goal undermine your short-term success.

3 XP when you steal or destroy an ally's information, technology, or resources to further your goal.

10 XP when your future goal comes to fruition, whether the consequences are what you had planned or not.

Keep your Secrets

Part of the burden of being in the Illuminati is never telling the other heroes, authorities, or even your loved ones about the group. Likewise, some of the things you find out would be better dealt with by the Illuminati than by other heroes—even those you trust.

1 XP when you withhold information from, or lie to, an ally.

3 XP when you reveal a secret another member of the Illuminati divulged to you.

10 XP when you side with the Illuminati to betray an old friend, or betray the Illuminati for an old friend.

ALTERNATE ILLUMINATI

Tony Stark could have invited other heroes to the Illuminati, or another hero might have even started the group. What if other members of the super hero community had been voting on the issues brought before the Illuminati?

- **T'Challa**: The first Illuminati meeting took place in Wakanda, but King T'Challa refused to join. If he'd become a member, would he have tried to keep the Illuminati from abusing the power they granted themselves, such as when they banished the Hulk to a distant planet?

- **Steve Rogers**: With his connections to S.H.I.E.L.D. and the great respect he earned from other heroes, Captain America could have been invited. Would his strong moral compass have led the Illuminati in a different direction?

- **Hank Pym**: Another brilliant scientist, Pym eventually became a major collaborator with Stark and Richards during the Civil War. What if Iron Man had brought in his Avengers teammate for the founding of the Illuminati? How would Pym's troubled life and constantly changing identity have affected the group?

- **Nick Fury**: The most legendary agent of all time could have brought the intelligence gathered by S.H.I.E.L.D. to the Illuminati. If he had used his skills at manipulation and espionage for the cabal, how might his reach have grown?

S.H.I.E.L.D.

The Strategic Hazard Intervention Espionage Logistics Directorate, better known as S.H.I.E.L.D., is the world's premier covert operations and superhuman law-enforcement organization. They have the best tech, the best-trained agents, and the best intelligence on just about every known superhuman operating on planet Earth. Led for decades by the legendary **Nick Fury**, S.H.I.E.L.D. has recently suffered major shake-ups, including a disastrous mission to Latveria that ultimately saw Fury resign as Director and go underground, leaving S.H.I.E.L.D. in the relatively untested hands of Director **Maria Hill**.

LOCATIONS

As a multinational force with a tremendous budget and some of the most dangerous superhuman criminals in its custody, S.H.I.E.L.D. has plenty of top-secret, high-tech bases that are ideal settings for Transition Scenes—and as the conflict over the SHRA comes to a head, Action Scenes as well.

S.H.I.E.L.D. Helicarrier

Designed by Tony Stark, Reed Richards, and Forge, the Helicarrier is S.H.I.E.L.D.'s primary base of operations, a massive aerial battleship BRISTLING WITH WEAPONS. A full contingent of agents are ALWAYS ON DUTY, and it also boasts STATE-OF-THE-ART MONITORING FACILITIES that can track superhuman activity anywhere on the globe and coordinate an appropriate response.

S.H.I.E.L.D. Safehouses

Equipped with the BEST SECURITY MONEY CAN BUY, these bases have EVERYTHING YOU NEED to conduct a covert war. During the first Act, Director Fury may share the location of one of the 28 top-secret safehouses with the Anti-Registration resistance, especially if the resistance is headed by one of his long-time associates (such as Captain America).

Avengers Tower

After the destruction of Avengers Mansion, Tony Stark donated the top three floors of his new skyscraper as a base of operations for the reassembled New Avengers. The building itself is NIGH INDESTRUCTIBLE, and the top three floors boast ALL THE COMFORTS OF HOME, if your definition of "home" includes hi-tech labs, Iron Man's Hall of Armor, and a gym to rival the Danger Room. Recently, it was revealed that the Sentry's base of operations, the Watchtower, is a part of Avengers Tower as well. This ominous black structure provides MYSTERIOUS MONITORING TECHNOLOGY that the Sentry shares with Stark's Avengers.

NOTABLE S.H.I.E.L.D. AGENTS

Any of these characters could be brought in as a Watcher character or a resource created by a player hero with S.H.I.E.L.D. connections.

DIRECTOR MARIA HILL

Affiliations
- SOLO ⑧
- BUDDY ⑥
- TEAM ④

Distinctions
- BULL-HEADED
- EYE IN THE SKY
- IN FURY'S SHADOW

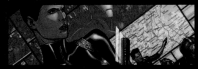

Power Sets

S.H.I.E.L.D. TECH

BODY ARMOR ⑧	GLOBAL MONITORING SYSTEMS ⑩
SWINGLINE ⑥	

SFX: *Focus.* Replace two dice of the same size in a dice pool with one stepped-up die.

Limit: *Compromised.* Shutdown a S.H.I.E.L.D. TECH power to add a D6 to the doom pool or step up the smallest doom die. Spend D6 from the doom pool to recover.

Hill's attitude toward the super hero community is decidedly cooler than Nick Fury's was. Rumors persist that she was given the post of Director of S.H.I.E.L.D. to keep "Fury loyalists" out of power within the Directorate, rather than any great faith in her ability.

Specs
COMBAT EXPERT ⑧	COVERT EXPERT ⑧
TECH EXPERT ⑧	VEHICLE EXPERT ⑧

TIMOTHY "DUM-DUM" DUGAN

Affiliations
- SOLO ④
- BUDDY ⑥
- TEAM ⑧

Distinctions
- ALL ABOUT THE BOWLER HAT
- OLDER THAN I LOOK
- TENACIOUS LEADER

Power Sets

HOWLING COMMANDO

CIRCUS STRONGMAN ⑥	RIFLE ⑥

SFX: *Let's Go, Commandos!* Step up or double a HOWLING COMMANDO power for your next action, then shutdown that power. Spend d6 doom or activate an opportunity to recover.

Limit: *Compromised.* Shutdown a HOWLING COMMANDO power to add a D6 to the doom pool or step up the smallest doom die. Spend D6 from the doom pool to recover.

One of Nick Fury's original Howling Commandos, "Dum-Dum" followed his friend to S.H.I.E.L.D., where he rose to the rank of Deputy Director. As tensions rise over SHRA, he becomes deeply conflicted over his role in the fracas and Maria Hill's leadership of S.H.I.E.L.D.

Specs
COMBAT EXPERT ⑧	COVERT EXPERT ⑧
MENACE EXPERT ⑧	VEHICLE EXPERT ⑧

CAPE-KILLERS

Affiliations
- SOLO ④
- BUDDY ⑥
- TEAM ⑧

Distinctions
- LOYAL TO S.H.I.E.L.D.
- TRAINED TO FIGHT SUPERHUMANS

Power Sets

STARK TECH ARMOR

BODY ARMOR ⑧	COMMS ⑥
SUBSONIC FLIGHT ⑥	TRANQUILIZER GUN ⑧

Officially the Superhuman Restraint Unit, the "Cape-Killers" are elite S.H.I.E.L.D. agents, equipped with armor and weapons designed by Tony Stark and specially trained to engage and subdue superhumans who fail to comply with the SHRA. Against more powerful heroes, they attack as a mob—increase their Affiliations to TEAM 4D8 and BUDDY 2D6.

S.H.I.E.L.D. MILESTONES

Characters associated with S.H.I.E.L.D.—or hoping to become so—may choose one or both of these Milestones.

Climbing the Ranks

You're on S.H.I.E.L.D.'s payroll by choice or by decree and you've taken on the duty of upholding the law, including the SHRA...

1 XP when your actions earn you a commendation from your superiors in S.H.I.E.L.D.

3 XP when you inflict stress on an Anti-Registration hero on orders from S.H.I.E.L.D.

10 XP when you're appointed Director or Deputy Director of S.H.I.E.L.D., or when you sacrifice your career with S.H.I.E.L.D. to do what you think is right.

Double Agent

...But you work for some other organization(s) who want you to keep tabs on whatever S.H.I.E.L.D. is up to. You may be called upon to feed wrong information to your supposed superiors or get involved in acts of sabotage.

1 XP when you pass confidential S.H.I.E.L.D. information to an Anti-Registration hero or pass intelligence on an Anti-Registration hero or group of heroes on to S.H.I.E.L.D.

3 XP when you suffer mental stress as part of an investigation to find a mole or when someone attempts to blow your cover.

10 XP when you reveal your true allegiance or convince your "allies" that you really are on their side once your cover is blown.

S.H.I.E.L.D. UNLOCKABLES

These unlockables are available to any hero following one of the S.H.I.E.L.D. Milestones presented above. At the Watcher's discretion, they might be available to other heroes with S.H.I.E.L.D. affiliation, even if they aren't following one of these Milestones.

▶ **[5 XP/10 XP] Thunderbolts:** For 5 XP, you can request that S.H.I.E.L.D. send in one of the Thunderbolts—super villains recruited by S.H.I.E.L.D. for black ops missions against Anti-Registration forces. The villain helps you out for one Action Scene, and is then recalled to the Helicarrier. For 10 XP, the Thunderbolt remains a supporting Watcher character for the rest of the Act.

▶ **[5 XP/10 XP] Life Model Decoy:** For 5 XP, you can declare that the hero you're playing has been a Life Model Decoy—a highly sophisticated, lifelike android—for some period of time, maybe since the beginning of the Act. The "real" hero can then show up in any Scene you like. For 10 XP, you can declare that any character who has died during the Event was actually an LMD and the real hero is alive and well and available for play.

▶ **[10XP] Stark Industries Upgrade:** For 10 XP, you receive a gadget, probably a costume, designed by Tony Stark to augment your superhuman abilities. You can step up two power traits in one of your Power Sets by +1 step, but the tech isn't 100% reliable. Whenever the Watcher adds a die to the doom pool by activating an opportunity, step up the die by +1.

▶ **[5 XP] Backdoor Computer Codes:** You gain access, either illicit or authorized, to the SHRA registration database. These codes give you a free D12 effect die you can apply once during the Act, either to create an asset or remove a complication without having to roll for it.

▶ **[5 XP/10 XP] Rogue Agents:** For 5 XP, you can declare that a group of unnamed S.H.I.E.L.D. agents present in the scene don't support the SHRA. They'll stand back, not engaging Anti-Registration heroes for the rest of the Scene, unless attacked. For 10 XP, they'll actively aid Anti-Registration heroes, *or* you can use the 5 XP unlockable against a named S.H.I.E.L.D. agent.

THE FRONT LINES

The battle for liberty, justice, and national security is fought on many fronts, both physical and social. There's the battle for public support, fought in the press. There are verbal battles in court and in Congress. And of course there are physical battles... well, everywhere. The following sections focus on the media and significant locations that serve as the backdrop of the Civil War.

THE MEDIA BATTLEGROUND

Among the many Big Apple information sources, the most delicious news bytes in the mighty Marvel Universe come from the newshounds at *The Daily Bugle*. Owned and operated by publisher J. Jonah Jameson, the *Bugle* is known throughout New York City, and to its many costumed vigilantes, as particularly anti-super-hero—especially against your Friendly Neighborhood Spider-Man.

The current chief competitor for the *Bugle* is *The Alternative*, which promotes a more objective stance. On the video side of the news, several local television stations, as well as 24-hour news media, play a major role in covering current events.

THE DAILY BUGLE

One of the forefront newspapers, *The Daily Bugle* is home to conservative slant, brutish and outspoken Publisher **J. Jonah Jameson**, and a slew of widely known reporters from one of the most-varied news bullpens in the United States.

Some of the most well-known journalists in the newspaper's longstanding existence include: Jameson, current Editor-in-chief **Robbie Robertson**, reporters **Ben Urich**, **Betty Brant**, **Eddie Brock**, and **Jessica Jones**, photographer **Russ Holmes**, and freelance photographer **Peter Parker**.

THE ALTERNATIVE

Chief competitor to the *Bugle*, *The Alternative* features more idealistic reporters, like **Sally Floyd**, who try to get to the grit of a story without placing a slant on the news. Floyd, photographer **Geoffy Creswell**, and the rest of the staff get strong support from Managing Editor **Neil Crawford**.

SIGNIFICANT JOURNALISTS

Neil Crawford

Data File

MASTER JOURNALIST 10

SOLO 4   **BUDDY** 6   **TEAM** 8

Managing Editor of *The Alternative*, Crawford stands up for his reporters, even in the face, literally, of S.H.I.E.L.D. Agent Eric Marshall.

Geoffy Creswell

Data File

ROOKIE PHOTOJOURNALIST 6

SOLO 8   **BUDDY** 6   **TEAM** 4

Photojournalist for *The Alternative*, nicknamed the "Swami of the Snapshot."

John "Johnny" Fernandez

Data File

EXPERT PHOTOJOURNALIST 8

SOLO 8   **BUDDY** 6   **TEAM** 4

Emmy-nominated journalist and a former national news media videographer with at least 15 overseas war zone tours, his last job was filming a New Warriors reality TV show.

Sally Floyd

Data File

EXPERT JOURNALIST 8

SOLO 8   **BUDDY** 6   **TEAM** 4

A leading reporter for *The Alternative*, Sally Floyd is concerned that civil comfort may one day win the war against civil liberty. She is generally trusted by super heroes because of her reputation for fair reporting.

Russ Holmes

Data File

ROOKIE PHOTOJOURNALIST 6

SOLO 8   **BUDDY** 6   **TEAM** 4

Photojournalist for *The Daily Bugle*.

J. JONAH JAMESON

Affiliations		Distinctions
Solo	6	Holds a Grudge
Buddy	4	Sensational Journalist
Team	8	You're Fired!

Specs

Business Expert 8   Menace Expert 8

Sometimes referred to as JJJ, Jameson is the owner and publisher of *The Daily Bugle*. He is a dinosaur from the ol' days of hard-hitting sensational journalism who uses the newspaper as a tool to push his hate of costumed heroes. It is his personal belief that "American security came under attack from an out-of-control pack of costumed freaks." Likewise, he's a big fan of disasters and anything else that will sell extra copies of one of the best-known daily newspapers in New York City. JJJ has spent most of his life with the *Bugle*, rising up through the ranks from copy boy to reporter to editor, before purchasing the business, and then ultimately the Goodman Building. Following the unmasking of his nemesis Spider-Man, Jameson takes it personally. JJJ officially supports the Superhuman Registration Act.

Peter Benjamin Parker

Longtime freelance photojournalist Peter Parker has submitted thousands of images to *The Daily Bugle*'s picture desk, mostly featuring costumed super heroes and villains. Parker was renowned for his ability to capture some of the best frames of New York's famous wall crawler. Even though Parker always believed he was on shaky ground with *Bugle* Publisher J. Jonah Jameson, he was far more liked than his alternate self, Spider-Man.

Spider-Man
Datafile
p. CW204

JOSEPH "ROBBIE" ROBERTSON

Affiliations		Distinctions
Solo	4	Journalistic Integrity
Buddy	6	Voice of Reason
Team	8	Years of Experience

Specs

Pysch Expert 8

Current Editor-in-Chief of *The Daily Bugle*, Robbie Robertson is the type of editor who builds strong working relationships with his reporters, frequently running interference between them and publisher J. Jonah Jameson. Robertson tends to be the one strong voice of reason on the *Bugle*'s staff whenever Jameson goes off on a rant. Robertson believes the Superhuman Registration Act is "as history changing as Watergate, the Moon landing, Vietnam War, and Iraq War all rolled into one." Robertson is a graduate of the Columbia School of Journalism.

BEN URICH

Affiliations		Distinctions
Solo	8	Fearless Reporter
Buddy	6	Hated by the Goblin
Team	4	Seen It All

Specs

Crime Expert 8   Pysch Expert 8

One of the most-respected reporters in *The Daily Bugle*'s history, Ben Urich earned his stripes as a criminal investigator. He's a friend and former co-worker of Peter Parker. Urich is an NYU journalism graduate.

PRESS MILESTONES

Characters associated with various media outlets may choose from one or both of these Milestones in addition to those on their datafiles, or those related to the Event.

On the Front Lines

Your involvement in the conflict, your ability to withstand its violence, and, more importantly, your willingness to stand in the spotlight makes you a natural source for media reporters.

- **1 XP** when you give an exclusive interview to a member of the media who's on the front lines.
- **3 XP** when you rescue members of the working media who are risking their lives (or yours) in a war zone.
- **10 XP** when you turn the media away from the Civil War in order to focus on something else, or you succeed in making yourself the central figure of the media's coverage of the Civil War to the exclusion of others.

Inside Source

The Civil War is not as clear-cut as people would like; you want to expose its darker secrets without blowing your cover or endangering your family and loved ones. You act as an off-the-record source for reporters and seek out proof to change public opinion about the underlying issues of the war.

- **1 XP** when you leak secret information that will aid a reporter in a breaking news story.
- **3 XP** when you risk your life to provide a journalist with valuable information that could affect the outcome of the Civil War.
- **10 XP** when you reveal Top Secret information from a major organization, such as the U.S. government, S.H.I.E.L.D., rogue heroes, Hydra, etc., that would forever change the face of the war, either way, and could be Pulitzer worthy for the reporter.

PRESS UNLOCKABLES

These unlockables are available to any hero following one of the Press Milestones presented above.

▶ **[5 XP/10 XP] Embedded:** Most major news sources are taking sides of Pro-Registration or Anti-Registration. For 5 XP, a journalist puts a hold on a story or photo for up to a few days. For 10 XP, the reporter kills a vital story or photos, keeps knowledge private, and possibly destroys all records.

KEY MARVEL UNIVERSE LOCATIONS

Superhumans of the Marvel Universe live and do battle in a multitude of settings. During the Civil War, many of those key locations are in New York City and Washington, D.C. The following iconic locations serve as inspiration for scenes set in either of these cities and include examples of Scene Distinctions to offer your players.

AVENGERS MANSION RUINS

Built by the Stark family, this 5th Avenue townhouse in Manhattan, located near Central Park and the Upper East Side, was destroyed by the Scarlet Witch's reality-warping powers. Due to financial troubles, Stark was unable to rebuild the mansion and it was left as a MEMORIAL TO THE AVENGERS who died during that crisis. In order to save costs, Stark moved the Avengers HQ to the Stark Tower, which he renamed Avengers Tower. The ruins may reveal ARTIFACTS FROM AVENGERS HISTORY or one or two HIDDEN CACHES OF TECHNOLOGY.

AVENGERS TOWER (FORMERLY STARK TOWER)

Industrialist Tony Stark's 93-story corporate headquarters in the heart of Manhattan—near Columbus Circle—has recently been converted into the Avengers Tower after the destruction of the Avengers Mansion. The tower features HIGH TECH SENSORS, DEFENSIVE COUNTERMEASURES, and several INSULATED NETWORKS. The roof includes the Sentry's Watchtower with its own set of MYSTERIOUS DISTURBANCE DETECTORS, as well as an AERO-PAD and a PROTECTIVE DOME. The top floors contain a WAR ROOM, which features a 360-DEGREE VIEW of the city and multiple STARK TECH WORKSHOPS. It has recently been home to Stark's butler Jarvis, co-worker Peter Parker, and Parker's family—wife Mary Jane Watson-Parker and Aunt May Parker. Depending on the status of the Avengers in the Civil War Event, it may become the headquarters of the Pro-Registration heroes, or seized by S.H.I.E.L.D. as their New York base of operations.

BAXTER BUILDING

Located on Madison Avenue in Midtown Manhattan—about 10 blocks from Avengers Tower—the 35-story Baxter Building is home to the world-famous Fantastic Four. Originally built in 1949 by the Leland Baxter Paper Company, the building is currently owned by Reed and Susan Storm Richards, better known as Mr. Fantastic and the Invisible Woman. Visitors are greeted on the 30th floor in the reception area by one of the tower's many ROBOTIC ASSISTANTS. The team's living quarters are on the 31st floor while the 33rd floor contains the ADVANCED SCIENTIFIC LABORATORY. The top floor features a HANGAR FOR THE TEAM'S VEHICLES. Battles have happened outside of, inside of, and literally through the many floors of the building. It's also the location of a PORTAL TO THE NEGATIVE ZONE, carefully guarded by many SECURITY FEATURES.

ADAPTING LOCATIONS

Many of these areas can be easily adapted to create other buildings and sites in New York, Washington, Phoenix, Stamford, or any other city you decide to set a scene in.

Sewers and subways are similar all over the planet. Take the digital billboards away and Time Squares can become the National Mall on a bad day. Add a few of the traits from New York's landmarks to get historical DC monuments, generic office buildings anywhere, or a super team's headquarters like Thunderbolts Mountain in Arizona.

OTHER MANHATTAN LOCATIONS

There are a variety of Manhattan locations your heroes may visit. In such cases, make up one or two interesting Scene Distinctions whenever you set scenes there.

- Bedford Towers
- Empire State University
- Fisk Towers
- Flatiron Building, Damage Control offices
- Grand Central Station
- Ground Zero
- Hellfire Club mansion
- Heroes for Hire office
- Holy Ghost Church
- Latverian, Wakandan, or Symkarian consulates
- Master Planner's undersea base
- Metropolitan Museum of Art
- One Roxxon Plaza
- Sanctum Sanctorum
- S.H.I.E.L.D. public HQ or the secret HQ
- United Nations
- X-Factor Investigations
- Yancy Street

DAILY BUGLE BUILDING

Formerly known as the Goodman Building and located between Midtown and East Side in Manhattan, the Daily Bugle Building is the HOME OF THE DAILY BUGLE newspaper. Currently owned by publisher J. Jonah Jameson, the building has gone through several owners including William Walter Goodman; the psychotic Norman Osborn, AKA the Green Goblin; and Thomas Fireheart, also known as the mercenary Puma. Numerous fights between Spider-Man and a variety of super villains have taken place here. These battles have even resulted in the building's destruction at the hands of the Green Goblin and its later reconstruction. It also offers a WARM WELCOME for Pro-Registration heroes thanks to Jameson's Pro-Registration slant. Regardless of his Pro- or Anti-Registration status, the newspaper office is never a welcome place for Spider-Man who is vehemently hated by Jameson—especially after his unmasking. Its overcrowded offices feature STACKS OF PAPERS, CLUNKY COMPUTERS, MASSIVE OFFICE FURNITURE, and WINDOWS EVERYWHERE.

EMPIRE STATE BUILDING

The Empire State Building is one of the most RECOGNIZABLE features gracing the skyline of the Big Apple. This TOWERING and ICONIC skyscraper has seen more than its fair share of action in the Marvel Universe. It's located in Chelsea, near Midtown Manhattan. One of the Big Apple's most popular tourist destinations, it often has LONG LINES waiting to use its many EXPRESS ELEVATORS. Its two observatories have PROTECTIVE GUARDRAILS to protect people from a DIRE FALL.

RYKER'S ISLAND

Ryker's Island is a HIGH SECURITY island jail complex. It imprisons superhuman criminals through EXTRAORDINARY SECURITY FEATURES such as POWER NEUTRALIZING AGENTS. It features large OPEN AREAS, including some that are EXPOSED TO THE ELEMENTS. Inside the multiple buildings you're likely to see VAULT-LIKE DOORS, TWISTED PASSAGES, and REINFORCED GUARD POSTS manned by HIGHLY TRAINED S.H.I.E.L.D agents. The jail is home to enemies of the Avengers, Fantastic Four, and Spider-Man. The Island and one of its sub-complexes, the Raft, are covered in detail in the *Breakout* mini-Event included in the **MARVEL HEROIC ROLEPLAYING BASIC GAME**.

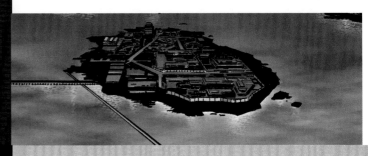

SEWER TUNNELS

Beneath the busy New York City streets lies a MAZE-LIKE NETWORK of sewers. These sewers are often used as escape or travel paths for heroes—like Spider-Man—when other means of travel are limited or when stealth is a key factor. They are also frequently used as hideouts for a variety of villains, like the Lizard. Sewers are one location where heroes can engage in combat and have a lot less chance of causing collateral damage—although they can be FLOODED, FILLED WITH TRASH and contain caches of MUTAGENIC TOXIC WASTE hidden by unscrupulous corporations.

STATUE OF LIBERTY

A true historical icon of the United States of America, the Statue of Liberty and Ellis Island are a BEACON OF HOPE to immigrants from around the world. Many super-powered fights seem to happen around this immediately recognizable national SYMBOL OF FREEDOM or inside its CRAMPED QUARTERS.

SUBWAY SYSTEM AND STATIONS

New York City has an intricate subway system, full of DANK TUNNELS, HIGH-VOLTAGE RAILS, HARRIED COMMUTERS, and CROWDED ENCLOSED SPACES. It's common for mobs of thugs to cause a scene in the subway. Sometimes heroes or villains use it as an underground SHORT CUT for a quick getaway or to elude a tail.

TIMES SQUARE

Located in Midtown Manhattan, not far from Hell's Kitchen, Times Square is a NATIONAL ICON, thanks to its televised New Year's Eve celebrations, MASSIVE DIGITAL BILLBOARDS, nearby Broadway shows, and frequently CONGESTED TRAFFIC. Superpowered battles that take place here have a HIGH RISK OF COLLATERAL DAMAGE. Passersby find themselves ducking into subway entrances or doing whatever they can to dodge FALLING DEBRIS during such confrontations.

WASHINGTON, D.C.

When battles get more political, they can be taken to the country's capital, Washington, DC. Its legendary TRAFFIC JAMS, scoop-obsessed POLITICAL REPORTERS, PROTEST RALLIES, ARDENT LOBBYISTS, and HARDBOILED POLITICIANS are all elements that superhumans might have to deal with over and above whatever brought them into the capital in the first place. Washington has several WIDE OPEN SPACES with plenty of GRANITE PILLARS and HISTORICAL LANDMARKS to allow for satisfying, if expensive, smackdowns.

Key locations include:
● Capitol Building
● Lincoln Memorial
● Pentagon
● Vietnam Memorial
● Washington Memorial
● White House

ACT ONE
ROAD TO CIVIL WAR

The political landscape has shifted. Where once hero registration was a fringe debate among outsiders and bigots, things have changed—now the heroes must decide what side they're on. The politically safe path of hero registration, though many fear it leads down the road to totalitarian oppression? Or resist registration at all costs, preserving liberty for heroes but potentially losing the goodwill and trust of the public? **Which side are you on?**

ACT ONE: ROAD TO CIVIL WAR

SCENE STRUCTURE

Act One has two parts. The Buildup section has four main Action Scenes introducing the heroes to the story and getting them together before the horrific tragedy of Stamford. The Key Scenes introduce Action and Transition Scenes that can be played in any order, ending in the final Transition Scene that gathers the heroes together before the SHRA passes at midnight.

Buildup
▶ Action: Titanium Man Attacks Washington
▶ Action: The Hammer Falls
▶ Action: Crusader Hijacks An Airplane
▶ Action: Appear Before Congress

Key Scenes
▶ Transition: Clean Up Stamford
▶ Action: Registration and Super Villains
▶ Action: What About Stamford?
▶ Transition: Where Is Nitro?
▶ Action: The Rally
▶ Action: Meeting With the CSA
▶ Action: Confronted by S.H.I.E.L.D.
▶ Transition: Meet and Discuss Before Registration

Remember that you can create additional Transition Scenes as needed to allow the heroes to rest, recover, gather additional resources, and recruit new heroes or support between any Action Scenes. The nature of these Scenes largely depends on the activity of the heroes, but they might take place at super hero headquarters such as the Baxter Building or Avengers Tower, at a hero's home, or at any other private or public location favored by the heroes.

HOOKS

With so many ways to set things in motion and so many playable characters, it might be challenging to find a way to bring the heroes together. One option is to frame an opening scene with the heroes and have the players tell you why they're all there. Here are a couple of other ways to get the ball rolling:

▶ **The Summons:** The characters are summoned—as individuals or as a group—to appear before Congress to discuss the provisions of the SHRA. When they show up, go straight into Titanium Man Attacks Washington or Appear Before Congress. If they refuse the summons, they may get a taste of Maria Hill's new managerial style—a squad of Cape-Killers show up, tasked with bringing them to Washington.

▶ **Recruitment:** The heroes are contacted by mysterious agents of one or several organizations—like A.I.M., Hydra, or S.H.I.E.L.D.—trying to recruit them for the upcoming crisis. Maybe the organization seems to know more about what's about to happen than the heroes themselves; curiosity may be reason enough to accept the offer and investigate what's going on. This can lead directly to The Hammer Falls or Crusader Hijacks an Airplane.

DOOM POOL

The doom pool begins at 2D6 for this Act.

DOOM POOL: **2D6**

BUILDUP: BEFORE STAMFORD

The following Action Scenes take place before the tragedy in Stamford, Connecticut. Depending on the heroes the players have chosen, one or more of these Scenes may be played out; every hero should have the opportunity to start the Event in at least one of these four Scenes.

ACTION: TITANIUM MAN ATTACKS WASHINGTON

This Scene establishes some or all of the heroes as a united front against threats that endanger the general population. It takes place in the nation's capital, so the heroes should have plenty of reasons to be present.

Titanium Man visits Washington with the express intention of killing Tony Stark. Unless Tony is one of the player heroes, Titanium Man's focus won't be on them. However, he'll go through anyone who happens to be in his way. He's confident of his own abilities, and he's unlikely to let up until he's clearly lost the fight—generally this means losing significant portions of his armor.

Like Iron Man, Titanium Man's power comes from his armor. He takes full advantage of his GODLIKE STRENGTH to pummel, slam, and throw his enemies, wrecking the Washington, D.C., landscape. His *Area Attack* SFX puts innocent lives in danger with every application of his CONCUSSIVE BLAST. He'll try to engage a single opponent at a time, even if that means picking one up and using SUPERSONIC FLIGHT to vacate the area.

TITANIUM MAN

Identity of Current User Unrevealed

Affiliations
SOLO 10
BUDDY 8
TEAM 6

Distinctions
EMPTY-HEADED
HIGH-POWERED MERCENARY
SHORTSIGHTED

POWERED ARMOR

CONCUSSIVE BLAST 10 CYBERNETIC SENSES 6
SUPERHUMAN DURABILITY 10 GODLIKE STRENGTH 12
SUPERSONIC FLIGHT 10

SFX: *Area Attack.* Against multiple targets, for each additional target add D6 and keep an additional effect die.

SFX: *Force Rings.* When inflicting an ENTRAPPED complication on a target, add a D6 and step up the effect die.

SFX: *Heavily Reinforced.* Spend a doom die to ignore physical stress or trauma.

SFX: *System Allocations.* Shutdown one POWERED ARMOR power to step up another POWERED ARMOR power. Spend a doom die to recover that power.

Limit: *Charged System.* Shutdown a power to add that power die to the doom pool. Activate an opportunity to recover.

Before his apparent death, Russian agent Boris Bullski used the first few Titanium Man suits against Iron Man over many years. Others adopted the identity and upgraded the suit to suit their agendas. Regardless of the wearer or version of the suit, the Titanium Man armor is always a powerful piece of offensive technology—though never quite as sophisticated as the Iron Man armor.

Specs
COMBAT EXPERT 8 COVERT EXPERT 8
MENACE EXPERT 8

OPTIONS WITH TITANIUM MAN

▶ If Tony is one of the heroes, consider spending doom dice to activate one or more of his Limits, shutting down his powers and making him more vulnerable to Titanium Man's onslaught, thus urging other heroes to defend Tony.

▶ Titanium Man isn't the brightest, and he's zealous about his anti-American agenda. Tactics to outsmart and distract him should be rewarded. Play up his SHORTSIGHTED and EMPTY-HEADED Distinctions.

▶ If the heroes are particularly patriotic, step up the devastation of Washington, D.C. With every strike—whether a hit or a miss—national monuments should serve as targets for collateral damage. Don't just throw the heroes around; spend those doom dice and throw them into chunks of American history. Make rubble. Make news.

▶ This is a great turning point. The heroes could look very good—or very bad. This can set the tone for the SHRA debate to come. If the heroes try to protect innocents, public opinion should shift to their side (whichever that side happens to be). If they put lives in unnecessary danger, the public will fight vehemently for registration, or worse.

ACTION:
THE HAMMER FALLS

While the SHRA debate rages on, other dangers threaten the United States. Alerted to the presence of Mjolnir—or at least something that fell from the skies—the heroes head to Oklahoma to investigate, placing them right in the middle of things as Doctor Doom arrives to seize his prize.

Doctor Victor Von Doom escaped from Hell when Thor's hammer, Mjolnir, crashed through multiple dimensions on its way to Earth. He pursued the weapon to Broxton, Oklahoma, where it left a sizable crater. Convinced he's worthy of the Mjolnir, Doom and a full force of mechanical minions are going for the hammer. His small army marches on the crater, and Doom forces his way through the heroes toward his prize. In his pursuit of godhood, he's dismissive of their resistance.

The research facility in Broxton, OK is HEAVILY PATROLLED, built around the crater where Thor's hammer was discovered. Temporary buildings are constantly being replaced by more permanent structures and the government is sparing nothing, so it's TECHNOLOGICALLY ADVANCED.

Doctor Doom is a skilled and challenging opponent. While his armor gives him SUPERHUMAN STRENGTH and he has SORCERY to fall back on, never forget that Doom's greatest asset is that DOOM'S GENIUS KNOWS NO EQUALS! Doom may sometimes become overconfident, but he should never be careless or ignorant. Always take advantage of his surroundings and take full advantage of any stress, assets, or complications in play. However, this isn't a hill Doom will die on—he'll escape if need be. And when he realizes he's not worthy of the hammer's power, he'll immediately retreat from the battle and flee.

DOCTOR DOOM

Victor Von Doom

Affiliations

Solo	10
Buddy	8
Team	6

Distinctions

Doom's Genius Knows No Equals!

Failure Is for Lesser Beings

Ruler of Latveria

Power Sets

BEHOLD THE GENIUS OF DOOM!

Cybernetic Senses 6	Energy Blast 10
Superhuman Durability 10	Superhuman Strength 10

SFX: *Always Prepared.* Spend a doom die to step up a Tech Master stunt or resource and recover mental or emotional stress.

SFX: *Impervious Force Field.* Spend a doom die to ignore physical stress or trauma.

SFX: *Multipower.* Add more than one Behold the Genius of Doom! power die to a pool. Step back each Behold the Genius of Doom! power die in that pool once for each die beyond the first.

SFX: *Plans within Plans.* When using a Behold the Genius of Doom! power to create assets, add a D6 and step up the effect die.

SFX: *Versatile.* Split Energy Blast into 2D8 or 3D6.

SFX: *You Are Not Worthy of Doom!* Spend 2D8 from the doom pool and reveal that the heroes have been fighting a Doombot instead of the real Dr. Doom.

Limit: *Epic Arrogance.* Step up the lowest die in the doom pool or add a D6 doom die to step up emotional stress from opponents that offend or otherwise anger Dr. Doom.

THE INDOMITABLE WILL OF DOOM

Master Sorcery 10	Psychic Resistance 10

SFX: *Iron Will.* Split Psychic Resistance into 2D8 or 3D6.

SFX: *Practiced Ritualist.* When inflicting a magical complication on a target, add a D6 and step up the effect die.

Limit: *Conscious Activation.* While stressed out, asleep, or unconscious, shutdown Master Sorcery. Recover that stress or wake up to recover that Master Sorcery. If physical trauma received, shutdown Master Sorcery until trauma recovered.

MECHANICAL MINIONS OF DOOM

Energy Blast 8	Enhanced Speed 6
Horde 8 8 8 8	Superhuman Durability 10
Superhuman Strength 10	

SFX: *Attack in Waves.* Using either Superhuman Strength or Blast against multiple targets, for each additional target add a D6 and keep an additional effect die.

Limit: *Limited Autonomy.* Defeat Horde dice (with D10 stress) to reduce Horde, Each Horde die may be treated as a separate target for *Area Attack* SFX.

Limit: *Too Proud for Teamwork.* Shutdown Behold the Genius of Doom! and The Indomitable Will of Doom to activate Mechanical Minions of Doom. Shutdown Mechanical Minions of Doom to recover Behold the Genius of Doom! and The Indomitable Will of Doom. Doom never uses his own powers against his robots' targets, nor does he accept their help with his.

Specs

Business Expert 8	Combat Expert 8
Cosmic Expert 8	Crime Expert 8
Medical Master 10	Menace Master 10
Mystic Master 10	Psych Expert 8
Science Master 10	Tech Master 10

Victor Von Doom went from being an orphaned child of an oppressed people and an expelled college student to the ruler of Latveria. A disastrous scientific experiment led to his expulsion from college and his life-long rivalry with Reed Richards of the Fantastic Four. While ruling Latveria, Doom has displayed unparalleled willpower and cruel genius, equipping the nation with cutting-edge defense technology and robot minions. He has gotten into conflict with many of the world's most powerful costumed defenders over the years and been a match for entire teams with his dangerous blend of scientific brilliance and sorcerous mastery. He crafted his armor and mask with a potent blend of technology and magic, and he never seems to take them off.

DOOMBOT

Affiliations

SOLO 8
BUDDY 4
TEAM 6

Distinctions

"I AM DOOM!"
PROGRAMMED FOR EVIL
ROBOTIC DUPLICATE

Doombots are advanced robots designed to mimic their creator, Dr. Doom. They are equipped with a number of advanced devices similar to those Doom uses in his armor. Doombots are programmed for utter loyalty to their master and can imitate him when ordered. Many heroes have "defeated" Dr. Doom, only to discover they were really facing a Doombot. When they become severely damaged or have outlived their usefulness, Doombots often self-destruct, but not before delivering a taunting message from Doom himself.

Power Sets

LATVERIAN SUPERTECH

CYBERNETIC SENSES	6	ENERGY BLAST	8
FLIGHT	6	SUPERHUMAN DURABILITY	10
SUPERHUMAN STRENGTH	10		

SFX: *Guise of Doom.* Step up or double any Latverian Supertech power as long as opponents believe it's actually Dr. Doom. Step back when next physical stress or trauma is received, revealing it's only a Doombot.

SFX: *Immunity.* Spend a D6 doom die to ignore stress, trauma, or complications caused by disease, poison, vacuum, hunger, thirst, fatigue, or psychic powers.

SFX: *Self-Destruct.* Against multiple targets, for each additional target add a D6 and keep an additional effect die. Add your physical stress to the pool and step up any doom dice added to this roll. Destroy the Doombot afterwards.

Limit: *Systems Failure.* Shutdown LATVERIAN SUPERTECH to step up lowest die in the doom pool or add D6 doom die. Activate an opportunity to recover.

Specs

COMBAT EXPERT	8	MENACE EXPERT	8
TECH EXPERT	8		

MJOLNIR

EXPERT SORCERY	8	GODLIKE DURABILITY	12
SUPERSONIC FLIGHT	10	TELEPORTATION	10
WEAPON	10	WEATHER SUPREMACY	12

SFX: *Anti-Force.* On a successful reaction against an energy-based attack, add a doom die equal to the reaction effect die to inflict your attacker's effect die against your attacker.

SFX: *Area Attack.* Against multiple targets, for each additional target add a D6 and keep an additional effect die.

SFX: *I Say Thee Nay!* Double or step up a MJOLNIR power for your next action, then step back that power. Activate an opportunity or participate in a Transition Scene to recover that power.

Limit: *Gear.* Shutdown MJOLNIR to gain 1 PP. Take an action vs. the doom pool to recover MJOLNIR.

OPTIONS WITH THE HAMMER FALLS

▶ Doom is crazy, not stupid. Smart heroes could try to convince him (i.e., inflict a complication or emotional stress) that the hammer's NOT WORTH THE FIGHT, because he can't take it even if he wins. His first response is that, if they think he can't take it, what do they lose if they simply GIVE HIM THE CHANCE?

▶ While Doom shouldn't be worthy of the hammer, what if a hero was? A player who wants to lift Mjolnir from the ground must prove his worth. A hero with 5 XP may take action using any traits that would prove "worthiness," opposed by the doom pool plus a D12 because of Mjolnir's enchantment. If the action succeeds, the hero spends 5 XP and gains the MJOLNIR Power Set for the remainder of the Scene. If the roll fails, that hero is not worthy, and may not make another attempt.

▶ Spend D8 doom to add a Doombot to the Scene. Doom created his Doombots and he knows their behaviors well. When fighting, he should take full advantage of their strengths. He'll use them to distract, to remove weaker heroes from the fight, or to give him support dice.

▶ Everyone wants Mjolnir. The public and military are giving full attention to the Broxton installation—all eyes are on the heroes. This could be an alternate inspiration for the SHRA movement.

IF I HAD A HAMMER...

● Wielding Mjolnir and wielding Mjolnir proficiently are separate matters. Most heroes will only get WEAPON D10, GODLIKE DURABILITY D12, the SFX: *I Say Thee Nay!*, and the Limit: *Gear*.

● Heroes with MYSTIC MASTER also gain access to the hammer's EXPERT SORCERY and the SFX: *Area Attack*.

● Heroes with COSMIC MASTER also gain access to TELEPORTATION and SFX: *Anti-Force*

● Additional Powers and SFX can be unlocked by spending 5 XP for each power or SFX the player wishes to unlock.

● After the Scene, the hammer ceases functioning, awaiting its true owner. However, if the player wants to really change his character, consider allowing him to spend 10 XP to replace a Power Set with MJOLNIR to become the new God of Thunder!

ACTION: CRUSADER HIJACKS AN AIRPLANE

In this Scene, the heroes face Crusader and his followers, who have hijacked an airplane.

Crusader (Arthur Charles Blackwood), incarcerated in the Raft until a recent breakout, has formed a small cult of thugs who share his extreme beliefs. Continuing his militant crusade against the super hero community for its dalliances with the dark arts, demigods, and demons, Crusader and his lackeys have hijacked a Federal Treasury C-130 filled with cash to finance his plans of bombing several superhuman organizations. Crusader's hope is to target Avengers Tower, the Baxter Building, the Xavier Institute, or a S.H.I.E.L.D. HQ with explosive devices. He fervently believes such an action will open the eyes of the public to see just how vile superhumans truly are.

Frame the Scene *in medias res*, with the heroes either on board the plane after Crusader and his thugs have seized it, or flying in under their own power to put an end to Crusader's terrorist acts. Ask them who put them up to this—S.H.I.E.L.D., an anonymous tip, or perhaps one of their other information sources. This is a great opening scene for heroes with obvious ties to magic or other dimensions, or for covert ops heroes who might enjoy the shot at playing air marshal. It's also a suitable Scene for a solo hero.

As soon as Crusader gets the impression the heroes are here to stop him, he changes plans. He orders his thugs to crash the plane anywhere— preferably a populated area, ideally one connected to the government or super heroes. The heroes therefore find themselves on a crashing plane that they have to try to land safely while dealing with PANICKED TREASURY AGENTS or UNRESPONSIVE CONTROLS. If they fail to land the plane, it may crash into something important, causing significant collateral damage. Landing doesn't end the drama, as the plane might have BURNING ENGINES or a FUEL LEAK, putting it on the verge of exploding. Survivors need to be evacuated as quickly as possible before the plane explodes. Whatever the results, this will gather significant press attention, likely influencing public opinion on the registration debate.

During the hijacking, Crusader's cult members join the fray until they realize they're overpowered. Some may be zealous enough to continue the fight, but most will back down out of fear.

CRUSADER'S CULTISTS

A mob of religious thugs who claim to do God's work but follow Crusader.

Affiliations

SOLO	8
BUDDY	4 4
TEAM	6 6 6 6 6

Distinctions

CULT MENTALITY
FANATICAL
ZEALOUS

Power Sets

CULT TRAITS

| GRAB | 8 | | SWARM | 8 |

SFX: *Area Attack.* Against multiple targets, for each additional target add D6 and keep an additional effect die.

LIMIT: *Cult Cohesion.* Defeat TEAM dice (with D8 stress) to reduce cultist mob.

CRUSADER

Arthur Charles Blackwood

Affiliations

SOLO **10**
BUDDY **8**
TEAM **6**

Distinctions

EDUCATED
SWORDSMAN
ZEALOT

POWER OF SPIRIT

Power Sets

| SUPERHUMAN DURABILITY **10** | SUPERHUMAN REFLEXES **10** |
| SUPERHUMAN STRENGTH **10** | SWORD **8** |

SFX: *Focus of Faith*. If a pool includes a Power of Spirit power, replace two dice of equal size with one stepped-up die.

SFX: *Spiritual Armor*. Spend a doom die to ignore physical stress or physical trauma unless caused by an opponent with the same faith.

Limit: *Faith-Based*. While stressed out, asleep, or unconscious, shutdown Power of Spirit. Recover that stress or wake up to recover that Power of Spirit. If emotional trauma received, shutdown Power of Spirit until trauma recovered.

Specs

COMBAT EXPERT **8**   MYSTIC EXPERT **8**

Former divinity student Arthur Blackwood received a vision that granted him miraculous power and the sword, shield, and armor of a knight. The vision compelled him to pursue a crusade against pagans and infidels, beginning with Thor. When he loses his faith, his sword becomes vulnerable and his powers abandon him. He has clashed with Luke Cage and Wolverine in the course of his recent acts of zealotry.

OPTIONS WITH CRUSADER HIJACKS AN AIRPLANE

▶ Instead of Crusader, the Watcher might choose to substitute a different villain. You could introduce Green Goblin very early in the Event by having him attempt to hijack the plane. Many of the villains in the *Breakout* Mini-Event in the **MARVEL HEROIC ROLEPLAYING BASIC GAME** would be perfect. Perhaps the whole thing is a stunt by Hydra or A.I.M. to fan the flames and influence public opinion in favor of the Superhuman Registration Act.

▶ Following the Scene, if Crusader survives, he may (after licking his wounds) move on to the next stage of his zealotry. You could include a Transition Scene where the heroes seek out the Crusader's compound as he recuperates. If Crusader goes forward with his plans, the heroes may need to find his PLANTED EXPLOSIVES before other heroes, government agents, or civilians get killed or injured.

▶ If you set this on a passenger airliner instead of a Federal plane, a brave Air Marshal (EXPERT AIR MARSHAL D8 [SOLO D8, BUDDY D6, TEAM D4] COURAGEOUS D8, SIDEARM D6) may choose to try to stop the villains before the heroes enter the action. While he might not have trouble taking out one or two of the cult members, Crusader takes him HOSTAGE in an attempt to keep the heroes at bay. Also, Crusader could take airline passengers as HUMAN SHIELDS, believing his life of service to his Creator is more important than their lives. This would be a great alternative to crashing the plane.

ACTION: APPEAR BEFORE CONGRESS

MORE OPENING SCENES

All of these scenes share a common premise: set up the climate in which the SHRA is being introduced, with super villains threatening the peace and super heroes forced to use their powers in ways that might endanger others or property. In lieu of the Action Scenes provided here, consider opening with one of the following:

- Hydra or A.I.M. seize a government building and take hostages.
- Kingpin hires a group of super villains to eliminate white-collar criminal rivals in the business district, in broad daylight.
- A hero is given Mutant Growth Hormone (MGH) without his consent and loses control of his powers, threatening a busy urban area.

This Action Scene doesn't involve big super hero battles; instead it showcases heroes' ability to handle themselves as idealists, public speakers, or social commentators. Alternately, they could be here as bodyguards or incognito as protestors.

The heroes are offered a chance to speak before Congress either for or against the Superhuman Registration Act. Either way, the purpose of this Scene is to persuade. About half of Congress stands one way, half stands the other, so there will likely be VOCAL HOSTILITY blurring the discussion. Passage or refusal of the Act will take a bipartisan effort. On something so impassioned, that's easier said than done. Name a few members of Congress. Have them give counterpoints or support for the heroes' testimony. While many of the Congress members should be reasonable, consider the absolute worst case scenarios of either side (see page CW14 for some ideas) and argue those points. Use hyperbole and fact bending to their advantage.

Congress: Big decisions and earth-shattering events happen in these HALLOWED HALLS. The halls and rooms of Congress are always CROWDED, full of NOSY JOURNALISTS, and both STUBBORN and OPPORTUNISTIC POLITICIANS. The wheels of politics never stop turning.

The individual Representatives and Senators on the opposing side of the SHRA debate from the heroes are collectively represented by a mob. To get aid from their Congressional allies, heroes need to establish them as resources for the Scene. For every D8 of mental or emotional stress done to the opposing group, the heroes can knock away a TEAM die. An *Area Attack* SFX or spending PP to keep multiple effect dice could take out multiple dice at once. Keep in mind, anything suspicious like an obvious display of mind-control powers or physical attacks will end the Scene and likely accelerate the passing of the bill.

Success doesn't mean that a specific side of the SHRA debate automatically wins, but it should drive the story from that point forward. Instead, the successful heroes unlock a FRIEND IN CONGRESS D8 asset that persists until the end of Act Two (when the Congressional ally finally caves to public opinion). If the bill passes, then the climate is considerably tenser when the tragedy occurs, making it even more of a firestorm than it otherwise would be (and uniting all of Congress behind the new act). This creates a persistent ATMOSPHERE OF FEAR D8 complication that can make all actions in opposition to the government or to win over their support much harder. It, too, lasts until the end of Act Two, after which it becomes more about S.H.I.E.L.D.'s drastic actions and less about government oversight.

CONGRESSIONAL COMMITTEE

A committee of legislators

Affiliations

TEAM
`6` `6` `6` `6` `6`

Distinctions

CONFLICTED

CONSTITUTIONAL AUTHORITY

PARTISAN

Power Sets

COMMITTEE TRAITS

BROWBEAT `8`   FILIBUSTER `8`

SFX: *Forum.* Against multiple targets, for each additional target add D6 and keep an additional effect die.

Limit: *Committee Cohesion.* Defeat TEAM dice (with D8 stress) to reduce mob.

OPTIONS FOR APPEAR BEFORE CONGRESS

▶ If the Scene gets boring, don't hesitate to have a super villain attack. Maybe Titanium Man is ready for round two, or you could grab a particularly contentious superhuman character from elsewhere in this Event or from the **BASIC GAME**.

▶ If you want the plot to seem more conniving, set up an attack where the opposition goes out of its way to make the heroes look bad in the eyes of Congress. Put onlookers' lives at stake. Give the heroes hard choices. Single out a Senator and make him or her a minor Watcher character instead of part of the mob.

▶ Numerous witnesses are packed into the House Gallery. If any of the heroes use a superhuman power, someone is bound to notice unless special care is taken. This is certain to cause outrage, which could end disastrously for the heroes' side of the argument.

KEY SCENES FOR ACT ONE

Once any or all of the Buildup scenes have been played out, the first Act is in full swing. These Action and Transition Scenes follow the Stamford tragedy, which the heroes should hear about off-camera (see The Explosion Heard Around the World). The YOUNG AVENGERS/RUNAWAYS SUPPLEMENT offers more options and alternatives for the Stamford Tragedy, including using the New Warriors as player heroes, but for the purposes of the core CIVIL WAR EVENT, the tragedy is assumed to happen as it was presented in the CIVIL WAR comic book series.

TRANSITION: CLEAN UP STAMFORD

This Transition Scene gives the heroes cause to recruit help, recover from a previous Action Scene, or acquire resources for later. It's also a perfect opportunity for some exposition.

After the tragedy at Stamford, there's a ton of cleanup to do. Bring in the human element—hit home with how terrible the events were for the locals and for the New Warriors. The heroes could support the actual cleanup and rebuilding efforts, or they might take a more public relations stance. No matter what direction they take, there's a lot of work to do. As Watcher, it's your job to show them that no matter how much work they put in it's not enough. Think back to all the tragic events you've seen in the news. Think about the most tear-jerking stories you've heard, and emulate that pathos. Tell individuals' stories. Show the broken homes. The death of 600 is a statistic; the death of an individual is a tragedy.

Stamford: There isn't much left of Stamford after the explosion. If anything, the rubble and the destruction serve as a depressing reminder of superhuman hubris. Much of the rubble is DANGEROUS and UNSTABLE.

There are several options for acquiring resources here, most of which can be tied to BUSINESS, COVERT, CRIME, or PSYCH Specialties:

▶ PUBLIC SUPPORT: With a good showing at Stamford, the heroes could sway public opinion in their favor. While it might not help sway Congress directly, it could buffer some of the fallout.

▶ SYMPATHETIC OPPOSITION: Whatever the heroes' stance on the Superhuman Registration Act, honest efforts at Stamford could help some of the opposition to sympathize with the heroes' cause. Played well, it could even garner some converts.

▶ FEDERAL AUTHORITIES: Stamford's knee-deep in federal attention. There's FBI, CIA, NSA, ATF, and everything else under the sun watching for slipups, for causes, and for potential threats to public safety. This is a great chance to make allies— or enemies—in these offices.

▶ LEADS: While the police reports make up entire filing cabinets by this point, there are still stories that haven't gotten attention. These stories could lead to important breaks, such as the location of Nitro.

▶ INSPIRATION: Stamford was a terrible tragedy, but the kind of work that can be done on its streets could be fulfilling and empowering for any hero. Even the most cynical lone wolf may feel renewed when seeing humans and superhumans working together to rebuild.

THE EXPLOSION HEARD AROUND THE WORLD: STAMFORD, CT

In Stamford, Connecticut, 60 children and 600 adults are killed at the conclusion of a televised battle between the **New Warriors**, a young team of heroes, and a number of super villains. **Nitro**, a villain able to explode his body with tremendous force, unleashes his power and levels dozens of city blocks, including a school and most of a residential area. This event polarizes most United States citizens, and indeed, most of the super hero world as well. Everything has changed, and there's no more ignoring registration. Congress immediately goes back into session to push the bill through.

Nitro's whereabouts after the battle are unknown, but the New Warriors (Night Thrasher, Namorita, Microbe, and Speedball) are declared dead, together with their film crew (including **Johnny Fernandez**) and the remaining villains on site (Cobalt Man, Coldheart, and Speedfreek).

For more on the New Warriors and alternatives to the Stamford Tragedy, see CIVIL WAR EVENT SUPPLEMENT: YOUNG AVENGERS/ RUNAWAYS

ACTION: REGISTRATION AND SUPER VILLAINS

This Scene can happen whenever a hero crosses paths with a villain without necessarily having to fight.

Getting heroes to agree or disagree to registration is one thing, and more than likely it can be handled with diplomacy and discussion. However, what about super villains? Anyone who has devoted his life to crime by choice or circumstances is not likely to register because it's the right thing—unless he's given very strong incentive to do so. Is it truly a moot point, as many of them feel, or is it worth fighting over? Changing a criminal's mind without bashing his head into a brick wall is likely going to involve conflict on an emotional or mental scale. Of course, things may end up being physical anyway—sometimes a brick wall is a great argument.

Villains are likely to resist the arguments of registration, even if offered immunity or a similar incentive, since it implies the villain will cooperate with the government and submit to government training. Some villains are going to be too STUBBORN, PRIDEFUL, or SCORNFUL to accept any kind of deals without conflict. This is most likely the case with highly intelligent villains such as Dr. Octopus. Other villains believe that REGISTRATION IS POINTLESS from a criminal viewpoint given that they're still going to be jailed and have their secret identity documented—they might become RECKLESS and ON THE EDGE when dealing with Pro-Registration forces. Many of the inmates that recently escaped from the Raft could fit that bill (see the *Breakout* Mini-Event in the **MARVEL HEROIC ROLEPLAYING BASIC GAME** or grab a villain from the Friends and Foes roster).

Finally, for hunted villains, registration could be the last chance for redemption in the eyes of the general population. Some villains may decide that now's the best time to switch sides and hope for a fate similar to the Thunderbolts. In such cases, the heroes may find themselves emissaries from S.H.I.E.L.D. to negotiate these villains' surrender and registration. Alternatively, villains may show up at an Anti-Registration safe house and try to convince the heroes of their honest intent to join their side. In both cases, villains will likely have NOTHING TO LOSE and be seen as UNTRUSTWORTHY at best, considered as HOPELESS CRIMINALS or MURDERERS at worst.

Friends and Foes
p. CW134

Thunderbolts
p. CW104

ACTION: WHAT ABOUT STAMFORD?

This Scene can take place anywhere a hero may run into a civilian, preferably when a hero is alone and the doom pool is very high, making it harder for the hero to resist accusatory questions.

Very few heroes live so removed from the real world that they never have brushes with civilians. In this Scene, the Watcher highlights one of the rare moments where a civilian isn't a part of the backdrop, but rather a consequence the hero simply cannot ignore.

Maybe a hero who unmasks is stopped on the street by a family member of one of the kids killed in Stamford. Perhaps a costumed hero or one whose public identity is known, like Luke Cage, answers the door to a pizza deliveryman who has a few questions to go along with the extra mushrooms and pineapple. While cleaning up from a previous battle, a hero might find himself being eyed by a young kid, who asks him, point blank, "Why did those kids die? Am I going to die, too?"

Really, that question, "What about Stamford?" should be on the lips of any citizen who sees a hero pass by. Describe the noise, the buzz, and the feeling that Everyone's Watching. All the focus is on this one civilian and the hero who has to answer the question. There can and should be follow up questions and accusations. "What's to stop it from being my daughter next?" "It could have been me." "You can't stop the bad guys, and when you try, things get worse." "How can we even tell who's good and who's bad?" "Are we supposed to just trust you?" There's a lot of Distrust After Stamford.

While some civilians may simply be Looking for Reassurance, others may actually want to hurt the heroes the only way they can. As the Watcher, your job is to push for emotional stress, especially if any of your heroes have been acting detached about the whole thing. It will heighten the drama and, of course, set the heroes up for deeper emotional impact later. Make it real. Make it hard to ignore. Don't hesitate to pull in doom dice to add Pesky Reporters listening in, or distraught citizens showing Heartbreaking Pictures.

This is an interesting Scene to pull on a lonely, high profile hero with few social skills.

TRANSITION: WHERE IS NITRO?

This Transition Scene involves asking questions and getting answers about the location of Nitro, the super villain responsible for Stamford.

Nitro (Robert Hunter) was incarcerated in the Raft and escaped during the *Breakout* Mini-Event. Holed up in Stamford, CT, he was among the villains targeted by reality TV heroes the New Warriors. He caused the violent explosion that killed hundreds of civilians. Now, he's on the run. S.H.I.E.L.D. and the U.S. Government want Nitro stopped and taken into custody to answer for his crimes. The Atlanteans want Nitro brought to justice for killing Prince Namor's cousin Namorita at Stamford.

To locate Nitro, heroes might need to investigate or call in resources. Your players might come up with creative ideas, such as making contact with the Atlanteans to trade information. Here are a few other options:

▶ **Business Resource:** By looking into Nitro's business activities, the hero follows a lead that takes her to the location of one of Nitro's former associates. Though the details don't come out at this time, the SHADY ASSOCIATE was an underling who dealt with Mutant Growth Hormone supplies for Nitro. Hoping to hide the true nature of the relationship, the associate points the hero in the right direction, then goes into hiding to stay off Nitro's radar.

▶ **Covert Resource:** Through S.H.I.E.L.D. resources, the hero learns of several suspicious activities that might be associated with Nitro. Further investigation and undercover work reveals those suspicions to be true. The hero has followed the leads right to Nitro's doorstep.

▶ **Crime Resource:** CONFUSED ex-con Bobbie the Mooch—who swears up and down he's "walking the straight and narrow these days" despite having several expensive watches in his possession—tells the hero where to find Nitro, as long as the hero promises not to call the cops on Bobbie. "See, I overheard Frank who was telling Dave about a conversation he had with John about this explosion...see?"

▶ **Menace Resource:** Pretty much the same as the CRIME RESOURCE version, but the hero first roughs up Bobbie the Mooch to get the information from him.

▶ **Psych Resource**: Journalists sometimes have shady sources—especially a trusted reporter who protects his sources. While offering up an exclusive interview to a journalist from *The Daily Bugle*, *The Alternative*, or some other news outlet, the reporter reveals a news tip he heard from a contact—the whereabouts of Nitro.

▶ **Tech Resource:** The hero searches through COMPLICATED digital records and cross-references event timelines with known information on Nitro. As a result, the hero narrows down the search and sees a pattern leading to the Act Two scene at Big Sur (see page CW88).

ACTION: THE RALLY

This Scene takes place during a rally in support of the Superhuman Registration Act.

The heroes have either been asked to oversee a Pro-Registration rally or are there simply to observe. The atmosphere at the rally is TENSE and OVERCROWDED. However, SYMPATHETIC CIVILIANS and some very brave superhumans have lined up across the street with their own signs and protests. Some heroes may even be included in the protest group, depending on how they've expressed their feelings about the proposed Act so far.

Things get ugly, and fast. People start screaming, policemen are on edge, and someone's bound to throw a projectile at the other side. If there are HURT CIVILIANS on either side of the conflict, or if the scene is ended with a 2D12 from the doom pool, the real losers are the heroes—the blame will very likely be put on them.

As the Watcher, be sure to present a variety of supporters at the rally from reasonable to fanatical. Describe signs that show pictures and names of innocent bystanders caught up in the Stamford tragedy and similar situations. Then point out a sign that reads "Tell Us Who the Freaks Are So We Know Where To Aim" with the picture of Anti-Registration leaders with cross-hairs over it. The people in this crowd are SCARED AND ANGRY, and many are going to be IRRATIONAL about it.

It's not all roses on the other side of the rally. In addition to civilians supporting the civil rights of superhuman Americans as well as civilian Americans, the rally may also attract anti-government radicals. Some of the more extreme signs might have slogans like "Live Gamma or Die," "Big Government Wants Superhuman Martial Law" or "Mutants Uber Alles." Although most of these people are acting on their own consciences, a hero may notice a mind-controller mentally manipulating some normal humans into a LIVID RAGE.

The heroes will need to make a few rolls against the crowd (either as a Mob or represented by the doom pool with appropriate Scene Distinctions or complications) to keep things peaceful. Feel free to spend doom dice to create complications that present difficult choices regardless of the side the heroes support, like a MUTANT ASSAULTED, VIOLENT RIOT COP, or an ENRAGED LYNCH MOB.

ACTION: MEETING WITH THE CSA

This Scene takes place in Washington, at an office in the Pentagon.

Being CLEVER BUREAUCRATS, the Commission on Superhuman Activities won't venture into a huge project like the registration of all superhumans lightly. They need a strong plan; the stronger it is, the easier it will be to sell the act to Congress.

The legendary former government liaison to the Avengers and current Acting Co-Chair of the CSA, **Henry Peter Gyrich**, has called the heroes in to discuss the Bill and its ramifications.

HENRY PETER GYRICH

Affiliations
SOLO	6
BUDDY	4
TEAM	8

Distinctions
HEAVY-HANDED BUREAUCRAT
NOT EASILY INTIMIDATED

Specs
| BUSINESS EXPERT | 8 | | CRIME EXPERT | 8 |
| MENACE EXPERT | 8 | | TECH EXPERT | 8 |

Gyrich has a long history with super heroes and is despised by many of them, although he really does love his country and wants only to uphold the law and ideals of the US Government. He deals with politicians all day, so the bluster of your average hero won't even raise his blood pressure. He's all business and dedicated to his agenda. That's not to say he can't be manipulated on a mystical or psionic level—he's not superhuman—but it won't be easy to get him to deviate much from his goals.

All he really wants from the heroes right now are lists of possible problems the government may face in rounding up all superhumans and, more importantly, solutions to those problems. He doesn't want to debate the morality of what the SHRA proposes—after all, he helped draft the original Bill and worked closely on the Mutant Registration problem. And, ultimately, Congress is the group that must address this. He just wants to know how to handle the process.

While heroes may do some unexpected things, the three most likely approaches to handling Gyrich are:

▶ **Pro-Registration heroes** may try to use this opportunity to maneuver themselves to the forefront of the operation. They may try to convince Gyrich that they'll be happy to oversee the program, and that it would be better to use their money and resources, rather than add additional strain on the tax-paying public—or however they want to spin it. Heroes can take him out of the Scene with a CONVINCED complication rather than completely stressing him out with mental or emotional "attacks."

▶ **Unaffiliated or independent heroes**, or those otherwise playing it close to the vest at this point, can simply try to get as much information from him as possible. Knowing what the government plans, should the Act pass, could be valuable no matter which side they end up choosing. This is most likely to be a mental "attack" against Gyrich. Stressing him out mentally gets the heroes the information they need, but makes him difficult to work with in the future. Overcoming him with a DAZZLED or SAID TOO MUCH complication gets less information for now, but leaves more room to pump him for information later.

▶ If the heroes insist on going whole hog in their **resistance to the Registration Act**, they may try to flip his loyalty. If they can completely exhaust him and leave him stressed out with emotional stress, they can turn him into a resource for later scenes.

ACTION: CONFRONTED BY S.H.I.E.L.D.

The Superhuman Registration Act hasn't passed yet. In this Scene, as a preliminary measure, S.H.I.E.L.D. moves in on a hero or group of heroes to "encourage" them to become a part of the Pro-Registration enforcement.

Maria Hill, Director of S.H.I.E.L.D, leads a crew of armored enforcers from the Superhuman Restraint Unit, AKA Cape-Killers. Hill and her squad confront the heroes and demand that they register immediately and agree to assist S.H.I.E.L.D. in policing the SHRA once it is passed. While Hill's goal isn't violence, it's a likely outcome if the heroes aren't compliant. Hill also seeks to "persuade" already publicly known heroes to come out in support of the coming Superhuman Registration Act.

You can frame this Scene on the S.H.I.E.L.D. Helicarrier, with the hero(es) having been invited there or perhaps stationed on board. Maria should have the home field advantage, in any case. It's up to the heroes to get out of the situation one way or another.

The restraint unit uses Stark Enterprises' armor and weaponry, loaded with nonlethal ordinance (tranq darts, stunguns, etc.). Maria's INFLEXIBLE IDEOLOGY comes into play heavily—she technically has no authority to demand anything until the SHRA passes. She doesn't want to compromise on this issue; she believes she's wholly in the right. She believes that human lives will be in danger if her mission fails.

S.H.I.E.L.D.
p. CW34

Maria Hill
p. CW35

Cape-Killers
p. CW35

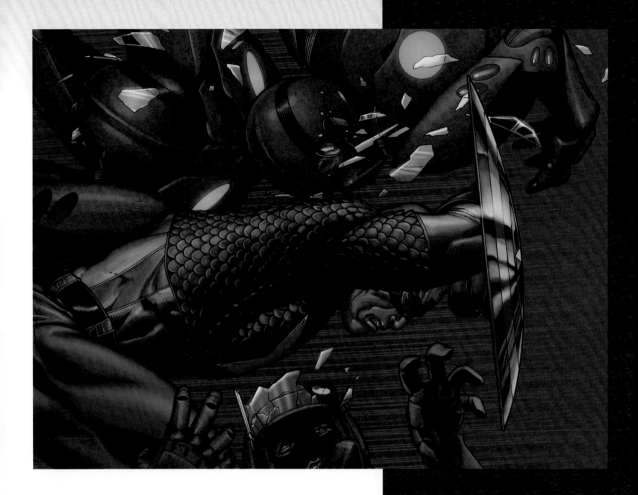

OPTIONS FOR CONFRONTATION WITH S.H.I.E.L.D.

▶ Maria Hill isn't a fool. She can tell a brush-off when she sees one. Convincing her to back off through trickery and deception should be met with challenge. Have her see through whatever the heroes' first ruse happens to be.

▶ The enforcers aren't fools, either. In fact, they've recently had violent altercations with other superhumans and assume the heroes are no different. They'll start discussion with the heroes in crosshairs and in a TRIGGER HAPPY mood.

▶ Maria is uneasy about her job. She's recently been appointed as Director of S.H.I.E.L.D. because Nick Fury vanished following a number of allegations and cover-ups, and she doesn't believe she was the right choice for the job. Playing on a potential NOT UP FOR THE JOB complication could either pacify or escalate the situation, depending on how the heroes play it.

TRANSITION: MEET AND DISCUSS BEFORE REGISTRATION

The issues of Act One have come to a head. In this Scene, the heroes meet to discuss how to resolve these issues before the Superhuman Registration Act passes or fails.

This Scene concludes Act One. You can have it run at the same time as Confronted By S.H.I.E.L.D. if you want to follow along with the comics, but that's by no means required

As Watcher, frame this Scene with as many player heroes as you like. Tell them they're meeting at a private location known to all the heroes. The Baxter Building, Avengers Tower, or Dr. Strange's Sanctum Sanctorum are all good options; the players can decide. Most of the heroes whose datafiles weren't chosen by the players should be here, as well as some of the more heroic Watcher characters. The heroes are in their heroic identities, but there won't be any civilians present other than characters like Jarvis or Wong. The heroes are free to talk about the imminent passing of the SHRA.

If the players haven't settled on their specific heroes (perhaps they've been playing several so far, just to "try them out"), or which side of the debate they wish to take, this Scene allows them an opportunity to settle this. Encourage them to feel out various personalities, arguments, philosophies, and ideologies. Let them settle on a diverse team, but be sure each hero has a direction in mind regarding Registration.

Consider whether Tony Stark and Captain America should be heading the two sides of the debate—for and against registration, respectively. Does this even come up? Are some of the players likely to choose a side right here, while it's still safe to do so? What do the other player heroes do in response? If a player hero chooses to be at the forefront of either side (either as Cap or Iron Man, or an alternate), be sure to suggest the possible consequences. But don't just tell them; use other heroes and pose those arguments. Let them know that extremists might hurt or kill them. Remind them that if they're public, their families and friends are fair game. Have someone question whether their support comes from a love of their public image, or from a love of the ideology. Just be sure to keep it in-character.

For a fun wrap-up to this scene, have Uatu the Watcher manifest nearby, a calm but monolithic observer over the fateful decisions being made at this meeting of heroes.

This Transition is a great place to gain perspective on the issues surrounding the Superhuman Registration Act. It's also a chance to pick up resources that could change the scope of the following Acts. Here's a list of potential resources the heroes can pick up, ready for the opening scenes of Act Two.

▶ BUSINESS **Resource:** There are a lot of affluent or company-connected heroes present, from Tony Stark and Nighthawk to Reed Richards and Danny Rand (assuming the heroes know that he's the guy behind Daredevil's mask). A hero could use BUSINESS to broker some sort of helpful financial assistance or backing with those characters.

▶ COMBAT **Resource:** A sparring session or two always helps a hero get in shape, but connections in the fighting community may also provide handy insight into other heroes' fighting styles, which is useful if conflict is expected.

▶ COSMIC **Resource:** Uatu the Watcher only appears in times of great importance or significance. Heroes with this knowledge might use it to inspire or motivate themselves and their allies. Perhaps there are signs and portents unseen to those who don't traffic with arcane forces. These, too, make inspirational resources for the coming crisis.

▶ COVERT **Resource:** Spy contacts abound among the super heroes present, so why not leverage those relationships to get some secrets or access to helpful files known only to covert organizations? Safehouses, passwords, routines...the list goes on.

▶ CRIME **Resource:** A conversation with a super hero who has connections with the law (or with the criminal underground) can generate any number of useful resources, from a sympathetic attorney to a guy inside Ryker's Island.

▶ SCIENCE, TECH, **and** VEHICLE **Resources:** Getting your hands on a gadget or piece of gear from a technology-related hero is always useful in times of impending conflict. With just a little conversation and one or two brokered deals, the heroes could come away with something cutting edge.

ACT TWO
REGISTRATION

The SHRA has passed, for good or ill, and the process to register all superhumans in the U.S. has started. The logistics and the initial consequences of Registration are the main focus of the titanic struggle during most of this Act. Dark implications abound as things snowball and people get hurt or killed in the process of enforcing or resisting the new law of the land.

SCENE STRUCTURE

Act Two builds up as S.H.I.E.L.D. begins enforcing the SHRA, pulling in newly registered heroes to flex its new regulatory muscles. It follows with a series of Key Scenes that see the Civil War unfold as heroes unmask, friends and villains are tracked down, crucial questions start being asked, and heroes from both sides attempt to attend a joyful but tense wedding in Wakanda. Action and Transition Scenes can be played in any order, but they ultimately lead to the final Scene at the Gefen-Meyer Petrochemical Plant. There the Act culminates in a bloody, massively violent confrontation that sends the war into the spiraling dive that is Act Three.

BUILDUP
▶ Action: Midnight Registration Day Roundup
▶ Transition: Find One of Nick Fury's Safehouses
▶ Action: Press Conference: Identity Revealed

KEY SCENES
▶ Action: Hunt Down or Elude a Friend
▶ Action: Home Invasion and Rebels Going Underground
▶ Transition: Wakandan Wedding Tensions
▶ Action: Transport/Rescue a Captured Superhuman
▶ Action: Confront the Authorities About Hero Prejudice
▶ Transition: Find/Uncover Hydra, A.I.M. Base, or Atlantis Agent
▶ Action: Nitro at Big Sur
▶ Transition: Investigate Atlantean Sleeper Agent Activity
▶ Action: Battle at Geffen-Meyer Petrochemical Plant

HOOKS

The most likely way to pull heroes kicking and screaming into this Act is to make them central characters in the early enactments of the SHRA as either enforcers or targets. This Act is structured to allow heroes to play the Event from the Pro- and Anti-SHRA sides of the conflict. With some tweaks, you can adjust for heroes who attempt to remain neutral in the conflict. That neutrality should be constantly challenged as registered heroes are pulled in by Federal Law Enforcement agencies without having a say in the matter. Unregistered heroes who don't want to get involved are eventually hunted down or contacted to join the resistance. Regardless of their initial allegiance, feel free to add additional Action and Transition Scenes to follow the story that you and your players shape. Together you direct the course of the Civil War.

DOOM POOL

The doom pool starts at 3D8 for this Act.

DOOM POOL: **3D8**

Doom Pool
p. OM14

BUILDUP

The following Scenes represent the first decisions and consequences of what devolve into the Civil War. Regardless of whether the heroes are neutral, Pro- or Anti-Registration, everyone eventually gets pulled in.

- **Registered:** You should start with **Midnight Registration Day Roundup**. If the heroes have qualms about acting against other heroes, consider playing through a variation of **Confronted by S.H.I.E.L.D.** from Act One to drive home the federal government's willingness to enforce the new regulation. Alternatively, you could start with **Press-Conference: Identity Revealed.**

- **Unregistered:** The heroes are among the first that S.H.I.E.L.D targets to get registered or be imprisoned. You can start with **Midnight** Registration Day Roundup or, if the heroes have already banded together as a group of rebels, you can go directly to **Find One of Nick Fury's Safehouses**.

S.H.I.E.L.D.
p. CW34

Maria Hill
p. CW35

Cape-Killers
p. CW35

ACTION: MIDNIGHT REGISTRATION DAY ROUNDUP

The clock has struck twelve, and Registration is now mandatory for all US-based super heroes. This Scene starts Act Two.

Now that the Superhuman Registration Act has passed, things start getting serious. S.H.I.E.L.D. has been empowered to take to the streets and round up superhumans unwilling to abide by registration. Maria Hill has ordered a group of recently registered heroes to lead a Superhuman Response Unit team—AKA Cape-Killers—to the house of a publicly known super hero.

Registered heroes are summoned to the Helicarrier and drafted into this mission. If they decide to defy orders, Maria Hill threatens to unleash the Cape-Killers on them for insubordination (just as she did in the last Act). She likely calls in for reinforcement from carrier-based heroes like Ms. Marvel, Black Widow, or Wonder Man if needed. Of course, the real issue in this confrontation is to either force Hill to stand her troops down to allow rational dialogue or find a way to escape the Helicarrier.

If the heroes are the targets of the raid, pick a posse of Pro-Registration characters (at least one less than heroes in the team) and a MOB OF CAPE-KILLERS (TEAM 4D8) to throw at them. Set up a few Scene Distinctions like CRAMPED STAIRWAYS, STURDY DOORS, or SECURITY SYSTEMS to represent the unregistered heroes' lodging or hideout. If the heroes are part of the raiding party, send them without Cape-Killers and pick a small group of independent minded but somewhat minor heroes that you think would likely resist registration, such as Battlestar, Gladiatrix, Solo, or Patriot.

The Scene ends when the unregistered heroes are taken into custody, escape, or take out the raiding party. If unregistered heroes have been captured, you can play the **Transport/Rescue a Captured Superhuman** Scene next. If the raiding heroes were defeated, Maria Hill's fury is immense and she assigns more resources to track down the rebels that made her look like a fool.

OPTIONS FOR MIDNIGHT REGISTRATION DAY ROUNDUP

▶ Hit fast. Hit hard. If you want to start things with a bang, don't hesitate to send more Cape-Killers and heroes into the fray.

▶ Maybe the expected opposition is a lot bigger or better organized than the intelligence Maria Hill has. You might want to add more characters on the Anti-Registration side to bolster up their numbers. Maybe the hideout is BOOBY TRAPPED or RIGGED TO COLLAPSE.

▶ If you have the chance, drop hints about Hydra involvement to foreshadow the next Scenes. Even a passing sentence during battle dialogue is enough.

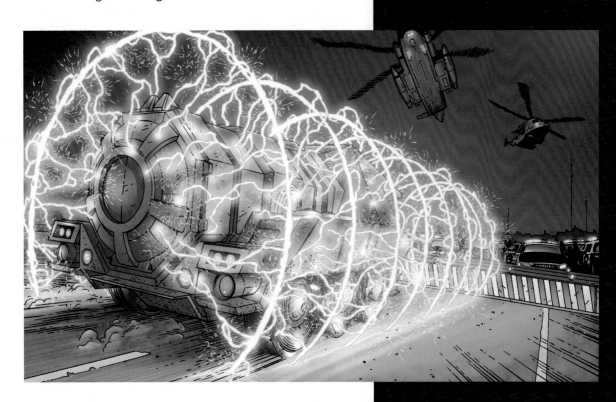

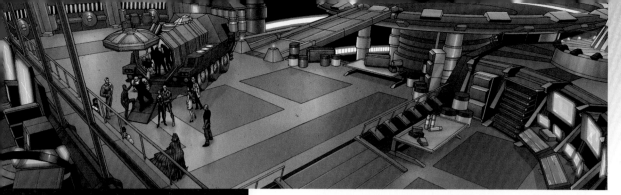

TRANSITION: FIND ONE OF NICK FURY'S SAFEHOUSES

As hostilities start, S.H.I.E.L.D. unleashes its resources to track movement all over the country. Finding a base of operations to retreat to and regroup is hard for the fledgling Anti-Registration movement. Play this Scene early in the Act as the rebels try to organize themselves.

During the events of the Civil War, Nick Fury hides out in a fallout shelter somewhere. He discloses the location of some of his safehouses to the leaders of the Anti-Registration movement as secret hideouts for their forces. While many potential bases of operations have been raided already, Fury's remaining ones are among the best hidden for the Resistance. Finding such a location could help prevent some of the violence of the upcoming conflict.

Very few people know where such safehouses are. If he hasn't in a previous Scene, Fury might contact trusted members of an Anti-SHRA team to help shepherd superhumans away from danger. He's not going to give anything to Pro-Registration heroes. A spy might perhaps overhear a discussion about such a location or a proficient psychic might read the mind of one of his trusted agents. A double-agent might let slip the information or someone being led to the safehouse could be followed.

The knowledge of the whereabouts of this safehouse can be applied in multiple ways:

Nick Fury
p. CW124

▶ BLACKMAIL MATERIAL: With the location, a Pro-Registration superhuman could blackmail Anti-Registration superhumans into conversion or obedience.
▶ SAFEST SAFEHOUSE: While it won't help on the offensive, having a good place to run and hide can always help from a tactical standpoint.
▶ SUPPORT NETWORK: Knowing where such safehouses are is a very important bit of information for both sides; those with the information are valuable contacts.
▶ LOVED ONES: Every moment the Superhuman Registration Act continues, relationships are strained for those superhumans that try to maintain a semblance of normalcy. For those Anti-Registration heroes, having a safe place reassures those loved ones and keeps their hopes alive.

ACTION: PRESS CONFERENCE: IDENTITY REVEALED

Play this Scene once violence has started. It's especially compelling if you have a hero interested in playing out the inner conflicts of revealing who lies behind the mask.

One or more super heroes whose identities have been kept a secret are heavily pressured by the leaders of the Pro-Registration movement to reveal their identity at a press conference. The Pro-Registration movement hopes to create momentum for their cause by presenting a more human image of formerly secretive heroes. This Scene's conflict focuses primarily on wrangling, manipulation, and peer pressure from multiple sides as one or several heroes struggle with whether or not to reveal who they really are.

Staging this complex Scene requires particular attention—it presents great story opportunities, yet can be played from many angles. The following advice should guide you.

WHAT SIDE ARE YOU ON?

If you frame the Scene for Pro-Registration heroes, the conflict revolves around leaders of the Pro movement acting directly on the heroes or on close friends. If framed from the Anti-Registration viewpoint, the action should focus on heroes trying to convince a newly registered friend—and likely ex-ally—not to unmask.

WHO'S THE RING LEADER?

If you haven't yet determined who's leading the Pro-Registration movement, Iron Man, Captain America, Mr. Fantastic, Ms. Marvel, the Wasp, or any characters with a PSYCH Specialty make good candidates. That leader can—and maybe should—be included in your group's Pro-Registration team. That hero is a key player in this Scene.

WHO'S IN THE SPOTLIGHT?

You must decide who has to resist the leader's rhetoric and dirty tricks, what hero or heroes are going to be pressured to unmask to the public. If the Scene is played with Pro-Registration heroes, decide with the rest of the group if one or more of them plays that central role or if one or more Watcher-controlled allies fill that role.

If the Scene is played with an Anti-Registration team, or if none of the members of a Pro-Registration team want to play that part, pick one Watcher-controlled hero that the team cares about or has dealt with in the past. Good examples of characters with secret identities that could unmask are Spider-Man, Daredevil (as either Matt Murdock or Danny Rand), or Iron Man.

WHAT IF A HERO WANTS TO UNMASK?

If a hero in your group is fine with revealing her secret identity and the rest of the group expresses no interest in arguing against her, then take the opportunity to turn this Scene into a Transition Scene. Let heroes tap into the media frenzy to create new resources. Discuss with them the possible repercussions. What will happen to the hero's day job, how does her family react, are other heroes following suit? Play out a few meeting between the heroes and those most affected by the situation before moving on to the next Action Scene.

SET THE ENTOURAGE

Once the central players of the Scene have been selected, decide what secondary characters round out this Scene. Pick or create buddies, friends, and family members that might play an active role in this Scene. For example, if Iron Man tries to convince Spider-Man to unmask, Peter Parker turns to his wife Mary Jane and his Aunt May for advice and insights. Make some of those minor characters into Scene Distinctions so that both sides can use them to their advantage.

FRAME THE CONFLICT

For this Scene to work, you need a Pro-Registration leader who's absolutely convinced that unmasking will push the cause forward. You need one or more heroes that are very reluctant and think this isn't such a good idea. You need allies, friends, and family members with strong opinions about the situation that can be manipulated by both sides of the issue.

This is mostly a mental and emotional conflict pitting the leader against the hero(es) expected to unmask. Both sides likely have allies who take action against the opposition, trying to discredit each other and bolster their own team.

Contrary to a standard super hero battle Scene, the action here should be drawn out over an undefined period of time—a montage of sorts where the heroes, friends, and families meet in various settings to discuss, argue, and possibly fight over this issue. For example, the heroes could meet in places like Washington, Stark Tower, a café, a hidden Anti-Registration base or in their homes.

CHOOSE THE LIKELY OUTCOMES

The outcome of this Scene is straightforward if the hero expected to unmask is Watcher-controlled—a stressed-out hero caves in and agrees to unmask. Unless the team intervenes physically, the hero reveals his identity to the world.

If the hero or heroes are controlled by players, you need to discuss with them what winning or losing this conflict accomplishes. You can't force a player to have his hero unmask regardless of the results of the conflict unless he agrees to it. See "Running the Scene" for suggested outcomes.

If a hero unmasks, think about how the various characters linked to this hero's background react to the news. Is there joy, outrage, cries for justice, or more? Is the hero sued? Are his loved ones hounded by the press or targeted by threats?

RUNNING THIS SCENE

Each action of this conflict should be a talking point, an argument, an expressed fear, a plea, a pledge of support, a veiled threat, or an outright manipulation of the truth. While many of these actions will be played through the use of Affiliations, Distinctions, and Specialties, no one should be above using super powers to gain an edge.

Don't hesitate to exploit minor characters by bringing them into the arguments of the Pro-Registration leader and Anti-Registration friends. Don't hesitate to create assets and complications that play with base emotions like You'll Risk Their Lives, Are They Safe Now?, Can You Trust Your Allies?, or We've Been Through Hell and Back.

The Scene ends as soon as either the Pro-Registration leader or one of the heroes gets stressed out, likely from emotional or mental stress. The stressed out leader loses his drive and gracefully accepts the other side's refusal. A stressed out hero cracks under the pressure and angst and puts a stop to the whole thing. He must decide if he goes ahead with unmasking or refuses to do so, putting a significant strain on his relationship with the leader. In that case, the leader expresses disappointment and likely expresses doubt about the hero's loyalty to the Pro-Registration cause. This is a key opportunity for a Pro-Registration team to change sides.

This is a good time to segue into a Transition Scene where heroes can recuperate and explore the outcome of what just transpired. See "What if a Hero Wants to Unmask?" for some advice about running such a Scene.

OPTIONS FOR IDENTITY REVEALED

▶ If your team is more focused on physical action, you can frame the Scene so that they prevent a hero from unmasking by taking him out right before the press conference. Alternatively, the heroes might be part of a Pro-SHRA security team, ready to intercept such an occurrence.

▶ The Pro- and Anti-SHRA leaders are under a lot of pressure. Some might start making rash moves, rationalizing that such actions will prevent further anguish downstream. One such leader hires or sends some thugs, A.I.M., or Hydra agents to rough up the allies and loved ones of the principal heroes involved in this Scene. They might even bring in some psychic-powered supers and use mind-control to gain an upper hand.

▶ If a hero cracks but refuses to unmask, the Pro-Registration movement creates a Life Model Decoy of the hero to unmask in her place. The real hero is now tracked as a criminal. Exposing the Decoy is the first step of a long process to convince the world that the hero isn't who they think she is.

KEY SCENES

This section covers several Action and Transition Scenes that build the conflict toward the climactic confrontation at the Geffen-Meyer Petrochemical Plant. You can play these out in any order, and even repeat some of them with minor changes, before getting to the Ambush at the plant.

ACTION: HUNT DOWN OR ELUDE A FRIEND

Play this Scene if you have a hero with at least one good friend, ally, or family member who sits on the opposite side of the conflict. You can also modify it to play any kind of chase Scene.

War pits brother against sister. Inevitably, old allegiances come into question during the conflict. If any of the heroes maintain strong relationships with other superhumans that haven't taken an active stand or are firmly on the other side, you can frame this Scene to play them off each other. Perhaps one seeks the other for an ultimate attempt at recruiting, or to warn them of an upcoming attack, or try to make them see reason.

Finding or eluding the friend is the first action to resolve in this Scene. Have the hunting heroes roll against the doom pool to establish if they find their quarry without alerting him. In a similar vein, a hunted hero rolls to see if she spots the hunter and can get an edge (i.e., an asset) in the upcoming chase or meeting. This is an opportunity to stage a chase Scene through Exposed Rooftops, Dark Alleys, or Congested Traffic.

If there's ever a reason to focus on banter during a conflict, this is it. Make sure the heroes know exactly what's at stake for their friend/enemy. Make them consider withdrawal. This Scene ends when the hunted hero is taken down, reasoned with, or escapes.

OPTIONS FOR HUNT DOWN OR ELUDE A FRIEND

▶ Always consider raising the stakes. The opponent shouldn't back down even if highly stressed. In fact, when nearly beaten, he should make a last-ditch effort to overcome the hero. While the fight doesn't have to be to the death, it can. This is a time for burning bridges.
▶ If things have been particularly negative and stark thus far, pick heroes that are easier to recruit to the cause. If the two are family members, ex-lovers, or have been through a lot together in the past, this is a good time to give reuniting a shot.
▶ Maybe the friend is being blackmailed or forced into compliance. Not only would this give sympathy for his actions, but it'd give the heroes a great reason to continue along the path against their opposition.

ACTION: HOME INVASION AND REBELS GOING UNDERGROUND

Play this after a few Scenes have taken place. This Scene establishes how protracted the conflict will be if the bigger issues aren't addressed soon.

As the war progresses, the rebels get driven deeper underground, grouping together for protection. The Pro-Registration superhumans have to uncover these clandestine headquarters in order to crack down on the opposition. This Scene represents one of many such raids by a team of Pro-Registration heroes acting on the info of a double-agent in an Anti-Registration team.

The UNEXPOSED BETRAYER Scene Distinction should play into this Scene for or against the heroes, depending on their side. If played from the Anti-SHRA side, you could use Cape-Killers or use other heroes the players have established relationships or rivalries with. Consider using the turncoat in the battle, to heighten the sense of shifting loyalties and tenuous trust. A hero with a Milestone based on shifting loyalty might want to play the role of the mole.

The Scene ends when some rebels are captured or when the Pro-Registration raiders are routed or defeated.

OPTIONS FOR HOME INVASION

▶ If played from the Anti-Registration side, make the best use of the betrayal. Be sure to showcase the actions of the turncoat. Give a chance for banter about the reasons behind the shift in allegiance. Be sure to play on guilt, anger, and fear of reprisal for a potential resource during a Transition Scene later.

▶ If the players are on the Pro-Registration side, bring home the pain of what Registration entails; perhaps one of the Anti-Registration superhumans sacrifices herself in a blaze of glory instead of submitting. Show the heroes that their side is by no means the "good" side.

▶ Bring in some collateral damage while the two sides fight. Show them that their petty bickering is causing problems outside of the war. Have villains attack or angry civilians intervene.

▶ You could add a trigger-happy mob of Cape-Killers who aren't overly concerned about who they take down. If you use this option, use the doom pool to reflect the problems caused by the Cape-Killers. Friendly fire is the least creative possibility. They may turn on friendlies or plant evidence to bring up their arrest counts.

TRANSITION: WAKANDAN WEDDING TENSIONS

MAKING THIS INTO AN ACTION SCENE

So many things could go wrong at the wedding that you might decide to make it into an Action Scene at any point. A hero who's had Too Much To Drink might start trouble or maybe one of Black Panther's old enemies (like Man-Ape) might decide to cause an incident. In any case, refer to the Wakanda section (page CW22) to help you get setting elements to frame the Scene.

This Scene is a pause of sorts—an Eye of the Storm moment where members of both sides can mingle without fighting. Stage this Transition Scene once the heroes have been through multiple conflicts and are deeply embroiled in the War; the wedding offers a reprieve during which they can examine their choices and see where other major characters stand in all this.

As the battle wages on, the toll—both emotional and physical—rises for both sides of the Civil War. The celebration of the wedding of Kenyan princess Ororo Munroe and King T'Challa, the Black Panther of Wakanda, in a neutral country provides a much needed break. Heroes can use the paradise-like setting of Wakanda to recover from previous confrontations.

This is a great occasion to frame non-violent meetings between heroes that fought each other mere days, or hours, before. The heroes may wish to even some score by saying something cuttingly brilliant to other guests. Sometimes there's nothing more satisfactory than chucking a glassful of champagne in the face of someone you thoroughly disagree with. If a hero feels up to it, he may even offer to act as Black Panther's best man and take the stage during the best man's speech.

The ceremony and ensuing celebrations are on neutral grounds, but they represent a volatile situation. A shift in the geopolitical situation and a concentration of power in the world has occurred. Tensions are high and could bubble over at any instant (see "Making This Into an Action Scene.") The place crawls with diplomats, heads of state, heroes, Pro-SHRA ex-villains, reporters, spies, and agents of all organizations.

The presence of so many people is a perfect opportunity for organizations to contact undercover agents and trade info and new directives. Play up this option if the team has one or several hidden agents in its ranks.

Finally, heroes can tap into their networks of contacts at the wedding or recruit new ones. Here are a few options:

▶ BUSINESS **Resource:** Casual conversations with business contacts will reveal that some huge technological projects backed by the federal government are underway in the continental US. An INSIDER SOURCE could be recruited to keep tabs on things if the heroes plan to investigate this soon.

▶ COVERT **Resource:** The covert world burns brightly and uncontrollably as every nation, intelligence outfit, secret society, and terrorist organization is trying to come to terms with the short and long term implications and opportunities of the war. Secrets are plentiful and many are willing to sell them. Now's the time for heroes to get their hands on SPY TECH and SECRET BLUEPRINTS.

▶ MEDICAL **Resource:** Wakandan medical technology is among the highest of the modern world. Characters who make a good case about protecting heroes and civilians alike in the war can get some NANOTECH FIRST AID KITS.

▶ TECH **Resource:** It's not just medical technology that's advanced. Thanks to being one of the foremost sources of Vibranium, Wakandan society is among the most advanced in the world. Heroes that call in favors or broker special deals may obtain some WAKANDAN BODY ARMOR, ADVANCED COMMUNICATIONS SYSTEMS, or some kind of COOL GADGET.

STORM

Ororo Munroe

Affiliations			Distinctions
SOLO	8		CLAUSTROPHOBIC
BUDDY	6		MERCURIAL
TEAM	10		STRONG-WILLED LEADER

Power Sets

GODDESS OF THE STORM

ELECTRICAL BLAST	10	ENHANCED REFLEXES	8
ENHANCED SENSES	8	ENHANCED STAMINA	8
PSYCHIC RESISTANCE	8	SUBSONIC FLIGHT	8
WEATHER SUPREMACY	12		

SFX: *Area Attack.* Against multiple targets, for each additional target add D6 and keep an additional effect die.

SFX: *Immunity.* Spend a doom die to ignore stress or trauma from extremes of temperature or electricity.

SFX: *Multipower.* Add more than one GODDESS OF THE STORM power die to a pool. Step back each GODDESS OF THE STORM power die in that pool once for each die beyond the first.

SFX: *Emotional Link.* Step back highest die in the doom pool to add emotional stress die to a pool including a GODDESS OF THE STORM power.

Limit: *Mutant.* When affected by mutant-specific complication or tech, step up the lowest die in the doom pool or add a D6 doom die.

Limit: *Emotional Tempest.* Change any GODDESS OF THE STORM power into a complication to recover emotional stress equal to that power's die rating. Activate an opportunity to recover that power.

Specs

COMBAT EXPERT	8	COSMIC EXPERT	8
COVERT EXPERT	8	MYSTIC EXPERT	8

American-born Ororo Munroe spent most of her early life in Cairo, Egypt. Orphaned at the age of 5, she became a street thief and, later, wandered Africa in search of adventure. Charles Xavier discovered her in Kenya, her ancestral home, where she was worshipped as a goddess due to her mutant power over the weather. Invited to join his new team of X-Men, she's been associated with them ever since. She recently left the team to pursue a romance with the Black Panther, and they are soon to be married in Wakanda.

ACTION: TRANSPORT/ RESCUE A CAPTURED SUPERHUMAN

Play this Scene as soon as key Anti-Registration heroes have been captured and an Anti-Registration team expresses its wish to free them. Alternatively, play this Scene to give Pro-Registration heroes a little change from hunting friends and heroes.

It's very likely at least one superhuman is captured and moved for imprisonment to Ryker's Island during this Act. Such times are perfect opportunities for the Anti-Registration rebellion to make an attempt to free the captive(s). This Scene is about the Anti-SHRA setting up an ambush of the transferring caravan in the streets of the city. The prisoner transport is handled by ARMORED CAR, escorted by one or more superhuman(s), HEAVILY-ARMED S.H.I.E.L.D. agents, and possibly a few Cape-Killers.

This Scene is a great opportunity for a team of heroes to free a previously captured teammate. If you haven't had a hero captured so far, consider the ramifications of who you put in the caravan and who is assigned to guard it. Adding a recently captured leader-type hero can lead to some later scuffles about how to lead the Anti-Registration movement.

S.H.I.E.L.D.
p. CW34

Cape-Killers
p. CW35

OPTIONS FOR TRANSPORT/ RESCUE A CAPTURED SUPERHUMAN

▶ All is not what it seems! The Pro-Registration movement knows about the rescue attempt and planned a counter ambush with stealthy heroes. Alternately, they might have planted a shape-shifting hero (like Hulkling) instead of the prisoner. Worse still, the prisoner might have shifted loyalties and is expected to act as a mole once she's freed.

▶ If the players are on the Anti-Registration side and have felt overwhelmed so far by the attacks from the Pro-Registration forces, this is a good chance to let them feel like they've got the upper hand. Offer less resistance than in other Scenes so far and try to ensure that the captive is freed early on so he is able to contribute on the heroes' side.

▶ If the players are on the Pro-Registration side, this is a chance to give them some comeuppance since they've so frequently been on the aggressive side. Be heavy-handed with the doom pool. This is a good time to vent it so the conclusion of Act Two isn't overwhelming. Remember that even if the heroes "lose," the goal of the attack is to free the captive, not to directly assault the heroes.

▶ If you wish to use this as a spectacle, use the doom pool and make things go wrong. Perhaps there's a crash and some of the caravan members die. Maybe there's a news crew watching, ready to paint the Pro- or Anti-Registration forces as overt villains.

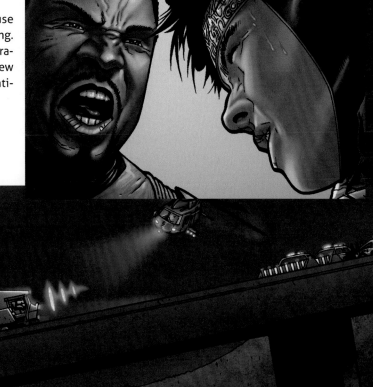

ACTION: CONFRONT THE AUTHORITIES ABOUT HERO PREJUDICE

OPTIONS FOR HERO PREJUDICE

- Though she's human, Maria Hill is not always reasonable. She may be looking for a quick score to prove her worth, or maybe Hydra or some other organization has compromised her. This could be a great lead into a conspiracy twist.
- Maybe Maria Hill isn't human after all. Maybe she's a Life Model Decoy with an implanted bomb sent to destroy the heroes. Maybe the decoy was taken over by Nick Fury instead as a way to secretly contact the heroes to lend them much needed support.
- With Director Hill possibly away from the security of the Helicarrier, a group of militant Anti-SHRA heroes unallied with the team launches an attack on everyone, bent on capturing or killing her.

S.H.I.E.L.D.
p. CW34

Maria Hill
p. CW35

Play this Scene once it's been clearly established that the heroes have been far more involved in battling heroes than villains. If the team members don't come up with the idea themselves, you can introduce it through a reporter or other source.

So far the action surrounding the Superhuman Registration Act has been to strike down heroes opposing registration. S.H.I.E.L.D. has hunted rebels in a disproportionate manner. This is particularly offensive to heroes from both sides because super villains have often been overlooked, ignored, or worse yet drafted into these assaults. In this Scene, a group of heroes confronts Director Maria Hill and S.H.I.E.L.D. about this prejudice.

Set the Scene on the Helicarrier, a secret S.H.I.E.L.D. base, or at a neutral rendezvous point where Maria agrees to meet Anti-Registration heroes under a temporary truce. She'll meet with prominent heroes with little hesitation, if only to show the righteousness of the Superhuman Registration Act. While she'll have guards, she won't promote violence.

It's not likely that she'll completely reverse her stance—she's an iron-willed woman with much to prove. However, she's likely to respond realistically to logical arguments that paint the future of her career in bleak terms. Her ambition and insecurities about being in Nick Fury's shadow can be used against her. She absolutely doesn't want to fail. In fact, she thinks she's not the right person for the job. Playing on her self-esteem and confidence will have great effect. On the other hand, threats will make her double down and strike harder, likely on those close to the aggressors.

Make this conflict about rational arguments and the importance of the Law. In the end, Maria Hill is human and can be reasoned with; heroes may be able to convince her to focus her S.H.I.E.L.D. forces on more logical targets. If the heroes resort to violence, the Scene should end poorly for them. Aim to capture the rogues, and focus heavily on the shift in public opinion against them.

TRANSITION: FIND/ UNCOVER HYDRA, A.I.M. BASE, OR ATLANTIS AGENT

Play this Scene when you want to explore and expose some of the plans of other organizations in the grander schemes of the Civil War.

If the heroes have gotten significant leads in any of the previous Scenes, the heroes might decide to hunt down some Hydra, A.I.M., or Atlantis agents that have been influencing the Civil War. All three groups have a vested interest in furthering or otherwise influencing this conflict. Furthermore, some of the heroes may have ties to one of them.

With this Transition, the heroes make headway toward uncovering the clandestine affairs affecting the efforts surrounding the Superhuman Registration Act. Much of this sets off the situation in Act Three.

Any of the three groups could help or hinder the heroes. Played properly, even negative intervention can be leveraged as an advantage in the right situation. While Hydra and A.I.M. have nefarious plans for the SHRA backlash, they can be valuable—if risky—allies. Their help could turn the tide of a battle. But then again, other heroes will look on with scrutiny if Hydra comes to their aid. Only the best of friends will turn a blind eye to such involvement. Here are some resources that heroes can obtain:

▶ NEGATIVE HYDRA ATTENTION: If the heroes go hunting for Hydra, they're likely to be noticed. If noticed, Hydra agents could show up at inopportune times. Spun correctly, these agents could serve either as a distraction or a helpful force.

▶ POTENTIAL HYDRA RECRUIT: If Madame Hydra sees potential in one of the heroes, she may try to bring him into her fold. This interest brings with it a few "favors" to help breed loyalty. In a time of need, Hydra agents or even Madame Hydra herself may show up to assist.

▶ AN ADVANCED IDEA: In the search and shuffle for A.I.M., the heroes stumble upon an amazing piece of technology. While it's limited in scope (i.e., a resource asset), and likely malfunctions after its initial use, it may very well turn the tide of a coming conflict.

▶ ATLANTEAN AID: While Prince Namor hasn't yet played his hand in the fight, he is fearsomely Anti-Registration and is willing to lend a few agents to aid in efforts to find Nitro or to prevent damage to his empire.

Hydra
p. CW29

A.I.M.
p. CW26

Atlantis
p. CW18

ACTION:
NITRO AT BIG SUR

The heroes discover that Nitro has taken refuge in a hidden cabin in Big Sur, California, to avoid the authorities. They must capture or "remove him from the picture."

The Explosion
Heard Around
the World
p. CW59

Where is
Nitro?
p. CW62

Following the events of Stamford, Connecticut, Nitro is pretty much Public Enemy Number One. If the heroes are working with S.H.I.E.L.D. to stop Nitro, they're going to need to do everything in their power to take him in alive. The U.S. Government wants to make an example out of him with a very public trial and sentencing. S.H.I.E.L.D. wants him taken into custody to serve the government's demands as well as its own agenda to incarcerate all Anti-Registration superhumans. Likely, S.H.I.E.L.D. sends agents along to help or "supervise" the takedown. Instead, the Watcher might allow the heroes to gain the assistance of a Pro-Registration hero.

On the other hand, if the heroes are working without S.H.I.E.L.D. help, they run the risk of encountering S.H.I.E.L.D. forces who might also be looking for Nitro—thus possibly resulting in a three-way confrontation. Bar that, the heroes are going to need to come up with a creative way to take down or capture Nitro. His explosive ability is not only dangerous to the heroes who go up against him but also to any civilians who might be around. Luckily, the hidden cabin is fairly secluded in a DENSE FOREST surrounded by a BLUFF making it HARD TO FIND and ISOLATED.

NITRO

Affiliations
SOLO 10
BUDDY 6
TEAM 8

Distinctions
EXPLOSIVE
MGH-ADDICT
RAINMAKER

PSIONIC PARTICLE PHYSIOLOGY

Power Sets

BLAST 8   FLIGHT 6
INTANGIBILITY 10   SUPERHUMAN STAMINA 10

SFX: *Detonation.* Against multiple targets, for each additional target add a D8 and keep an additional effect die, then shutdown BLAST and activate FLIGHT and INTANGIBILITY. Shutdown FLIGHT and INTANGIBILITY to recover BLAST.

SFX: *Explosive Fists.* If a pool includes BLAST, add D6. Remove the highest rolling die and step up the effect die.

SFX: *Ka-Boom.* If the doom pool includes at least 2D12, add the doom pool to an attack action including BLAST and *Detonation* SFX. End the Scene and remove 2D12 from the doom pool. Recover BLAST in the next Transition Scene.

Limit: *Divided.* Step up the lowest die in the doom pool or add a D6 doom die to step up any containment-related complication received while INTANGIBILITY is active. If that complication exceeds D12, shutdown all SFX.

Limit: *Gaseous Form.* FLIGHT and INTANGIBILITY start and remain shutdown until *Detonation* SFX activated.

Specs

CRIME EXPERT 8   SCIENCE EXPERT 8
TECH EXPERT 8

Robert Hunter

Electrical engineer Robert Hunter was given his powers by the Kree Lunatic Legion in order to become their agent on Earth. He was defeated by the Kree Captain Mar-Vell, but later reappeared as a super villain working for various criminals. Recently, he escaped confinement at the Raft when Electro freed all of the prison's inmates. Secretly given access to Mutant Growth Hormone by contract company Damage Control, Inc., his powers are more explosive than ever.

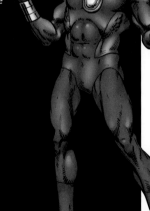

S.H.I.E.L.D. AGENT SQUAD

Affiliations

TEAM
6 6 6 6 6

Distinctions

CONFIDENT
HIGHLY-TRAINED

S.H.I.E.L.D. Agents are highly trained military spec-ops forces with specialized training on how to combat superhumans.

Power Sets

S.H.I.E.L.D. TRAITS

BODY ARMOR 6   COMMS 6

SMALL ARMS 6

SFX: *Concentrate Fire.* The entire S.H.I.E.L.D. Agent Squad targets the same Anti-Registration superhuman. Add 2D6 and keep an additional effect die.

Limit: *Squad Breakdown.* Defeat TEAM dice (with D8 stress) to reduce squad.

FOLLOWING UP ON NITRO'S STORY

The Scene ends when Nitro is captured or escapes. If they triumph, the heroes can interrogate Nitro to learn more about the events that have transpired from Stamford, Connecticut, to the present. You might represent this with a Transition Scene or simply reveal the following:

▶ Nitro had his powers increased due to a shipment of Mutant Growth Hormone (MGH) from a certain Walter Declun.

▶ If the heroes contact Namor or are on good terms with Atlantis, they discover Declun is the CEO of Damage Control, Inc.—a company formed to clean up the messes that result all-too-often from superhuman conflicts. See Act Three for more about this corrupt businessman.

▶ If the heroes don't talk to Namor, they need to discover that through other means—though Nitro claims he has no knowledge of Declun's employer.

▶ Heroes may choose to interrogate Anne Marie Hoag, Damage Control president. If so, they learn Declun and investors took a controlling interest in the superhuman cleanup business. Hoag also knows Damage Control won the recovery contract for Stamford and another contract to evaluate and train Pro-Registration superhumans.

OPTIONS WITH NITRO AT BIG SUR

▶ Atlanteans try to grab Nitro instead. This is some serious business for the Atlanteans. Prince Namor's cousin Namorita was killed during Nitro's explosion in Stamford. It's often said that, "Revenge is a dish best served cold." If so, seafood is on the menu. Janus, the Atlantean agent from the Sourcebook section, leads a handful of Atlantean agents.

Janus
p. CW20

▶ Your version of the Event might have yet another faction with a vested interest in seeing Nitro brought to justice or to revenge. Maybe some close friend of the New Warriors has digressed from lamentations to rage and seeks vengeance.

▶ During the engagement, you may choose to have a family of campers hiking in the area. The family might simply be collateral damage or they could provide an opportunity to either side of the Registration Act. A member of the family might be an influential U.S. senator. The Watcher can decide if this senator is Pro- or Anti-Registration. The heroes' actions of saving the senator's life and/or family could sway support for or against the act.

TRANSITION: INVESTIGATE ATLANTEAN SLEEPER AGENT ACTIVITY

IS NITRO INVOLVED?

The sleeper agents have been activated and they're on the move. What is their secret mission? Are they merely here to observe the culture of the surface dwellers, as some claim? More likely, they're intended to serve a protective or sinister purpose. Atlantis and the surface have been on shaky terms since their re-introduction. In light of the events at Stamford, which included the death of Prince Namor's cousin Namorita, the Atlanteans are not likely to sit idly by while her murderer lives. Using the Atlantean sleeper agents would be an excellent way to co-vertly track down Nitro to bring him back to Atlantis for either justice or vengeance. By this point, Namor's anger makes him a force to fear.

Atlantis
p. CW18

S.H.I.E.L.D. agents and New York's finest have discovered suspicious activity around the city and it becomes the heroes' job to unravel the truth. Play this Scene right before the final Scene of Act Two, as it leads into a number of Scenes in Act Three and can tie into the Nitro storyline.

It started with an aquarium shop owner going missing and the destruction of his store. While police might suspect Soviet Union sleeper agents left over from the Cold War, S.H.I.E.L.D. investigators are looking into a more likely scenario.

If the heroes are Pro-Registration, S.H.I.E.L.D. representatives will request—or command—they follow a suspected Atlantean sleeper agent. Otherwise, the heroes might stumble upon some suspicious activity while on patrol.

▶ BUSINESS **Resource:** The hero meets with a nervous business contact who has ties with the head of the warehouse district. "I think you're going to find this interesting," she says as she hands the hero a file folder. These files list all of the warehouses, owners, and leaseholders in the warehouse district. Upon close examination of the list, one of the entries seems a bit "fishy."

▶ COVERT **Resource:** The heroes discover a stealthy Atlantean sleeper agent. Keeping surveillance on the agent, the hero ends up following the Atlantean to the warehouse district.

▶ CRIME **Resource:** Unable to get any information out of the usual crime resources, the heroes turn to the media. While trading information or offering an interview with a HARD-NOSED crime reporter, the heroes learn there have been reports among criminal circles of suspicious smuggling activity. This smuggling includes some odd-looking, advanced weapons. The trail leads to a warehouse.

▶ MENACE **Resource:** Once again, a CONFUSED Bobbie the Mooch serves a purpose—after some roughing up. It turns out that Bobbie spends some of his time down in the warehouse district and has seen some unusual things. "See, Frank and I were hanging out to, um, do some fishing down by the docks, see? I catch this blue shape out of the corner of my eye. Frank, he doesn't see a thing. But I swear it, I do. It was a blue man." The heroes also notice that Bobbie doesn't smell like fish in the slightest, though he certainly could use a bath.

▶ PSYCH **Resource:** This is identical to the MENACE Resource, only kinder, and probably involves some cash.

▶ TECH **Resource:** Pretty much the same as the BUSINESS Resource option but without the meet-and-greet.

ACTION: BATTLE AT GEFFEN-MEYER PETROCHEMICAL PLANT

Play this Scene when you're ready to end the Act. This is the grand confrontation between both sides of the conflict that changes the tide of the war.

In order to draw as many NYC-based Anti-SHRA heroes out of their hideouts as possible, the leaders of the Pro-SHRA movement stage a colossal trap at the Geffen-Meyer Petrochemical Plant by sending out distress signals about explosions and fire. While there is an explosion and an ensuing fire, the damages are under tight control by the ambushers and no one has gotten hurt...yet.

While the Pro-SHRA leaders ostensibly want to talk, they're ready to dish out the required level of violence to knock everyone out and bring them in custody. That's why they planned a little thunderous surprise.

This is another complex Scene to frame given the potential scale. Dozens of heroes show up and S.H.I.E.L.D. has a very strong presence with more than 500 Cape-Killers flying and skulking around the site. Framing this Scene requires special care so you can run it as easily as possible.

PRO- OR ANTI-SHRA?

By now the heroes have likely picked a side; if they're still trying to be neutral, they'll be considered Anti-SHRA by the ambushers. Pro-SHRA heroes will be expected to make their Anti-SHRA counterparts surrender or, failing that, fight to capture them. Anti-SHRA will likely go into this Scene expecting to save plant workers, but they'll rapidly notice that no workers are calling for help on any radio frequencies.

BATTLE ROYALE CASTING CALL

The scale of this Scene can be staggering. With most of the NYC-located super heroes present, you aren't expected to play all confrontations. You should focus on a smaller but significant part of the conflict. If the players have chosen leaders in their factions, focus on the meeting of these leaders and their direct entourage. Pick enough heroes to create an interesting conflict—perhaps four or five—but not so many that the Scene will be unwieldy for you to run. For example, you might want to focus on using members of an established team like the Fantastic Four, the Avengers (Iron Man, Wasp, Yellow Jacket, Ms. Marvel, Wonder Man, etc.) or the Secret Avengers (Captain America, Luke Cage, Falcon, Goliath, Wolverine, etc.).

LIKELY OUTCOMES

With the number of resources at the disposal of the Pro-Registration side, defeat is unlikely although not impossible. Once Ragnarok attacks (see below), chaos breaks out as dozens of Anti-SHRA heroes fall to the clone's attack. Anti-SHRA heroes will likely need to organize a retreat or create a big enough diversion to leave the site without having to face S.H.I.E.L.D.'s reserves. Whatever happens, many friends will be lost, some possibly for good.

RUNNING THE SCENE

The Scene starts with both sides meeting. Anti-Registration heroes realize they're trapped as a few minor characters fall under a hail of S.H.I.E.L.D. tranquilizer darts. Pro-Registration heroes are ready for the worst, but rational discourse is still possible—though probably not for long.

The Geffen-Meyer Petrochemical Plant is a dangerous location filled with reservoirs of EXPLOSIVE CHEMICALS and other HIGHLY TOXIC and FLAMMABLE material. Although it's been evacuated, some hapless citizen or overly adventurous reporter can become TRAPPED IN WRECKAGE or SEVERELY HURT.

Keep in mind that many other heroes (and S.H.I.E.L.D. agents) are in this Scene. Work the consequences of their actions into the Scene Distinctions and Complications you create with the doom pool. There will be an amazing amount of collateral damage in this Scene—exploit as much of it as you can.

Try not to let the combat be the entire Scene, though. Allow heroes to retreat and regroup, to de-escalate the battle to a point where discussions can start again. Have the opposing side propose a truce. Remain in conflict mode, but instead of punches and beams of destruction, have the battle move to cutting words, impassioned arguments, and bitter accusations.

ENTER CODENAME: LIGHTNING

If the discussion stalls or if the Pro-SHRA forces are losing ground, start the battle over. Have someone slip and lose her temper. Have someone say something inflammatory and unforgivable. Kick everything into high gear and then unleash the Pro-SHRA's secret weapon, something so terrible everyone may have to band together to overcome it—a cybernetic clone of Thor, looking exactly like the real thing (currently believed to be dead). He wields the power of the Thunder God, but without the reason or compassion. While the clone's intended purpose is to help with the Registration effort, a nefarious intervention by mysterious agents twisted its programming to more destructive ends. It takes a collaborative effort from both sides to stop it.

This Scene ends when all Anti-SHRA heroes have been captured or have escaped or when the Pro-SHRA opposition is defeated or captured. At this point, a significant lull occurs in the conflict, allowing the Anti-Registration heroes to escape.

RAGNAROK

Affiliations

Solo 10
Buddy 8
Team 6

Distinctions

I Am the Odinson!
Killer Cyborg
Thunderous Temper

Power Sets

ASGARDIAN DNA

Enhanced Reflexes	8	Enhanced Senses	8
Enhanced Speed	8	Godlike Stamina	12
Godlike Strength	12	Superhuman Durability	10

SFX: *Immunity.* Spend a doom die to ignore stress, trauma, or complications from disease, poison, and fatigue.

SFX: *Invulnerability.* Spend a doom die to ignore physical stress.

SFX: *Mighty Blow.* Spend a doom die to double Godlike Strength for one action.

Limit: *Richard Wagner, 1813-1883.* Shutdown an Asgardian DNA power or step up mental stress from Ragnarok's creators or handlers to step up the lowest die in the doom pool or add a D6 doom die.

STARK TECH MJOLNIR

Electric Blast	10	Supersonic Flight	10
Weapon	10	Weather Control	8

SFX: *Area Attack.* **When using a** Stark Tech Mjolnir **power** against multiple targets, for each additional target add a D6 and keep an additional effect die.

SFX: *I Don't THINK So!* Step up or double a Stark Tech Mjolnir power for the next action, then step back that power. Activate an opportunity to recover that power.

Limit: *Gear.* Shutdown Stark Tech Mjolnir and step up the lowest die in the doom pool or add a D6 doom die. Spend a doom die to recover Stark Tech Mjolnir.

Specs

Combat Expert	8	Cosmic Expert	8
Mystic Expert	8		

Codename: Lightning

Codename: Lightning—grown in a vat from the Asgardian DNA found in a single strand of Thor's hair and bolstered by cybernetic technology—is the secret weapon of S.H.I.E.L.D. against Anti-Registration forces. The Thor clone believes himself to be the real thing, although he's many times more brutal, arrogant, and merciless. Codename: Lightning's creators built a functional equivalent of Thor's hammer, Mjolnir, out of Stark technology. The clone Thor may direct the raw power of the elements with this technological counterfeit of Thor's legendary hammer.

OPTIONS FOR BATTLE AT GEFFEN-MEYER

▶ This is the Act's climactic Scene. Make it as dramatic as you like. While it's unlikely to happen to the heroes themselves, don't hesitate to describe how minor characters—friends and allies—get captured, seriously hurt, or killed. A death, possibly the first since hostilities started, sends a shock through the superhuman community. This should happen at the hands of the Thor Clone (or his substitute; see below).

▶ Don't hesitate to play up the intrigue aspects of this event by granting special advantages to any heroes with ties to one of the organizations involved in the war. Maybe Hydra, A.I.M. or Nick Fury grants a hero with a special piece of tech (a D8 asset) against an opposing hero, like an ELECTRO-SCRAMBLER for Iron Man's armor or a PSYCHIC WARBLER to disorient an opponent.

▶ While the default location for the fight is the Geffen-Meyer Petrochemical Plant, you can use other locations that present similar dangers. If you've ever looked at a location and felt it would be frightening and dangerous, that's a good example. A power plant, an airplane hangar, or a skyrise condo could all work well.

▶ You don't have to use Ragnarok here at all. As alternatives, the "weapon of mass destruction" used in this battle could be the Hulk Robot or, perhaps, the Sentry.

HULK ROBOT

Affiliations
SOLO 10
BUDDY 8
TEAM 6

Distinctions
DOOM'S TECH
RAMPAGING
RETROFITTED

Students at M.I.T created a robot mascot modeled after the Hulk. Accidentally charged with cosmic power, the robot became sentient and proved a dangerous opponent. It was rebuilt by Dr. Doom and sent against the Thing; later, the Jester added a number of prank-themed modifications. Currently, it's essentially a cosmic-powered engine of destruction, barely under the control of S.H.I.E.L.D.

COSMIC-POWERED CREATION

Power Sets
ENHANCED SENSES 8   GODLIKE DURABILITY 12
GODLIKE STRENGTH 12   LEAPING 10
MIMIC 10   SUPERHUMAN STAMINA 10

SFX: *Area Attack.* When using a COSMIC-POWERED CREATION power against multiple targets, for each additional target add a D6 and keep an additional effect die.

SFX: *Energy Absorption.* On a successful reaction against an energy-based action, convert opponent's effect die into a COSMIC-POWERED CREATION stunt or step up a COSMIC-POWERED CREATION power until used in an action. If opponent's action succeeds, spend a doom die to use this SFX.

SFX: *Immunity.* Spend a doom die to ignore stress, trauma, or complications from disease, fatigue, poison, or psychic attack.

SFX: *Invulnerability.* Spend a doom die to ignore physical stress or trauma.

SFX: *Multipower.* Add more than one COSMIC-POWERED CREATION power die to a pool. Step back each COSMIC-POWERED CREATION power die in that pool once for each die beyond the first.

Limit: *Cosmic Adaptation.* MIMIC may only be used to create assets mimicking energy or cosmic-based Power Sets.

Limit: *Overload.* After using the MIMIC power or *Energy Absorption SFX*, shutdown any COSMIC-POWERED CREATION power to step up the lowest die in the doom pool or add a D6 doom die. Activate an opportunity to recover the power.

Specs
COMBAT EXPERT 8

ACT THREE
ROCKET'S RED GLARE

The Superhuman Civil War escalates beyond Registration and enforcement. With so much at stake, S.H.I.E.L.D. unveils two bold new plans: **Prison 42**, a superhuman prison in the Negative Zone; and the new **Thunderbolts**, an elite team of superhumans composed of some of the deadliest villains, conscripted to work for the SHRA. At the same time, the events that triggered the Civil War itself have brought Atlantis into the fray and have revealed the dark side of super villain involvement. With such drastic initiatives from the Pro-Registration side and increased challenges for the Anti-Registration side, the question now becomes: **Whose side do you fight for?**

ACT THREE: ROCKET'S RED GLARE

SCENE STRUCTURE

Like the two previous Acts, Act Three has two parts. The Buildup section has three main Action Scenes that bring several of the interlacing plots together—SHRA, Atlantis/Nitro, and the growing 24-hour media coverage. The Key Scenes introduce Action and Transition Scenes that can be played in any order, ending in the final Action Scene that pits every side against the others in an inevitable battle for the fate of the nation and possibly the world.

BUILDUP
▶ Action: The Goblin Attacks
▶ Action: The New Thunderbolts
▶ Action: The Media and SHRA

KEY SCENES
▶ Action: The Atlantean Envoy
▶ Transition: Investigate Damage Control
▶ Transition: Baxter Building Infiltration
▶ Action: Atlantis Prepares For War (STORY ENDING SCENE)
▶ Transition: Talking to S.H.I.E.L.D. About the Goblin
▶ Transition: Interviewing Superhumans
▶ Action: Hostile Takeover (STORY ENDING SCENE)
▶ Action: Final Battle with A.I.M. or Hydra (STORY ENDING SCENE)
▶ Action: Negative Zone Prisoner Bust
▶ Action: Breaking into the Negative Zone Prison (FINAL SCENE)

As always, remember that you can create additional Transition Scenes as needed to allow the heroes to rest, recover, gather additional resources, and recruit new heroes or support between any Action Scenes. You can also use information provided in Transition Scenes to frame new Action Scenes not included here, which becomes especially important as multiple plot threads converge.

HOOKS

It's a good idea to recap some of the Scenes from the last Act for your players so that everyone's aware of where they are when things get decidedly worse. Identify which of the heroes are aligned with the SHRA or authorities, which are opposed, and which are either neutral or ambivalent. This should inform which of the three Action Scenes in Buildup are appropriate.

DOOM POOL

The doom pool begins at 3D8 for this Act. Remember to re-fresh all Plot Points for player heroes and have the players settle on new Milestones if any were closed out in the last Act.

Doom Pool
p. OM14

DOOM POOL: 3D8

BUILDUP

The following Action Scenes primarily focus on Pro-Registration, Anti-Registration, and independent groups. Each of them builds on Scenes from the first two Acts.

- Heroes chasing down leads on Atlantean sleeper cells or otherwise working for the authorities should start with **The Goblin Attacks**.
- Anti-Registration freedom fighters or turncoats are going to have **The New Thunderbolts** to deal with.
- And if neither Scene sounds ideal, have reporters or media producers approach them for **The Media and SHRA**.

ACTION: THE GOBLIN ATTACKS

This Scene focuses on former villain and now secret C.S.A. operative Norman Osborn, AKA the Green Goblin. Osborn's off his nanotech-implant leash thanks to a mysterious benefactor, so he doesn't have the same complication the other Thunderbolts have (see **The New Thunderbolts** *on page CW104). His mission: blow up some Atlanteans.*

The Scene takes place at night in the warehouse district. Heroes who investigated the Atlantean sleeper cells in Act Two should be included in this Scene, regardless of their relationship to the SHRA. Pro-Reg heroes may also be here as part of their S.H.I.E.L.D. assignment based on intelligence their superiors have gathered; Anti-Reg heroes might be here having heard the same intel, likely as a result of tapping S.H.I.E.L.D.'s network transmissions. The chief antagonist here is the Green Goblin, but see **Options with the Goblin Attacks** for alternatives.

An Atlantean sleeper cell has set up a compound in a WAREHOUSE FULL OF CRATES and is using it to coordinate further activity. An armed guard force is present, but most of them are unarmed Atlantean covert agents like those the heroes may have encountered earlier. You can include any established Atlantean characters here, such as Janus, to make things interesting. The heroes might use their powers to keep tabs on the Atlanteans, or they might observe the goings-on through a ROOFTOP SKYLIGHT, or perhaps the heroes are still searching for the compound. The action kicks off with the chilling whine of the Goblin's goblin-glider and the first deet-deet-deet of a pumpkin bomb as it hurtles through the night.

For Osborn, this is a hit-and-run mission. He'll target heroes with his attacks, if he sees them; otherwise his first action is to reduce the mob of Atlanteans by one die. This also creates a TRAPPED ATLANTEANS Scene Distinction that the heroes may want to focus on and blows a LARGE HOLE IN THE ROOF of the warehouse. If the conflict with the heroes takes more than an action sequence or two, Osborn disengages and tries to flee as he has been ordered. He leaves once the mob of Atlanteans is eliminated, in any case. If it looks as if the heroes might defeat Osborn (or your alternate villain), don't forget you can use the doom pool to end the Scene and allow the cackling fiend to escape—by spending 2D12 out of the doom pool and handing out 2 XP to each affected player. Refer to the **Options with the Goblin Attacks** for more suggestions.

ATLANTEAN AGENTS

Affiliations

TEAM
6 6 6 6 6

Distinctions

LOYAL TO ATLANTIS
SLEEPER CELL

Power Sets

AGENT TRAITS

ATLANTEAN WEAPONS 8	ENHANCED STRENGTH 8
ENHANCED SWIMMING 8	ENHANCED DURABILITY 8

SFX: *Area Attack.* Against multiple targets, for every additional target add a D6 and keep an additional effect die.

Limit: *Unit Cohesion.* Defeat TEAM dice (with D8 stress) to reduce mob.

Limit: *Gills.* Step back traits by −1 when not immersed in water. When dehydrated, shutdown all traits other than ATLANTEAN WEAPONS and step up lowest doom die or add D6 to the doom pool. Recover all traits when returned to water.

GREEN GOBLIN

Norman Osborn

Affiliations
SOLO 10
BUDDY 6
TEAM 8

Distinctions
A MONSTER HIDES WITHIN
OBSESSED WITH SPIDER-MAN
POWER AT THE COST OF SANITY

Power Sets
GOBLIN AUGMENTATIONS
ENHANCED DURABILITY 8   **ENHANCED REFLEXES** 8
SUPERHUMAN STAMINA 10   **SUPERHUMAN STRENGTH** 10

SFX: *Planner.* Spend a doom die to step up a TECH MASTER or CRIME MASTER stunt or resource and recover mental or emotional stress.

SFX: *Seething Rage.* Step up or double any GOBLIN AUGMENTATIONS power for one action. If the action fails, spend a doom die equal to or greater than the normal rating of the power die.

Limit: *Barely Restrained Madness.* Step up the lowest die in the doom pool or add a D6 doom die to step up emotional stress from opponents that offend or mock Osborn.

WICKED GOBLIN ARSENAL
ELECTRICAL BLAST 8   **SUBSONIC FLIGHT** 8
SUPERHUMAN DURABILITY 10   **WEAPONS** 8

SFX: *Pumpkin Bombs.* Against a single target, step up or double a WEAPONS die. Remove the highest rolling die and use three dice for the total.

SFX: *Ghost Grenades.* When using WEAPONS to inflict an OBSCURING complication on a target, add a D6 and step up WEAPONS die.

SFX: *Razor-Rangs.* Step back the highest die in an attack action pool to add a D6 and step up physical stress inflicted.

Limit: *Gear.* Shutdown WICKED GOBLIN ARSENAL to step up the lowest die in the doom pool or add a D6 doom die. Spend a doom die to recover WICKED GOBLIN ARSENAL.

Specs
BUSINESS EXPERT 8   **COMBAT EXPERT** 8
CRIME MASTER 10   **MENACE MASTER** 10
PSYCH EXPERT 8   **SCIENCE EXPERT** 8
TECH EXPERT 8

Raised in an abusive home, Norman Osborn learned that only hard work and brutal ruthlessness achieve goals. In achieving his own goals, this genius chemist and engineer stepped on whoever was in his way. His mind and body warped by an experimental formula he tested on himself, he created the Green Goblin identity and built an elaborate criminal operation from the shadows. Coming into conflict with Spider-Man, Osborn developed an obsession with the hero.

Support Actions by Watcher Characters p. OM53

During the battle, the remaining Atlanteans lend support to the heroes by returning fire at Osborn with their Atlantean rifles. Have them hand over an appropriate trait as a support asset to any heroes who are attacking Osborn. This counts as their action. As long as the heroes make no attack toward the Atlanteans, they won't consider the heroes to be a threat. They won't hesitate to turn on the heroes if they're attacked, however, even accidentally. If the heroes are on the roof of the warehouse or flying overhead, there could be some close calls as Atlantean WEAPON-FIRE shoots by.

The heroes may also choose to rescue the Atlanteans pinned under fallen beams and crates. They can target the TRAPPED ATLANTEANS Scene Distinction with rescue-oriented actions, thus eliminating it, or attempt some other creative action that achieves the same result. Osborn doesn't concern himself with heroes who are trying to pull off such a rescue; he's only worried about creating as much carnage as he can before he flies off. If the heroes manage to free the Atlanteans, replace TRAPPED ATLANTEANS with a GRATEFUL ATLANTEANS D8 resource for their next appropriate Scene.

If the Scene ends via the 2D12 doom pool method, the heroes are knocked unconscious by a pumpkin bomb and fall among the Atlantean bodies. They're able to make out the Green Goblin's laughter and visage through the smoke before falling unconscious. If the heroes don't fall, they might be able to track the Goblin for a while, but he eventually eludes them because his controller has further plans for him. The Atlanteans are taken into custody by the authorities, unless the heroes get them out of the warehouse first.

OPTIONS WITH THE GOBLIN ATTACKS

▶ You could use another super villain in place of the Green Goblin. That villain, like the Goblin, might have nanotech implants tampered with by the unknown source connected to the C.S.A., or the villain might have his own motivations for his actions. For instance, if the heroes didn't stop Crusader in Act One, he might still be on the loose and may believe bringing the Atlanteans into the war would kill even more of the abominations known as super heroes, as well as Atlanteans. If Nitro's still on the run, maybe he attacks the Atlanteans, hoping to both put a stop to their revenge efforts over Namorita's death and create a further distraction for the heroes.

▶ Replace the Atlanteans with another organization, if you want to change up the plot. Perhaps the plot in your campaign isn't as complex and S.H.I.E.L.D. or the C.S.A. might control the Green Goblin (or another villain) to simply make hit-and-run attacks on suspected Anti-Registration holdouts. If your own campaign involves the tipping of the scales that results in the X-Men entering the fray, perhaps the attack takes place at the Xavier Institute to send the mutants a message about the cost of getting involved.

▶ Instead of allowing Osborn to escape, you might choose to allow the heroes to capture the Green Goblin. The heroes could then learn that this Green Goblin is, in fact, Osborn, and not another copycat. Osborn denies any knowledge of why he did what he did. This could lead down a completely different story arc, sending the heroes to investigate S.H.I.E.L.D. activities regarding prisoners and nanotechnology and Operation Thunderbolt (see **The New Thunderbolts** for more of this). If this happens, a substitute villain may be required for future Action Scenes involving the Green Goblin. Alternately, the Goblin identity could still be used if someone else dons Osborn's mask. Good choices include Jack O' Lantern, the Jester, or (for a real twist) Diamondback.

▶ You can follow this Action Scene with a Transition Scene that lets the heroes follow up on the Goblin's current status. By creating a COVERT or CRIME EXPERT resource, the heroes learn from their sources that Osborn is still behind bars. S.H.I.E.L.D. representatives or Osborn's legal team claim there's no way the heroes could have encountered the real Green Goblin. A COVERT or CRIME MASTER resource tells a different story; Osborn's been drafted as an operative in the ultra-secret Operation Thunderbolt program.

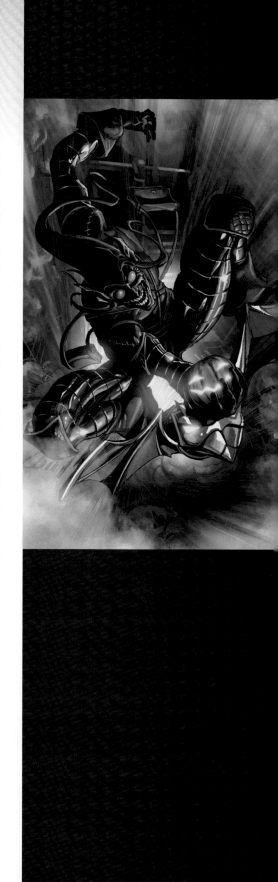

ACTION: THE NEW THUNDERBOLTS

This Scene kicks off Act Three for Anti-Registration or neutral player heroes who are opposed to the government, S.H.I.E.L.D., or the Pro-Registration movement. It can also easily be modified to work with Pro-Registration heroes.

When S.H.I.E.L.D. and the Commission on Superhuman Activities find that corralling the Anti-Registration rebellion is harder than it sounds, they take to recruiting super villains by offering them clemency deals in exchange for their cooperation. Those super villains became the new Thunderbolts and are charged with moving against the rebellion. The whole T-Bolt Division is classified; the names and identities of these operatives are not revealed to the public.

When one or two of the Anti-Registration heroes are active outside of their headquarters or home base, a Cape-Killer Unit spots them. You can play this out a little or just have the heroes try to avoid them, which isn't difficult. The unit contacts S.H.I.E.L.D. and a squad of Thunderbolts shows up. Some heroes may already be familiar with these operatives, either because they were previously on Zemo's team, or because the heroes have come to blows against them in the past. Choose any two of the T-Bolts provided here, plus one for every hero present in the Scene.

The T-Bolts have been given strict instructions to bring in any rogue heroes alive. This doesn't mean some of them won't do everything they can within the limits of the nanotechnology in their bloodstream to mess the heroes up a lot. If Songbird is present, she's a moderating influence, trying to convince the heroes to surrender. If Moonstone's leading the field team, she's likely to cause as much vicious emotional stress as physical. Without either of these experienced leaders, the squad has little to no plan of attack other than beating the daylights out of the heroes.

THE THUNDERBOLTS

Originally a team of super villains masquerading as heroes and working for Baron Helmut Zemo, the Thunderbolts has become a true hero team in its own right over the years. They've worked alongside the Avengers and often clashed with them, usually because of their close ties with the C.S.A. Shortly before the Civil War, Zemo's team fell apart from internal conflict and S.H.I.E.L.D. infiltration; the current team's membership includes some of the older team, but the new members are all convicted superhuman criminals kept in line with nanotechnology injected into their bloodstream and a hefty parole stipend.

With the exception of Moonstone (field leader), Radioactive Man, Songbird, and Swordsman, every Thunderbolt conscript has a NANOTECH IMPLANT D10 persistent complication that can be triggered when they act in opposition to their mission parameters. As Watcher, you should feel free to add other characters to the team as needed. The **50 STATE INITIATIVE EVENT SUPPLEMENT** includes more details on playing the Thunderbolts as heroes.

CAPE-KILLER UNIT

Affiliations	Distinctions
TEAM 8️⃣8️⃣8️⃣8️⃣8️⃣	**LOYAL TO S.H.I.E.L.D.**
	TRAINED TO FIGHT SUPERHUMANS

Power Sets

UNIT TRAITS
BODY ARMOR 8️⃣   **COMMS** 6️⃣
SUBSONIC FLIGHT 6️⃣   **TRANQUILIZER GUN** 8️⃣

SFX: *Area Attack.* Against multiple targets, for every additional target add a D6 and keep an additional effect die.

Limit: *Unit Cohesion.* Defeat TEAM dice (with D8 stress) to reduce mob.

BULLSEYE

Lester (full name unknown)

Affiliations
- SOLO **8**
- BUDDY **6**
- TEAM **4**

Distinctions
- COLD-BLOODED ASSASSIN
- DEADLY ACCURACY
- KILLER GRUDGES

Power Sets

EVERYTHING IS A WEAPON

ENHANCED DURABILITY **8** WEAPON **8**

- **SFX:** *Focus.* If a pool includes an EVERYTHING IS A WEAPON power, replace two dice of equal size with one stepped-up die.
- **SFX:** *I Never Miss.* If a pool includes an EVERYTHING IS A WEAPON power, spend a doom die to reroll.
- **SFX:** *Trick Shot.* Against a single target, step up or double WEAPON. Remove the highest rolling die and use three dice for the total.
- **SFX:** *Whatever's on Hand.* When using an asset, step up or double the asset die. If the asset is persistent, step it back for the rest of the Scene.
- **Limit:** *Psychotic.* Step up mental stress taken to add a doom die to the stepped-up die.

Specs

- ACROBAT EXPERT **8**
- COVERT EXPERT **8**
- MENACE EXPERT **8**
- COMBAT MASTER **10**
- CRIME EXPERT **8**
- PSYCH EXPERT **8**

A former major-league pitcher, Bullseye is one of the world's foremost killers-for-hire. This sadistic sociopath can turn anything into a weapon. Other than his brief sports career and time with the National Security Agency, little is known about Bullseye. His accounts of his childhood and family history are wildly varied and contradictory. His bones are augmented with Adamantium implants, making him even more formidable. Bullseye's mastery of ranged weapons borders on the supernatural—he's maimed and killed with playing cards and toothpicks. His conflicts with Daredevil are brutal, extremely personal, and legendary.

JACK O'LANTERN

Steven Mark Levins

Affiliations
- SOLO **4**
- BUDDY **8**
- TEAM **6**

Distinctions
- CAREER CRIMINAL
- FREELANCE TERRORIST
- RUTHLESS MERCENARY

Power Sets

HALLOWEEN-THEMED ARSENAL

CYBERNETIC SENSES **6** ELECTRIC BLAST **6**
ENHANCED DURABILITY **8** FLIGHT **8**
WEAPON **8**

- **SFX:** *Pumpkin Bombs.* Against multiple targets, for each additional target add a D6 and keep an additional effect die.
- **SFX:** *Ghost Grabbers & Gas Grenades.* When inflicting a complication on a target, add a D6 and step up the effect die.
- **Limit:** *Gear.* Shutdown HALLOWEEN-THEMED ARSENAL power to step up the lowest die in the doom pool or add a D6 doom die. Spend a doom die to recover that power.

Specs

- COMBAT EXPERT **8**
- MENACE EXPERT **8**
- CRIME EXPERT **8**

Steven Levins began his costumed career working for the Red Skull along with then partner Blackwing. Now Levins has replaced the first Jack O'Lantern—the late Jason Macendale, murdered by the Hobgoblin. Levins has had a varied criminal career, working for numerous crime bosses and evil masterminds. He's battled many heroes, including Spider-Man, Captain America, Union Jack, and Falcon. He sports a heavily armored costume and numerous weapons and gadgets, including electric blasters, pumpkin bombs, and "pogo-glider" hover platform.

JESTER

Jody Putt

Affiliations
- SOLO 8
- BUDDY 4
- TEAM 6

Distinctions
- GRAND AMBITIONS
- LOSER LEGACY
- WANTS RESPECT

Power Sets

DEADLY TOYS

WEAPON 8

- **SFX**: *Bag of Tricks.* When inflicting a complication on a target, add a D6 and step up the effect die.
- **SFX**: *This One'll Kill Ya.* Spend a doom die to step up TECH EXPERT stunts or resources and recover emotional stress.
- **Limit**: *All Out of Tricks.* Shutdown DEADLY TOYS to step up the lowest die in the doom pool or add a D6 doom die. Spend a doom die to recover DEADLY TOYS.

Specs

- ACROBATICS EXPERT 8
- TECH EXPERT 8
- CRIME EXPERT 8

Successor to the first Jester, Jonathan Powers, Jody Putt was given weaponry designed by Dr. Doom. Putt formed the eclectic Assembly of Evil, including Fenris, Hydro-Man, Rock, and a robot Hulk. The villains were defeated by Cloak, Dagger, and the Avengers. Jester is a fair combatant and skilled acrobat who uses a number of toy-themed weapons and gadgets including trick yo-yos, toy robots, and exploding juggling balls.

LADY DEATHSTRIKE

Yuriko Oyama

Affiliations
- SOLO 8
- BUDDY 4
- TEAM 6

Distinctions
- CYBORG SAMURAI ASSASSIN
- OYAMA FAMILY HONOR
- VENGEFUL

Power Sets

CYBERNETICS

ADAMANTIUM CLAWS 10	CYBERNETIC SENSES 8
ENHANCED REFLEXES 8	ENHANCED STRENGTH 8
SUPERHUMAN DURABILITY 10	SUPERHUMAN STAMINA 10

- **SFX**: *Adamantium Bonding.* On a successful reaction against an edged or blunt attack action, convert opponent's effect die into a CYBERNETICS Enhancements stunt or step up a CYBERNETICS power until used in an action. If opponent's action succeeds, spend a doom die to use this SFX.
- **SFX**: *Death Rage.* Add a doom die to an attack action. After that action, step back the doom die and return it to the doom pool.
- **SFX**: *Healing Factor.* Spend a doom die to recover your physical stress and step back your physical trauma.
- **SFX**: *Multipower.* Add more than one CYBERNETICS power die to a pool. Step back each CYBERNETICS power die in that pool once for each die beyond the first.
- **Limit**: *Metal Body.* On a magnetic or electrical attack, change any CYBERNETICS power into a complication to step up lowest doom die or add a D6 doom die. Activate an opportunity or remove the complication to recover the power.
- **Limit**: *Systems Failure.* Shutdown highest-rated power to add that power die to the doom pool. Activate an opportunity to recover that power.

Specs

ACROBATICS EXPERT 8	COMBAT MASTER 10
COVERT EXPERT 8	MENACE EXPERT 8
TECH EXPERT 8	VEHICLE EXPERT 8

Lady Deathstrike is the daughter of Lord Dark Wind, creator of the Adamantium bonding process used on Wolverine. She fought Wolverine, but he defeated her and left her for dead. Making her way to the Mojoverse, Yuriko found Spiral's Body Shoppe, which transformed her into a killer cyborg through a mix of magic and technology. She has clashed repeatedly with Wolverine, whom she sees as an insult to her father's grand discovery.

MOONSTONE

Affiliations
- Solo **8**
- Buddy **4**
- Team **6**

Distinctions
- **Bound to Power**
- **Coldhearted Schemer**
- **Manipulative**

Power Sets

LIFESTONE AUGMENTED FORM

Energy Blast **10**		Intangibility **10**
Subsonic Flight **8**		Superhuman Durability **10**
Superhuman Reflexes **10**		Superhuman Stamina **10**
Superhuman Strength **10**			

- **SFX:** *Area Attack.* Against multiple targets, for each additional target add a D6 and keep an additional effect die.
- **SFX:** *Dazzling Burst.* When inflicting a Blinded complication or mental stress on a target, add a D6 and step up Energy Blast.
- **SFX:** *Puppets on a String.* Spend a doom die to step up a Psych Master stunt or resource and recover mental or emotional stress.
- **Limit:** *Holds a Grudge Forever.* Step up the lowest die in the doom pool or add a D6 doom die to step up emotional stress from opponents that offend or mock Sofen.

Specs
Combat Expert **8**	Medical Expert **8**
Menace Expert **8**	Psych Master **10**

Karla Sofen

Karla Sofen swore she would never put another person's needs before her own. As a psychiatrist, she tricked the original Moonstone into rejecting the stones that gave him his powers and took them for herself. As the new Moonstone, she derives her powers from a symbiotic bond with an ancient Kree artifact. She worked with a number of partners before winding up with Zemo and his Thunderbolts.

RADIOACTIVE MAN

Affiliations
- Solo **6**
- Buddy **4**
- Team **8**

Distinctions
- **Chinese Patriot**
- **Highly Pragmatic**
- **Smarter than He Looks**

Power Sets

RADIOACTIVE BODY

Enhanced Stamina **8**	Radiation Mastery **10**
Superhuman Durability **10**	Superhuman Stamina **10**
Superhuman Strength **10**		

- **SFX:** *Creative Applications.* When inflicting a complication on a target, add a D6 and step up the effect die.
- **SFX:** *Energy Absorption.* On a successful reaction against an energy-based attack, convert your opponent's effect die into a Radioactive Body stunt or step up a Radioactive Body power until used in an action. If opponent's action succeeds, spend a doom die to use this SFX.
- **SFX:** *Hypnotic Lights.* Step back the highest die in an attack action pool to add a D6 and step up mental stress inflicted.
- **Limit:** *Radiation-Based.* When stressed out by energy-draining or radiation-inhibiting tech, step up the lowest die in the doom pool or add a D6 doom die and shutdown Radioactive Body.

Specs
Combat Expert **8**	Menace Expert **8**
Psych Expert **8**	Science Expert **8**
Tech Expert **8**	

Chen Lu

Chinese physicist Chen Lu developed a process that transformed him into the Radioactive Man. A covert asset for his government, Chen was a founding member of the Masters of Evil, but now works for the Thunderbolts to present a "reformed" image to the world.

The Radioactive Man is able to manipulate radiation along a broad spectrum for direct energy discharges, blinding heat emissions, and the infliction of radiation poisoning. In addition, the radiation greatly enhances his physical strength and resilience.

SONGBIRD

Affiliations

SOLO **4**
BUDDY **6**
TEAM **8**

Distinctions

ABANDONMENT ISSUES
FORMER PROFESSIONAL WRESTLER
REFORMED CRIMINAL

SONIC HARNESS

Power Sets

ENHANCED DURABILITY **8**　　ENHANCED REFLEXES **8**
ENHANCED STAMINA **8**　　　　SONIC BLAST **8**
SONIC CONTROL **8**　　　　　SUBSONIC FLIGHT **8**

SFX: *Sonic Constructs.* When inflicting a sonic-type complication on a target, add a D6 and step up your effect die.

Limit: *Gear.* Shutdown SONIC HARNESS to step up the lowest die in the doom pool or add a D6 doom die. Spend a doom die from the doom pool to recover SONIC HARNESS.

Specs

COMBAT EXPERT **8**　　　　CRIME EXPERT **8**
MENACE EXPERT **8**　　　　PSYCH EXPERT **8**

Melissa Gold

Melissa Gold ran away from a troubled home, turning to crime before entering the professional wrestling world as "Screaming Mimi." Later recruited as "Songbird" for Baron Zemo's Thunderbolts, she has since worked against Zemo and tried to retire several times, only to be dragged back in by circumstance. Songbird is a trained combatant, physically enhanced by the Power Broker. A harness adapted from Klaw's sonic technology allows her to unleash destructive sonic discharges and create solid objects from sound, including wings for flight.

SWORDSMAN

Affiliations

SOLO **4**
BUDDY **8**
TEAM **6**

Distinctions

BROKEN TWIN
EX-SUPER TERRORIST
SKILLED SWORDSMAN

GENETICALLY ENGINEERED TWIN

Power Sets

KINETIC BLAST **10**

SFX: *Second Wind.* Before making an action including a genetically Engineered Twin power, spend a doom die the same size or larger than current physical stress to recover it and step up the genetically Engineered Twin power for this action.

Limit: *Twisted Family Tree.* Step up the lowest die in the doom pool or add a D6 doom die to step up emotional stress involving the loss of his sister or relations with his father.

SWORDS & BLADES

ENHANCED DURABILITY **8**　　　　SWINGLINE **6**
WEAPON **8**

SFX: *Focus.* If a pool includes a Swords & Blades power, replace two dice of equal size with one stepped-up die.

SFX: *Master Swordsman.* On a successful reaction against a close combat-based attack action, convert opponent's effect die into a SWORDS & BLADES stunt or step up WEAPON until used in an action. If opponent's action succeeds, spend a doom die to use this SFX.

Limit: *Gear.* Shutdown a SWORDS & BLADES power to step up the lowest die in the doom pool or add a D6 doom die. Spend a doom die to recover that power. If shutting down WEAPON, shutdown GENETICALLY ENGINEERED TWIN as well and step up the lowest die in the doom pool twice or add a D8 doom die.

Specs

ACROBATICS EXPERT **8**　　　COMBAT MASTER **10**
COVERT EXPERT **8**　　　　MENACE EXPERT **8**

Andreas von Strucker

Children of Hydra Leader Baron Wulfgang von Strucker, twins Andrea and Andreas operated as the super-terrorists known as Fenris. Andrea was killed revealing that the Thunderbolts leader Citizen V was actually supervillain Baron Zemo. Andreas was then mind controlled by Purple Man and joined the Thunderbolts as Swordsman. Recently freed of this control, he remained with the group. Once able to generate destructive blasts when touching his sister, as Swordsman he retains this by using her tanned skin for his sword's hilt. His costume also sports numerous hidden blades.

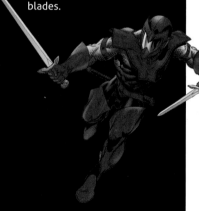

TASKMASTER

Affiliations
Solo 8
Buddy 4
Team 6

Distinctions
SHADOWY PAST
SKILLED INSTRUCTOR
VILLAINOUS MERCENARY

The Taskmaster is an experienced mercenary and trainer of super-powered operatives, but it is his unique abilities that make him a significant threat. Able to duplicate the skills of anyone he has seen, he has copied and fought Daredevil, Captain America, Hawkeye, and many others. He uses weaponry modeled after many of these heroes to augment his abilities. However, Taskmaster's power comes with a cost; the more skills he absorbs, the less he remembers his own past.

DUPLICATE ARSENAL

Power Sets

SUPERHUMAN DURABILITY 10   WEAPON 8

- **SFX:** *Area Attack*. Against multiple targets, for each additional target add a D6 and keep an additional effect die.
- **SFX:** *Dangerous*. Step back the highest die in an attack action pool to add a D6 and step up physical stress inflicted.
- **SFX:** *Trick Arrows*. When inflicting a complication on a target, add a D6 and step up the effect die.
- **Limit:** *Gear*. Shutdown a DUPLICATE ARSENAL power to step up the lowest die in the doom pool or add a D6 doom die. Spend a doom die to recover that power.

PHOTOGRAPHIC REFLEXES

ENHANCED REFLEXES 8   MIMIC 10

- **SFX:** *Copycat*. In a reaction against an opponent using a COMBAT or ACROBATICS Specialty, spend a doom die to add a die equal to the opponent's COMBAT or ACROBATICS to a dice pool.
- **SFX:** *Library of Moves*. Spend a D6 from the doom pool to step up or double a Photographic Reflexes asset.
- **Limit:** *Natural Mimic*. Mimic can only copy trained or skill-based powers or Specialties.

Specs

ACROBATICS MASTER 10	COMBAT MASTER 10
CRIME EXPERT 8	COVERT MASTER 10
MENACE EXPERT 8	PSYCH EXPERT 8
VEHICLE EXPERT 8	

VENOM

Affiliations

SOLO 8
BUDDY 4
TEAM 6

Distinctions

BRUTAL KILLER
UNRELENTINGLY SAVAGE
VENGEFUL

Mac Gargan

Once a P.I. hired by J. Jonah Jameson to investigate Spider-Man, Mac Gargan was later transformed at Jameson's request into the super villain Scorpion. This drove Gargan mad, and he spent years fighting Spider-Man and other heroes. When the alien Venom symbiote left its past host, Eddie Brock, it approached Gargan and offered to meld with him. Desiring the power the symbiote promised, he accepted. Now Gargan possesses the powers of Spider-Man and is even more dangerous, savage, and insane than he was before. **Note:** Spider-Man's *Spider-Sense SFX* doesn't help him against Venom.

SYMBIOTE

ENHANCED DURABILITY 8
SUPERHUMAN REFLEXES 10
WALL-CRAWLING 6

SHAPESHIFTING 6
SWINGLINE 6

SFX: *Claws.* Step back the highest die in an attack action pool to add a D6 and step up physical stress inflicted.

SFX: *Envelop.* When inflicting a restraining or immobilizing complication on a target, add a D6 and step up the effect die.

Limit: *Sonic Vulnerability.* After making a reaction against fire-based or sonic-based attacks, take emotional stress equal to the attack's effect die, regardless of physical stress taken.

SCORPION POWERS

SUPERHUMAN DURABILITY 10
SUPERHUMAN STRENGTH 10

SUPERHUMAN STAMINA 10

SFX: *Focus.* If a pool includes a SCORPION POWERS power, replace two dice of equal size with one stepped-up die.

Limit: *Exhausted.* Shutdown any SCORPION POWERS power to step up the lowest die in the doom pool or add a d6 doom die. Activate an opportunity to recover that power.

Specs

ACROBATIC EXPERT 8
CRIME EXPERT 8

COMBAT EXPERT 8
MENACE EXPERT 8

OPTIONS FOR THE NEW THUNDERBOLTS

This is by default an Anti-Registration Scene, but it could easily be modified. Heroes working closely with S.H.I.E.L.D. are made aware of the top secret "Operation Thunderbolt" after the major battle in the last Act. With many heroes joining the Anti-Registration side due to the dark turn of events, and the Fifty State Initiative not yet up and running, recruiting operatives with experience in dealing with superhumans is key.

▶ Rather than framing this Scene as an attack against player Anti-Registration heroes, you might choose to have **Pro-Registration heroes assigned to "ride along" with the Thunderbolts** on one of their first assignments. This is a great opportunity to bring up the moral dilemma of working with convicted criminals—in some cases, the heroes' own foes.

▶ You could **make this a Transition Scene**, one in which the heroes learn about the existence of the T-Bolt Division within S.H.I.E.L.D. before it goes live. Resources earned by this investigation include Operation Thunderbolt plans, operative lists, information on the nanotechnology that's being used to keep them in line, or a sympathetic former ally on the Thunderbolts team (Songbird is a good choice).

▶ One or more characters already locked up in the Raft (or Prison 42 in the Negative Zone) might be injected with nanotech and **enlisted into the Thunderbolts**. This could include player heroes. This Scene might therefore serve as a great way to start a new Thunderbolts-centric group.

ACTION: THE MEDIA AND SHRA

This is a quick and easy Scene that can and should ramp up the tension and the stress for the characters in Act Three, no matter what side of the Civil War the characters are on. It may also be used again later as the heroes face the media, attend a press conference, or are confronted by members of the press who catch them off guard.

A reporter named **Bill Price** from *The Daily Bugle*—who has every intention of winning a Pulitzer—corners the heroes either in a group or alone. The reporter is hard hitting and has a whole slew of "gotcha" questions meant to catch the hero off guard as well as expose the truly terrible aspects of how SHRA has developed. Even heroes who want the SHRA scrapped may have to confront their own failings along the way.

BILL PRICE, EXPERT JOURNALIST 8

SOLO 8   BUDDY 6   TEAM 4
      PERSISTENT 8   FACT-CHECKING 10
      COLLEGE BOXING 6

This is a good chance for you to frame a Scene that reveals the heroes' personalities and ideologies without putting them at a risk of personal injury. Your weapons in this Scene are your knowledge of the heroes, what matters to them, and the situations where they failed. Pin Spider-Man to the wall about supporting Registration for so long. How does Mr. Fantastic's wife feel about indefinite detention of people like her, and why hasn't she been standing beside her husband in support of Iron Man? Would Storm like to go on record with what she really thinks about Goliath's death? Obviously, all of this will be conditional on how these heroes have been represented so far in your game. Set up triggers for Milestones here as much as you can.

Ask the player a hard question, and then pick up the dice and heap on the mental and emotional stress. If the hero avoids stress, find another line of questions. If the hero takes stress while answering a question, follow that line of questions, so that the escalation feels organic.

OPTIONS FOR THE MEDIA AND SHRA

There are so many ways to re-frame this Scene; you can use it over and over. Make it short, sweet, and about something that's central to the heroes (something in their Milestones or Distinctions). Here are some other options:

- If the heroes get fairly beaten up in a way that might evoke sympathy, give them the option to spend 1 PP to grab a persistent asset or resource related to the Scene. Maybe the report has SWAYED PUBLIC OPINION. Or perhaps the reporter himself is now pulling for the heroes and their side. Maybe laying them bare like that has inspired him to right the wrongs committed in this war.
- Bring up something the heroes haven't really been paying attention to so far, or that hasn't come out in play. What are these rumors of a Negative Zone prison for superhumans who fail to register? What about mutants? Have the heroes tracked down who was responsible for Stamford yet? Where's the Hulk?
- Switch Bill Price out for **Sally Floyd** of *The Alternative* (page CW38) who's trying to get another angle on the whole SHRA thing by becoming "embedded" with the Anti-Registration crowd.

KEY SCENES FOR ACT THREE

This section covers a variety of Action and Transition Scenes that all build the tension rapidly toward a final confrontation. You can play these out in any order, and even repeat some of them with minor changes, before getting to a final confrontation between the Pro-Registration and Anti-Registration forces, most likely in **Breaking Into the Negative Zone Prison**. You don't want to force such a finale, of course; with these Scenes, enough seeds should be planted that the players make their own decisions that lead them to that big finish.

Several of these Scenes tie into multiple story threads. You can connect Atlantis, Damage Control, A.I.M./Hydra, Pro-Registration, and Anti-Registration storylines together with many of them. There should also be satisfying endings to all of these threads in this Act, some of them even working as alternate climax Scenes for the whole Event if your group seems headed that way.

ACTION: THE ATLANTEAN ENVOY

This Scene takes place on land, near an inlet from the ocean. Most people are here to seek peace between Atlantis and the land; Norman Osborn, however, has shown up to intervene.

A group of super heroes with international or diplomatic connections has organized a meeting between an Atlantean delegation and surface leaders to discuss and apologize for the recent attack on Atlanteans (see **The Goblin Attacks**, page CW100). Reporters from *The Daily Bugle* and *The Alternative* are among those in the press pool. The heroes introduce the surface leaders to the media and begin the summit despite the Atlantean representatives not yet having arrived.

This group could be the player heroes, assuming they meet the qualifications (Black Panther, for example, is an internationally recognized hero, and the Fantastic Four have long maintained relations with Atlantis) but fugitive heroes definitely won't be included. Alternately, the player heroes could simply be present to monitor the envoy, or they're following the trail of Nitro and the Atlanteans from Act Two. If the organizing heroes are all Watcher characters, they should take the back seat to the player heroes in the ensuing action.

As the press asks questions, there's a stir from the NEARBY WATER. From the stir emerges the Atlantean delegation, headed by Ambassador Govan. The sea dwellers move to the RAISED PLATFORM, are greeted by the representative heroes and the surface leaders, and are introduced to a translator. Ambassador Govan begins a speech, declaring that the Atlanteans who were attacked were on a peaceful exploration mission to study human culture.

Near the PRESS POOL, there are some seats filled with important locals and some standing room for onlookers. Heroes with at least ENHANCED SENSES D8 and who are familiar with Norman Osborn (out of costume) may spot him in the DENSE CROWD as he stands up and yells—giving them a split second to try to stop him as he draws a weapon. If not, he draws a gun and shoots Govan in the shoulder. He's not in control of his actions; this is a setup, his nanites having been reprogrammed just as they were in **The Goblin Attacks** Action Scene earlier. It's notable that he doesn't kill the envoy, just wounds him.

Chaos breaks out as the Atlantean bodyguards jump into a defensive stance and Govan takes cover behind bodyguards and chairs. Surface security, likewise, leaps into action. The FRIGHTENED CROWD spreads in all directions as someone yells, "Is that Norman Osborn?"

STOPPING OSBORN

A hero may choose to take down Osborn, who goes down with a struggle (hero's action vs. Osborn's reaction) but without using any of his Green Goblin powers. He keeps yelling, "I didn't do it. It wasn't me!" If the hero stopped Osborn before he could fire his weapon, the situation calms down faster but the Atlanteans still flee out of fear.

PROTECTING THE ATLANTEANS

A hero may choose to protect the Atlanteans. If so, it may be possible to try to mend the situation, build a positive relationship with the Atlanteans, or at least keep things from getting worse. This would also include providing Medical aid for the injured.

PROTECTING THE PRESS AND CROWD

As things get crazy, members of the media and crowd may be threatened in the panic. A hero may choose to protect them in hopes of building a positive relationship with a member of the press. This would also include providing Medical aid for the injured. If a hero is protecting the press and crowd, this could also help avoid collateral damage.

OPTIONS FOR THE ATLANTEAN ENVOY

As it stands, this Action Scene is quite scripted: the envoy shows up; Osborn takes a shot; everyone scrambles to arrest or restrain Osborn. How can you switch things up? Here are some suggestions:

▶ **You can replace Osborn** with another Thunderbolt operative, S.H.I.E.L.D. agent, or a Life Model Decoy. Osborn is the patsy for a conspiracy, so if the heroes are already familiar with the assassin it makes it personal. If the heroes had captured Osborn earlier in the Act, and he's still in custody, then you definitely need a replacement.

▶ **If you're not using Atlantis**, your stand-in organization or group needs to be the one sending the olive branch. Wakanda or some other nation would be just as valid here, so long as there's a credible threat from that nation if they're motivated to declare war.

▶ **One of the heroes could be the assassin**. Take the player aside and let him know what's going on; his hero has been injected with compromised nanotechnology, his mission is to put a stop to the Atlantean diplomatic mission, and then he's going to forget the whole thing. It's a tricky play, but a lot of fun if it works.

▶ **If the heroes were involved heavily in the Nitro/Atlantis situation** in Act Two, bring in some of those Watcher characters here. Maybe Janus or another of the Atlantean sleeper cell agents is present. Maybe Nitro surfaces again if he's still rogue. Because it's a press event, add someone in from a media Scene.

TRANSITION: INVESTIGATE DAMAGE CONTROL

Hostile
Takeover
p. CW120

In an earlier Scene, the heroes should have learned that Nitro was being supplied Mutant Growth Hormone (MGH) by Walter Declun, CEO of Damage Control, Inc. In this Scene, the heroes must investigate Damage Control to put a stop to Declun and the dangerous sale of MGH.

Describe this as a montage of poking around and asking informants, specifically Bobbie the Mooch, with a whole list of possible resources available to the heroes. It also gives the heroes the opportunity to recruit any new heroes or recover from stress. Follow this Transition Scene with the **Hostile Takeover** *Action Scene.*

▶ Business **Resource:** The hero speaks with shady business associates of Damage Control to determine Declun's location and any related information about MGH production. They learn he's planning to appeal to the board of directors of Damage Control, Inc., to purchase Roxxon's Long Island facility, which would increase MGH distribution under cover of standard operations.

▶ Covert **Resource:** The disguised hero infiltrates Damage Control, Inc., to discover the information from the inside about Declun's involvement with MGH production and distribution.

▶ Crime **Resource:** Bobbie the Mooch gets another chance. At first, Bobbie is hesitant to admit anything. After some serious threats involving a trip to prison, the "ex-con" breaks down. "I had no idea what you was lookin' for, honest...see? Me an' Frank been workin' for Declun. He makes us run deliveries of some new substance. He kept goin' on about it and Frank and me would just look at each other with that look, ya know? I...aw, damn. That's what helped kill those kids at Stamford, wasn't it?" Bobbie's remorse seems sincere at the realization. He tells the hero everything he knows about how to reach Declun and the production facility.

▶ Menace **Resource:** Bobbie the Mooch gets intimidated, and caves in almost immediately. "Whoa! Whoa. See, I woulda told you sooner but I didn't want Nitro comin' after me and Frank," Bobbie pleads. "We was workin' for Declun, see? He had us make some deliveries of some new substance. He kept goin' on about it and Frank and me would just look at each other with that look, ya know? I had no idea that's what you was lookin' for, honest...see?" He tells the hero how to reach Declun and the facility.

▶ Psych **Resource:** Rather than threaten Bobbie the Mooch with prison, a hero pleads with him to help bring in those responsible for the Stamford disaster. After hearing that, Bobbie puts two and two together and realizes what really happened. He then breaks down as in the Crime resource.

▶ Tech **Resource:** Hacking into Damage Control's high-security computer system, the hero learns of Declun's involvement with MGH production and his tenuous position as CEO of Damage Control.

TRANSITION: BAXTER BUILDING INFILTRATION

Reed Richards, or another genius working with S.H.I.E.L.D., has built a prison in the Negative Zone. For the Anti-Registration forces, the location of this prison is integral to protecting those oppressed by the Superhuman Registration Act. To get that location, the heroes break into the Baxter Building and pull the data from its stores.

This Scene assumes a couple of things. One, Reed Richards/ Mr. Fantastic is working on the Pro-Reg side as he does in the comics. Two, the Negative Zone prison is accessed from a number of secure locations, but primarily the Baxter Building, headquarters of the Fantastic Four. If either of these is a problem, check out Options, below.

You can handle this Scene as a Transition, to guarantee it gives the basic amount of success necessary. The players can decide what additional resources they can pull from the raid, in preparation for the move against the prison in the Negative Zone.

This transition works as a lead in to the big finish, allowing the players to recruit whichever heroes they want to take into the final confrontations. If you want, capture the hero that broke in, if the players aren't using that datafile for the move on the Negative Zone. Let them rescue that hero, who transmits the necessary data before capture; see **Negative Zone Prisoner Bust** (page CW126) for details on that.

▶ Covert **Resource:** With detailed floor plans and security details as an alternative resource, the prison might not be as daunting a break-in as it otherwise could be.
▶ Cosmic **Resource:** The general coordinates would be enough to hunt down a Negative Zone gate. But with detailed directions and layout, the zone would be an open book. Navigation would be no problem at all, and could mean more efficient tactical movement.
▶ Tech **Resource:** The Baxter Building houses more than just the plans for the Negative Zone. Inside, an intruder could stumble upon some of Reed Richards' advanced technology. This could offer a major surprise in the coming battles. Richards and the Pro-Registration movement aren't prepared to face Richards's own technology.

OPTIONS WITH BAXTER BUILDING INFILTRATION

There are several ways to adjust this Transition Scene. The best way, of course, is to use it to respond to the players' interest in finding out what super-prison the authorities have built to contain the captured Resistance heroes.

● You could easily make this an Action Scene centered on a single hero or small team of heroes. The Baxter Building is no joke. Its security is renowned for being Top of the Line. If a hero is Caught on Film breaking in, she'll be recognized as an amazing burglar, and someone who's not afraid of the best possible security measures.
● It doesn't have to be the Baxter Building. In Arizona, there's a training ground for new government-sponsored super heroes, the fledgling Avengers Initiative. It's basically a boot camp, but it's also a S.H.I.E.L.D. base and thus has much the same sophisticated technology and archives as the Baxter Building. Maybe that's where the Negative Zone gate is located.
● Not only can the heroes dig up the location of the Negative Zone prison, they can also find evidence of Hydra or A.I.M. influence on the project, at your discretion. This could ruin the Pro-Registration agenda if played properly and lead into the **Final Battle with A.I.M. or Hydra** Action Scene.

ACTION:
ATLANTIS PREPARES FOR WAR

Atlantis
p. CW18

Regardless of whether the attack on Atlantean Ambassador Govan was successful, the Atlanteans are preparing for war. Likely, the attempt on Govan's life was the final straw. Tensions have been escalating ever since Namorita's death at Stamford.

This Scene is heavily weighted toward interpersonal social conflict, with the heroes having to use their wits, diplomacy, and whatever resources they have on hand to keep Atlantis from launching an attack on the coastline of North America.

The Atlantean
Envoy
p. CW112

IF THE HEROES ARE FRIENDS OF ATLANTIS

If the heroes stopped Norman Osborn from shooting Govan in **The Atlantean Envoy** or if the heroes helped protect the Atlanteans, there's the possibility of either recruiting Atlantis to the heroes' side in the Civil War or of resolving things peacefully. Any hero who has proven to be a friend gets at least a fair listen from the Atlanteans. It might even be enough for an audience with the Sub-Mariner himself. While Namor is still angry over the loss of Namorita, he doesn't really want an all-out war with the surface. Or does he? A reasonable Namor will work with an ally for the betterment of both Atlantis and the surface.

IF THE HEROES ARE STRANGERS

If the heroes are basically unknown to the Atlanteans, they're not likely to even get the time of day. The only option here is to try to resolve the matter peacefully, but that won't be easy. If the Atlanteans won't even speak to the heroes, they may need to find an ally the Atlanteans will speak with and offer some type of sanction. The Fantastic Four or one of the other Illuminati (assuming the heroes even learn about this secretive group) know Namor best.

Heroes may decide to reveal information about the Mutant Growth Hormone used by Nitro and a possible link to Damage Control, Inc. This information might cause Namor to re-evaluate the factors that led to his cousin's death and divert his anger from the surface world and instead to Walter Declun. Namor already knows Declun is Damage Control's CEO and he might aid the heroes in taking down Declun in their final confrontation (see **Hostile Takeover**, page CW120).

Attempting to make contact with a hostile Atlantis leads to a confrontation. Heroes must be prepared for a possible conflict with Atlantean warriors. If they can avoid casualties and convince the Atlanteans that they come in peace, they might still be given an audience. This may also be a hero's last chance to improve her reputation with Atlantis. On the other hand, if this route ends in Atlantean casualties, Namor will have no choice but to launch a full invasion against the surface—it would be viewed as an outright act of war.

OPTIONS WITH ATLANTIS PREPARES FOR WAR

The following suggestions give you more ways to include this Scene's conflict in the larger Civil War:

▶ If Namor is won over by the heroes, he might aid them against the other side in the battle over the SHRA. Atlantis' warriors are already geared up for battle; this gives them an outlet for that aggression. Namor can handle the fallout later, in his usual arrogant manner.

▶ If Namor is a player hero, you can determine whether or not this entire Scene is actually about him and his allies confronting surface heroes and getting information about Damage Control, about Norman Osborn, or about any number of other threads connected to Stamford. Perhaps this Scene is where the players unlock Namor as a player hero in preparation for the big climactic battle of Act Three.

▶ A peace treaty with Atlantis might be brokered by clever players, one that not only benefits their side in the Civil War but opens up more opportunities later. Perhaps Namor offers sanctuary to heroes who seek refuge from the SHRA, or maybe he determines that Atlantis offers superior technology in the effort to curtail unregistered superhumans.

THE CONSPIRACY REVEALED?

As the Watcher, you may choose to change up the story from what's presented in the Civil War comics. Instead of Tony Stark orchestrating Osborn's bizarre activities via reprogrammed nanotechnology, perhaps Namor plotted the whole Event as an excuse to invade the surface or simply to seek vengeance for Namorita's death. Perhaps S.H.I.E.L.D. or Nick Fury did all of this behind Tony Stark's back as a way to keep him guessing, to keep him in line, or as a diversion for other subversive activities. Or, maybe Osborn really was in jail the whole time and it was the Chameleon posing as him? The possibilities are vast. Consider using your players' own theories as the truth, if for no other reason than to give them the satisfaction of putting all the pieces together. Now... what are they going to do with this information?

S.H.I.E.L.D.
p. CW34

Maria Hill
p. CW35

TRANSITION: TALKING TO S.H.I.E.L.D. ABOUT THE GOBLIN

By this point, the heroes have unraveled most of the intricate details of the overall plot of the Event. This Scene lets them grab one or two resources in preparation for any of the final conflict Scenes.

One of the main questions that should be niggling at the heroes, whether they're for or against the Registration Act, is this: "Why was Norman Osborn released?"

While it may have been unclear during the first Green Goblin attack whether it was really Osborn (it was), the attack on the Atlantean delegates was most certainly Osborn unless you switched him out for another character. This means he was released from high-security prison and acting under S.H.I.E.L.D. orders via Operation Thunderbolt. If so, what purpose could there be in releasing this psychotic murderer known publicly as the Green Goblin? The heroes may even suspect that S.H.I.E.L.D., Tony Stark, Namor, or some other entity is truly behind this fiasco.

If Norman is pardoned by S.H.I.E.L.D., do the heroes want to know why? S.H.I.E.L.D. won't likely offer any response to such questioning. They may admit Osborn was under the control of someone else, which is why they pardoned him, but they aren't likely to reveal that person's identity, even if they do know.

Through media, Atlantean, or other resources, the heroes may be able to delve deeper and find out the truth that S.H.I.E.L.D. won't reveal. Investigative reporters have likely uncovered some of the biggest secrets behind the Civil War. While normally those truths would come to light via publication or broadcast, the stories may be in editorial limbo, embargoed, or in the hands of reporters keeping secrets. Whether they would be willing to release that information depends on their relationship with the hero. Likewise, the hero's relationship with Atlanteans might uncover secrets that Atlantis is keeping.

If you chose to allow the heroes to capture Osborn during the first Green Goblin attack, the heroes may not need a media source to track things back to Stark, Namor, or whomever you've decided is the mastermind of that particular story arc and plot.

TRANSITION: INTERVIEWING SUPERHUMANS

This Scene can take place at any point in Act Three, provided the characters have access to incarcerated superhumans in holding or perhaps on their way to the Negative Zone prison.

Even in the best situations, players may miss something important, and heroes may make choices that back them into corners that you, as the Watcher, weren't anticipating. By this point, it is highly unlikely that the heroes are still neutral or even trying to be neutral. That's not to say their affiliations are publically known, but certainly they should know on some level where their allegiances reside.

If for some reason the heroes are still undecided before an important Scene in Act Three, this Transition can be used to help sway them the rest of the way and give them justification for creating resources, recruiting new heroes, or recovering from mental and emotional stress.

Present a good and decent hero, someone they could admire and look up to, on his way to the Negative Zone prison. Hammer home the people the hero was trying to protect and how much he believed in the rights of other superhumans to live in whatever sort of secrecy they desire. Tell the players a story about a local superhuman—a mutant or otherwise low-powered nobody—who was dragged out of her home and beaten, maybe killed, by an angry mob; maybe this person was guilty of nothing more than being born different.

Or, if they're leaning toward favoring registration, put them in an interview with someone really vile—a super villain who couldn't be stopped any other way, one who avoided every other legal loophole and politics to avoid detention and even thrived in that environment. Thanks to the Superhuman Registration Act, this villain is being stopped once and for all. There was no other way, and a lot of people are going to live thanks to his incarceration.

Additionally, if there's some clue or piece of information the heroes have missed, now is a good time to plant that seed again through the superhuman interview. It's a handy time to catch them up and, if need be, point blank ask the players, "What do you think your hero is missing? What does she need to get the job done from here?"

OPTIONS WITH INTERVIEWING SUPERHUMANS

- This Scene could also be framed as an Action Scene if the heroes want to actually engage with the inmate or captured superhuman character. If this sounds more interesting to them, frame it as an antagonistic meeting; maybe Pro-Registration heroes confront a villain they rounded up. A player hero who has taken a stand could be interviewed by a player hero who's still on the fence.

- Under the context of a secure meeting at Prison 42 in the Negative Zone, the players might continue to set up the foundation for their ultimate breakout attempt or determine if they've got a mole on their side. This is the perfect setup for resources based on information and contacts.

- The meeting doesn't have to be set in prison. It could be a rooftop conversation, a gathering of fugitives in a warehouse by the East River, a heart-to-heart in the Inhuman city of Attilan, or anywhere else that works as a breather in the action (even if it's not so lighthearted).

ACTION: HOSTILE TAKEOVER

Investigate
Damage
Control
p. CW114

In this Scene, armed with all the evidence about Damage Control's involvement in Stamford, use of Mutant Growth Hormone, and its interest in promoting the Civil War, the heroes take the battle right to the boardroom of Damage Control, Inc.

Walter Declun, CEO of Damage Control, Inc., and supplier of Mutant Growth Hormone to Nitro (and possibly others), is well connected. He's got S.H.I.E.L.D. and the White House on speed dial and he thinks he's untouchable. All he wants to do is sow the seeds of more chaos and destruction so Damage Control can pick up lucrative government contracts.

The heroes learn that Declun is meeting with the DAMAGE CONTROL BOARD OF DIRECTORS in their UPSCALE MANHATTAN SKYSCRAPER to swiftly pass a measure to purchase ROXXON OIL'S Long Island facility, which the heroes may already have learned about (it'll be a cover for MGH production). The heroes may have evidence to present to the board or perhaps they just want to show up and take down Declun.

Declun is unhinged, as anyone would be if confronted with charges of criminal activity and causing the tragedy in Stamford. When the heroes arrive at the boardroom, the board sticks around long enough to hear the heroes' initial claims of Declun's wrongdoing before he dismisses them. Declun, sensing the heroes may get hands-on, injects himself with CONSIDERABLY MORE MGH THAN IS SAFE, and becomes a super-powered threat.

WALTER DECLUN
(MGH-Enhanced)

Affiliations

SOLO	10 10 10
BUDDY	8 8
TEAM	6

Distinctions

COLDHEARTED CEO
FRIENDS IN HIGH PLACES
RECKLESS

MGH ENHANCEMENT

Power Sets

ENHANCED SPEED	8	ENHANCED STAMINA	8
LEAPING	8	SUPERHUMAN DURABILITY	10
SUPERHUMAN STRENGTH	10		

SFX: *Area Attack.* Against multiple targets, for each additional target add a D6 and keep an additional effect die.

SFX: *Now I'm Really Mad!* Step up or double any MGH EN-HANCEMENT power for one action. If the action fails, step back that power. Activate an opportunity to recover that power.

Limit: *Side Effects.* Change any MGH ENHANCEMENT power into a complication to step up the lowest die in the doom pool or add a D6 doom die. Activate an opportunity or remove the complication to recover that power.

Specs

BUSINESS MASTER	10	CRIME MASTER	10
MENACE EXPERT	8	PSYCH EXPERT	8

OPTIONS FOR HOSTILE TAKEOVER

This could be a simple knockdown drag-out fight in an office building, but the players might take it in a different direction. Here are some other suggestions:

▶ Business-savvy heroes such as Danny "Daredevil" Rand or Tony "Iron Man" Stark have enough clout that they might try to shut Declun out of his company through clever corporate methods, which would be a good option. This would be an action against the doom pool with Damage Control's HERO-PROOF BUREAUCRACY adding to the doom pool's dice (or used by the players for a D4 + Plot Point). Of course, this might not stop Declun personally, but it would bring his empire down around his ears.

▶ Declun might have MGH in the form of an aerosol gas and spray the whole board of directors with it, creating a MOB OF CRAZED MGH-ADDICTED SUPERHUMANS 3D6 to act as an additional obstacle.

▶ If the heroes are Anti-Registration, Declun calls in the Cape-Killers to help him as he attempts to get away. He can leap right out of the skyscraper and into the city while S.H.I.E.L.D's Superhuman Response Unit rappels in on cables.

▶ If the heroes are Pro-Registration, after Declun is caught he calls in some favors and gets out early—though clever heroes might pull some strings of their own (such as from a friendly Congressperson) and have him locked up in Prison 42 as a dangerous unregistered villain.

▶ Atlantis might get involved, with one or more Atlanteans showing up to bring Declun to justice. This is useful if the heroes are looking overwhelmed.

ACTION: FINAL BATTLE WITH A.I.M. OR HYDRA

A.I.M.
p. CW26

Hydra
p. CW29

With this Scene the heroes have one good chance to destroy one of the world's biggest terrorist organizations. This Scene can happen at any point in Act Three. It's a particularly important Scene if any of the characters have Milestones related to Hydra or A.I.M., so don't skip it.

As the Civil War rages toward its catastrophic climax, even tightly operated and successful superhuman-run terrorists groups are weakened. Monitoring, arrests, crackdowns—no one can operate the way they used to. Both Hydra and A.I.M. are suffering from funding issues and are the weakest they have ever been. If the heroes are going to strike, there will be no better time.

▶ SHRA and Congressional oversight has led to some heavy pressure on military contracts and technology contracts both public and private.

▶ As a result of that—as well as heavy tactics from S.H.I.E.L.D. and the arrests of unregistered superhumans—A.I.M. has been suffocating under its own weight. Money, political pressure, and the threat of incarceration have forced A.I.M.'s scientists to go even deeper underground and the organization's ability to fund itself is limited.

▶ The many advantages of cell activities are now working against Hydra as whole swaths of the organization vanish into the Negative Zone with no contact, another consequence of the hyper-vigilant SHRA.

Frame your Scene considering the information below and choose a shadowy, espionage-themed location that suits the organization and the player heroes. These places should have CRATES OF SMUGGLED TECH, GUARDS ON HIGH ALERT, DARK RECESSES, or ESCAPE ROUTES.

HITTING HYDRA

Hydra has its Tentacles in Many Places near the end of the Civil War with double agents in almost every major group and organization. Exposing any of those double agents can shift the balance dramatically. S.H.I.E.L.D., the Avengers, even SHRA and Congress all have ties to Hydra, whether they know it or not. A final fight with **Madame Hydra** is possible; with so few of the heads of Hydra left, her death or capture would be crippling.

Dealing with **Baron Von Strucker** is a much bigger challenge, since killing him is a non-option. However, capturing him—and locking him up in Prison 42 in the Negative Zone—means that, with luck, the Baron can finally be put out of business forever.

Any attack on a Hydra installation (such as Hydra Island, or one of its secret urban bases) means dealing with dozens of Hydra goons, probably a super villain or two (usually a mutate, failed genetics experiment, or super-spy with gadgets), and the threat of explosives, poison gas, toxins released into the water supply, and double-crossing agents.

HITTING A.I.M.

While they may have fewer personnel, A.I.M. facilities are still guarded by Advanced Security Systems. Finding and subduing M.O.D.O.K. is possible, but it won't be easy. The death and destruction of the war is incredibly stimulating for a monster created only to kill. However, A.I.M.'s weakening is also a sore point that the player heroes can use against him. Anti-Registration heroes may even be able to grab some of A.I.M.'s tech and use it for their own purposes later in the Act.

Any A.I.M. raid means facing high-tech gadgets, villains in armored suits, mobs of A.I.M. troopers, scientists with unpredictable electronic gear, and killer robots. An A.I.M. base is likely underground, possibly even right underneath some national landmark or iconic location.

ENTER NICK FURY

Former S.H.I.E.L.D. Director Nicholas Fury isn't dead or locked up. He's exactly where he wants to be in the Civil War—keeping out of sight and making sure he keeps track of who's doing what. His INTEL IS LEGENDARY. You should assume he has his IRONS IN ALL THE FIRES. This is a good time for him to emerge, perhaps as a source of information, perhaps as an ally against whichever organization the heroes are going to hit. Is he the real deal? Or is it a Life Model Decoy of the real Nick Fury? Either way, many heroes with connections to S.H.I.E.L.D. prior to Maria Hill (Captain America, Ms. Marvel, Spider-Woman, and so on) may be glad to see him.

NICK FURY

Nicholas Joseph Fury

Nick Fury distinguished himself during WWII, then joined the CIA and worked for years as an intelligence operative. His eyepatch is due to damage from a Nazi grenade. Eventually he joined S.H.I.E.L.D., starting as an agent and rising to director. He counts Captain America as one of his oldest friends, though the two don't always see eye to eye. Recently Fury ran an unsanctioned black op into Latveria. The fallout from his "Secret War" cost Fury directorship of S.H.I.E.L.D. He's currently in hiding, with numerous agencies seeking his arrest. So far, S.H.I.E.L.D. has kept this development quiet.

Affiliations

SOLO	6	
BUDDY	4	
TEAM	8	

Distinctions

EX-DIRECTOR OF S.H.I.E.L.D.
GRIZZLED VETERAN
WHATEVER IT TAKES

Power Sets

INFINITY FORMULA

ENHANCED REFLEXES 8   ENHANCED STAMINA 8

SFX: *Old Soldiers Never Die.* Spend a doom die to recover physical stress of equal size and step back physical trauma.

SFX: *Seen It All.* Spend a doom die to ignore stress, trauma, and complications caused by aging, shock, surprise, or fear.

Limit: *World-weary.* Step up emotional stress taken from loss, tragedy, or betrayal to step up the lowest die in the doom pool or add a D6 doom die.

33RD DEGREE S.H.I.E.L.D. OFFICER

ENHANCED DURABILITY 8   WEAPON 8

SFX: *LMD.* When stressed out in a Scene, spend a doom die to reveal that it was actually a Life Model Decoy. Fury can no longer act in the Scene but takes no trauma.

SFX: *Spymaster.* Spend a doom die to step up a COVERT MASTER stunt or resource and recover mental or emotional stress.

Limit: *Gear.* Shutdown a 33RD DEGREE S.H.I.E.L.D. OFFICER power to step up the lowest die in the doom pool or add a D6 doom die. Spend a doom die to recover.

Specs

COMBAT MASTER	10	
MENACE EXPERT	8	
VEHICLE MASTER	10	

COVERT MASTER	10
PSYCH EXPERT	8

OPTIONS FOR FINAL BATTLE WITH A.I.M. OR HYDRA

The key for this Scene is making it tie in to the heroes' activity in the Civil War. To that end, here are some more suggestions for mixing it up:

▶ One or more prominent figures in the Pro- or Anti-Registration movement are secretly A.I.M. or Hydra agents. This is best handled with Watcher characters, but make good use of the Milestones and unlockables for A.I.M. and Hydra.

▶ The underlying technology and science behind a lot of the SHRA's resources may turn out to be from A.I.M., rather than Stark or Reed Richards or Hank Pym. If none of these brilliant geniuses are working for S.H.I.E.L.D. in support of the SHRA, perhaps S.H.I.E.L.D. has been depending on A.I.M. scientists for its gear...and now the heroes are able to exploit this knowledge or bring it to light.

▶ What if A.I.M. and Hydra are working together to present themselves as weak or disorganized, all the while waiting for the Civil War to eliminate most of their common enemies? The heroes may discover, as they take the battle to A.I.M. or Hydra's doorstep, that these organizations are not only stronger than they look, but a united force.

▶ What if A.I.M. or Hydra are working with Damage Control, Inc.? You could tie up a number of threads this way, especially if Walter Declun is actually a high-ranking operative. See **Hostile Takeover** for more on Declun.

A.I.M. Unlockables
p. CW28

Hydra Unlockables
p. CW31

ACTION: NEGATIVE ZONE PRISONER BUST

This Scene deals with an initial attempt at thwarting a transfer of prisoners to the Negative Zone's Prison 42, and what the heroes do about it.

The heroes are on site as a group of prisoners are carted off to a Negative Zone gateway in S.H.I.E.L.D. armored personnel carriers. While there are certainly second-string villains in the midst of these prisoners, not every superhuman in the group is a vile criminal. Many simply refused to register or didn't have a chance before bounty hunters rounded them up. You can frame the Scene with the heroes as part of the group transferring the prisoners, or they may be prisoners themselves. They might also be here having attained codes to get close to the Negative Zone gateway (either at Ryker's Island or in the Baxter Building).

Still, it only takes a few bad apples to ruin the bunch, and for some of the particularly rotten criminals in the group, this is their last chance at freedom. A breakout is going to happen. Whether the heroes choose to help or hinder the escape is what turns the tide in this Scene.

The gateway could be either at Ryker's or the Baxter Building, but the former is preferable. It's part of the Ryker's Island penitentiary complex, within a building the SIZE OF A 747 HANGAR. The gateway takes up the far end of the building; a ramp leads up to it and "42" is clearly marked on the side in giant numerals. It has ADAMANTIUM-REINFORCED POWER CABLES D12 and hums loudly. Technicians and Cape-Killers are everywhere. The captured superhumans need to make their move before they pass through the gateway, after which the security and location in another dimension makes escape almost impossible.

IF THE HEROES CHOOSE TO HELP WITH THE ESCAPE:

▶ They'll have to deal with a mob of S.H.I.E.L.D. Cape-Killers led by a pair of elite officers who deeply believe in what they're doing. They've seen enough of what a superhuman can do to know that registration and incarceration is the only chance "normal humans have."

▶ The Cape-Killer unit isn't without backup. Once the doom pool gets to at least 2D10, you can spend D10 doom to introduce support in the form of two operatives of Thunderbolt Division plus an additional operative for every D10 doom you spend.

IF THE HEROES TRY TO PREVENT THE ESCAPE:

▶ At first, only a select group of second-string villains attempt to escape. Treat them as a mob with DESPERATE as a D8 complication. They can and will do anything—including taking hostages and human-shields—in order to escape indefinite detention. The Watcher can and should describe them fighting dirty to get free. Who could blame them, really? If they're taken to the Negative Zone, they may never come back.

▶ If that isn't bad enough, if the fight persists long enough for the doom pool to hit 2D10, you can spend D10 doom to trigger the more passive prisoners to rise up to join the villainous mob. Not because they want to, but because it becomes increasingly clear that life isn't fair, and no one is going to help them but themselves. Add a second mob to the first with the POSSIBLY INNOCENT Distinction.

CAPE-KILLER UNIT

Affiliations

TEAM 8 8 8 8 8

Distinctions

LOYAL TO S.H.I.E.L.D.
TRAINED TO FIGHT SUPERHUMANS

Power Sets

UNIT TRAITS

| BODY ARMOR 8 | COMMS 6 |
| SUBSONIC FLIGHT 6 | TRANQUILIZER GUN 8 |

SFX: *Area Attack.* Against multiple targets, for every additional target add a D6 and keep an additional effect die.

Limit: *Unit Cohesion.* Defeat TEAM dice (with D8 stress) to reduce mob.

Data File

MASTER OFFICER 10

SOLO 6   BUDDY △   TEAM 8
CAPE-KILLER ARMOR 8   HARD-EDGED 8

MOB OF CONVICTS
Various second-stringers, thugs, and bad guys

Affiliations

TEAM 8 8 8 8 8

Distinctions

DANGEROUS
DESPERATE

Power Sets

MOB TRAITS

| GRAB 8 | SWARM 8 |

SFX: *Area Attack.* Against multiple targets, for every additional target add a D6 and keep an additional effect die.

Limit: *Unit Cohesion.* Defeat TEAM dice (with D8 stress) to reduce mob.

ACTION: BREAKING INTO THE NEGATIVE ZONE PRISON

This Action Scene is the climax of Act Three and the fight that the heroes have likely been building up to since their last big conflict at the end of Act Two. It may be broken into multiple Action Scenes depending on how you want to play it, but this section handles it as a single Scene by default.

With this—our big finish—the Anti-Registration forces move against Reed Richards' prison in the Negative Zone. They do so through a gateway at Ryker's Island. However, thanks to a mole within the Secret Avengers, S.H.I.E.L.D. and the Pro-Registration superhumans know of the attempt and prepare an ambush. One of the Anti-Reg members was a mole for the other side (possibly even one of the player heroes, depending on their Milestones) and manages to release the captives. This no-holds-barred, all-star free-for-all frames the conclusion of the Civil War Event.

Frame the Scene initially in the futuristic entry lobby/processing area of Prison 42, the Negative Zone prison. The Anti-Registration side squares off with the Pro-Registration side, including the Thunderbolts; the heroes have a whole prison-full of potential allies if they can somehow open the cell security doors and let them out. Prison 42 is PACKED WITH ADVANCED TECHNOLOGY and includes a number of CONFINED SPACES to hinder big fights like this from happening, so each of these is an immediate concern.

This fight is all about options and possibilities. Since everything the players have done so far leading up to this fight determines who's involved, what the stakes are, and what happens, here are a number of suggestions, but please don't feel limited. **This is the finale.** Don't be afraid to go wild with the doom pool. Complications such as CROWDED and CONFUSING rule the day. With any action, expose weaknesses. Hit every opportunity, use those D4 Distinctions for the Watcher characters, and remember to group minor characters into large mobs for ease of play.

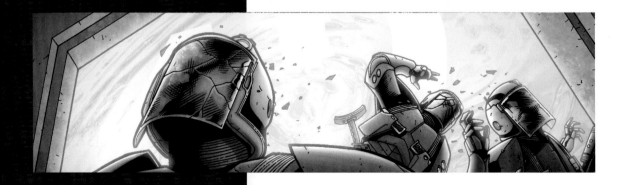

OPTIONS FOR BREAKING INTO THE NEGATIVE ZONE PRISON

▶ This fight should be epic. Drag it to the streets. As things get heated, teleport the entire melee into the streets of New York. Cloak could do this, for example; so might Cable, Deadpool, or Doctor Strange. Be sure that it's a worldwide spectacle, even before any major consequences have occurred. The media is alert and the people are watching.

▶ If the characters push into the Negative Zone, they could end up anywhere with a Negative Zone gate. Be creative. You could use this phenomenon to separate the heroes and increase tension for the big finale.

▶ This is the last Scene in the third and final Act. Unless the players go to amazing lengths to end the fight, there will be death. For Watcher characters, consider being stressed out a near-fatality. Treat this as a Limit on the entire Scene—you can earn D6 doom by having one of the Watcher characters die after being stressed out physically, or you can offer a PP to a player...a reprehensible act for most heroes! A number of bit players should fall in the battle, and at least one major player. The ideal would be a leader—Captain America, Iron Man, or whoever is leading the sides in your story. As a leader dies, the fight should draw to a close. That should be the tipping point. If necessary, use 2D12 to End the Scene at this point.

▶ Raise the stakes. Refer back to previous Scenes. For example, if you used Ragnarok or the Hulk Robot in the fight at the end of Act Two, bring him back. He might return for further destruction, or he might come back fixed and ready to fight for a side. Use every opportunity to remind the players of their past accomplishments and failings.

▶ Remember alliances and rivalries. Hit home with them. If two heroes have been at each other's throats so far, now is the time to bring that to a head. They fight more viciously than ever before, possibly ending in death. Characters they've helped previously step in to take blows or to dish them out.

▶ Betrayal happens at the worst times. These aren't always willful. Maybe a loyal hero was hypnotized, lied to, or mentally controlled to betray their team. This keeps things from being too black and white, and guarantees that fighting ability alone won't win the war.

▶ Use the spotlight. When two heavy hitters go at each other, bring the focus on them for a moment. Be vivid in describing the blow-by-blows. And be sure that no victory is weak or without consequence.

CONCLUSION: WAR'S END

With the dramatic final Scenes of **Act Three**, the Super Hero Civil War draws to a close. There are multiple potential endings to an Event this large and all-encompassing, depending not only on the sides the heroes have taken in the conflict but the resolution of their Milestones and the whims of the dice. The following suggestions tie into the major threads of **Act Three**, but many more are possible.

PRO-REGISTRATION TRIUMPHANT

▶ If the Pro-Registration side triumphs in the climactic battle, the Super Hero Registration Act remains law.

▶ Anti-Registration heroes and any as-yet undecided rogue superhumans are brought in or remain fugitives.

▶ If an opposition leader has been killed or captured, the Anti-Registration fire has temporarily gone out, but enough public opinion may have been swayed in their direction that the SHRA continues to be a divided issue in Congress all the way through the next election cycle.

ANTI-REGISTRATION SCORES THE UPPER HAND

▶ If the Anti-Registration side claims a victory, the outcome is mixed.

▶ SHRA forces are weakened, which leads to further destabilization across the country. Riots, public demonstrations, and similar reactions are likely.

▶ S.H.I.E.L.D. attempts to distance itself from the operation, shifting more and more responsibility onto the U.S. Government and thus the C.S.A. who are tasked under the Act to enforce it.

▶ If the public and the media have largely been on the Anti-Registration heroes' side, the SHRA is overturned.

WAR UNITES THE FACTIONS

▶ Atlantis, A.I.M. or Hydra may have declared war on the United States and other surface nations. If this happens, the two sides of the Super Hero Civil War may initiate a ceasefire and unite against this imminent threat.

▶ The SHRA is probably still intact, but the draconian registration requirements might be relaxed as a nationwide amnesty is put into place.

▶ Notable heroes on either side of the conflict may be convinced of the need for a single unified super hero agency, whether strong armed or not. The Avengers Initiative may be rolled out, but as a volunteer force akin to the U.S. Armed Forces.

PUBLIC DEMANDS CEASEFIRE

▶ There may be no clear outcome other than the public deciding that this constant battle is morally wrong.

▶ Much like the Anti-Registration victory, riots and protests rule the day until the Pro- and Anti-Registration forces can agree on a ceasefire and a better resolution.

▶ Much like in the comics, perhaps a prominent Anti-Registration hero is assassinated when brought to trial, leading to a very different outpouring of public sentiment.

▶ The C.S.A. may create a volunteer-driven Avengers Initiative, with enforcement of super hero activity handed over to individual states, taking it out of Federal hands.

AFTERMATH: CASUALTIES OF WAR

With so much having passed in the space of only a few months, the super hero community is likely changed forever. Some heroes have died, villains have become heroes, powers have been changed, hero teams have divided or split apart. Regardless of the outcome, your own Marvel Universe should reflect the weight of these choices and consequences if you decide to continue the story.

MIGHTY AVENGERS

The Pro-Registration heroes might come together after the Civil War with the backing of the U.S. government and the C.S.A. to serve as the Mighty Avengers, the leading team of registered superhuman agents. Their job is to do what the Avengers have always done—unite against a common threat that no single hero can withstand.

SECRET AVENGERS

In many outcomes, there's still a super hero resistance. Even if the Anti-Registration side triumphed, not all of the heroes involved seek a handshake and a pardon. Their ideologies have been forever cemented in opposition to authority and control, and as long as the government, S.H.I.E.L.D., or anyone else still seeks to control them, they work from the shadows to continue the fight.

YOUNG AVENGERS

The next generation of heroes has seen the worst of their elders during the Civil War. Is it time for them to step up and join that community? Might they seek out other young heroes and band together as their own non-partisan group, or will they side with one faction or the other?

AVENGERS INITIATIVE

In a post-Civil War America, where the SHRA is still active, heroes need to be trained to use their abilities responsibly and in the service of their country. Even if the SHRA is repealed, the Avengers Initiative could arise as a means of settling the dispute between heroes and the government; perhaps on the state level, an Initiative team acts to police its own as an elite force responsible for dealing with superhuman threats.

THUNDERBOLTS

Many villains were promised millions of dollars and a clean slate, no record, if they signed up to be a T-Bolt. This team, potentially one of the largest single groups of superhumans in the nation, may continue after the Civil War in any number of ways. The default is that Norman Osborn is given a director's title and the group operates completely under the C.S.A. as a "scared straight" elite team. But the directorship could easily be handed to somebody else: Clint Barton, Luke Cage, Songbird, Yellowjacket, even Nick Fury! The future of these heroic former villains is wide open.

MUTANT NATION

After the Civil War proves that having powers and being different is still a problem, the remaining mutants who have survived M-Day must decide what to do with themselves. There are many options: fall under the C.S.A.'s mandate; go underground, perhaps the Morlock Tunnels of New York City; flee to another country, such as the Savage Land or Canada; or, like in the comics, form their own Utopia.

SUPPLEMENTING CIVIL WAR

Three supplements are available to further flesh out storylines, characters, and Scenes for the Civil War. Each is a trade paperback book published by Margaret Weis Productions.

- The *Fifty State Initiative Event Supplement* includes ideas to move the story forward with the Avengers Initiative, the Thunderbolts, and the mercenary Heroes for Hire. It includes full hero datafiles for many of these heroes who aren't given the spotlight in this core Event Book, as well as new heroes who appear in the pages of *Avengers: The Initiative*.

- The *Young Avengers/Runaways Event Supplement* deals with teen heroes and renegades caught up in the Civil War. It includes new hero datafiles and characters for many of the teenage super heroes together with the full New Warriors lineup in case you want to turn back the clock to the beginning of the Civil War. What if Speedball wasn't the only survivor of Stamford? What if they were the core of the resistance or the Thunderbolts?

- The *X-Men Event Supplement* covers the survivors of the Decimation and M-Day and their own struggles with registration and authority during the Civil War. It includes many new characters from the pages of *Uncanny X-Men*, *New X-Men*, and *X-Factor*, as well as more details about the Office of National Emergency O*N*E and its Sentinels.

FRIENDS AND FOES

The following section provides game statistics and brief bios of many of the superhuman operatives and rogues active during the Civil War, any of whom may stand against the player heroes or stand with them in the conflict. There are many of them, and you're not expected to use them all, but if you want to expand Civil War beyond the three Acts provided these characters make that easy to do.

Each datafile is written up as a minor character, which is to say that the Affiliations are set at D4/D6/D8. If you want to use them as major characters, just step up each of those Affiliation dice. If you use them as minor characters, you may choose to draw a line through one of their Distinctions, or keep all three.

For those players looking for a challenge, you might offer them one or more of these characters as player heroes. Many of them are heroes in their own right, albeit not as prominent as those listed with the hero datafiles. Remember to adjust their SFX and Limits to reflect using Plot Points instead of doom dice, and step up their Affiliations just as if you were using them as major characters. Players should rely solely on the Event Milestones when choosing Milestones for upgraded characters.

ANT-MAN

Eric O'Grady

Affiliations			Distinctions
SOLO	8		IRREDEEMABLE JERK
BUDDY	4		RELUCTANT LEGACY
TEAM	6		TERRIBLE S.H.I.E.L.D. AGENT

G.I.ANT ARMOR

INSECT CONTROL	6	ENHANCED DURABILITY	8
ENHANCED STRENGTH	8	FLIGHT	6
SHRINKING	10	WALL-CRAWLING	6

SFX *Jet-Flame Burst.* Step up or double FLIGHT for an attack action, then shutdown FLIGHT. Activate an opportunity to recover FLIGHT.

SFX: *Multipower.* Add more than one G.I.ANT ARMOR power die to a pool. Step back each G.I.ANT ARMOR power die in that pool once for each die beyond the first.

Limit: *Gear.* Shutdown G.I.ANT ARMOR power to step up the lowest die in the doom pool or add a d6 doom die. Spend a doom die to recover that power.

Limit: *Small Problem.* Change any G.I.ANT ARMOR power into a complication to step up the lowest die in the doom pool or add a d6 doom die. Activate an opportunity or remove the complication to recover that power.

Specs			
COMBAT EXPERT	8	COVERT EXPERT	8
CRIME EXPERT	8	VEHICLES EXPERT	8

Remarkable mostly for his moral failings and ability to shirk responsibility, Eric O'Grady became the newest Ant-Man by stealing prototype armor designed by Hank Pym. O'Grady seems mostly concerned with spying on attractive women and stealing things. As a S.H.I.E.L.D. agent, Ant-Man is trained in combat, surveillance, and espionage; he's familiar with most S.H.I.E.L.D. procedures, vehicles, weaponry, and personnel. O'Grady has encountered few members of the super hero community so far, but he has spied on Ms. Marvel in the shower—something she's unlikely to forgive if she ever finds out.

ARAÑA

Anya Corazon

Affiliations			Distinctions
SOLO	8		BRAVE
BUDDY	6		NAÏVE
TEAM	4		ROOKIE HERO

EXOSKELETON

ENHANCED DURABILITY	8	ENHANCED REFLEXES	8
ENHANCED SPEED	8	ENHANCED STAMINA	8
SUPERHUMAN STRENGTH	10	WALL-CRAWLING	6

SFX: *Desperate Battler.* Step up or double any EXOSKELETON power for one action. If your action fails, take mental or emotional stress equal to the power trait's original rating.

Limit: *Exhausted.* Shutdown any EXOSKELETON power to step up the lowest die in the doom pool or add a D6 doom die. Activate an opportunity to recover that power.

Limit: *Inexperienced.* Step up the lowest die in the doom pool or add a D6 doom die to step up emotional stress inflicted by violence or hard decisions.

HOMEMADE GRAPPLING HOOKS

SWINGLINE	6	WEAPON	6

SFX: *Grapple.* When inflicting a restraint- or immobilization-type complication on a target, add a D6 and step up the effect die.

Limit: *Gear.* Shutdown HOMEMADE GRAPPLING HOOKS to step up the lowest die in the doom pool or add a D6 doom die. Spend a doom die to recover HOMEMADE GRAPPLING HOOKS.

Specs			
ACROBATICS EXPERT	8	COMBAT EXPERT	8

Recruited by the mysterious Spider Society, teenager Anya Corazon clashed with the Sisterhood of the Wasp. Discovering that the Spider Society had misled her, she passed her role on to another and is now forging a new path as a hero. Araña can spontaneously form a protective exoskeleton around her body, and her physical abilities are noticeably greater than human. She also uses homemade grappling hooks with spider-shaped heads.

ASP

Cleo Nefertiti

Affiliations

SOLO	4
BUDDY	6
TEAM	8

Distinctions

DANGEROUS BEAUTY

LOOKS OUT FOR HER FRIENDS

"REFORMED" VILLAIN

RADIANT BIO-ELECTRICITY

Power Sets

ENHANCED STAMINA 8	VENOM BLAST 8

SFX: *Hands to Yourself.* On a successful reaction against a close-combat attack action, inflict physical stress with the effect die at no doom pool cost. Spend a doom die to step it.

SFX: *Paralyzing Blast.* When inflicting a paralyzing or movement-hindering complication on a target, add a D6 and step up the effect die.

Limit: *Mutant.* When affected by mutant-specific complication or tech, step up the lowest die in the doom pool or add a d6 doom die.

Specs

ACROBATIC EXPERT 8	COVERT EXPERT 8
CRIME EXPERT 8	PSYCH EXPERT 8

Egyptian mutant and exotic dancer Cleo Nefertiti took the name Asp when she joined the Serpent Society. She fought numerous heroes, including Captain America and the members of Alpha Flight, before she left the Serpent Society to form the mercenary group B.A.D. Girls with Diamondback and Black Mamba. Asp's mutation makes her body a battery of dangerous bio-electricity. Prolonged contact with her skin is harmful, even potentially fatal. Strenuous activity recharges her energy; she prefers dancing, but anything that raises her metabolic rate works.

BANTAM

Robert Velasquez

Affiliations

SOLO	8
BUDDY	4
TEAM	6

Distinctions

COULD HAVE BEEN A CONTENDER

EASILY ANGERED

SKILLED BOXING TRAINER

POWER BROKER AUGMENTATION

Power Sets

ENHANCED DURABILITY 8	SUPERHUMAN STAMINA 10
SUPERHUMAN STRENGTH 10	

SFX: *Lose It.* Add a doom die to an attack action. After that action, step back the doom die and return it to the doom pool.

Limit: *Anger Issues.* Add a D6 to the doom pool and step up emotional stress caused by anger or loss of control.

Specs

COMBAT EXPERT 8	MENACE EXPERT 8

Puerto Rican native Robert Velasquez was a talented but undersized boxer. Desperate to win, he let crime boss Armando Aviles convince him to accept the Power Broker's augmentation process. Bantam gained great strength and endurance at the cost of being easily enraged and uncontrollable. After accidentally killing a fellow boxer, he first fought against and then teamed with Captain America to bring down Aviles' syndicate. He now works as a boxing trainer and does some small-time heroics on the side.

BATTLESTAR

Lemar Hoskins

Affiliations

Solo	4
Buddy	8
Team	6

Distinctions

Ex-Soldier
Never Gives Up
Patriotic

Power Sets

POWER BROKER AUGMENTATION

| Enhanced Durability | 8 | Enhanced Reflexes | 8 |
| Superhuman Stamina | 10 | Superhuman Strength | 10 |

SFX: *Focus.* If a pool includes a Power Broker Augmentation power, replace two dice of equal size with one stepped-up die.

SFX: *Second Wind.* Spend a doom die to recover physical stress of an equal die size.

Limit: *Patriot.* Step up the lowest die in the doom pool or add a d6 doom die to step up emotional stress inflicted by government forces or popular opinion.

ADAMANTIUM ALLOY SHIELD

| Superhuman Durability | 10 | Weapon | 6 |

SFX: *Shield Throw.* Step up and double Weapon for one action, then shutdown Adamantium Alloy Shield. Activate an opportunity to recover Weapon.

Limit: *Gear.* Shutdown an Adamantium Alloy Shield power to step up the lowest die in the doom pool or add a d6 doom die. Spend a doom die to recover that power.

Specs

| Acrobatics Expert | 8 | Combat Expert | 8 |
| Menace Expert | 8 | | |

Along with his ex-Army buddies—including John Walker (USAgent)—Chicago-born Lemar Hoskins underwent a human augmentation process created by the infamous Power Broker. When Walker took over as Captain America for a time, Lemar became his partner. Unhappy with being called "Bucky," he became Battlestar. Lemar is a brave man and a devoted patriot, though he sometimes finds himself torn between his devotion to patriotic ideals and various U.S. Government organizations and policies. As Battlestar, he carries an Adamantium alloy shield modeled after Captain America's original triangular one.

BLACK MAMBA

Tanya Sealy

Affiliations

Solo	4
Buddy	6
Team	8

Distinctions

Loyal Friend
Plays Both Sides
Sexy Serpent

Power Sets

DANGEROUS CHARMS

| Darkforce Control | 8 | Psychic Resistance | 8 |
| Telepathy | 8 | | |

SFX: *Deadly Embrace.* Against a character already suffering mental stress, emotional stress, or a complication from another Dangerous Charms roll, step up Darkforce Control.

SFX: *Shadows of the Mind.* When causing mental stress, emotional stress, or complications based around the target's desires and fears, step up Telepathy.

Limit: *Conscious Activation.* While stressed out, asleep, or unconscious, shutdown Dangerous Charms. Recover that stress or wake up to recover Dangerous Charms. If mental trauma received, shutdown Dangerous Charms until trauma recovered.

Specs

| Covert Expert | 8 | Crime Expert | 8 |
| Menace Expert | 8 | Psych Expert | 8 |

A former call girl turned super villain turned mercenary hero, Black Mamba gets her powers from a device implanted in her brain that allows her to craft illusions, read thoughts, and control Darkforce. Black Mamba left the Serpent Society to form the mercenary—and decidedly less villainous—group B.A.D. Girls with Asp and Diamondback. The three friends play the dangerous middle ground between hero-for-hire and mercenary. Black Mamba isn't above breaking the law, but she's also risked her life to save heroes or foil the plans of other villains—when her conscience gets the better of her.

BLACK WIDOW

Affiliations

SOLO	8
BUDDY	4
TEAM	6

Distinctions

DANGEROUS LIAISONS

NATURAL LEADER

RUSSIAN SUPERSPY

RED ROOM CONDITIONING

Power Sets

ENHANCED DURABILITY 8   ENHANCED REFLEXES 8

ENHANCED STAMINA 8

- **SFX:** *Focus.* If a pool includes a RED ROOM CONDITIONING power, replace two dice of equal size with one stepped-up die.
- **SFX:** *Immunity.* Spend a doom die to ignore stress, trauma, or complications from aging, disease, or psychic attack.
- **Limit:** *Deep Programming.* Step up the lowest die in the doom pool or add a D6 doom die to step up emotional stress inflicted by intelligence agencies and their directors.

WIDOW'S GEAR

ELECTRIC BLAST 8   SWINGLINE 8

WALL-CRAWLING 6

- **SFX:** *Full Auto.* In a pool including a ELECTRIC BLAST die, add D6. Remove the highest-rolling die and step up the effect die.
- **SFX:** *Widow's Bite.* Spend a doom die to step up ELECTRIC BLAST to D10; step back to 2D6 for subsequent actions. Activate an opportunity to recover.
- **Limit:** *Gear.* Shutdown WIDOW'S GEAR and step up the lowest die in the doom pool or add a D6 doom die. Spend a doom die to recover WIDOW'S GREAR.

Specs

ACROBATICS MASTER	10	COMBAT EXPERT	8
COVERT MASTER	10	MENACE EXPERT	8
VEHICLES EXPERT	8		

Natasha Romanova

Former Soviet black ops agent Natasha Romanova defected to the United States and joined S.H.I.E.L.D., becoming one of its most decorated and trusted agents. Decades of overcoming Russian conditioning have made her guarded, but she remains loyal to S.H.I.E.L.D. and fond of American heroes such as Iron Man, Hawkeye (Clint Barton), and Captain America.

BROTHER VOODOO

Jericho Drumm

Affiliations
Solo **6**
Buddy **8**
Team **△**

Distinctions
Bound to Dead Brother's Spirit
Esteemed Psychologist
Voodoo Houngan

Power Sets

LORD OF THE LOA

Animal Control **8**   Fire Control **8**
Plant Control **8**   Sorcery Mastery **10**
Teleport **8**

- SFX: *Call on the Loa.* Step up or double any LORD OF THE LOA power for one action. If the action fails, move a die to the doom pool equal to or greater than the normal rating of the power die.
- SFX: *Immunity.* Spend a D6 doom die to ignore stress, trauma, or complications from fire or heat.
- Limit: *Conscious Activation.* While stressed out, asleep, or unconscious, shutdown LORD OF THE LOA. Recover that stress or wake up to recover that LORD OF THE LOA. If emotional trauma received, shutdown LORD OF THE LOA until trauma recovered.
- Limit: *Whims of the Loa.* Shutdown LORD OF THE LOA power to step up the lowest die in the doom pool or add a D6 doom die. Spend a doom die to recover LORD OF THE LOA.

GHOST OF DANIEL DRUMM

Enhanced Durability **8**   Enhanced Strength **8**
Mind Control **10**

- SFX: *Second Wind.* Spend a doom die to recover physical stress of an equal die size.
- Limit: *Two Souls, One Body.* Shutdown MIND CONTROL to use ENHANCED STRENGTH and DURABILITY. Shutdown ENHANCED DURABILITY and ENHANCED STRENGTH to recover MIND CONTROL.

Specs
Combat Expert **8**   Medical Expert **8**
Mystic Master **10**   Psych Master **10**

Joined to his murdered brother's spirit and imparted with vast mystic knowledge and powers, psychologist and scholar Jericho Drumm became Brother Voodoo, Lord of the Loa. Since then, he's fought evil spirits, stopped A.I.M. from creating a zombie army, and recently helped foil a vampire take-over of New Orleans. Brother Voodoo can call upon the Loa for a variety of tasks, including controlling animals, teleporting, and summoning smoke and fire. His brother Daniel's ghost can possess others or use his strength to boost Jericho's own. He occasionally counsels others with a mix of voodoo mysticism and modern psychology.

DIAMONDBACK

Rachel Leighton

Affiliations
Solo 4
Buddy 8
Team 6

Distinctions
Bad Girl Attitude
Romantic at Heart
Skilled Mercenary

Power Sets

GIRL'S BEST FRIEND

Enhanced Durability 8   Weapon 8

- SFX: *Acid-Tipped Diamonds.* Step back the highest die in an attack action pool to add a D6 and step up physical stress inflicted.
- SFX: *Diamond Burst.* Against a single target, step up or double WEAPON die. Remove the highest rolling die and use three dice for the total.
- SFX: *Explosive Diamonds.* Against multiple targets, for each additional target add a D6 and either keep an additional effect die or add a D6 doom die for every two additional targets.
- Limit: *Gear.* Shutdown a GIRL'S BEST FRIEND power to step up the lowest die in the doom pool or add a D6 doom die. Spend a doom die to recover that power.

Specs
Acrobatics Master 10   Combat Expert 8
Covert Expert 8   Crime Expert 8
Vehicles Expert 8

Rachel Leighton joined Taskmaster's academy for training criminals and mercenaries after a severe beating by gang leader Crossbones. Sporting special diamond-shaped throwing weapons, she joined the Serpent Society as Diamondback. But Captain America's good looks and heroism charmed Rachel—she betrayed her companions and aided the Star-Spangled Avenger. After a brief romantic and professional partnership, the pair is still on good terms. With Black Mamba and Asp, Rachel founded the mercenary group B.A.D. Girls. Her throwing diamonds have an array of functions, including acid and explosives. Her brother Danny is the villain-for-hire known as Cutthroat.

DOC SAMSON

Leonard Samson

Affiliations
Solo 8
Buddy 4
Team 6

Distinctions
Famous Psychiatrist
Green-Haired Goliath
Reluctant Super Hero

Power Sets

GAMMA-AUGMENTED POWERHOUSE

Enhanced Speed 8   Leaping 8
Superhuman Durability 10   Superhuman Stamina 10
Superhuman Strength 10

- SFX: Invulnerability. Spend a doom die to ignore physical stress or trauma.
- Limit: *Exhausted.* Shut down any GAMMA-AUGMENTED POWERHOUSE power to step up the lowest die in the doom pool or add a D6 doom die. Activate an opportunity to recover.

Specs
Combat Expert 8   Medical Expert 8
Menace Expert 8   Psych Master 10

While working as Bruce Banner's psychiatrist, Dr. Leonard Skivorski was exposed to the gamma radiation siphoned away from Banner. Together with his gamma-enhanced size and strength, the doctor's hair became long and green, inspiring him to change his name to "Samson." He's superhumanly resilient and can run and leap at far greater levels than humanly possible. He's a famously accomplished psychiatrist with substantial contacts in academic and government circles, including S.H.I.E.L.D and Project: P.E.G.A.S.U.S.

ECHO

Affiliations

Solo 8
Buddy 6
Team 4

Distinctions

Anything You Can Do...
Identity Crisis
Masterless Samurai

PHOTOGRAPHIC REFLEXES

Power Sets

Enhanced Reflexes 8   Enhanced Senses 8
Mimic 10

SFX: *Copycat.* In a close-combat attack or reaction roll where the opponent is using Combat or Acrobatics Specialties, spend a doom die to step up or double a Photographic Reflexes power or stunt.

SFX: *Perfect Counter.* On a successful reaction against a close-combat attack action, inflict physical stress or target an asset with the effect die at no doom pool cost. Spend a doom die to step it up.

Limit: *Deaf.* Step up the lowest die in the doom pool or add a D6 doom die to step up complications relating to darkness or visual impairment.

Limit: *Natural Mimic.* Mimic can only copy trained or skill-based powers or Specialties.

WAYS OF THE WARRIOR

Enhanced Durability 8   Weapon 8

SFX: *Deadly Weapons.* Step back the highest die in an attack action pool to add a D6 and step up physical stress inflicted.

Limit: *Gear.* Shutdown a Ways of the Warrior power to step up the lowest die in the doom pool or add a D6 doom die. Spend a doom die to recover that power.

Specs

Acrobatics Master 10   Combat Master 10

Maya Lopez

Covert Expert 8
Crime Expert 8

Maya Lopez was born deaf but with the ability to mimic any physical action or skills she sees. She was raised by Wilson Fisk, the Kingpin of Crime, who told Maya that Daredevil killed her father. Maya sought revenge, but on discovering Fisk was the true killer, she blinded and nearly killed him instead. She and Daredevil were romantically involved but she broke it off to wander the world in search of her true purpose. For a time, she adopted the costume and name of Ronin, a masterless samurai. She helped the New Avengers battle the Hand ninja in Japan, and has stayed behind to watch over that situation.

EQUINOX

Terry Sorenson

Affiliations
Solo 8
Buddy 6
Team 4

Distinctions
DRIVEN TO VILLAINY
PRONE TO VIOLENCE
UNSTABLE

Power Sets

ALTERED FORM

COLD CONTROL 8	HEAT CONTROL 8
SUPERHUMAN DURABILITY 10	SUPERHUMAN STRENGTH 10
THERMAL BLAST 10	

SFX: *Multipower.* Add more than one Altered Form power die to a pool. Step back each Altered Form power die in that pool once for each die beyond the first.

Limit: *Strain of His Powers.* Step up the lowest die in the doom pool or add a D6 doom die to step up emotional stress from situations where he overuses his powers without rest.

Specs
MENACE EXPERT 8

When one of David Sorenson's experiments exploded, it caught his son Terry in the blast, changing him rather than killing him. As Equinox, Terry Sorenson is noticeably inhuman, partly covered in icy armor and partly in flame. Desperate and already emotionally unstable due to the strain of his powers, Terry turned to crime to gain the funds he needed for a cure. He fought a number of heroes before getting help from Henry Pym and Project: P.E.G.A.S.U.S., which gave him a degree of control over his abilities.

GLADIATRIX

Robin Braxton

Affiliations
Solo 4
Buddy 6
Team 8

Distinctions
BRASH
EX-PRO WRESTLER
SOMETHING TO PROVE

Power Sets

POWER BROKER AUGMENTATION

ENHANCED DURABILITY 8	SUPERHUMAN STAMINA 10
SUPERHUMAN STRENGTH 10	

SFX: *Grapple.* When inflicting a restraining or immobilization complication on a target, add a D6 and step up the effect die.

Limit: *Undisciplined.* If a pool includes a Power Broker Augmentation power, both 1s and 2s on those dice count as opportunities, but only 1s are excluded from being used for totals or effect dice.

Specs
COMBAT EXPERT 8   MENACE EXPERT 8

Formed Unlimited Class Wrestling Federation member Robin "Gladiatrix" Braxton worked with the all-female wrestling group the Grapplers until it disbanded. Transformed into a superhuman powerhouse by the Power Broker, Gladiatrix has tussled with Captain America, B.A.D. Girls, Paladin, and the Soviet Super Soldiers. The Avengers briefly considered her for membership, but rejected her due to a lack of discipline and training. Gladiatrix is a skilled wrestler, but lacks other notable skills and experience.

GOLDBUG

Affiliations
SOLO 8
BUDDY 6
TEAM 4

Distinctions
MIDAS TOUCH
STRATEGIC THINKER
STUCK ON A THEME

Matthew Gilden

Turning his obsession with gold into a motivation and theme for super-villainy, Matthew Gilden became Gold-bug. Using an array of gold-themed gadgets—such as a gun that traps targets in a sheath of gold—and vehicles like an insect-inspired hovership, Goldbug has fought Spider-Man, the Hulk, Luke Cage, and others. Keenly intelligent and technically proficient, Goldbug is often undone by his slavish devotion to his theme.

GOLDEN GEAR

Power Sets
ENHANCED DURABILITY 8   ENHANCED STRENGTH 8
TRANSFORMATION 6

SFX: *Bugship.* Spend a doom die to step up a VEHICLES asset or stunt.

SFX: *Golddust Gun.* When inflicting an immobilization complication on a target, add a D6 and step up the effect die.

Limit: *Gear.* Shutdown a GOLDEN GEAR power to step up the lowest die in the doom pool or add a D6 doom die. Spend a doom die to recover that power.

Specs
CRIME EXPERT 8   TECH EXPERT 8
VEHICLES EXPERT 8

HAWKEYE

Affiliations
SOLO 6
BUDDY 4
TEAM 8

Distinctions
CHIP ON HER SHOULDER
DANGEROUSLY BRAVE
SOCIETY GIRL

Kate Bishop

After suffering a brutal attack in Central Park, young Kate Bishop threw herself into physical training to work through the emotional trauma. Encountering members of the Young Avengers and following them to the ruins of the Avengers HQ, she "appropriated" the leftover equipment of the original Hawkeye (and other Avengers), taking the fallen hero's nickname for her own. Highly skilled in archery, swordsmanship, and unarmed combat, Kate comes from a wealthy family and uses their resources as she needs them.

EXCEPTIONAL TRAINING

Power Sets
ENHANCED REFLEXES 8

SFX: *Versatile.* Split ENHANCED REFLEXES into 2D6.

Limit: *Exhausted.* Shut down EXCEPTIONAL TRAINING power to step up the lowest die in the doom pool or add a D6 doom die. Activate an opportunity to recover.

SPECIAL EQUIPMENT

ENHANCED DURABILITY 8   WEAPON 6

SFX: *Blades and Broadheads.* Step back the highest die in an attack action pool to add a D6 and step up physical stress inflicted.

SFX: *Trick Arrows.* When inflicting a trick-arrow-related (usually grappling or blinding) complication on a target, add a D6 and step up the effect die.

Limit: *Gear.* Shutdown SPECIAL EQUIPMENT to step up the lowest die in the doom pool or add a D6 doom die. Spend a doom die to recover.

Specs
ACROBATICS EXPERT 8   COMBAT EXPERT 8
MENACE EXPERT 8   PSYCH EXPERT 8
VEHICLES EXPERT 8

HULKLING

Teddy Altman

Affiliations

Solo	4
Buddy	8
Team	6

Distinctions

In Love with Wiccan
Levelheaded
Prince of Two Worlds

KREE/SKRULL HYBRID

Power Sets

Flight	6	Growth	6
Shapeshifting	10	Shrinking	6
Superhuman Durability	10	Superhuman Stamina	10
Superhuman Strength	10		

- **SFX:** *Claws and Spines.* Step back the highest die in an attack action pool to add a D6 and step up physical stress inflicted.
- **SFX:** *Resilient Body.* Spend a doom die to ignore physical stress or trauma.
- **Limit:** *Exhausted.* Shut down KREE/SKRULL HYBRID power to step up the lowest die in the doom pool or add a D6 doom die. Activate an opportunity to recover.

Specs

Cosmic Expert	8	Psych Expert	8

When the Super-Skrull unexpectedly arrived to "retrieve" Teddy Altman, Teddy learned he was the son of Kree hero Captain Mar-Vell and Skrull Princess Anelle, smuggled to Earth by his nurse, who had acted as his mother for years. His Skrull-inherited shapeshifting allows him to impersonate people perfectly and grow wings, claws, armor plates, and other physical modifications, while his strength exceeds that of any normal Kree.

KINGPIN

Wilson Fisk

Affiliations

Solo	8
Buddy	6
Team	10

Distinctions

Manipulative
Speed Belying His Size
Utterly Ruthless

SELF-MADE MAN

Power Sets

Enhanced Durability	8	Enhanced Strength	8

- **SFX:** *Boss of Bosses.* Spend a doom die to step up a CRIME MASTER stunt or resource and recover mental or emotional stress.
- **SFX:** *Criminal Empire.* When using BUSINESS or CRIME MASTER to create scene assets or complications, step up the effect die.
- **SFX:** *Grappling.* When inflicting a restraining- or immobilization-type complication on a target, add a D6 and step up the effect die.
- **Limit:** *Your Reach Exceeds Your Grasp.* Spend a resource, asset, or complication created by Kingpin to step up the lowest die in the doom pool or add a D6 doom die.

Specs

Business Master	10	Combat Master	10
Crime Master	10	Menace Master	10
Psych Expert	8		

Wilson Fisk rose from nothing to a formidable figure in organized crime. Publicly an affluent spice merchant, the self-titled Kingpin of Crime runs a vast criminal empire well-protected by an army of high-priced attorneys and loyal henchmen. Fisk's only real soft spot is his wife Vanessa—he's even worked with bitter rival Daredevil when she's threatened. Currently imprisoned, he's trying to "out" Daredevil as attorney Matt Murdoch and secure his own release before one of his numerous enemies brings him down. Fisk's massive bulk may seem obese and slow, but he's a skilled combatant in excellent physical condition.

LECTRONN

Tommy Samuels

Affiliations
- SOLO **8**
- BUDDY **4**
- TEAM **6**

Distinctions
- ALIENS EVERYWHERE
- GUILT-RIDDEN
- HEROIC SCHOOLTEACHER

Power Sets

ATOMIC-POWERED ABILITIES

ELECTRON BLAST **8**	ENHANCED DURABILITY **8**
SUBSONIC FLIGHT **8**	SUPERHUMAN STRENGTH **10**

SFX: *Energy Absorption.* On a successful reaction against an energy-based attack action, convert opponent's effect die into an ATOMIC-POWERED ABILITIES stunt or step up an ATOMIC-POWERED ABILITIES power until used in an action. If opponent's action succeeds, spend a doom die to use this SFX.

Limit: *Self-Doubt.* Step up the lowest die in the doom pool or add a D6 doom die to step up emotional stress caused by doubt, guilt, or self-worth.

Specs

COSMIC EXPERT **8**

High school English teacher Thomas "Tommy" Samuels was stricken by polio until an alien cured him and conferred superhuman powers upon him. He spent several years active as a super hero, until he retired due to crippling self-esteem problems. His wife Amy Jo was spirited away in an invasion by extradimensional aliens because he was out of practice. He has once again taken up the heroic identity of Lectronn, hoping one day to rescue his wife and, in the meantime, recover his confidence.

PATRIOT

Elijah Bradley

Affiliations
- SOLO **4**
- BUDDY **6**
- TEAM **8**

Distinctions
- LEGACY OF LIBERTY
- NATURAL LEADER
- YOUNG AVENGER

Power Sets

BLOOD OF THE SUPER-SOLDIER

ENHANCED DURABILITY **8**	ENHANCED REFLEXES **8**
ENHANCED STAMINA **8**	ENHANCED STRENGTH **8**

SFX: *Immunity.* Spend a doom die to ignore stress, trauma, or complications from poison, disease, or fatigue.

SFX: *Second Wind.* Spend a doom die to recover physical stress of an equal die size.

Limit: *Patriotic Legacy.* Step up emotional stress inflicted by government forces, popular opinion, or personal heroes to step up the lowest die in the doom pool or add a D6 doom die.

STAR-SPANGLED ARSENAL

SUPERHUMAN DURABILITY **10**	WEAPON **6**

SFX: *Throwing Stars.* Against a single target, step up or double WEAPON. Remove the highest rolling die and use three dice for the total.

Limit: *Gear.* Shutdown STAR-SPANGLED ARSENAL power to step up the lowest die in the doom pool or add a D6 to the doom pool. Spend a D6 from doom pool to recover.

Specs

ACROBATICS EXPERT **8**	COMBAT EXPERT **8**
PSYCH EXPERT **8**	

Elijah "Eli" Bradley grew up inspired by his family's heroic legacy as US-sponsored super-soldiers. Joining together with the heirs of other heroic legacies, Eli helped form the Young Avengers. Sporting a costume inspired by his grandfather's, he became Patriot. Eli first gained powers by abusing Mutant Growth Hormone (MGH), a super-steroid. Severely injured in battle, Eli received a blood transfusion from his grandfather, gaining abilities like his grandfather and Captain America. He carries a replica of his grandfather's triangular shield and star-shaped shuriken into battle.

PENANCE

Affiliations

SOLO	8
BUDDY	4
TEAM	6

Distinctions

BROKEN NEW WARRIOR
HAUNTED BY STAMFORD
"I HAVE TO SUFFER"

Robert "Robbie" Baldwin

Sole survivor of the New Warriors team involved in the Stamford disaster, Robbie Baldwin reinvented himself in the wake of the tragedy. No longer the happy-go-lucky Speedball, he became Penance—his costume has one internal spike for each of the 612 victims of Stamford; the 60 longest spikes represent the kids. Penance seeks both punishment and redemption for Stamford. The combination of Robbie's costume, his severe injuries at the hands of guards and inmates while incarcerated, and the bullet fragments lodged near his spine from a failed assassination attempt fuel Penance's purpose and powers.

Power Sets

PENANCE ARMOR

ENHANCED DURABILITY 8

> **SFX:** *Area Attack.* Against multiple targets, for each additional target add a D6 and keep an additional effect die.
>
> **SFX:** *Power in Pain.* Step up your emotional or physical stress to step up and double a SPEEDBALL EFFECT power.
>
> **Limit:** *612.* Step up the lowest die in the doom pool or add a D6 doom die to step up mental stress or trauma taken from authorities, public opinion, or confronting victims of superhuman actions.
>
> **Limit:** *Gear.* Shutdown PENANCE ARMOR to step up the lowest die in the doom pool or add a D6 doom die. Spend a doom die to recover PENANCE ARMOR.

SPEEDBALL EFFECT

KINETIC BLAST 8   **LEAPING** 8

SUPERHUMAN DURABILITY 10

> **SFX:** *Invulnerability.* Spend a doom die to ignore physical stress or trauma.
>
> **SFX:** *Rebound Attack.* On a successful reaction against a kinetic-based attack action, convert opponent's effect die into a SPEEDBALL EFFECT stunt or step up KINETIC BLAST until used in an action. If opponent's action succeeds, spend a doom die to use this SFX.
>
> **Limit:** *Uncontrollable.* Change any SPEEDBALL EFFECT power into a complication and step up the lowest die in the doom pool or add a d6 doom die. Activate an opportunity or remove the complication to recover the power.

Specs

ACROBATICS EXPERT 8   **COMBAT EXPERT** 8

PLUNDERER

Affiliations
SOLO ⑧
BUDDY ⑥
TEAM ④

Distinctions
BLACK SHEEP OF THE FAMILY
BRITISH ARISTOCRAT
TREACHEROUS PIRATE

Parnival Plunder

Younger brother of Lord Kevin Plunder (AKA Ka-Zar), Parnival Plunder seized the family's ancestral holdings and stockpile of Antarctic Vibranium (Anti-Metal) and used this to fuel his own criminal ambitions as a modern-day pirate. Discovering his presumed-dead brother alive in the Savage Land, he has tried since to destroy Ka-Zar and exploit the resources of his brother's adopted home. He has clashed with others as well, most notably Daredevil. The Plunderer is wealthy, resourceful, and treacherous, often using agents, pawns, and proxies.

ANTI-METAL ARSENAL
WEAPON ⑧

Power Sets

SFX: *Pirate King.* Spend a doom die to step up a Crime Master or Vehicle Expert stunt or resource and recover mental or emotional stress.

SFX: *Vibra-Ray.* When using an Anti-Metal Arsenal power in an attack action against metallic objects or characters, add a D6 and step up effect die.

Limit: *Gear.* Shutdown an ANTI-METAL ARSENAL power to step up the lowest die in the doom pool or add a D6 doom die. Spend a doom die to recover that power.

Specs

BUSINESS EXPERT ⑧		COMBAT EXPERT ⑧	
COVERT EXPERT ⑧		CRIME MASTER ⑩	
MENACE EXPERT ⑧		TECH EXPERT ⑧	
VEHICLES EXPERT ⑧			

PRODIGY

Affiliations
SOLO ⑧
BUDDY ⑥
TEAM ④

Distinctions
EMOTIONALLY VOLATILE
JOCK
TRYING TO BE A BETTER HERO

Ritchie Gilmore

Captain of his school's wrestling team, Ritchie Gilmore was one of the four heroes brought together by the Black Marvel to form the Slingers. Sporting a mystically powered version of a costume briefly worn by Spider-Man, he became Prodigy. As Prodigy, Ritchie was a fairly effective but obsessive hero—and a callous teammate and leader. Confronted with his attitude problems, Prodigy has been taking steps to do better but his tendency to drink too much and act without thinking things through makes this a rocky road.

MYSTIC COSTUME

Power Sets

 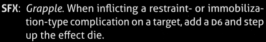

FLIGHT ⑥		LEAPING ⑧	
SUPERHUMAN STAMINA ⑩		SUPERHUMAN STRENGTH ⑩	

SFX: *Grapple.* When inflicting a restraint- or immobilization-type complication on a target, add a D6 and step up the effect die.

SFX: *Multipower.* Add more than one MYSTIC COSTUME power die to a pool. Step back each MYSTIC COSTUME power die in that pool once for each die beyond the first.

Limit: *Gear.* Shutdown a MYSTIC COSTUME power to step up the lowest die in the doom pool or add a D6 doom die. Spend a doom die to recover power.

Specs

ACROBATICS EXPERT ⑧   COMBAT EXPERT ⑧

THE SENTRY

Robert "Bob" Reynolds

Affiliations

Solo	8
Buddy	6
Team	4

Distinctions

Golden Guardian of Good

Neutral Observer

Phobic

Power Sets

Power of a Million Exploding Suns

Godlike Durability	12	Godlike Stamina	12
Godlike Strength	12	Light Blast	10
Light Supremacy	12	Superhuman Senses	10
Superhuman Speed	10	Space Flight	12

SFX: *C.L.O.C.* In a pool including a Tech resource, remove the largest die from that pool and use three dice for the total.

SFX: *Multipower.* Add more than one Power of a Million Exploding Suns power die to a pool. Step back each Power of a Million Exploding Suns power die in that pool once for each die beyond the first.

SFX: *Unleashed.* Double any Power of a Million Exploding Suns power for one action. If the action fails, spend a doom die equal to or larger than the normal rating of the unleashed die.

Limit: *Fear of the Void.* Use the two lowest-rolling dice for the total of a reaction roll to step up the lowest die in the doom pool or add a d6 doom die.

Limit: *Growing Dread.* If a pool includes a Power of a Million Exploding Suns power, both 1s and 2s on those dice count as opportunities, but only 1s are excluded from being used for totals or effect dice.

Specs

Combat Expert	8	Cosmic Expert	8
Psych Expert	8	Tech Expert	8

Bob Reynolds was the most powerful active super hero for over a decade, until his catastrophic alter ego, the Void, shattered his confidence. To save everyone he loved, Bob used his vast powers to remove himself from the world's memory. Recently, Bob re-emerged into an era that knows nothing of him, crippled with phobias but ready to rejoin the super hero community. He is unwilling to take any sides in a conflict between heroes, however, lest the Void return and destroy everything. He is aided in his mission by C.L.O.C., a Centrally Located Organic Computer.

SHROUD

Maxmillian Quincy Coleridge

Affiliations
SOLO 8
BUDDY 4
TEAM 6

Distinctions
KEEN TACTICIAN
MYSTERIOUS VIGILANTE
TRAINED BY THE CULT OF KALI

Power Sets

KISS OF KALI

ENHANCED REFLEXES 8   ENHANCED STAMINA 8
SUPERHUMAN SENSES 10

- **SFX:** *Immunity.* Spend a doom die to ignore stress, trauma, or complications from attacks targeting sight or vision.
- **SFX:** *ESP.* Spend a doom die to add SUPERHUMAN SENSES (or step up if already in a pool) and reroll.
- **Limit:** *Sensory Overload.* Shutdown any KISS OF KALI power to step up the lowest die in the doom pool or add a D6 doom die. Activate an opportunity to recover that power.

MASTER OF DARKNESS

DARKFORCE MASTERY 10   FLIGHT 6
INVISIBILITY 6

- **SFX:** *Area Attack.* Against multiple targets, for each additional target add a D6 and keep an additional effect die.
- **SFX:** *Blinding Darkness.* When inflicting a vision-imparing complication on a target, add a D6 and step up the effect die.
- **Limit:** *Conscious Activation.* While stressed out, asleep, or unconscious, shutdown MASTER OF DARKNESS. Recover that stress or wake up to recover that MASTER OF DARKNESS. If mental trauma received, shutdown MASTER OF DARKNESS until trauma recovered.

Specs

ACROBATICS EXPERT 8   COMBAT MASTER 10
COVERT EXPERT 8   CRIME MASTER 10
MENACE EXPERT 8   VEHICLES EXPERT 8

After his parents' murders, young Max Coleridge devoted his life to fighting crime. He learned martial arts in the Far East and joined the mysterious Cult of Kali. The "Kiss of Kali," a brand marking him as one of the cult's chosen, blinded Max and gave him supernatural extrasensory perception. Returning stateside, Max became the Shroud, and his latent ability to summon Darkforce awakened. He posed as a super villain and crime boss, using this status to bring down real criminals. He has resumed more traditional super heroics and developed a relationship with Arachne. He often uses explosive boomerang-like "bombarangs."

SOLO

Affiliations

Solo	8
Buddy	6
Team	4

Distinctions

Ex-Special Forces
Man Without a Country
"While Solo Lives Terror Dies!"

Power Sets

OMEGA STRIKE PROGRAM

Enhanced Reflexes 8   Teleport 8

SFX: *Push Limits.* Step up and double Teleport for one action, then shutdown Omega Strike Program. Activate an opportunity to recover Omega Strike Program.

Limit: *Fanatic.* Step up mental or emotional stress or trauma relating to acts of terrorism to step up the lowest die in the doom pool or add a D6 doom die.

PERSONAL ARMORY

Enhanced Durability 8   Weapon 8

SFX: *Full-Auto.* Against a single target, step up or double Weapon. Remove the highest rolling die and use three dice for the total.

Limit: *Gear.* Shutdown a Personal Armory power to step up the lowest die in the doom pool or add a D6 doom die. Spend a doom die to recover.

Specs

Combat Master 10   Covert Expert 8
Crime Expert 8   Menace Expert 8

James Bourne

After James' lover was killed in a terrorist attack, he joined Omega Strike and was trained in counter-terrorism tactics and covert operations; cybernetics granted him the ability to teleport short distances. James left Omega Strike after his team was killed during an operation. Armed with military-grade weapons and body armor, he began a one-man war on terror as Solo, until he accidentally killed an innocent girl. Grief-stricken, Solo turned himself in and went to prison. Recently released, Solo started up his one-man war once again. His current whereabouts are unknown, but he's presumably still working to annihilate terrorism.

SPEED

Affiliations

Solo	8
Buddy	4
Team	6

Distinctions

Cocky
Headstrong
Juvie Record

Power Sets

HYPERFAST EXISTENCE

Godlike Reflexes 12   Godlike Speed 12

SFX: *All Over the Place in the Blink of an Eye.* Against multiple targets, for each additional target add a D6 and keep an additional effect die.

SFX: *Can't Touch This.* Double a Hyperfast Existence power for one reaction to an attack action. If the reaction fails, spend a doom die equal to or greater than the normal rating of the power die.

SFX: *Hyperkinetic Vibrations.* Step back the highest die in an attack action pool to add a D6 and step up physical stress inflicted.

SFX: *Machine Gun Punches.* Against a single target, step up or double a Godlike Reflexes die. Remove the highest rolling die and use three dice for the total.

Limit: *Exhausted.* Shut down Hyperfast Existence power to step up the lowest die in the doom pool or add a D6 doom die. Activate an opportunity to recover.

Limit: *Hothead.* Step up the lowest die in the doom pool or add a D6 doom die to step up emotional stress from opponents that provoke or otherwise tick off Speed.

Specs

Crime Expert 8

Thomas Shepherd

The product of a broken home, Thomas Shepherd had already developed his powers and used them destructively when the Young Avengers found him in a high-tech juvenile facility and offered him a place on their team as "Speed." Thomas lives up to his codename, demonstrating the ability to move much faster than Mach 1. Another trick he is fond of showing off is generating hyperkinetic vibrations by accelerating molecular motion in matter to an explosive degree.

STATURE

Solo	4		**Ant-Man's Daughter**
Buddy	6		**Emotional Teenager**
Team	8		**Naïve Courage**

Affiliations · *Distinctions*

NOW I'M BIG

Power Sets

Enhanced Stamina	8	**Growth**	10
Superhuman Durability	10	**Superhuman Strength**	10

SFX: *Gargantuan.* Step up or double a Now I'm Big power for an action. If the action fails, spend a doom die equal to or larger than the normal rating of the power die.

Limit: *Angry Young Woman.* Change Growth into an anger-related complication to step up the lowest die in the doom pool or add a d6 doom die.

NOW I'M SMALL

Enhanced Reflexes	8	**Shrinking**	10

SFX: *Can't Hit Me Now.* Step up or double an Now I'm Small power for the next reaction. If the reaction fails, spend a doom die equal to or larger than the normal rating of the power die.

Limit: *Guilt Complex.* Change Shrinking into a guilt-related complication to step up the lowest die in the doom pool or add a d6 doom die.

Limit: *Mutually Exclusive.* Shutdown Now I'm Big **to activate** Now I'm Small. Shutdown Now I'm Small **to recover** Now I'm Big.

Specs

Psych Expert 8

Cassie Lang grew up wanting to follow in the footsteps of her dad, Ant-Man Scott Lang. Devastated by her dad's death during the dissolution of the old Avengers, Cassie planned to run away when she encountered the Young Avengers. A mood swing during that encounter triggered powers related to her repeated exposure to Pym particles. She discovered her emotions influence her power to grow and shrink. Currently she's working out the difficulties of leading a costumed career that her mother and stepfather *strenuously* object to.

STINGRAY

Walter Newell

Affiliations

SOLO	6
BUDDY	8
TEAM	4

Distinctions

DEVOTED TO HIS WORK
SEA-BASED HERO
WORLD-CLASS OCEANOGRAPHER

Oceanographer and marine researcher Walter Newell has worked with Prince Namor, the Sub-Mariner, to develop numerous underwater inventions, including the battlesuit that lets him be Stingray, part-time hero and protector of the oceans. He married Diane Arliss, sister to Tiger Shark. The couple has twin children, Tommy and Lisa. Though usually focused on undersea research, salvage, and rescue operations, Stingray has aided many heroes over the years, mostly fighting villains operating in the world's oceans. He currently co-administrates an undersea research facility—a joint Atlantean-Human project dubbed Hydropolis—with his wife.

Power Sets

AMPHIBIOUS BATTLESUIT

CYBERNETIC SENSES	6	ELECTRIC BLAST	8
ENHANCED DURABILITY	8	FLIGHT	6
SUPERHUMAN STRENGTH	10	SWIMMING	10

SFX: *Artificial Cartilage.* Step up ENHANCED DURABILITY for a reaction roll against blunt, explosive, or crushing force, then step back. Activate an opportunity to recover.

SFX: *Immunity.* Spend a D6 doom die to ignore physical stress or trauma caused by pressure, suffocation, or electricity.

SFX: *Multipower.* Add more than one AMPHIBIOUS BATTLESUIT power die to a pool. Step back each AMPHIBIOUS BATTLESUIT power die in that pool once for each die beyond the first.

Limit: *Systems Malfunction.* Shutdown an AMPHIBIOUS BATTLESUIT power to step up lowest die in the doom pool or add a D6 doom die. Activate an opportunity to recover that power.

Specs

BUSINESS EXPERT	8	SCIENCE EXPERT	8
TECH MASTER	10	VEHICLES EXPERT	8

THUNDERCLAP

Stanley George Johnson

Affiliations

SOLO	8
BUDDY	4
TEAM	6

Distinctions

DODGES RESPONSIBILITY
SONIC-POWERED SALESMAN
WANNABE SUPER HERO

An unsuccessful London electronics salesman, Stanley Johnson decided to try his hand at super-heroics. Creating a costume that generated targeted sonic booms, he traveled to New York to debut as Thunderclap. He teamed up with Spider-Man, against the wall-crawler's wishes. Despite doing far more harm than good, Thunderclap received credit by the *Daily Bugle* for the criminals Spidey actually apprehended. Thunderclap hasn't been seen much in recent years, but he's presumably still practicing his own brand of mostly ineffectual super-heroics.

Power Sets

SONIC GAUNTLETS

SONIC BLAST	10	SONIC RESISTANCE	10

SFX: *Area Attack.* Against multiple targets, for each additional target add a D6 and keep an additional effect die.

SFX: *Boom!* When inflicting a deafening or intense sound-based complication on a target, add a D6 and step up the effect die.

Limit: *Gear.* Shutdown a SONIC GAUNTLETS power to step up the lowest die in the doom pool or add a D6 doom die. Spend a doom die to recover that power.

Specs

 TECH EXPERT | 8

TYPEFACE

Thomas Gordon

Affiliations
- Solo 8
- Buddy 4
- Team 6

Distinctions
- Ex-Military
- Not All There
- Would-Be Revolutionary

LETTER-THEMED ARSENAL

Weapon 8

- **SFX:** *Area Attack.* Against multiple targets, for each additional target add a D6 and keep an additional effect die.
- **Limit:** *Gear.* Shutdown Letter-Themed Arsenal to step up the lowest die in the doom pool or add a D6 doom die. Spend a doom die to recover Letter-Themed Arsenal.

Combat Expert 8   Covert Expert 8

Ex-soldier Thomas Gordon lost his mind shortly after losing his job at Ace Signs. Armed with letter and word-themed weapons, he began a one-man campaign of sabotage and vandalism against advertisements and signs as Typeface. Stopped by Spider-Man, Typeface eventually settled down, even helping the web-slinger once. Now a recovering mental patient and would-be vigilante, Typeface resurfaces from time to time. Despite his strange theme, Thomas is a skilled combatant and a fair strategist. He's also just pretty nuts.

VISION

Affiliations
- Solo 4
- Buddy 6
- Team 8

Distinctions
- In Love with Stature
- Mix of Advanced and Future Tech
- Synthezoid

ARTIFICIAL FORM

Electronic Senses 8	Enhanced Durability 8
Enhanced Strength 8	Flight 6
Intangibility 10	Shapeshifting 8
Solar Blast 8	Superhuman Stamina 10

- **SFX:** *Computerized Intellect.* When creating intellect-related assets, add a D6 and step up the effect die.
- **SFX:** *Disruption.* When including Intangibility in an attack action, add a D6 and step up the effect die.
- **Limit:** *Inexperienced with Emotion.* Step up emotional stress in situations when attempting to use or understand human emotions to step up the lowest die in the doom pool or add a D6 doom die.

HYPER-DENSITY

Superhuman Durability 10   Superhuman Strength 10

- **SFX:** *Diamond-Hard Body.* Step up or double any Hyper-Density power for one action. If the action fails, spend a doom die equal to or larger than the normal rating of that power die.
- **Limit:** *Mutually Exclusive.* Shutdown Flight and Intangibility to activate Hyper-Density. Shutdown Hyper-Density to activate Flight and Intangibility.
- **Limit:** *Too Heavy.* Change Hyper-Density into a complication and step up the lowest die in the doom pool or add a D6 doom die. Activate an opportunity or remove the complication to recover Hyper-Density.

Combat Expert 8   Science Expert 8
Tech Expert 8

The new Vision is a synthetic body formed from neuro-kinetic armor originating at least a thousand years in the future and housing an "artilect" (artificial intellect) that operates as a mix of the old Vision's persona programming and Iron Lad's brain patterns. The synthetic body is functionally superior to a human body's performance and can alter its density to become intangible or hyper-dense. It also possesses holo-morphic functions enabling cosmetic disguise and a solar-based energy discharge.

WICCAN

Billy Kaplan

Affiliations
Solo 4
Buddy 8
Team 6

Distinctions
COMPLICATED ORIGIN
DOESN'T REALLY UNDERSTAND HIS POWERS
IN LOVE WITH HULKLING

MAGICAL REALITY ALTERATION
Power Sets

EXPERT SORCERY 8   LIGHTNING BLAST 8

SUBSONIC FLIGHT 8

SFX: *Area Effect.* Against multiple targets, for each additional target add a D6 and keep an additional effect die.

SFX: *Magic Mantra.* When using a MAGICAL REALITY ALTERATION power to create magical assets or inflict magical complications, add a D6 and step up the effect die.

SFX: *Multipower.* Add more than one MAGICAL REALITY ALTERATION power die to a pool. Step back each MAGICAL REALITY ALTERATION power die in that pool once for each die beyond the first.

SFX: *Power at a Cost.* Step up EXPERT SORCERY for the rest of the Scene. For every step up, spend a doom die equal to the new die size, then inflict a Scene-based complication equal to the new die size on all present.

SFX: *Versatile, but Dangerous.* Split EXPERT SORCERY into 2D6 or 3D4.

Limit: *Conscious Activation.* While stressed out, asleep, or unconscious, shutdown MAGICAL REALITY ALTERATION. Recover that stress or wake up to recover MAGICAL REALITY ALTERATION. If emotional trauma received, shutdown MAGICAL REALITY ALTERATION until trauma recovered.

Limit: *Exhausted.* Shutdown any MAGICAL REALITY ALTERATION power to step up the lowest die in the doom pool or add a D6 doom die. Activate an opportunity to recover that power.

Specs
MYSTIC EXPERT 8   PSYCH EXPERT 8

The son of a pair of well-educated and highly successful parents, Billy Kaplan led a fairly normal life, albeit one where he suffered school bully-ing with some frequency. His powers manifested after he met and received healing and guidance from the Scar-let Witch. Wiccan now possesses a limited ability to alter reality at will, chanting a mantra cen-tered on what he wants to happen. He also has potential for developing great mystical ability, though he remains mostly untrained in that regard.

WILDSTREAK

Tamika Bowden

Affiliations
Solo 8
Buddy 6
Team 4

Distinctions
OLYMPIC-CLASS GYMNAST
PARAPLEGIC
PERSONAL MISSION

ENHANCING EXOSKELETON
Power Sets

ENHANCED DURABILITY 8   ENHANCED REFLEXES 8

ENHANCED SPEED 8   ENHANCED STAMINA 8

ENHANCED STRENGTH 8

SFX: *Focus.* If a pool includes an ENHANCING EXOSKELETON power, replace two dice of equal size with one stepped-up die.

SFX: *Multipower.* Add more than one ENHANCING EXOSKELETON power die to a pool. Step back each ENHANCING EXOSKELETON power die in that pool once for each die beyond the first.

Limit: *Power Loss.* Shutdown any ENHANCING EXOSKELETON power to step up the lowest die in the doom pool or add a D6 doom die. Activate an opportunity to recover that power.

Specs
ACROBATICS MASTER 10   COMBAT EXPERT 8

CRIME EXPERT 8

Crippled after her father refused to work for crime boss "Big" John Bus-celli, Tamika Bowden lost her dreams of Olympic gold. Wishing to restore his daughter's mobility, her inventor father designed an exoskeleton to re-store and amplify her physical abili-ties. Devoted to making a difference and bringing down Buscelli, Tamika became Wildstreak. Working mostly on her own, she has met some other heroes, notably the Thing and Thunder-strike. She focused most of her hero-ics on taking down Buscelli's syndicate, crippling the crimi-nal's operations like he did her body.

HERO DATAFILE

For the CIVIL WAR Event, we've provided a number of heroes suitable for this major period in the history of the Marvel Universe. Many of these heroes are members or past members of various teams such as the Avengers or Fantastic Four, while others remain independent. Your players are free to decide their current membership during the course of the game as sides are chosen and battles are fought. Each datafile includes a pair of Milestones that represent recurring plotlines specific to the hero.

For the sake of continuity, note that these datafiles reflect the heroes after the *House of M*, shortly before the passing of the Superhuman Registration Act. Two heroes, **Black Panther** and **Sub-Mariner**, are not available at the beginning of Act One but may be unlocked using XP during the Event or recruited from specific Scenes in Act Two. As always, each hero datafile may be tweaked or adjusted to suit the needs of your players. Refer to Chapter Four of the OPERATIONS MANUAL for definitions, guidelines, and rules for doing so.

Hero datafiles that are not chosen by players may be converted into Watcher characters for use as antagonists or occasional allies. Remember to switch their SFX and Limits to reflect using doom dice instead of Plot Points. Even if the players don't use them, these heroes remain major characters and should keep their Affiliations at their listed ratings.

- Ⓐ = Avengers
- ④ = Fantastic Four
- 🛡 = S.H.I.E.L.D.
- ⊗ = X-Men
- ◯ = Unaffiliated at the time of Civil War

ARACHNE

STRESS / TRAUMA

Affiliations

SOLO **6**　　BUDDY **8**　　TEAM **10**

Distinctions

DEVOTED MOTHER
PART-TIME HERO
RELUCTANT GOVERNMENT AGENT

4 +1 PP　or　**8**

Power Sets

SPIDER-SERUM

SUPERHUMAN REFLEXES **10**	ENHANCED SENSES **8**
ENHANCED STAMINA **8**	SUPERHUMAN STRENGTH **10**

SFX: *Focus.* If your pool includes a SPIDER-SERUM power, you may replace two dice of equal size with one stepped-up die.

Limit: *Exhausted.* Shutdown any SPIDER-SERUM power to gain 1 PP. Recover by activating an opportunity or during a Transition Scene.

PSI-WEBS

ENHANCED DURABILITY **8**	SWINGLINE **8**
WALL-CRAWLING **6**	WEAPON **8**

SFX: *Ensnare.* When inflicting a web-related complication on a target, add a D6 and step up your effect die.

SFX: *Web Control.* When creating web-related assets, add D6 and step up your effect die.

Limit: *Conscious Activation.* While stressed out, asleep, or unconscious, shutdown PSI-WEBS. Recover PSI-WEBS when you recover that stress or wake up. If you take emotional trauma, shutdown PSI-WEBS until you recover that trauma.

Specialties

ACROBATIC EXPERT **8**	COMBAT EXPERT **8**
COVERT EXPERT **8**	MENACE EXPERT **8**
PSYCH EXPERT **8**	

[You may convert Expert D8 to 2D6, or Master D10 to 2D8 or 3D6]

P △4 6 8 10 12
M △4 6 8 10 12
E △4 6 8 10 12

Milestones

GOVERNMENT TIES

1 XP when you take down a wanted criminal or fugitive.

3 XP when you find a loophole in your governmental ties so you can break the law.

10 XP when you either bring in another hero wanted by the authorities or refuse and become a fugitive yourself.

SUPER MOM

1 XP when you either tell your daughter a story about your adventures or tell your allies a story about your daughter.

3 XP when you treat an enemy like a petulant child.

10 XP when you either incorporate your life as a mother fully into your super heroics or keep your daughter well away from your masked adventures.

XP

History

Recruited by college friend Valerie Cooper, struggling single mom Julia Carpenter participated in an experiment by the Committee for Superhuman Affairs (CSA), unaware its purpose was to create superhuman covert operatives. Julia gained a number of superhuman powers and joined the CSA under the codename Spider-Woman. One of the heroes abducted to an alien world by the extra-dimensional and godlike Beyonder, she unwillingly fought in his "Secret Wars." It was here she met many of Earth's premiere heroes, impressing several of them with her power, courage, and skill.

Returned to Earth, Julia worked alongside former super criminals in the government-run Freedom Force. When they tried to arrest the Avengers on trumped-up treason charges, she quit the team and chose to aid the heroes instead. Julia eventually became an Avenger herself, serving on the team's West Coast branch. Due to her double life of secret identities and long absences, she lost custody of her daughter Rachel to her ex-husband. When he was later killed, she was reunited with her child.

Villainess Charlotte Witter attacked Julia and stole her powers and the Spider-Woman mantle. Depowered and severely injured, Julia retired from super heroics completely. Eventually she recovered, her powers restored with the aid of Max Coleridge, the mysterious vigilante known as the Shroud. Julia gave up the Spider-Woman moniker out of deference to the returned Jessica Drew, but she returned to heroics part-time as Arachne. Her primary focus is her personal life—her daughter and Coleridge, who she's grown very close to.

Personality

Julia is capable, compassionate, and totally devoted to her loved ones. After several bad experiences, she doesn't trust most government organizations or officials, particularly those with ties to her old bosses at the CSA. She often finds herself working with them anyway—just not always enthusiastically—since their resources and influence help her protect and provide for her daughter. Her love for Rachel is both her greatest source of inner strength and a weakness the ruthless can exploit.

Abilities & Resources

Arachne's physical abilities are similar to Spider-Man and Spider-Woman—superhuman agility and strength, extraordinary senses and endurance. In addition, with her psychokinetic powers she can create web-like psychic constructs to ensnare foes, create swinglines, and crawl on walls like a spider. Trained as a government agent and spy, she's skilled in close combat, espionage operations, stealth, and acrobatics.

Julia is on good terms with most other arachnid-themed heroes, including Peter Parker, Jessica Drew, and one-time Spider-Woman Mattie Franklin. She has close friends and allies among the Avengers, particularly Ms. Marvel, Wonder Man, and Iron Man. Recently, she's also grown close to the mysterious Shroud. Though she's a former member of the CSA's Freedom Force team, she really doesn't consider that group as allies or friends. She does have contacts within various government agencies, however. She's still close to her parents, Walter and Elizabeth Cornwall, who take care of her daughter on occasion.

BLACK PANTHER

Affiliations	Solo **10**	Buddy **6**	Team **8**

Distinctions

King of Wakanda
Peerless Strategist
World-Class Intellect

△ 4 +1 PP or **8**

Power Sets

WAKANDAN TECHNO-RAIMENT

Cybernetic Senses **6**	Enhanced Durability **8**
Wall-Crawling **6**	Weapon **8**

SFX: *Ebony Blade.* If your attack action pool includes a Weapon power, you may step back the highest die to add a D6 and step up the physical stress inflicted.

SFX: *Energy Absorption.* On a successful reaction against an energy-based action, convert your opponent's effect die into a Wakandan Techno-Raiment stunt or step up a Wakandan Techno-Raiment power until used in an action. If your opponent's action succeeds, spend 1 PP to use this SFX.

SFX: *Mystic Armory.* At the cost of creating a resource, you may step up or double Weapon or Enhanced Durability for the duration of a resource.

Limit: *Gear.* Shutdown a Wakandan Techno-Raiment power to gain 1 PP. Take an action vs. the doom pool to recover.

CHOSEN OF THE PANTHER GOD

Enhanced Reflexes **8**	Enhanced Senses **8**
Enhanced Stamina **8**	Enhanced Strength **8**

SFX: *Focus.* If your pool includes a Chosen of the Panther God power, you may replace two dice of equal size with one stepped-up die.

SFX: *Panther Champion.* Before you take an action including a Chosen of the Panther God power, you may move your mental and emotional stress dice to the doom pool and step up the Chosen of the Panther God power for this action.

Limit: *Fit to Rule.* May not spend PP when making reaction rolls during ritual or mystical combat or when facing challenges to your title.

Specialties

Acrobatic Master **10**	Combat Master **10**
Covert Master **10**	Menace Expert **8**
Mystic Expert **8**	Science Expert **8**
Tech Expert **8**	Vehicles Expert **8**

[You may convert Expert D8 to 2D6, or Master D10 to 2D8 or 3D6]

Milestones

LEARNING ABOUT MUTANTS

1 XP when you ask Storm, or a mutant ally, a question about mutant history or culture.

3 XP when you get into a conflict with a mutant or an enemy of mutant-kind.

10 XP when you either join an X-team as an honorary member or create a team for you and your wife to lead.

SHREWD INTELLECT

1 XP when you use Science Expert to create an asset for an Action Scene.

3 XP when you utilize Wakandan technology to do physical stress to an opponent.

10 XP when you either decide to use Wakandan science to change the world for the better or take away Wakandan-made Vibranium tools and weapons that are outside of your nation's boundaries.

PP

STRESS / TRAUMA

P △4 6 8 10 12
M △4 6 8 10 12
E △4 6 8 10 12

XP

History

Latest in a long line of warrior-statesmen, T'Challa rules the African nation of Wakanda as their champion and king, the Black Panther. His nation's advanced technology and the world's only abundant source of the mysterious metal Vibranium has meant centuries of isolation and secrecy. This changed when opportunistic fortune hunter, Ulysses Klaw, killed T'Chaka, T'Challa's father and then current Black Panther. Swearing to avenge his father and take his place as the new Black Panther, T'Challa studied and trained, eventually passing the trials of leadership and ascending to the throne.

Deciding a more proactive stance on world affairs was needed to protect his people, T'Challa interacted more with the outside world than his predecessors. First, he allied with the Fantastic Four against Klaw. Later, he joined the Avengers and became a valued member. He often returns to Wakanda to deal with affairs of state, coup attempts, tribal conflicts, and other issues. However, he eventually leaves again to aid his allies, monitor external threats to his people, and stay connected to the world. Recently, T'Challa has been focused on affairs of state, including the continuation of the royal line. To this end he rekindled his childhood romance with Ororo Monro,(AKA Storm). The couple are now engaged to be married, and the wedding is scheduled for the coming months.

Personality

Black Panther is a man who was both born to and earned his right to rule. As such, he is confident and used to being heeded, but also doesn't see birthright or destiny as a key element of character. His people's chosen protector, he is always aware of potential threats against Wakanda—even from among his allies and teammates. This often creates a distance between himself and others, as he must always stand vigilant and slightly apart. However, once someone earns his trust, he treats them not just as a friend but family, using all his considerable resources to aid them.

Abilities & Resources

A lifetime of training, as well as the rare herbs involved in the ceremony that made him king, have given Black Panther physical abilities at peak human level. His senses possess animal-like acuity and he is an expert hunter and tracker. T'Challa is a master of various martial arts, an accomplished acrobat, a trained scientist, and a master of stealth and infiltration. He has one of the best tactical minds in the world and is a keen student of human nature. He augments these considerable abilities with numerous weapons and inventions, many using advanced Wakandan technology and Vibranium as key elements; he recently acquired the Black Knight's Ebony Blade, adding it to his arsenal.

As King of Wakanda, T'Challa has incredible resources. His people possess vast technological and cultural advancements on par with or exceeding most Western nations. *Dora milaje*—ceremonial wives-in-training and highly skilled bodyguards—often attend him. He personally counts as friends and allies some of the greatest heroes in the world. Most notable among these are Captain America, fiancée Storm, and the Fantastic Four. Black Panther can call upon all of his former Avengers allies for aid, though he and Tony Stark sometimes clash ideologically.

CABLE

Affiliations SOLO **10** BUDDY **6** TEAM **8**

Distinctions

COMPLICATED HISTORY
MAN ON A MISSION
TIME TRAVELER

4 +1 PP or **8**

PP

STRESS / TRAUMA

Power Sets

HEAVILY-ARMED CYBORG

BIG GUNS **8**   CYBERNETIC SENSES **10**

ENHANCED REFLEXES **8**   SUPERHUMAN DURABILITY **10**

SUPERHUMAN STAMINA **10**   SUPERHUMAN STRENGTH **10**

TELEKINETIC CONTROL **8**   TELEPORT **10**

SFX: *Man with the Plan.* Spend 1 PP to borrow the highest die in the doom pool as an asset for your next action, then step back and return that doom die.

SFX: *Multipower.* Add more than one HEAVILY-ARMED CYBORG power to your pool. Step back each HEAVILY-ARMED CYBORG die in your pool once for each die beyond the first.

Limit: *Gear.* Shutdown a HEAVILY-ARMED CYBORG power trait to gain 1 PP. Take an action vs. the doom pool to recover.

Limit: *Techno-Organic Virus.* When you take mental or emotional stress, change any HEAVILY-ARMED CYBORG power into a complication to gain 1 PP. Activate an opportunity or remove the complication to recover that power.

BURNED-OUT MUTANT TELEPATH

PSYCHIC RESISTANCE **10**

SFX: *Immunity.* Spend 1 PP to ignore stress, trauma, or complications from psychic attacks.

SFX: *Latent Power.* When a HEAVILY-ARMED CYBORG power is shutdown, spend 1 PP to recover and step up that power as a BURNED-OUT MUTANT TELEPATH power for the remainder of the scene.

Limit: *Mutant.* When affected by mutant-specific complications and tech, earn 1 PP.

Specialties

COMBAT MASTER **10**   COSMIC EXPERT **8**

COVERT MASTER **10**   MENACE EXPERT **8**

TECH EXPERT **8**   VEHICLE MASTER **10**

[You may convert Expert D8 to 2D6, or Master D10 to 2D8 or 3D6]

P △4 6 8 10 12 **M** △4 6 8 10 12 **E** △4 6 8 10 12

Milestones

THERE'S ALWAYS ANOTHER WAR

1 XP when you make a battle plan with your allies.

3 XP when you put fellow soldiers into the line of fire for the sake of the mission.

10 XP when you sacrifice friends or family for the mission, or when you choose family or friends over the mission.

SO MANY THREADS...

1 XP when you seek out a friend or enemy from your timeline.

3 XP when you describe the horrors of your world to an ally or enemy from this time.

10 XP when you either take actions that preserve your timeline or find a new path that dissolves your timeline into oblivion, leaving you a refugee from another reality, a man without a world.

XP

History

Cable was born Nathan Summers, the son of Scott Summers (AKA Cyclops) and Jean Grey's clone Madelyne Pryor-Summers, as part of a long-term plan by Mr. Sinister against the mutant En Sabah Nur (AKA Apocalypse). To thwart Sinister, Apocalypse infected the baby with a techno-organic virus, but the time-traveling Mother Askani took Nathan into the future to cure him. There, he learned to resist the virus and trained to become a weapon against Nur, who had taken over the Earth of that future timeline. Cable's fight against his enemy would span eons, as he jumped through time to fight Apocalypse at different points in history.

Eventually, Summers ended up in the 20th century, decades before his own birth. As part of his overall strategy, he worked as a mercenary, honing skills while amassing resources, contacts, and allies. He came into contact with the X-Men, indirectly at first, then finally meeting his father at a point when Cable was actually older than Cyclops.

Over time, he achieved his hard-won goal of defeating Apocalypse, only to find new causes thereafter. Recently he became the leader of a peaceful Pacific island community named Providence.

Personality

Nathan Summers is a hard man, forged by difficult times and countless trials. At heart, he's simply a soldier, doing what he must to complete the mission at hand. Robbed of any chance at a normal existence, he has little that passes for a life outside of whatever struggle currently occupies his time. Molded by his experiences on the battlefield and in the shadows of clandestine communities, Summers is less upstanding and noble in his tactics and actions than most heroes. He has little problem making hard, even brutal, decisions when the situation calls for them. Cable has sacrificed much, regrets much, and has learned to live with it all while fighting on.

Abilities & Resources

Cable's original mutant powers were telepathy and telekinesis. Although he possessed the potential to manifest tremendous levels of both, he spent most of his energy containing the techno-organic virus that ravaged his body. After burning out his original powers, he switched to technology as substitutes for them. The Dominus Objective is a cyberpathic connection to the infonet, which he uses in place of his telepathy, and the Cone of Silence is a prototype force field generator and gravimetric sheath that functions much like his telekinesis did.

As a result of the techno-organic virus, Summers is functionally a cyborg, with significant physical enhancements. He's never without large guns and other tools of his violent trade, and he frequently relies on his "body-sliding" teleport technology. Also, Cable usually has little difficulty getting his hands on time-travel equipment when he needs it. Even without his powers and tech, Summers is a highly experienced soldier and covert operator with well-developed leadership and tactical skills.

Over the years he has amassed numerous hidden caches of resources in various locations and times, as well as many contacts and allies. Significant among these are "Professor," the consolidated AI brain of a Celestial ship, and Blaquesmith, a diminutive time-traveling mentor who has saved Cable's life many times.

CAPTAIN AMERICA

Affiliations

Solo **6** Buddy **8** Team **10**

Distinctions

Moral Compass
Resolute Tactician
Sentinel of Liberty

4 +1 PP or **8**

Power Sets

SUPER-SOLDIER PROGRAM

Enhanced Durability **8**   **Enhanced Reflexes** **8**

Enhanced Stamina **8**   **Enhanced Strength** **8**

SFX: *Immunity.* Spend 1 PP to ignore stress, trauma, or complications from poison, disease, or fatigue.

SFX: *Last-Ditch Effort.* Step up or double any SUPER-SOLDIER PROGRAM die on your next roll, or spend 1 PP to do both, then shutdown that power. Activate an opportunity to recover the power or during a Transition Scene.

SFX: *Second Wind.* Before you take an action including a SUPER-SOLDIER PROGRAM power, you may move your physical stress die to the doom pool and step up the SUPER-SOLDIER PROGRAM power for this action.

Limit: *Patriot.* Step up emotional stress inflicted by government forces or popular opinion to gain 1 PP.

VIBRANIUM-ALLOY SHIELD

Godlike Durability **12**   **Weapon** **8**

SFX: *Area Attack.* Against multiple opponents, for every additional target add a D6 and keep an additional effect die.

SFX: *Ricochet.* Against a single target, step up or double a WEAPON die. Remove the highest rolling die and use three dice for your total.

Limit: *Gear.* Shutdown VIBRANIUM-ALLOY SHIELD to gain 1 PP. Take an action vs. the doom pool to recover.

Specialties

Acrobatic Expert **8**   **Combat Master** **10**

Covert Expert **8**   **Psych Expert** **8**

Vehicle Expert **8**

[You may convert Expert D8 to 2D6, or Master D10 to 2D8 or 3D6]

Milestones

BORN LEADER

1 XP when you give an order to an ally.

3 XP when you take advice from an ally or utilize an ally-created asset to stress out a villain.

10 XP when you either create a new branch of the Avengers and select a leader for the team or step away from the Avengers, choosing an ally to take over as leader.

LIVING FLAG

1 XP when you say something about how America has changed.

3 XP when you take stress attempting to change America for the better.

10 XP when you either take a prominent position in the American government or military or set the Captain America mantle aside, declaring someone else more fit for the job of fighting for America while wearing and being the nation's flag.

STRESS / TRAUMA

P
4
6
8
10
12

M
4
6
8
10
12

E
4
6
8
10
12

XP

Steve Rogers [public]

History

Born in the early 20th Century in New York City to poor Irish parents, Steve Rogers grew up sickly. Despite his heartfelt desire to aid his country in its struggle against the Axis powers, his frailties disqualified him from active military service. However, his unyielding determination and moral character resulted in his being chosen for the top-secret Operation: Rebirth project. Dr. Abraham Erskine's Super-Soldier process transformed Rogers into a peerless physical specimen—a success that would never be reproduced thereafter, due to Erskine's subsequent murder at the hands of a Nazi spy. Trained and equipped as a spy-busting propaganda asset to counterbalance Germany's Red Skull, Rogers became Captain America. Accompanied by his partner Bucky Barnes, Captain America fought alongside the Sub-Mariner and the original Human Torch as the Invaders.

While trying to stop a rocket weapon of Baron Zemo's, Barnes apparently died and Rogers was lost to the icy waters of the North Atlantic. The Super-Soldier formula put Rogers into a state of suspended animation, while the world thought him dead for decades. Eventually discovered and revived by the Avengers in more recent times, Captain America has had to adapt to a world half a century different than the one that shaped him.

Personality

Captain America is the moral measure against whom most other heroes compare themselves. He is the hero's hero—fearless, selfless, noble, and unyielding. Rogers *lives* the ideals he represents— they aren't simply a code he espouses and works to uphold. Equality and fairness, justice and liberty for all—these are fundamental to Cap's basic character, not just words, and his every action demonstrates this.

Abilities & Resources

Operation: Rebirth transformed Rogers into the pinnacle of physical perfection. Captain America's body operates at the maximum of human physical potential, giving him levels of strength, endurance, and agility that would shame world-class athletes. His body also makes him effectively immune to poison, disease, and fatigue. In addition, he is highly trained in all aspects of military and tactical skill, and his close-quarter combat skills combine with his physical abilities to make him one of the single best hand-to-hand fighters alive. Rogers possesses extensive battlefield experience and years working in the intelligence community, and he is a natural leader with virtually unmatched powers of inspiration.

Captain America wears a scale-mail uniform of sophisticated anti-ballistic materials and carries a circular shield. This shield is one-of-kind, the accidental alloying of steel and Vibranium, practically indestructible and known to dampen kinetic energy impact entirely. In addition to using it defensively, Rogers has mastered its use as a throwing weapon.

Steve Rogers has always enjoyed a close relationship with S.H.I.E.L.D., through former Director Nick Fury and sometime romantic partner Sharon Carter (AKA Agent 13). Of late, however, Fury's replacement Maria Hill has been less accommodating and many of his S.H.I.E.L.D. resources have been limited. He uses customized vehicles such as a high-tech van and a heavily modified motorcycle, both gifts from the Black Panther's people. Cap's reputation, particularly among the superhuman community, is unmatched—no other figure commands the degree of respect and loyalty among heroes that he does.

CLINT BARTON

Affiliations

SOLO 8 BUDDY 6 TEAM 10

Distinctions

CHECKERED PAST
COCKY ROGUE
PEERLESS MARKSMAN

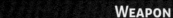 4 +1 PP or 8

Power Sets

EXCEPTIONAL TRAINING

ENHANCED REFLEXES 8   **ENHANCED SENSES** 8

ENHANCED STAMINA 8

SFX: *Fortune Favors the Bold.* If your pool includes an EXCEPTIONAL TRAINING power, spend 1 PP to reroll.

Limit: *Headstrong.* When your opponent includes your existing mental or emotional stress in a dice pool, step up that stress to gain 1 PP. If the opponent's action or reaction fails, step back that stress.

☐ BOW AND TRICK ARROWS (HAWKEYE)

ENHANCED DURABILITY 8   **WEAPON** 8

SFX: *Shoot to Kill.* Add a D6 to your attack action pool and step back the highest die in pool. Step up physical stress inflicted.

SFX: *EMP Arrow.* Against multiple robot or computerized opponents, for every additional target add a D6 and keep an additional effect die.

SFX: *Adamantium Arrow.* When your target uses a DURABILITY power in their reaction pool, step up physical stress inflicted.

SFX: *Tear Gas Arrow.* Against multiple opponents, for every additional target add a D6 and keep an additional effect die.

SFX: *Explosive Arrow.* Step up or double WEAPON for one action. If the action fails, add a die to doom pool equal to the normal rating of your power die.

Limit: *Gear.* Shutdown BOW AND TRICK ARROWS to gain 1 PP. Take an action vs. doom pool to recover.

☐ NINJA ARSENAL (RONIN)

ENHANCED DURABILITY 8   **WEAPON** 8

SFX: *"I'm Just That Good."* If your pool includes a NINJA ARSENAL power, you may replace two dice of equal size with one stepped-up die.

SFX: *"Watch Me Work."* Against multiple targets, for every additional target add a D6 and keep an additional effect die.

SFX: *Weapon Savant.* Against a single target, step up or double a NINJA ARSENAL die. Remove the highest rolling die and use three dice for your total.

Limit: *Gear.* Shutdown NINJA ARSENAL to gain 1 PP. Take an action vs. doom pool to recover.

☐ SIZE-CHANGING FORMULA (GOLIATH)

ENHANCED STAMINA 8   **GROWTH** 10

SUPERHUMAN DURABILITY 10   **SUPERHUMAN STRENGTH** 10

SFX: *Area Attack.* Against multiple targets, for every additional target add a D6 and keep an additional effect die.

SFX: *Push Your Limits.* Add D6 to the doom pool to step up or double a SIZE-CHANGING FORMULA power for your next roll.

Limit: *Huge.* When your great size becomes a complication for you, gain 1 PP.

Limit: *Fatigue.* Every time after the first that you change height in a scene, take D6 physical stress.

Choose one of the following power sets, depending on which costumed identity Clint chooses to adopt.

Specialties

ACROBATIC EXPERT 8   **COMBAT MASTER** 10

COVERT EXPERT 8   **CRIME EXPERT** 8

MENACE EXPERT 8   **VEHICLE EXPERT** 8

[You may convert Expert D8 to 2D6, or Master D10 to 2D8 or 3D6]

History

Orphaned young, Clint and his brother Bernard ran away to join the circus. There Clint met the men who would mentor him, the original Swordsman and Trick-Shot. Both men noticed Clint's natural abilities and trained him, but Trick-Shot had the greater influence, beginning Clint's lifelong love of archery. Inspired after watching Iron Man in action, Clint Barton left his brother and the circus, donning a colorful costume to fight crime as Hawkeye. Unfortunately, during Barton's first outing, the authorities mistook him for one of the criminals he was attempting to stop, and the young man ultimately found himself fighting the very hero who had inspired him in the first place: Iron Man.

After some unhappy times on the wrong side of the law, Clint approached the Avengers in an attempt to reform his image, and Iron Man sponsored him for membership. Hawkeye was part of the first serious set of changes in the team's line-up, a situation that saw him, Captain America, and their teammates forced to prove themselves worthy of name "Avengers" repeatedly.

Hawkeye has been on and off the roster of the Avengers over the years, but he has always returned to his allies, even when his choices and moral decisions cost him personally. Barton died as an Avenger, sacrificing himself aboard a Kree warship to save his comrades, a consequence of reality distorted by the Scarlet Witch. More recent manipulation by the Scarlet Witch returned him to the living, confused and uncertain. Although his allies suspect he is back from the dead, Clint has yet to reveal himself to his former teammates.

Personality

Clint Barton is two-parts swashbuckler and one-part showman. Win or lose, he's going to do it his way and with *style*. He may fight the good fight, but he has fun doing it and shows off every chance he gets. Brash, headstrong, recklessly brave, and sometime much too confident in his own abilities for his safety, Barton is never without a retort and wisecracks on a level that rivals Spider-Man at his most annoying. His friends and allies also see leadership qualities in him to which he himself sometimes seems blind.

Abilities & Resources

Regardless of what costumed identity he's using—and he's gone through several during his career—Barton remains one of the finest marksmen on the planet. His peers are few, limited to such villains as Trick-Shot, Bullseye, and Taskmaster. His impressive archery skills are often supplemented by a wide variety of trick arrows provided by Stark and others, but even without them, he's a highly experienced and well-trained martial artist and master of many weapons. This is a man used to fighting alongside Thor and Iron Man—and looking good while doing so—with nothing other than his skill and courage to complement their power and technology.

In addition to a broad background of expertise and an unhealthy level of personal bravery, Clint Barton also possesses many contacts in the intelligence and superhuman communities. Most of the world still believes the man once known as Hawkeye is dead. If he does reassume a heroic identity, he could easily become Hawkeye again (or Goliath, as he has been at least once in the past) or don the recently vacated costume of Ronin.

THE ONE AND ONLY...

1 XP   when you talk trash to a super villain and the doom pool has at least 2D8 in it.

3 XP   when your refusal to back down when obviously outclassed or overpowered either causes you to take stress or allows one of your allies to gain XP from one of their Milestones.

10 XP   when you publically take full credit for defeating a superior enemy or acknowledge the aid of your allies.

THE NEW MASK

1 XP   when you hide your identity or utilize new methods in order to reinforce your new identity.

3 XP   when you share you true identity with an ally.

10 XP   when you adopt this new mask as your new super hero persona, or take off the new mask in order to take on an older identity.

Milestones

CLOAK

PP

Affiliations	Solo **8**	Buddy **10**	Team **6**

Distinctions

THE DEMON INSIDE
IN LOVE WITH DAGGER
STREET KID

4 +1 PP   or   **8**

Power Sets

LIVING DIMENSIONAL INTERFACE

DARKFORCE CONTROL **10**	ENHANCED STAMINA **8**
ENHANCED STRENGTH **8**	INTANGIBILITY **10**
TELEPORT **8**	

SFX: *Area Attack.* Against multiple targets, for every additional target add a D6 and keep an additional effect die.

SFX: *Engulf.* When inflicting an ENTRAPPED complication on a target, add a D6 and step up your effect die.

SFX: *Life Drain.* If your attack action against organic targets includes INTANGIBILITY, add a D6 and step up your effect die.

Limit: *Growing Hunger.* If you pool includes a LIVING DIMENSIONAL INTERFACE power, both 1 and 2 on your dice count as opportunities, but only 1s are excluded from being used for totals or effect dice.

Limit: *The Predator.* Whenever you successfully stress out a target using LIVING DIMENSIONAL INTERFACE, you must choose to take D6 emotional stress or feed your target to the Predator and add a D6 to the doom pool.

Specialties

CRIME EXPERT **8**	MENACE EXPERT **8**

[You may convert Expert D8 to 2D6, or Master D10 to 2D8 or 3D6]

Milestones

THE DEMON NEVER SLEEPS

1 XP when you first use your *Life Drain* SFX in a Scene.

3 XP when your *Growing Hunger* Limit first adds a D10 or larger to the doom pool in a Scene.

10 XP when you either choose to feed someone to the Predator, despite the pleas of your friends, or stress yourself out to resist doing so.

CLOAKED PORTAL

1 XP when you teleport an ally into or out of trouble.

3 XP when you teleport an ally or innocent bystander out of danger.

10 XP when you either teleport everyone on your side of the conflict into a major battle or take a large contingent from your team into safety when they are in terrible danger.

P
△ 4
6
8
10
12

M
△ 4
6
8
10
12

E
△ 4
6
8
10
12

XP

History

Growing up on the rough streets of Boston, Tyrone "Ty" Johnson tried to stay on the straight and narrow, despite frequent temptations to an easier but less law-abiding life. Then he and his friend Billy witnessed a deadly robbery. Police saw them leaving the scene and ordered them to stop. Tyrone's lifelong stutter interfered as he tried to protest their innocence, and the police opened fire, killing Billy. Tyrone ran, from the police and his old life.

He ended up in New York City. At the Manhattan Port Authority, Tyrone met Tandy Bowen—a runaway from a rich family in the Midwest—when he stopped another runaway from robbing her. They quickly became close friends. When a group of strangers offered Tandy shelter, Tyrone went along to protect her. He failed again, as the strangers worked for the Maggia crime syndicate and forced the two runaways to become guinea pigs for a new form of synthetic heroin. Unlike the other subjects of the test, Tyrone and Tandy survived, the trauma triggering their powers.

The pair began operating as the vigilantes Cloak and Dagger. At first merciless in their methods, the pair slowly became less ruthless as the unique bond of their powers drew them closer together. Tandy's powers as Dagger influenced her towards less murderous ends; over time she guided Cloak to less extreme actions as well.

Cloak and Dagger never stray far or long from one another. They always return to the streets of New York, providing aid and hope to the continuous stream of runaways and other denizens of the street in dire need of both.

Personality

Tyrone is shy and unassuming; but as Cloak, his stutter disappears and his voice deepens, projecting a dark and foreboding demeanor. Cloak gives the impression of tightly restrained power—hungry and full of violent potential—always looking for an outlet. Tyrone is deeply protective of Dagger and takes great risks to keep her safe, even from himself.

Abilities & Resources

Tyrone's physical form is a "door" to the "Darkforce Dimension." He can move through that dimension, teleporting from one point to another in the real world. Cloak can carry passengers when he uses the conduit to teleport, but passengers travel at their own peril. The darkness leeches at their life force and fills them with dread and nameless horror during the trip. Cloak can also summon billowing clouds of darkforce that psychically numb and fill people with fear. At its fullest, this darkness can completely drain the life from victims caught in it, killing them. Tyrone sometimes feels compelled to this act of psychic vampirism by the Predator—his name for the entity his powers link him to. Dagger's light can sate this hunger temporarily. As Cloak, Tyrone is normally intangible and must solidify through force of will. He also seems to gain a small amount of height, and his strength increases significantly.

Cloak and Dagger have good relationships with many other "street-level" heroes such as Spider-Man and Daredevil, but little in the way of resources beyond their powers and allies.

DAGGER

Affiliations

Solo ⑧   Buddy ⑩   Team ⑥

Distinctions

In Love with Cloak
Inner Light
Naïve

④ +1 PP   or   ⑧

Power Sets

CHANNELING THE LIGHT

Enhanced Reflexes ⑧	Enhanced Stamina ⑧
Light Daggers ⑧	Light Mastery ⑩

SFX: *Area Attack.* Against multiple targets, for every additional target add a D6 and keep an additional effect die.

SFX: *Healing.* Add Light Mastery to your dice pool when helping others recover stress. Spend 1 PP to recover your own or another's physical stress or step back your own or another's physical trauma.

SFX: *Soul Shock.* When using Light Daggers to inflict emotional stress, add a D6 and step up your effect die.

SFX: *Versatile.* Replace Light Mastery die with 2D8 or 3D6 on your next roll.

Limit: *Only Humans.* Light Mastery only works on human targets. Earn 1 PP when you take an action against non-human targets.

Limit: *Overcharged.* Shutdown any Channeling the Light power to gain 1 PP. Activate an opportunity to recover the power or during a Transition Scene.

Specialties

Acrobatic Master ⑩   Combat Expert ⑧

Crime Expert ⑧   Psych Expert ⑧

[You may convert Expert D8 to 2D6, or Master D10 to 2D8 or 3D6]

Milestones

ATTACKING THE DARKNESS

1 XP when you first use your *Soul Shock* SFX on a character in a Scene.

3 XP when you use *Healing* SFX to help someone recover emotional stress or trauma.

10 XP when you either stress yourself out helping another hero recover or you help a foe recover trauma.

RUNAWAY

1 XP when you talk with your dearest friend about an exit strategy from your current living situation.

3 XP when you use your powers to defend your current home.

10 XP when you either set down roots and decide to call this place your home or run away again, taking only one dear friend with you when you go.

PP ☐

STRESS / TRAUMA

P △ 4 6 8 10 12

M △ 4 6 8 10 12

E △ 4 6 8 10 12

XP ☐

History

Originally from a wealthy suburb of Cleveland, Ohio, Tandy Bowen seemed to have the perfect life, with her famous former-model mother and wealthy father providing for her every material need. However, it was a loveless household; her mother pursued her own vain desires and her father abandoned the family in search of spirituality.

Tandy ran away from home after losing the boyfriend she viewed as her only source of love. Eventually, she arrived in New York. During an unsuccessful robbery attempt by other runaways, Tandy met Tyrone Johnson, her rescuer and the man who became her dearest and only true friend. He came along to protect her when she was approached by a group offering shelter. The men turned out to be enforcers for the Maggia criminal syndicate, and the offer of shelter only a ruse to recruit unsuspecting runaways to test a synthetic form of heroin. A toxic reaction to the drug triggered Tandy's latent mutant powers, saving her life. Together, she and Tyrone managed to escape. Once the two learned how to control their powers, they returned to wreak vengeance on their captors and became the ruthless vigilantes known as Cloak and Dagger.

Over time, the nature of Dagger's powers and their connection to her own inner light had a positive influence on her behavior, softening her outlook. Through her soothing influence, she and Cloak toned their violence down to a level more acceptable to their sometime allies among the Big Apple's other street-level defenders, such as Spider-Man and Daredevil. Despite wanting more from life than simply being Cloak's crime-fighting partner, her feelings of responsibility for the young people the two protect and her bond with Tyrone always pull Dagger back to Cloak and their quixotic crusade.

Personality

Tandy is literally full of life, a positive and buoyant point of hope and inspiration for those around her. She is highly energetic, with an easy smile and expressive body language. Fiercely devoted to Tyrone, she's tried many times to pull him away from the streets and toward more positive environs, only to persuade herself to be patient, waiting for the better opportunity that her infectious sense of optimism assures her is always right around the corner.

Abilities & Resources

Dagger can tap into her internal source of life force, or "inner light." She generates far more life force than a normal person, and that surplus enhances her agility and stamina. Her signature move is to create daggers of light to throw at people, mentally controlling the daggers in flight. These light daggers disrupt a target's life force, enough to kill or stun, but they only work on human targets. She can also illuminate a large area with her light, as well as heal others or purge various drugs and toxins from a person's body.

The demonic predator entity connected to Cloak's darkness can feed from Tandy's light, filling the harmful void Cloak's hunger creates. Dagger is always safe when teleporting through Cloak's darkness, and she can share that protection with other passengers.

In addition to her powers, Tandy Bowen is an experienced dancer with gymnastic training.

DAREDEVIL

Affiliations	Solo **8**	Buddy **10**	Team **6**

Distinctions

DEVIL'S ADVOCATE
INDIFFERENT BILLIONAIRE
LIVING WEAPON OF K'UN-LUN

4 +1 PP or **8**

Power Sets

BILLY CLUB

ENHANCED DURABILITY **8**　　　SWINGLINE **6**

WEAPON **6**

- **SFX:** *Rebound.* Against a single target, step up or double your WEAPON die. Remove the highest rolling die and use three dice for your total.
- **SFX:** *Grapple.* When inflicting a complication on a target, add a D6 and step up your effect die.
- **Limit:** *Gear.* Shutdown BILLY CLUB to gain 1 PP. Take an action vs. the doom pool to recover.

HEART OF SHOU-LAO

ENHANCED REFLEXES **8**　　　ENHANCED SPEED **8**

ENHANCED STAMINA **8**　　　ENHANCED STRENGTH **8**

- **SFX:** *Iron Fist.* Double or step up ENHANCED STRENGTH for one action. If that action fails, shutdown ENHANCED STRENGTH. Activate an opportunity to recover or during a Transition Scene.
- **SFX:** *Chi Focus.* If your pool includes a HEART OF SHOU-LAO die, you may replace two dice of equal size with one stepped-up die.
- **SFX:** *Chi Healing.* Add ENHANCED STAMINA to your dice pool when helping others to recover stress. Spend 1 PP to recover your own or another's physical stress or step back your own or another's physical trauma.
- **Limit:** *Conscious Activation.* While stressed out, asleep, or unconscious, shutdown HEART OF SHOU-LAO. Recover HEART OF SHOU-LAO when you recover that stress or wake up. If you take mental trauma, shutdown HEART OF SHOU-LAO until you recover that trauma.

Specialties

ACROBATIC MASTER **10**　　　BUSINESS EXPERT **8**

COMBAT MASTER **10**　　　COVERT EXPERT **8**

MYSTIC EXPERT **8**　　　PSYCH EXPERT **8**

[You may convert Expert D8 to 2D6, or Master D10 to 2D8 or 3D6]

Milestones

DRAGON BEHIND THE DEVIL

- **1 XP** when you use your Combat or Mystic Specialties to aid another hero.
- **3 XP** when you take stress in a battle where you did not use the Iron Fist.
- **10 XP** when you either nominate another hero as Iron Fist, so that you can fully become Daredevil, the champion of Hell's Kitchen or take off the Daredevil costume and let Foggy know that you can no longer participate in this charade.

IRON PEN

- **1 XP** when you use your Business Expert in a conflict.
- **3 XP** when you hire an ally to make the world a better place.
- **10 XP** when you either seize another character's business assets or merge with another character's company.

PP

STRESS / TRAUMA

P △ 4 6 8 10 12

M △ 4 6 8 10 12

E △ 4 6 8 10 12

XP

Daniel "Danny" Thomas Rand-K'ai [secret]

History

Years ago, Daniel Rand's father found the legendary city of K'un-Lun. Saving the life of the city's ruler, Wendell Rand stayed in K'un-Lun for a time before desiring to return to the United States. Years later, Wendell took his son Daniel, his wife Heather, and his friend and business partner, Harold Meachum, on a journey back to K'un-Lun. When Meachum betrayed them, Daniel's parents died, and he survived only due to the timely intervention of agents of K'un-Lun. Seeing the boy's need for focus and desire for vengeance, the city's ruler Yü-Ti directed the famed martial arts master Lei Kung the Thunderer to train the boy.

Danny Rand trained in K'un L'un, eventually defeating the dragon Shou-Lao and gaining the power of the Iron Fist, the city's protector and champion. Returning to the United States, Iron Fist avenged his father and took over the family business, Rand International. He also met hero-for-hire Luke Cage (AKA Power Man). The two became unlikely friends and partners, working together as freelance super heroes for years. Eventually the two dissolved their business partnership but not their friendship. Danny then wandered the world, seeking enlightenment and resolving various issues with his troubled past.

Recently, Iron Fist has returned to the United States once more. With the identity of Daredevil, Danny's long-time friend and fellow hero, leaked to the public, Iron Fist has stepped into the role himself to support the illusion that Matt Murdock is not Daredevil.

Personality

Danny Rand is disciplined, motivated, and idealistic. He seeks an enlightened existence through meditation, spiritual exploration, and the study of martial arts. Not that he doesn't like to have fun—he has a romantic streak, and though somewhat stiff and naïve in his early days, years spent hanging with Luke Cage have given Danny street smarts and a sharp sense of humor. He's also willing to go the extra mile to help his friends, even if this means challenging the authorities and covering up the paper trail with even more paper.

Abilities & Resources

Trained to be the current Immortal Weapon for the fabled city of K'un-Lun, Iron Fist is one of the world's greatest martial artists. He has mastery over his body's internal energies, or *chi*. Danny can channel this energy to heal, augment his physical and mental abilities, and transform each hand "like unto a thing of iron," making them capable of delivering devastating blows. His abilities also extend his life and grant him exceptional resistance to disease and toxins, though these can still affect him and weaken his chi. Danny is also a shrewd businessman, accomplished acrobat, and trained investigator.

As the current Immortal Weapon of K'un-Lun, Iron Fist can draw upon the resources and secret knowledge of that fabled hidden city. Danny also runs his family's multinational corporation, Rand International, though its fortunes rise and fall. Iron Fist is a long-time partner and best friend of Luke Cage and has many connections in the super hero community. Chief among these allies are Daredevil and the Daughters of the Dragon, Colleen Wing and Misty Knight. Misty and Danny have a long romantic history, though the two are currently not together.

DEADPOOL

Affiliations	Solo 10	Buddy 8	Team 6

Distinctions

Completely Unpredictable
The Merc with a Mouth
Totally Insane

4 +1 PP   or   8

Power Sets

TOYS FOR BOYS

Teleport 8   **Weapon** 8

SFX: *Unnecessary Sales-Boosting Violence.* Against a single target, step up or double a Toys for Boys die. Remove the highest rolling die and use three dice for your total.

SFX: *They Can Cut Through A Tank...Honest!* Step back the highest die in your attack action pool to add a D6 and step up physical stress inflicted.

SFX: *I Can Use Two At Once!* On your next action or reaction, replace a Weapon die with 2D6.

Limit: *Gear.* Shutdown a Toys for Boys power to gain 1 PP. Take an action vs. the doom pool to recover.

WEAPON X AUGMENTATION

Enhanced Reflexes 8   **Enhanced Strength** 8

Godlike Stamina 12   **Psychic Resistance** 12

SFX: *Healing Factor.* Spend 1 PP to recover your physical stress and step back physical trauma.

SFX: *Immunity.* Spend 1 PP to ignore telepathy or mind control.

SFX: *Breaking the Fourth Wall.* When one of your opportunities is activated to add a D6 to the doom pool, replace it with a D4. Spend 1 PP to do this to an existing D6 in the doom pool.

Limit: *Unstable.* Step up mental stress to gain 1 PP.

Specialties

Acrobatics Expert 8   **Combat Master** 10

Covert Master 10   **Menace Expert** 8

Psych Expert 8

[You may convert Expert D8 to 2D6, or Master D10 to 2D8 or 3D6]

Milestones

NEVER CAN TELL...

1 XP when you first use your *Unstable* Limit in any Scene.

3 XP when you alter your pattern of insane joking to say something lucid, smart, and logical in the midst of super heroic chaos and weirdness.

<unauthorized user edit>: Great thing about this is not only do you get to be reasonable but it sets up an even better crazier joke for later!

10 XP when you arbitrarily switch sides in a conflict or reject a reasonable and attractive offer to remain with your allies.

MYSTERIOUS PAST

1 XP when you reference a past connection with another character, real or imagined.

3 XP when you put another character at serious risk in order to explore your past connection with that character.

10 XP when you discover a significant fact about your past and have a serious emotional or mental breakthrough, or you discover a significant fact about your past and decide it isn't a big deal at all because mental breakthroughs are hard work.

PP

STRESS / TRAUMA

P
4
6
8
10
12

M
4
6
8
10
12

E
4
6
8
10
12

XP

Wade Wilson [public]

History

The Weapon X program altered mercenary Wade Wilson, heightening his physical abilities and giving him a healing factor similar to Wolverine. This made him an effective operative, but side effects from his transformation disfigured him and unbalanced his mind. As Deadpool, Wade became a government operative and later a killer for hire.

<unauthorized user edit>: I'm also the lost son of the Asgardian trickster god Loki. Why doesn't anyone mention that?

Deadpool worked as a mercenary and assassin for years, alternating between trying to recover his lost past and ignoring it entirely. Over time, Wilson has become less of a villain and more of an adventurer for hire—albeit a very unorthodox and unstable one. He has fought both with and against various heroes and villains, most notably Cable, Wolverine, and Agent X.

Personality

Wilson switches allegiances frequently, even in the middle of a fight. He also talks constantly, cracking jokes and making odd references. He frequently talks to an unseen "audience" as though he's a fictional character. Underneath this behavior is a deeply scarred man unsure of what is real and what is an elaborate delusion caused by his superhuman abilities.

<unauthorized user edit>: Okay, I suppose that's fair. But hey, it keeps things interesting, right, folks?

Abilities & Resources

Deadpool's healing factor allows him to recover from dismemberment, even decapitation, if the severed pieces are reattached. This power also greatly increases his lifespan and resistance to drugs and disease. Rampant and unrestrained cell growth causes his cerebral tissues to recover quickly from psychological trauma and renders him incredibly resistant to psychic powers such as mind control and telepathy. Wilson's physical abilities are also augmented, giving him increased strength and agility.

In addition to his powers, Deadpool is a highly trained soldier, assassin, and covert operative. He is particularly adept with bladed weapons and firearms, and fights so unpredictably that even skilled tacticians have a hard time following his moves. He also possesses various pieces of advanced technology, most notably a teleportation device. He has used an image inducer in the past to conceal his scarred features and appear normal.

<unauthorized user edit>: I also make a great tiramisu and knit cunning wool hats.

Deadpool has worked with numerous heroes and villains, from Cable to Taskmaster. Due to his personality problems and insanity, it's hard to consider most of these people allies much less friends, though he might call on some of them for help in a pinch. In addition to temporary partnerships, Deadpool has a couple of close confidants, most notably his manager Sandi Brandenburg and the troubled genius known as Weasel.

<unauthorized user edit>: I'm also multilingual and once shot a man in Reno just...because someone paid me. Please don't play me as if I'm an idiot. That'll really annoy me. Toodles!

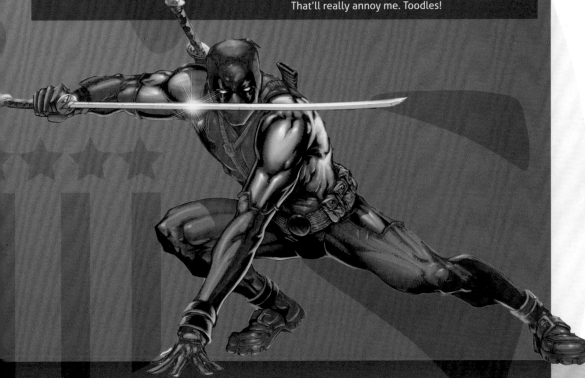

DOCTOR STRANGE

Affiliations	Solo 10	Buddy 8	Team 6

Distinctions
Former Surgeon
The Price of Magic
Earth's Arcane Defender
4 +1 PP or 8

Power Sets

DISCIPLE OF THE ANCIENT ONE

Enhanced Durability 8		Mystic Blast 10
Mystic Resistance 10		Supreme Sorcery 12
Telepathy 8		Transmutation 10

SFX: *Alliterative Invocations.* When using a stunt to create magical assets or complications, add a D6 and step up your effect die.

SFX: *Area Attack.* Against multiple targets, for every additional target add a D6 and keep an additional effect die.

SFX: *Multipower.* Add more than one Disciple of the Ancient One power to your pool. Step back each Disciple of the Ancient One die in your pool once for each die beyond the first.

Limit: *The Extent of Sorcery.* When you add Supreme Sorcery to any pool, you may only create assets and complications as your effect.

ASTRAL TRAVELER

Intangibility 12	Invisibility 10

SFX: *Without Form.* Spend 1 PP to ignore physical stress caused by anyone attacking your astral form by mundane means.

Limit: *The Empty Vessel.* When your dice pool includes an Astral Traveler power, adding a power from any other Power Set costs 1 PP. Your physical form remains where you left it, and for as long as you remain out of sight of it any stress or complications that target it directly are stepped up.

MYSTIC REGALIA

Flight 6	Mystic Senses 12
Teleport 10	

SFX: *Cloak of Levitation.* When including Flight in any reaction against attacks, remove the highest rolling die and add a third die to your total.

SFX: *Eye of Agamotto.* Add a doom die to your next action including a Mystic Regalia or Disciple of the Ancient One power. After your action, step up the doom die and return it to the doom pool.

SFX: *Mystic Library.* When you create a Mystic or Cosmic related resource or stunt, step up the lowest doom die to step up the stunt or resource.

Limit: *Mystic Feedback.* Shutdown Mystic Regalia to gain 1 PP. Take an action vs. the doom pool to recover.

Specialties

Combat Expert 8	Cosmic Expert 8
Medical Master 10	Menace Expert 8
Mystic Master 10	Psych Expert 8

[You may convert Expert D8 to 2D6, or Master D10 to 2D8 or 3D6]

Milestones

MYSTIC ADVISOR

1 XP when you offer advice to an ally.

3 XP when you include an ally in a mystical ritual.

10 XP when you use your magic powers against an ally because you think they either disregarded your advice or took that advice too far.

SUMMONER SUPREME

1 XP when you discuss the greater Powers at work in a given situation or which Powers could be brought to bring about change.

3 XP when you use Mystic Master or Supreme Sorcery to call on an entity from another plane of existence as a resource or stunt.

10 XP when you either make a binding pact with a Power from another plane of existence or banish it from Earth.

History

Stephen Strange was always destined for greatness. An early experience helping his injured sister inspired Stephen to be a doctor, a career at which he excelled. Family tragedies hardened his heart even as his easy success swelled his ego to towering proportions. At the peak of his career, an auto accident robbed him of the use of his hands. Too arrogant to accept working as an assistant or consultant, Strange burned through his fortune and contacts desperately trying to find a way to mend his hands. This quest sent him to the far reaches of the Earth and ultimately into the hall of the Ancient One. There Stephen faced his destiny, and when he chose altruistic reasons to aid the Ancient One, Strange passed the first of many tests to prove himself worthy of his future title.

Stephen spent decades under the Ancient One's tutelage before returning to the world outside to practice his mystic arts. Defeating the likes of Mordo and Dormammu further honed his skills, and when the time came for his master to leave the mortal realm behind, Stephen Strange took the Ancient One's place as the Sorcerer Supreme, mystical defender of Earth's dimension.

Personality

A calm, reserved, and often stoic presence, Stephen is a master of self-control. He knows the terrible cost of even his smallest errors in judgment. At the cost of his own happiness and relationships, Strange keeps himself constantly apart from those he protects. His cold exterior is a necessary shell to contain the passions and emotions that otherwise may interfere with the concentration and focus his arts require. In his heart, two forces wage war—arrogance due to his many achievements and guilt resulting from his many failures.

Abilities & Resources

Doctor Strange is the Sorcerer Supreme of Earth's dimension. He's one of the most powerful practitioners in the cosmos, understanding magic on a level most mages can't comprehend. He sets his own rules, performing magic that other sorcerers think to be impossible. Stephen interacts with universal entities as a respected near-equal; Eternity stated that Strange's power dwarfs other mortals. He can teleport himself and others anywhere in the cosmos, destroy enchantments cast by godlike beings, and hold his own in both physical and mental duels versus Dormammu and Nightmare.

As Sorcerer Supreme, Strange possesses the Eye of Agamotto and the Book of the Vishanti, powerful artifacts that expand his mystical knowledge beyond any mortal limitations. His Cloak of Levitation grants him the ability to fly without tapping his own power, and his heavily warded Sanctum Sanctorum on Bleeker Street is home to countless artifacts acquired by Strange and his predecessors.

Beyond his mystical talents, Stephen Strange is also a formidable martial artist and was once one of the premiere neurosurgeons in the world; though his hands are no longer suited for surgical tasks, he retains his considerable medical knowledge. He has many allies in both the mystical and costumed communities, such as his manservant Wong and various incarnations of the Defenders.

FALCON

Affiliations

| Solo | 8 | Buddy | 10 | Team | 6 |

Distinctions

Loyal Partner
Socially Conscious
Troubled Past

4 +1 PP   or   8

Power Sets

PSYCHIC ALTERATION

| Bird Control | 8 | Enhanced Senses | 8 |

SFX: *Redwing.* Target an additional opponent and either add a D8 to your pool or step up your effect die. Keep an additional effect die.

Limit: *"Snap" Wilson.* Step up mental or emotional stress relating to your criminal past to gain 1 PP.

FLIGHT HARNESS

| Enhanced Durability | 8 | Enhanced Senses | 8 |
| Subsonic Flight | 8 | Weapon | 6 |

SFX: *Boost.* Spend 1 PP to step up or double FLIGHT HARNESS power for one die roll.

SFX: *Stealth Technology.* When including a FLIGHT HARNESS power in an action or reaction to avoid electronic detection or tracking, step up or double COVERT EXPERT. Spend 1 PP to do both.

Limit: *Gear.* Shutdown FLIGHT HARNESS Power Set to gain 1 PP. Take an action vs. the doom pool to recover.

Specialties

Acrobatics Expert	8	Combat Expert	8
Covert Expert	8	Crime Expert	8
Psych Expert	8		

[You may convert Expert D8 to 2D6, or Master D10 to 2D8 or 3D6]

Milestones

PAY IT FORWARD

1 XP when you help out a kid mixed up in the same kind of trouble that tempted you before becoming the Falcon.

3 XP when you make amends for something you did in your past or help another do the same.

10 XP when you help a fellow super hero make the world a better place through an act of kindness or convince a villain to turn over a new leaf as a hero.

WINGED AVENGER

1 XP when you first take to the air during a battle.

3 XP when you save a teammate from stress due to falling or engage in a dogfight with multiple flying enemies.

10 XP when you change the tide of a battle by providing air superiority or take a complication that prevents you from flying.

History

Harlem-born Sam Wilson's early encounters with racism and the death of his father pushed him into crime. Taking the nickname "Snap," the embittered young man became a hustler and thug and likely would have remained so, if not for ex-Nazi super villain the Red Skull. The Skull used the reality-altering properties of the fabled Cosmic Cube to transform Wilson into the perfect friend and partner for his archenemy, Captain America, as part of a plot to destroy the star-spangled Avenger. The Skull's plan backfired, and Sam continued on as the Falcon, partner of Captain America.

As the Falcon, Wilson has worked mostly with Cap and S.H.I.E.L.D, joining the Avengers occasionally. Over the years the Falcon has become a formidable hero in his own right.

Recently, the world-changing powers of the Scarlet Witch pushed Sam back into his "Snap" persona, and the hero became more violent, moody, and angry. However, the hero's will and his bond with his friends allowed him to push past these problems and continue as the high-flying Falcon.

Personality

The Falcon is brave, self-sacrificing, and devoted to social justice. His friendship with Captain America has nurtured these qualities, making the once-criminal Wilson a true hero. Despite this, Sam often questions if putting on a costume is the best way to help people. A social worker in his civilian identity, he has given up being the Falcon at various points to devote himself fully to his community.

Wilson's life is defined most by his relationship to Captain America. The two men, despite different backgrounds, form one of the most effective and famous partnerships ever. This is reinforced by Cap's old-school ethics and Wilson's modern social perspectives, which combine to form a whole greater than the sum of its parts.

Abilities & Resources

The Cosmic Cube augmented Sam's natural avian affinity. He has an empathic link with birds, communicating with them and seeing through their eyes. This link is particularly strong with his own falcon, Redwing, but the Falcon has controlled whole flocks and used a city's bird population to locate a target.

The Falcon's skills are equally impressive. His street fighter's instincts combine with years of training with Captain America make him a formidable gymnast and martial artist. His experience in social work and his criminal background make Wilson a shrewd, no-nonsense counselor and advocate.

The Falcon's original costume included turbines and glider wings for flight. Fellow hero Black Panther recently gifted Wilson with a sophisticated flying harness of Wakandan manufacture. This "hard light" version uses solidified energy and magnetism to provide flight. The new costume incorporates sensors, body armor, and shielding from most mechanical detection, such as radar or satellite tracking. The costume also possesses a hidden "talon" for climbing or combat.

In addition to Captain America and Black Panther, the Falcon has several allies among the hero community, including many Avengers. Wilson has worked for S.H.I.E.L.D. in the past and still has connections with the organization, though mostly through long-time associate Nick Fury. While often a reluctant team player, he has joined the Avengers more than once and he worked with the Defenders briefly.

GOLIATH

Affiliations

SOLO **6**   BUDDY **10**   TEAM **8**

Distinctions

BRILLIANT BIOCHEMIST
HUMBLE HERO
STANDING ON THE SHOULDERS OF GIANTS

4 +1 PP   or   **8**

Power Sets

SIZE-CHANGING FORMULA

ENHANCED STAMINA **8**   GROWTH **10**

SUPERHUMAN DURABILITY **10**   SUPERHUMAN STRENGTH **10**

SFX: *Area Attack*. Against multiple targets, for each additional target add a **D6** and keep an additional effect die.

SFX: *Multipower*. Add more than one SIZE-CHANGING FORMULA power to your pool. Step back each SIZE-CHANGING FORMULA die in your pool once for each die beyond the first.

SFX: *Push Your Limits*. Add D6 to doom pool to step up or double a SIZE-CHANGING FORMULA power for your next roll.

SFX: *Human Shield*. When a nearby ally or friend takes physical stress, you may step up that stress to take it yourself instead.

Limit: *Huge*. Change any SIZE-CHANGING FORMULA power into a complication to gain 1 PP. Activate an opportunity or remove the complication to recover that power.

Limit: *Fatigue*. Every time after the first that you change height in a scene, take D6 physical stress.

Specialties

COMBAT EXPERT **8**   MEDICAL MASTER **10**

SCIENCE MASTER **10**   PSYCH EXPERT **8**

TECH EXPERT **8**

[You may convert Expert D8 to 2D6, or Master D10 to 2D8 or 3D6]

Milestones

GIANT AMONG MEN

1 XP when you take stress meant for someone else.

3 XP when you add an asset that allows an ally to inflict trauma on a villain or inflict trauma by utilizing a complication set up by an ally.

10 XP when you take trauma from using your *Human Shield* SFX to protect another or you allow an ally to take trauma when you could have saved them.

BRAINS OVER BRAWN

1 XP when you use SCIENCE, MEDICAL, or TECH specialties to create an asset or complication.

3 XP when you help a friend or ally recover from a problem involving their powers.

10 XP when you quit a super hero team in order to devote yourself to science or when you reject a great opportunity for research in order to remain a hero.

History

Born in the poverty-stricken neighborhood of Watts in Los Angeles, military veteran and scientist Bill Foster eventually became head of Stark Industries' biochemistry division. Working with fellow scientist—and super hero—Henry Pym, Foster helped cure Pym when his growth powers malfunctioned. Later Bill used his knowledge of Pym's work to develop his own growth formula. Desperate to restore a failed marriage, Foster concocted an ill-advised plan to win his wife back by becoming the super hero known as Black Goliath. This brought him to the attention of Luke Cage, briefly as an enemy and then as an ally.

Unable to repair his marriage, Foster continued as a hero until an encounter with a villain gave him terminal radiation poisoning. Taking a position with Project: P.E.G.A.S.U.S. in the hopes they might be able to cure him, the hero changed his costumed identity to Giant-Man. Foster's heroism was ultimately his salvation, as several heroes worked to save him. Eventually cured with a transfusion from the radiation-immune Spider-Woman, he retired from super heroics and worked as a consultant to the Avengers' West Coast branch. Later Bill came into the employ of the High Evolutionary, regained his powers and helped stop the Evolutionary's mad plan to forcibly evolve humanity, then retired again.

In recent years Foster, now known simply as Goliath, has lost and regained his powers, worked to aid various heroes with his scientific expertise, and occasionally engaged in traditional heroics. Preferring work as a researcher, he is more than willing to become Goliath if the cause is right.

Personality

Goliath is a mix of ambition and selflessness. Devoted to research and scientific advancement, he has shown repeatedly that he will fight and sacrifice to aid others, risking injury and death many times to help fellow heroes. Foster himself has self-esteem issues when it comes to his status as a hero, often stating he's a "second rater" and deciding his efforts are better focused on research, but he's repeatedly shown a willingness to step up and fight against significant threats. This behavior results in Bill being more admired and respected than he might personally believe.

Abilities & Resources

Altered by his formula, Goliath can grow to massive heights. In this form he possesses superhuman strength and resistance to injury. Early in his career Foster could only increase to 15 feet tall, but recently this limit disappeared. He's also one of the most brilliant scientists in the world, ranking among such luminaries as Pym and Richards. His military background and training with other heroes has made him an effective hand-to-hand combatant, especially at giant size.

For someone who thinks of himself as a "second-rater," Foster has an amazing resume of scientific and super heroic accomplishments that have gained him the admiration of an impressive array of friends and allies, from Black Panther to Iron Man. He was a highly valued employee of Stark Industries, as well as a consultant for both the Project: P.E.G.A.S.U.S. and the Avengers. Having saved both heroes in the past, Bill is a good friend of the Thing and Hank Pym, as well as Pym's ex-wife, Janet van Dyne (AKA Wasp). Spider-Woman temporarily sacrificed a portion of her own powers to save Goliath, an example of the high regard his peers have for his keen scientific mind and heroic heart.

HERCULES

Affiliations

SOLO **10**   BUDDY **8**   TEAM **6**

Distinctions

BRASH DEMIGOD
PARTY ANIMAL
PRINCE OF POWER

4 +1 PP   or   **8**

Power Sets

LION OF OLYMPUS

ENHANCED SPEED **8**   GODLIKE STAMINA **12**

GODLIKE STRENGTH **12**   LEAPING **6**

SUPERHUMAN DURABILITY **10**

SFX: *Area Attack.* Against multiple targets, for every additional target add a D6 and keep an additional effect die.

SFX: *Boundless Strength.* Double GODLIKE STRENGTH for an action. If the action fails, add the highest rolling die to the doom pool.

SFX: *Grappling.* When inflicting a PHYSICALLY RESTRAINED complication to a target, add a D6 and step up your effect die.

SFX: *Golden Mace.* Add a D6 to the doom pool to step up a COMBAT resource.

SFX: *Immortal.* Spend 1 PP to ignore stress, trauma, or complications caused by aging, disease, poison, radiation, or vacuum.

Limit: *Hubris.* Step up mental or emotional stress, trauma, or complications caused by pride or overconfidence to gain 1 PP.

P
△ 4
6
8
10
12

M
△ 4
6
8
10
12

Specialties

COMBAT EXPERT **8**   COSMIC EXPERT **8**

MENACE EXPERT **8**   MYSTIC EXPERT **8**

[You may convert Expert D8 to 2D6, or Master D10 to 2D8 or 3D6]

E
△ 4
6
8
10
12

Milestones

CONTESTS OF STRENGTH

1 XP when you joyously congratulate an opponent for a blow that inflicts physical stress on you.

3 XP when you engage in a contest of might against another character with GODLIKE STRENGTH and prevail.

10 XP when you fight a foe who wields a D12 from one of their Power Sets without accepting any help from your allies, or admit that you cannot defeat this foe with your own Zeus-granted strength and accept your ally's aid.

IMMORTAL FRIENDSHIP

1 XP when you declare another character a true friend and companion.

3 XP when you help your ally recover from emotional or mental stress through food, drink, and fellowship.

10 XP when you avenge a fallen comrade or take trauma in avenging your comrade's fall.

History

Hercules is in fact the famed Greek hero of legend. His father Zeus elevated him to godhood among the Olympians as a reward for his various acts of mortal heroics. The god-prince wandered for centuries, having adventures both among mortals and elsewhere. From time to time he displeased Zeus and was banished from Olympus until he either learned his lesson or his father relented. During his travels he met the Norse god Thor, and the two became both friends and rivals. Eventually he found worthy companions among the super heroes of the late 20th Century and began to operate as a super hero.

In modern times, Hercules worked with a number of heroes. He joined the Avengers and also helped form the short-lived Champions of Los Angeles. He's fought the Hulk to a stalemate and matched might with all Earth's powerhouses at one point or another. Hercules has traveled to other planets as well, once even fighting on behalf of one—Ego, the Living Planet—against Galactus' herald, Firelord. A brutal attack by the Masters of Evil once left him half-dead and brain damaged, but his Avengers allies managed to restore him.

More recently, the dissolution of the Avengers and the loss of several of its members hit Hercules hard. Tricked by his stepmother Hera, he recreated his famous labors as a reality TV show. A war between the Olympians and the Japanese gods seemed to sober him up, and since then he has returned to Earth, looking for a good cause, a good fight, and a good party—if not always in that order.

Personality

Hercules is a hero in the classic Greek sense—brave, powerful, and more than a bit proud. He loves to test his strength against worthy opponents and uses his powers to aid others without hesitation. Sometimes this leads to errors in judgment, but he's never malicious or willfully neglectful. He sometimes condescends to mortals, especially women, but he's quick to correct this behavior if confronted by true friends and valiant allies. Threats or insults to such companions bring great anger in him.

Underneath Hercules' boisterous exterior lurk great regrets. He has lost children, lovers, and friends over his immortal existence. Although he usually hides this pain behind boasts and occasional buffoonery, it also drives him to fiercely defend those he cares about.

Abilities & Resources

Hercules' strength is legendary, matching Thor, the Hulk, Gladiator, and others. His Olympian physiology makes him highly resistant to harm and effectively immortal. In addition to his powers, Hercules has centuries of experience, is a skilled warrior, and is particularly adept at wrestling. He also possesses a mace of indestructible Adamantine forged by the god Hephaestus himself.

Hercules has many allies from across the cosmos, including his fellow Olympians; the gods of many other pantheons respect him. He can count many heroes as friends and battle brothers, including Thor, the Thing, Captain America, and Hawkeye. Although on good terms with his teammates in the Avengers and the now-defunct Champions, some of the more technically minded like Iron Man see him as a bit of a fool.

HUMAN TORCH

Affiliations SOLO **6**   BUDDY **10**   TEAM **8**

Distinctions
HOTHEADED HERO
NEVER GROWS UP
SHAMELESS FLIRT

4 +1 PP or **8**

Power Sets

FLAME ON!

FIRE MASTERY **10**   FLAME BLAST **10**

SUPERSONIC FLIGHT **10**

- **SFX:** *Area Attack.* Against multiple targets, for every additional target add a D6 and keep an additional effect die.
- **SFX:** *Fiery Body.* On a succesful reaction against a physical attack, inflict physical stress with your effect die at no PP cost. Spend 1 PP to step it up.
- **SFX:** *Immunity.* Spend 1 PP to ignore stress or trauma from fire, heat, or cold.
- **SFX:** *Multipower.* Add more than one FLAME ON! powers to your dice pool. Step for back each FLAME ON! die in your pool once for each die beyond the first.
- **SFX:** *Nova Flame.* Step up or double your FLAME ON! powers for that scene, or spend 1 PP to do both. Take second-highest rolling die of each subsequent action or reaction as physical stress.
- **Limit:** *Extinguished.* Shutdown all FLAME ON! powers vs. a flame-retardant attack to gain 1 PP. Activate an opportunity to recover or during a Transition Scene.

Specialties

ACROBATICS EXPERT **8**   COSMIC EXPERT **8**

TECH EXPERT **8**   VEHICLES EXPERT **8**

[You may convert Expert D8 to 2D6, or Master D10 to 2D8 or 3D6]

Milestones

DANGEROUS LOVE

- **1 XP** when you choose to flirt with a non-heroic Watcher character.
- **3 XP** when your heroic activities put your chosen character in danger, or your commitment to your chosen character puts your team in danger.
- **10 XP** when your involvement with your chosen character changes them irreversibly, or you break off your relationship in order to protect your chosen character.

WORLD'S COOLEST SUPER HERO

- **1 XP** when you talk to a young super hero about a problem and tell them how you dealt with something similar.
- **3 XP** when you create an asset that allows a young super hero to shine in battle, doing stress or trauma to an enemy.
- **10 XP** when you either gather a group of young super heroes and form a team or gather a group of young super heroes and form a rock band.

PP

STRESS / TRAUMA

P 4 6 8 10 12
M 4 6 8 10 12
E 4 6 8 10 12
XP

History

Joining his big sister Sue on an experimental space flight, young Johnny Storm gained fantastic powers after cosmic rays bombarded their ship. The four crewmembers became the Fantastic Four, with Johnny's fire-based powers leading him to take the name "The Human Torch." The Fantastic Four became one of Earth's most prominent super hero teams and the Human Torch one of Earth's most famous heroes.

Johnny's life since becoming a hero has been full of adventure and opportunity. He's traveled the cosmos with the Fantastic Four, been a race car driver for a time, and watched his girlfriend Frankie Raye become Nova, the Herald of Galactus. He worked briefly as an actor and a firefighter, finished college, engaged in various solo heroics, and even married the Skrull Lyja while she was disguised as the Thing's then ex-girlfriend, Alicia Masters. Through it all, Johnny has kept his cheerful attitude, though his impulsive nature and penchant for practical jokes have sometimes annoyed his teammates. Despite often seeming immature and irresponsible, the Human Torch has helped save the world many times over and is a beloved member of the Fantastic Four.

Personality

The Human Torch loves being a super hero. He dates supermodels, pals around with various costumed heroes, and fights evil with a daredevil attitude and youthful exuberance. Recently confronted about his tendency to shirk "boring" responsibilities, he is slowly becoming more mature and adult. He still loves pranks and jokes, with teammate the Thing a favorite target. Johnny loves his sister Sue and the other members of the Fantastic Four dearly, and would do anything to aid them.

Abilities & Resources

The Human Torch can project fire from any part of his body. He can use this power to hurl fiery blasts, engulf his entire body in flames, and make shapes composed of fire. He can even "sculpt" flames, allowing him to form decoys of himself. His fiery aura protects him from projectiles and allows him to fly. He can extinguish part of it in order to safely carry passengers or objects and still fly. He can control fire as well, using it to create cages, rings, and other shapes. His body is fireproof, and he can absorb nearby fire and heat at will. The Human Torch can even voluntarily overload himself, creating a "Nova Flame" that is much hotter and more powerful than Johnny normally projects, but doing this exhausts him quickly. In addition to his powers, Human Torch is an experienced race car driver and mechanic.

As a member of one of Earth's most famous super hero teams, Johnny Storm has a lot of friends and allies. Chief among them are his teammates and family. He is especially close to his sister Sue Storm, the Invisible Woman, and he and the Thing have a brotherly rivalry going back years. Johnny has also become good friends with Iceman and Spider-Man, heroes close to his own age, who understand his attitudes and impulsive behavior better than most. Despite his well-deserved reputation as a hothead, the Human Torch can still call on many heroes for assistance, especially fellow New York-based ones such as previous members of the currently defunct Avengers.

INVISIBLE WOMAN

Affiliations

SOLO `6`   **BUDDY** `8`   **TEAM** `10`

Distinctions

COMPASSIONATE
IMPLACABLE WILL
MOST DANGEROUS TEAM MEMBER

`4 +1 PP` or `8`

Power Sets

FORCE PROJECTION

FLIGHT `6`   **FORCE BLAST** `10`

GODLIKE DURABILITY `12`   **INVISIBILITY** `12`

SFX: *Area Attack.* Against multiple targets, for every additional target add a D6 and keep an additional effect die.

SFX: *Force Constructs.* When using FORCE PROJECTION to create assets, add a D6 and step up your effect die.

SFX: *Multipower.* Add more than one FORCE PROJECTION power to your pool. Step back each FORCE PROJECTION die in your pool once for each die beyond the first.

SFX: *Reactive Power.* Spend 1 PP to add a FORCE PROJECTION power to another character's dice pool before rolling. If that character takes physical stress, take D6 mental stress.

SFX: *Force of Will.* When using GODLIKE DURABILITY in your dice pool, redirect physical stress to mental stress at no cost. Redirect effect dice targeting your FORCE PROJECTION assets to yourself as mental stress. Spend 1 PP to step back either redirected stress.

Limit: *Conscious Activation.* While stressed out, asleep, or unconscious, shutdown FORCE PROJECTION. Recover Force Projection when you recover that stress or wake up. If you take mental trauma, shutdown FORCE PROJECTION until you recover that trauma.

Specialties

COSMIC EXPERT `8`   **COVERT EXPERT** `8`

PSYCH MASTER `10`   **SCIENCE EXPERT** `8`

[You may convert Expert D8 to 2D6, or Master D10 to 2D8 or 3D6]

Milestones

INDEPENDENT

1 XP when you stand up to another hero.

3 XP when you prove one of your decisions was best for your team.

10 XP when you stress out the last foe in an action scene, or another character acknowledges your assistance was essential in saving the day.

EMOTIONAL CENTER

1 XP when you first use your *Reactive Power* SFX in a scene.

3 XP when you help another hero recover stress inflicted in a scene in which you were present.

10 XP when you either accept membership on a team that includes a hero you have helped recover or turn down an offer of membership unless that hero is excluded.

PP

STRESS / TRAUMA

P △4 6 8 10 12

M △4 6 8 10 12

E △4 6 8 10 12

XP

History

The children of a successful Long Island physician, Susan Storm and her brother Johnny lost their parents to a car accident. Their mother died from her crash injuries, and their father spiraled into guilt-fed self-destruction after failing to save his wife. Moving to California to live with her aunt, Sue met Reed Richards when he stayed as one of her aunt's boarders. Smitten, she would meet him again years later and start a relationship with him. That relationship was strong enough that she was able to convince Richards to allow her and her brother along on the fateful spaceflight that gave all of them superhuman abilities.

As a member of the Fantastic Four, Sue initially proved a convenient hostage or stumbling block. Over time, as her powers and confidence grew, that changed *dramatically*. By the time Susan Storm became a happily married Susan Richards and mother to young son Franklin, she was a vital member of the team. After an emotionally grueling experience under Psycho-Man's control, a newly confident Sue, now aware that the extent of her powers was much greater than previously thought, changed her codename from "Invisible Girl" to "Invisible Woman."

Susan is the mother of two extraordinary children, Franklin and Valeria. She is unique among her peers for the additional distinction of juggling active motherhood alongside her responsibilities as a costumed hero.

Personality

The Invisible Woman is often referred to as the soul of the Fantastic Four. Her strong will and immutable emotional core anchors the team through practically any challenge. Over time she has grown from a shy young girl to a powerful and self-confident woman with established leadership abilities and the respect of the super-hero community. She also acts as the conscience and voice of wisdom for her husband when his motives or actions are buried under blind logic and over-rationalization. Despite a long-held attraction to Namor the Sub-Mariner, Sue remains utterly loyal to her husband and her family.

Abilities & Resources

In the early years of the Fantastic Four, Susan's abilities seemed limited to bending light around her or others, making her or her targets invisible to the naked eye. As time passed, it became apparent that this was only one aspect of her power to generate a psionic force-field malleable to her will. This field can protect her from attack, expand outward in domes or spheres to protect others, or simply be formed into a number of crude—but practically indestructible—geometric shapes for uses ranging from ramps and movable platforms to bludgeoning ranged attacks. Given her level of control, this force-field projection is highly versatile and potentially quite dangerous. Even the team's enemies have more than once acknowledged that the Invisible Woman is probably the most powerful member of her team.

Sue has access to all of the Fantastic Four's facilities and equipment, as well as the significant goodwill and reputation bestowed on her and her teammates by New York City and the world.

IRON MAN

Affiliations	SOLO 10	BUDDY 6	TEAM 8

Distinctions

BILLIONAIRE PLAYBOY
CUTTING EDGE TECH
HARDHEADED FUTURIST

4 +1 PP or 8

Power Sets

EXTREMIS ENHANCILE

CYBERNETIC SENSES 10	ENHANCED SPEED 8
ENHANCED STAMINA 8	SUPERHUMAN REFLEXES 10

TECHNOLOGY CONTROL 8

- **SFX:** *Healing Factor.* Spend 1 PP to recover your physical stress and step back your physical trauma.
- **SFX:** *Situation Control.* Step up or double an EXTREMIS ENHANCILE power for your next action, then remove lowest die from the doom pool and take it as mental stress.
- **Limit:** *Conscious Activation.* While stressed out, asleep, or unconscious, shutdown EXTREMIS ENHANCILE powers (but not *Healing Factor* SFX). Recover EXTREMIS ENHANCILE powers when you recover that stress or wake up. If you take mental trauma, shutdown EXTREMIS ENHANCILE powers until you recover that trauma.

POWERED ARMOR

WEAPON SYSTEMS 10	SUPERHUMAN DURABILITY 10
SUPERHUMAN STRENGTH 10	SUPERSONIC FLIGHT 10

- **SFX:** *Area Attack.* Against multiple targets, for every additional target add a D6 and keep an additional effect die.
- **SFX:** *Boost.* Shutdown highest-rated POWERED ARMOR power to step up another POWERED ARMOR power. Activate an opportunity to recover or during a Transition Scene.
- **SFX:** *EMP.* For each tech-based target you chose, add a d6 to the doom pool. Roll WEAPON SYSTEMS + doom pool as an attack action against each target. Shutdown POWERED ARMOR. Activate an opportunity to recover or during a Transition Scene.
- **SFX:** *Energy Absorption.* On a successful reaction against an energy-based attack action, convert opponent's effect die into a POWERED ARMOR stunt or step up a POWERED ARMOR power until used in an action. If opponent's action succeeds, spend 1 PP to use this SFX.
- **SFX:** *Unibeam.* Step up or double WEAPON SYSTEMS on your next roll, or spend 1 PP to do both, then shutdown WEAPON SYSTEMS. Activate an opportunity to recover or during a Transition Scene.
- **Limit:** *Charged System.* Shutdown highest-rated power to gain 1 PP. Activate an opportunity to recover or during a Transition Scene.

Specialties

BUSINESS MASTER 10	SCIENCE EXPERT 8
TECH MASTER 10	VEHICLE EXPERT 8

[You may convert Expert D8 to 2D6, or Master D10 to 2D8 or 3D6]

Milestones

CAN'T BUY HAPPINESS

- **1 XP** when you suggest a solution to a problem that involves either Stark technology or millions of dollars.
- **3 XP** when you inflict mental stress on an ally who disagrees with your methods.
- **10 XP** when you either take a position of great power or realize that some people do not have access to your considerable resources and dedicate all of them to social justice.

IRON MENTOR

- **1 XP** when you use a Transition Scene to arm an ally with Stark technology.
- **3 XP** when you create an asset in an Action Scene that allows an ally armed by you to inflict stress against an opponent.
- **10 XP** when you either found and lead your own team of Iron Men and Women or strip those you mentored of their Stark technology, encouraging them to walk their own path without your aid.

PP

STRESS / TRAUMA

P
A 4
6
8
10
12
M
A 4
6
8
10
12
E
A 4
6
8
10
12

XP

History

Much like his father before him, Tony Stark was born into privilege and wealth that shaped him into both a jaded, cynical playboy and a successful industrialist. His worldview changed when he was grievously wounded and taken captive while touring a war-torn area where Stark Industry weapons were being tested. From parts his captors wanted made into weapons, Tony cobbled together the first Iron Man suit and used it to escape. His eyes now opened by his first-hand knowledge of the bloody and violent legacy behind his family's wealth, as well as by witnessing the death of the man who helped him build the suit, Stark had a change of soul. He turned the same focus he had previously used to build his family's business toward helping humanity directly with the same technology.

As Iron Man, Stark was a founding member of the Avengers. He has helped support the team either personally or financially during its many incarnations. Though his personal problems have occasionally forced him from the team, as well as cost him multiple businesses and multiple fortunes, he has always rebuilt and eventually returned to his allies in the good fight.

Personality

Tony Stark is a dichotomy. On the one hand, he is a caring humanitarian, a brave and philanthropic soul who works tirelessly for a better world, and on the other, he is a womanizer and recovering alcoholic who tries to bury his insecurities and fears in an endless parade of meaningless relationships or at the bottom of a bottle. Stark's towering intellect carries with it a degree of arrogance, and Stark sometimes has trouble grasping why people don't simply see the world as he does. This makes him self-assured in his conclusions but also hardheaded and more than a bit self-righteous.

Abilities & Resources

A brilliant futurist and engineer, Tony Stark has few intellectual peers, even in a world with minds like Reed Richards and Henry Pym.

As Iron Man he wears a sophisticated suit of powered armor that he constantly upgrades and redesigns to keep at the cutting edge. His latest suit incorporates impact-resistant ceramic plate armor and full-spectrum repulsor technology that allows it to fly, assemble itself around him, and project concussive blasts. It also greatly enhances his physical strength.

Recently, in order to stop a technological terrorist threat, Tony injected himself with a nanite-powered payload called Extremis, which rewrote his nervous system and reconfigured many of his internal organs in order to store essential elements of the Iron Man armor within his body. He is now directly linked to his armor via a personal area network, which not only gives him lightning-fast response time but also unparalleled access to worldwide data networks.

The Stark fortune is legendary, and Tony's periods of insolvency brief. Whatever their current form, his businesses always give him access to brilliant minds other than his own and usually substantial manufacturing capabilities on a global scale. He also has a loyal circle of friends who have braved terrible challenges for him—James Rhodes, his former pilot and sometimes bodyguard who wears the War Machine armor; Virginia "Pepper" Potts, his former assistant and lasting close friend; and Harold "Happy" Hogan, his former chauffeur, sometimes bodyguard, and constant confidant.

LUKE CAGE

Affiliations

Solo **6**   Buddy **10**   Team **8**

Distinctions

COME GET SOME!
HERO FOR HIRE
STREET SMART

4 +1 PP or **8**

Power Sets

UNBREAKABLE

SUPERHUMAN DURABILITY **10**   SUPERHUMAN STAMINA **10**

SUPERHUMAN STRENGTH **10**

SFX: *Area Attack.* Against multiple targets, for every additional target add a D6 and keep an additional effect die.

SFX: *Second Wind.* Before you make an action including an UNBREAKABLE power, you may move your physical stress die to the doom pool and step up the UNBREAKABLE power for this action.

SFX: *Versatile.* Replace any UNBREAKABLE power with 2D8 or 3D6 on your next roll.

Limit: *Difficult Recovery.* Add your SUPERHUMAN DURABILITY die to the opposing roll when others try to recover your physical stress.

P

A **4**
6
8
10
12

M **4**

Specialties

BUSINESS EXPERT **8**   COMBAT EXPERT **8**

COVERT EXPERT **8**   CRIME EXPERT **8**

MENACE MASTER **10**

[You may convert Expert D8 to 2D6, or Master D10 to 2D8 or 3D6]

6
8
10
12

E

A **4**

Milestones

NEW AVENGER, NEW IDEAS

1 XP when you discuss how the current situation connects to the history of the Avengers with a veteran of the team.

3 XP when you insist the Avengers work in a new way.

10 XP when you either commit to being an Avenger and move into Avengers Tower with your family or leave the Avengers and go back to Heroes for Hire and knocking heads with Danny.

200 DOLLARS FROM DOOM

1 XP when you offer a direct, blunt approach to a complicated problem.

3 XP when you start trouble by punching a bad guy in the face or inflict mental stress on a hero who is over-thinking his problems and being an angst-ridden idiot.

10 XP when you either defeat an enemy through direct physical confrontation or take a step back and elect to use more subtle methodology.

6
8
10
12

XP

History

Framed and imprisoned for a crime he didn't commit, ex-gang member Carl Lucas hoped for a chance at escape or parole. When Lucas volunteered for an experiment in cell regeneration and disease control, a vengeful racist prison guard sabotaged the experiment. Instead of death or injury, the experiment transformed Lucas, giving him superhuman strength and resistance to injury. Using his new-found powers to escape, he changed his name to Luke Cage and became the "hero for hire" known as Power Man, later finding a lifelong friend and long-term business partner in fellow hero Iron Fist.

Eventually, Luke cleared his name but chose to put his old life as Carl Lucas behind him and remain Luke Cage. For years, he and Iron Fist worked as partners, often doing heroic jobs for mundane pay. Luke also joined super hero groups such as the Defenders and the Fantastic Four, though usually preferring to assist such teams as needed instead of staying a long-term member.

Over the years, Luke has grown to become a respected member of the super hero community. He's married to ex-super-hero Jessica Jones and they have a new baby together, Danielle. He stands shoulder to shoulder with the Earth's mightiest heroes without missing a beat. He rarely goes by Power Man anymore, preferring to face foes as the man he was forced to become and chose to remain, Luke Cage.

Personality

Luke is an honest, often blunt, strong-willed man. He has the instincts of a street hustler and the heart of a hero. He is extremely devoted to his friends and family, but also cares for his community. He loves "sticking it to the man" and will go out of his way to fight, embarrass, or confront those who think their power and privilege lets them cheat or abuse others. After all, this is the guy who once flew all the way to Latveria to confront Dr. Doom about an unpaid bill.

Abilities & Resources

Luke Cage is superhumanly strong, and his body tissues have the density and strength of steel, making him highly resistant to injury. He also recovers from injury more quickly and completely than a normal human. Cage is a trained combatant, using a mix of street brawling and martial arts training learned from his friend Iron Fist and others. Cage is also an experienced businessman, able to turn his superhuman abilities into profit more readily than most heroes, though his kind heart often leads him to take cases for little or no money.

Luke has numerous allies he can call on for aid. Chief among them are his girlfriend, Jessica Jones, and his best friend and partner, Danny Rand AKA Iron Fist. Luke has also worked with the Fantastic Four, the Defenders, the Daughters of the Dragon, and Spider-Man on numerous occasions. Outside the super hero community, Luke is considered a great hero and role model among many of the poorer sections of New York and other major cities, as well as within the African-American community.

MISTER FANTASTIC

Affiliations Solo 8 Buddy 6 Team 10

Distinctions
ABSENT-MINDED PROFESSOR
BY THE NUMBERS
FAMILY MAN

 4 +1 PP or 8

Power Sets

HYPERELASTICITY

ENHANCED REFLEXES 8 ENHANCED SPEED 8

STRETCHING 10 SUPERHUMAN DURABILITY 10

SFX: *Area Attack.* Against multiple targets, for every additional target add a D6 and keep an additional effect die.

SFX: *Grapple.* When inflicting a complication on a target, add a D6 and step up your effect die.

SFX: *Rebound.* Against a single target, step up or double a STRETCHING die. Remove the highest rolling die and add use three dice for your total.

SFX: *Versatile.* Replace a STRETCHING die with 2D8 or 3D6 on your next roll.

Limit: *Exhausted.* Shutdown any HYPERELASTICITY power to gain 1 PP. Activate an opportunity to recover or during a Transition Scene.

Specialties

COSMIC MASTER 10 MEDICAL EXPERT 8

SCIENCE MASTER 10 TECH MASTER 10

VEHICLES EXPERT 8

[You may convert Expert D8 to 2D6, or Master D10 to 2D8 or 3D6]

Milestones

LOVE AND SUPER SCIENCE

1 XP when you use super science to do something to show that you care about someone.

3 XP when you take stress from an argument with a family member or loved one.

10 XP when take the big step and once and for all either prioritize love over science or prioritize science over love.

SCIENCE SAVES THE WORLD

1 XP when you use Medical, Science, or Tech Specialties to create an asset that will help an ally.

3 XP when you put science aside in order to end a threat with the Hyperelasticity Power Set.

10 XP when you either use science to contribute something new to the world or use science to stop a global, extinction-level threat.

History

Brilliance runs in the Richards family. Before he mysteriously disappeared, Nathaniel Richards' amassed a fortune through his scientific expertise and patents. He left that fortune to his son Reed, a genius that showed himself his father's worthy successor at a young age. After accumulating numerous degrees and academic distinctions, Reed ultimately turned the family fortune toward his dream of advancing humanity's spaceflight capabilities. When the government threatened to shut down the program, Reed took reckless action. Alongside his college friend and pilot, Ben Grimm, and with the Storm siblings, Sue and Johnny, rounding out a minimal crew, Richards launched a prototype spacecraft employing an experimental drive and shielding. Fate intervened and the ship's crew experienced high levels of unidentified exotic cosmic rays. Crash landing back on Earth, Reed discovered that their exposure to those energies had changed all four of them. They were now superhuman, and his best friend was trapped within a monstrous form.

Rather than risk them being considered as freaks and outcasts from humanity, Richards instead worked to brand them as heroes in the public eye. Their open identities, philanthropic works, and, above all, their exciting adventures and explorations as the "Fantastic Four" cemented that image firmly in the world's awareness.

Over the years, Reed has taken the fruits of his genius and turned them into a business enterprise with deep enough pockets to fund the Fantastic Four's most exotic explorations and adventures. He divides his time between going on these adventures, representing his team and family to the world as the most commonly seen "face" of the Fantastic Four, and performing the research and invention that ultimately finances the team. Reed has one other set of responsibilities— he and Susan Storm eventually married and had children, so Reed is unusual among his peers as he must also juggle marriage and fatherhood alongside his other roles.

Personality

Reed Richards is driven by a limitless scientific curiosity—he is always learning, always inventing, always exploring new avenues of research. Richards is unaccustomed to failure, so the results of Reed's spaceflight experiments, which stripped his loved ones of a normal life and condemned his best friend to carry a monster's face, haunt Richards constantly. That guilt makes him overly protective of his family and pushes him harder into tireless scientific exploration, to expand his knowledge of *everything*— just so he never makes such a mistake again. Reed wants to be a loving husband, a doting father, and a faithful friend, but his obsessive scientific pursuits sometimes cause him to neglect the very family and friends he is trying to protect.

Abilities & Resources

Mr. Fantastic possesses an elastic form down to the cellular level. He can reshape his body mass into numerous shapes and stretch his extremities over a thousand feet. He can contort his body into a lengthy coil or a springy sphere, or even flatten himself into a kite-like shape. He can also exert some finer control, distending his facial features or forming his fingers into makeshift tools. However, these changes to shape and form are limited to gross morphology, making it difficult to adapt for disguise or other precise or cosmetic uses.

Even without his powers, Reed Richards is arguably the single greatest scientific genius on Earth, noticeably outstripping even his peers Tony Stark, Bruce Banner, and Henry Pym.

Richards is one of the four shareholders for his patents and other revenue sources tied to the Fantastic Four and their discoveries. The proceeds sustain the Baxter Building facilities, various off-site labs, and numerous advanced vehicles, as well as provide sufficient funds for Richards and his family to live comfortably without outside assistance or normal employment.

MOON KNIGHT

Affiliations	Solo **10**	Buddy **8**	Team **6**

Distinctions

Dangerous Past
Fist of Khonshu
Who is Marc Spector?

4 +1 PP or **8**

Power Sets

LUNAR ARSENAL

Enhanced Durability **8**	Glider Cape **6**
Swingline **6**	Weapon **8**

- **SFX:** *Focus.* If your pool includes a Lunar Arsenal die, you may replace two dice of equal size with one stepped-up die.
- **SFX:** *Moon Copter Extraction.* Shutdown a LUNAR ARSENAL power to leave your current scene in an outdoor or exposed location. Spend 1 PP to recover power and join the next scene after it begins.
- **Limit:** *Gear.* Shutdown a LUNAR ARSENAL power to gain 1 PP. Take an action vs. the doom pool to recover.

AVATAR OF VENGEANCE

Enhanced Reflexes **8**	Enhanced Stamina **8**
Enhanced Strength **8**	

- **SFX:** *Lunar Might.* Activate an opportunity to step up ENHANCED STRENGTH until the end of the Scene.
- **SFX:** *Call for Vengeance.* Add a doom die to a dice pool including an AVATAR OF VENGEANCE die, then take the die as mental stress.
- **Limit:** *Under a Full Moon.* Shutdown LUNAR MIGHT when the moon isn't full; recover with a full moon.
- **Limit:** *Unstable.* Change any AVATAR OF VENGEANCE power into a complication to gain 1 PP. Activate an opportunity or remove the complication to recover that power.

Specialties

Acrobatic Expert **8**	Business Expert **8**
Combat Master **10**	Covert Master **10**
Menace Expert **8**	Mystic Expert **8**
Vehicles Expert **8**	

[You may convert Expert D8 to 2D6, or Master D10 to 2D8 or 3D6]

Milestones

GOD OF VENGEANCE

- **1 XP** when you allow Khonshu's desire for vengeance to distract you from something or someone important to you.
- **3 XP** when you inflict trauma in the name of your god.
- **10 XP** when you kill a dangerous foe or reject Khonshu's edicts and spare that foe, explaining your mercy to the enemy and what you expect in return.

SOMEONE HAS TO DO THE FUN STUFF

- **1 XP** when you use a resource die to take down a street-level criminal or criminal organization.
- **3 XP** when you oppose, confront, or challenge another hero in the course of dealing with the criminal underworld.
- **10 XP** when you turn in the boss of a major criminal organization, or you expose enough of that organization to cripple its operations.

PP

STRESS / TRAUMA

P 4 6 8 10 12

M 4 6 8 10 12

E 4 6 8 10 12

XP

Marc Spector [secret]

History

Marine-turned-mercenary Marc Spector didn't have to die to meet his god, but it was close. Attacked by fellow mercenary Raoul Bushman while serving in Africa, Spector hovered near death when Khonshu appeared. The ancient Egyptian god of vengeance and the moon saved Spector, in exchange for him becoming the god's avatar on Earth. Returning to the States, Marc invested his mercenary gains and adopted an array of high-tech weapons and a costume styled after Khonshu. He also adopted alternate identities to cover up his past, including millionaire Steven Grant and no-nonsense cabbie Jake Lockley.

Spector, now calling himself Moon Knight, began his heroic career by taking down a criminal conspiracy called the Committee. During those early days, he encountered a number of strange foes, such as Werewolf by Night, Morpheus, Midnight Man, and Stained Glass Scarlet. After a short retirement, Marc renewed his connection to Khonshu and found himself armed with new mystical weaponry and driven by visions to right various wrongs. Joining the Avengers briefly, he returned to solo heroics and eventually sacrificed himself to save friends and loved ones.

However, Spector didn't stay dead long, as Khonshu once again revived his champion. Since resuming his career as Moon Knight, he has concentrated on street-level heroics and bringing down more mundane threats.

Personality

Driven by conflicting desires of redemption and revenge, Marc Spector seeks to atone for his violent past by helping others; but he also hears Khonshu's calls for vengeance. This internal struggle, combined with numerous alternate identities, gives Moon Knight a multifaceted and somewhat disturbed personality. He often has visions of Egyptian priests, past foes, and recently Khonshu himself. Whether these visions are genuine or a product of his multiple personalities is unclear. Spector's mental issues often make it difficult for him to form lasting partnerships, romantic or professional.

Abilities & Resources

Moon Knight is one of the most skilled combatants in the world, having mastered various forms of armed and unarmed combat. He is also a skilled pilot, acrobat, businessman, and covert operative who speaks several languages. His contact with Egyptian gods, werewolves, and sorcerers has given him a keen understanding of magic and mysticism. He also possesses a gift from his patron god—enhanced physical abilities that reach superhuman heights during the full moon.

As Moon Knight, Spector sports crescent-shaped darts, a grapple, batons that can be configured into nunchaku or a fighting staff, and an armored costume equipped with a cape capable of gliding short distances. He also uses custom-made helicopter-type vehicles known as the Moon Copter and the Angel Wing. In the past Moon Knight employed heavily reinforced Adamantium armor and mystical weapons, but he currently uses neither.

Marc Spector is a millionaire with numerous contacts in high society, the art world, and various mercenary organizations. His close friends and allies include his old pilot buddy Jean-Paul "Frenchie" DuChamp and his former assistant and girlfriend Marlene Alraune. He has worked with numerous heroes, most notably the Avengers, Spider-Man, and the Punisher. For a time he even had a sidekick, Midnight, but Midnight eventually turned against him and is currently believed to be deceased.

MS. MARVEL

Affiliations	Solo **8**	Buddy **6**	Team **10**

Distinctions

BATTLE-TESTED HERO
LETTER OF THE LAW
TAKE-CHARGE ATTITUDE

4 +1 PP or **8**

Power Sets

KREE GENETICS

ENERGY BLAST **8**		SUBSONIC FLIGHT **8**
SUPERHUMAN DURABILITY **10**		SUPERHUMAN STAMINA **10**
SUPERHUMAN STRENGTH **10**		

SFX: *Energy Absorption.* On a successful reaction against an energy-based attack action, convert your opponent's effect die into a KREE GENETICS stunt or step up a KREE GENETICS power until used in an action. If opponent's action succeeds, spend 1 PP to use this SFX.

SFX: *Multipower.* Add more than one KREE GENETICS power to your pool. Step back each KREE GENETICS die in your pool once for each die beyond the first.

SFX: *Second Wind.* Before you take an action including a KREE GENETICS power, you may move your physical stress die to the doom pool and step up the KREE GENETICS power for this action.

Limit: *Overload.* Shutdown a KREE GENETICS power to gain 1 PP. Activate an opportunity to recover or during a Transition Scene.

Specialties

COMBAT EXPERT **8**	COSMIC EXPERT **8**
COVERT EXPERT **8**	PSYCH EXPERT **8**
VEHICLES EXPERT **8**	

[You may convert Expert D8 to 2D6, or Master D10 to 2D8 or 3D6]

Milestones

CHAIN OF COMMAND

1 XP when you give an order to an ally in the heat of battle.

3 XP when you cause stress utilizing an asset created by one of your allies.

10 XP when you take the leadership role of an established team or create a new team to lead into battle.

KREE-FUELED POWER HOUSE

1 XP when you fly directly into the most obviously powerful enemy on the field.

3 XP when you use brute force to create an asset for an ally.

10 XP when you either defeat an enemy by using SUPERHUMAN STRENGTH to inflict trauma or when you defeat an enemy by absorbing their energy with the *Energy Absorption* SFX.

PP

STRESS / TRAUMA

P
4
6
8
10
12

M
4
6
8
10
12

E
4
6
8
10
12

XP

Carol Danvers [public]

History

Born the daughter of a father that wouldn't accept women as the equal of men, Carol Danvers worked hard to change his attitude. She dreamed of becoming an astronaut one day, traveling from world to world. Finally fed up with her father's blindness regarding her abilities, she left home after high school and joined the Air Force, ready to prove herself to the world. She became an accomplished pilot and eventually joined military intelligence, where she also excelled as a spy, working on missions alongside people like Ben Grimm and Logan.

She left the USAF to take a job as security head for NASA. There she became involved in one of the many covert fronts for the Kree-Skrull War, allying herself with the Kree hero Mar-Vell. Exposed to a Kree device designed to alter reality, Carol found her body modified into a half-Kree superhuman form and took the name "Ms. Marvel." Continuing encounters with superhumans and aliens made her job untenable and when forced finally to leave NASA, she wrote a tell-all book that propelled her into the world of journalism. As Ms. Marvel, she worked alongside a number of heroes and teams, eventually joining the Avengers after helping them fight Ultron. Later, circumstances pushed her to distance herself from the Avengers, and the mutant Rogue stole Carol's powers and memories, leaving Ms. Marvel for dead. Working with the X-Men to regain what she had lost, she fell victim to the alien Brood, who mutated her into a cosmic-level energy channeler. After a stint as "Binary," wandering the cosmos alongside the Starjammers, she returned to Earth, exhausting her cosmic powers to save Earth's sun.

Without her Binary powers, Carol was back to being *merely* superhuman, and she operated for a time under the name "Warbird." She returned to the Avengers for a while, fighting her way through a bout with alcoholism brought on by her many emotional traumas. She left the team to take a position in Homeland Security, but again returned to fight the Scarlet Witch, whose assault resulted in the team disbanding.

After an experience in an alternate universe where Carol was one of the world's most popular heroes, she has fully embraced her heroic identity once again and rejoined the Avengers as Ms. Marvel.

Personality

Ms. Marvel has spent a good portion of her life fighting through a series of insecurities. She tends to overcompensate, and while she doesn't grandstand unnecessarily, she may take unwise risks or impulsive actions to prove herself to those around her. The victim of multiple emotional and psychic violations, she also tends to lead with her fists, projecting a buffer of violence between her and anything she perceives as a threat. When in doubt in a situation, she will generally default to her military training and the mindset it conditioned.

Abilities & Resources

Danvers has gone through more than one set of superhuman abilities during her career. Currently, she possesses a respectable degree of superhuman strength and durability. She can also fly, emit powerful energy discharges, and both absorb and channel ambient electromagnetic energy to amplify her other abilities.

Aside from her powers, Ms. Marvel is a highly trained combatant and an accomplished military officer, spy, and pilot. Also, Carol has friends, associates, and contacts everywhere—she has worked with the Avengers, the Defenders, the X-Men, S.H.I.E.L.D., alongside a number of individual heroes, and at varying times has been a member of the military, the intelligence community, and Homeland Security.

NIGHTHAWK

Affiliations

SOLO **8**   BUDDY **6**   TEAM **10**

Distinctions

HEART OF THE TEAM
NEEDS TO WEAR THE MASK
TRUST FUND BABY

4 +1 PP   or   **8**

Power Sets

ALCHEMICAL AUGMENTATION

ENHANCED REFLEXES **8**   ENHANCED SENSES **8**

ENHANCED STAMINA **8**   ENHANCED STRENGTH **8**

SFX: *Second Wind.* Before you make an action including an ALCHEMICAL AUGMENTATION power you may move your physical stress die to the doom pool and step up the ALCHEMICAL AUGMENTATION power for this action.

SFX: *From Dusk Til Dawn.* Step up ENHANCED STRENGTH when using it between sunset and sunrise.

Limit: *Exhausted.* Shutdown any ALCHEMICAL AUGMENTATION power to gain 1 PP. Activate an opportunity to recover or during a Transition Scene.

WINGED SUIT

CYBERNETIC SENSES **6**   SUBSONIC FLIGHT **8**

LASER CANNONS **8**   SUPERHUMAN DURABILITY **10**

SFX: *Sensor Suite.* Spend 1 PP to add CYBERNETIC SENSES (or step up if already in your pool) and reroll all dice on a reaction.

SFX: *Talons.* Add a D6 to your pool for an attack action and step back the highest die in the pool. Step up physical stress inflicted.

Limit: *Gear.* Shutdown WINGED SUIT to gain 1 PP. Take an action vs. the doom pool to recover.

Specialties

BUSINESS EXPERT **8**   COMBAT EXPERT **8**

MYSTIC EXPERT **8**

[You may convert Expert D8 to 2D6, or Master D10 to 2D8 or 3D6]

Milestones

THE HERO BEFORE THE MAN

1 XP when you talk to a hero about joining an eclectic team.

3 XP when you convince a group of disparate heroes to form an ongoing team or keep such a team from disbanding.

10 XP when you either make a great personal sacrifice to show the team the meaning of heroism or abandon your team or heroic identity in order to save yourself.

THE ROAD TO REDEMPTION

1 XP when you talk to an ally about seeing a noble side to a villain or enemy.

3 XP when you inflict emotional stress on a villain, causing them to abandon their criminal ways.

10 XP when you leave a team you consider villainous or join a team you consider heroic.

History

Born the heir to the Richmond family fortune, Kyle Richmond grew up in a loveless but wealthy home. The accompanying rashness and lapses in judgment that came with being spoiled helped him leave a trail of broken hearts, bad decisions, and disappointed expectations behind him. Only after hitting rock bottom emotionally did Richmond start trying to improve himself. After being denied entry into the army, he threw himself into a torturous program of physical training. This was when the Grandmaster chose Richmond to play the part of "Nighthawk" in the gamesman's Squadron Sinister, a counterpart to the extra-dimensional heroes, the Squadron Supreme, who the Grandmaster had faced previously. With the Grandmaster's encouragement, Richmond sought the alchemical resources he used to augment his physical abilities and used his family fortune to create advanced weapons and vehicles.

Though he started his costumed career as a criminal, he ultimately turned hero when he chose to sacrifice his life to stop the alien Nebulon's attempts to destroy humanity. Saved through a mystical ritual by the original Defenders, Richmond threw himself into his new role with gusto. He aided many heroes, especially his close allies in the constantly changing Defenders team. Surviving a roller coaster of personal challenges—including paralysis during daylight hours and multiple attempts to wreck his businesses, as well as a time when even his allies thought him dead—Richmond ultimately persevered. Helping his friends in the Defenders save themselves from their old enemy Yandroth, he returned to action, most recently aiding the Thunderbolts before leaving them due to personal problems with Baron Zemo.

Personality

Richmond is the poster boy for redemption through guts and gumption. Starting as a spoiled rich boy, he learned to be a selfless hero through great trials and hardships. Those trials strained his self-image, though, and he doesn't really have much sense of identity beyond being Nighthawk these days. It's his reason to get up in the morning, and he's uncomfortable even imagining life after heroics. He applies that same determination in his loyalty to his friends, standing behind the "Defenders" name and the friends he made working on that team regardless of circumstances.

Abilities & Resources

Nighthawk's augmented physical abilities and sensory capacity are derived from past alchemical infusions. His strength and other athletic traits are increased further at night. He once also possessed precognitive visions, but does not currently.

Kyle has used the Richmond family fortune to equip himself with an advanced skin-tight armored suit with artificial wings and jet-powered flight capabilities. Adding to his already heightened physical resilience, the suit and wing construction allow him to survive substantial incoming damage. Sensor systems in the cowl expand his already augmented senses and give him a number of digital inputs on top of his natural perception. The wings house computer-aimed laser weapons, and the gloves possess titanium claws.

Nighthawk benefits from extensive self-training in combat and acrobatics, as well as no small background in occult research. In addition to the resources that come with extensive personal wealth, Kyle has cultivated contacts in a number of fields and on various super teams.

PUNISHER

Affiliations	Solo 10	Buddy 8	Team 6

Distinctions

Dead Inside
Former Marine
Obsessed Vigilante

4 +1 PP or 8

Power Sets

WAR ON CRIME

ENHANCED DURABILITY 8 **WEAPON** 8

- **SFX:** *Battle Van.* Add a D6 to the doom pool to step up a COMBAT or VEHICLES-related resource.
- **SFX:** *Explosives.* Against multiple targets, for every additional target add a D6 and keep an additional effect die. For each complication you create using your effect dice, step up that effect die and add D6 to the doom pool.
- **SFX:** *Full Auto.* Against a single target, step up or double a WAR ON CRIME die. Remove the highest rolling die and use three dice for your total.
- **SFX:** *Take Your Shot.* Spend 1 PP or take D6 physical stress to step up or double your WEAPON die.
- **SFX:** *Welcome Back, Frank.* Step up your physical stress die and move it to the doom pool. Spend 1 PP to do the same to physical trauma.
- **Limit:** *Gear.* Shutdown a WAR ON CRIME power or SFX to gain 1 PP. Take an action vs. the doom pool to recover.
- **Limit:** *Tragic Past.* When reminded of a past tragedy, step up mental or emotional stress to gain 1 PP.

Specialties

COMBAT MASTER 10	COVERT MASTER 10
CRIME EXPERT 8	MENACE MASTER 10
PSYCH EXPERT 8	VEHICLES EXPERT 8

[You may convert Expert D8 to 2D6, or Master D10 to 2D8 or 3D6]

Milestones

UNCOMPROMISING

- **1 XP** when you explain to an ally how they are being weak and why it will get people killed.
- **3 XP** when you stick to your mission even when compromised by innocent bystanders or obstacles.
- **10 XP** when you convince a fellow hero to accept your methods or you decide to alter your methods out of deep respect for another hero and tell them so.

WAR ZONE

- **1 XP** when you declare war on an enemy.
- **3 XP** when you use a Transition Scene to arm yourself or your allies.
- **10 XP** when you either take trauma in pursuit of your war or you are captured by the enemy.

CIVIL WAR

PP

STRESS / TRAUMA

P 4 6 8 10 12

M 4 6 8 10 12

E 4 6 8 10 12

XP

History

The life of Frank Castle shattered when the mob killed his wife and children for witnessing a gangland execution. Distraught and vengeful, Frank donned a costume styled on an enemy sniper he'd fought during the war and became the killer vigilante known as the Punisher. Using his Marine training and various military-grade armaments, the Punisher waged a one-man war on crime. He targeted everything from street thugs to super villains, though he often focused on organized crime figures.

Frank has spent years bringing down criminals, terrorists, and those who harm the innocent. His methods are brutal and decisive, making it hard for him to work with costumed heroes. In fact, many such heroes have attempted to capture or stop the vigilante. He has been presumed dead many times; however, Castle always manages to come back from certain death or capture to return to his mission.

Recently, the Punisher began working his way through various criminal syndicates around New York, killing soldiers and crime family heads alike. He will likely continue along this path unless some new injustice demands his attention.

Personality

A war hero and loving father whose personal tragedies turned him into a vengeful killer, Frank Castle is completely devoted to his mission to punish the guilty and kill criminals. He occasionally displays a softer side when dealing with innocents, but generally he is a cold, obsessive man who finds little joy in life. He believes in swift, brutal justice, though he can be frighteningly patient, if the situation warrants. Ultimately, the Punisher is devoted to making criminals pay dearly for the harms they cause.

Frank appreciates the good intentions of super heroes and what they try to do, but he considers them naïve and ultimately ineffective. He sees the numerous escapes and the ever-increasing number of victims that seem to pile up around super villains and criminals as evidence that his methods are both logical and required. The Punisher possesses a deeper respect for heroes with military backgrounds or those who work aggressively to keep crime off the streets, such as Captain America, Moon Knight, and Daredevil.

Abilities & Resources

The Punisher has no superhuman abilities, but he's a veteran soldier in peak physical condition. A master of various forms of close combat and a marksman with numerous weapons, Frank uses whatever tools are required for his mission, but favors military-style firearms and explosives. He wears body armor to protect himself from small arms and other attacks, and even uses specialized vehicles, most notably his armored "battle van."

The Punisher has few friends, but he's had a few allies or temporary partners. He's teamed up with Moon Knight and Wolverine on more than one occasion, and fought both with and against Daredevil and Spider-Man. Frank's more mundane contacts include everyone from computer hackers to police officers. Unfortunately, these individuals often meet bad ends, sometimes even at the hands of Castle himself. He doesn't have many old military buddies left, though he might still be able to scare up a few to aid him.

SHE-HULK

Affiliations

SOLO **8**   BUDDY **6**   TEAM **10**

Distinctions

CRUSADING ATTORNEY
IMPULSIVE
JADE GIANTESS

4 +1 PP or **8**

Power Sets

GAMMA-IRRADIATED BLOOD

GODLIKE STRENGTH **12**   LEAPING **8**

SUPERHUMAN DURABILITY **10**   SUPERHUMAN STAMINA **10**

SFX: *Area Attack.* Against multiple targets, for every additional target add a D6 and keep an additional effect die.

SFX: *Break the Fourth Wall.* When one of your opportunities is activated to add a D6 to the doom pool, replace it with a D4. Spend 1 PP to do this to an existing D6 in the doom pool.

SFX: *Collateral Damage.* Add a D6 to the doom pool to step up or double a GAMMA-IRRADIATED BLOOD power.

SFX: *Lose Yourself.* Step up or double a GAMMA-IRRADIATED BLOOD power for your next action and take D6 emotional stress.

Limit: *Puny Human.* Shutdown GAMMA-IRRADIATED BLOOD to gain 1 PP. Activate an opportunity to recover or during a Transition Scene.

Specialties

COMBAT EXPERT **8**   COSMIC EXPERT **8**

CRIME MASTER **10**   PSYCH EXPERT **8**

VEHICLES EXPERT **8**

[You may convert Expert D8 to 2D6, or Master D10 to 2D8 or 3D6]

Milestones

GIRLS JUST WANT TO HAVE FUN

1 XP when you name another character as a former romantic partner or reference some wild times you had.

3 XP when you help another character recover mental or emotional stress, or recover your own mental or emotional stress by flirting, partying, or socializing.

10 XP when you get serious with a romantic partner or break off a relationship to maintain your independence.

OBJECTION!

1 XP when you use your legal expertise to aid another character.

3 XP when you agree to defend someone in court, regardless of guilt or innocence.

10 XP when you defend a law or regulation in court, despite your personal feelings, or give up being an attorney in order to oppose it.

History

A transfusion from her cousin, Dr. Bruce Banner, saved attorney Jennifer Walters' life, but sharing blood with the human alter ego of the Hulk changed her life forever. Becoming a green-skinned, super-powered She-Hulk, Jennifer stopped the criminals who put her in the hospital. At first unable to change unless she was angry or afraid, she eventually gained control of her changes.

As She-Hulk, Jennifer joined the Avengers, became the Thing's replacement on the Fantastic Four for a time, and provided legal counsel for Heroes for Hire. Remaining in her human form less and becoming more comfortable as She-Hulk, she became incapable of changing forms. Indifferent, Walters even appeared in court in her green-skinned form, an act that garnered much attention in the legal community. She went on strange adventures, fought bizarre foes such as the Headman and Doctor Bong, and romanced several partners, notably Luke Cage and Wyatt Wingfoot.

Recently, the reality-altering havoc unleashed by her fellow Avenger Scarlet Witch caused Jennifer to lose control of herself as She-Hulk. After destroying the android Vision, her friend and teammate, she fled the team. Afraid to assume her jade-hued alter ego, Jennifer laid low until fellow gamma-irradiated Dr. Leonard Samson cured her instability. Accepting a job with Goodman, Lieber, Kurtzberg, & Holliway—contingent on her practicing law only in human form—Jennifer has returned to both heroics and her legal career.

Personality

While more subdued as Jennifer Walters, She-Hulk is fun-loving, passionate, idealistic, and daring. She loves being a super hero and prefers to stay in her powered form. She likes the attention being a 6'7" emerald bombshell gets her and enjoys fighting villains and traveling to exotic places. The damage wrought during another recent loss of control has made Jennifer a bit more thoughtful and careful, but she still tends to act decisively and sometimes recklessly.

She-Hulk is a loyal friend and teammate and tries to help others whenever she can. She is also passionate about her profession, believing in a defendant's right to a fair trial, due process, and other key principles of the legal system.

Abilities & Resources

As She-Hulk, Jennifer possesses incredible strength, endurance, and resistance to physical damage. As her powers grew over the years, she became one of the strongest beings on Earth. Jennifer is a skilled hand–to-hand fighter, having been trained by Captain America. Her legal skills are top-notch, ranking among such famed attorneys as Matt Murdock and her co-worker Mallory Book. Her time with the Avengers and Fantastic Four, as well as some odd personal adventures, give her impressive experience with aliens and cosmic phenomena.

In addition to the Fantastic Four and the Avengers, She-Hulk is very close to her cousin, Bruce Banner. Her connection to the Hulk is more volatile. She remains on decent terms with most of her romantic partners, which may or may not include the villain Juggernaut. As an attorney, she's defended heroes and villains from both civil and criminal charges and has contacts in the legal community as a whole. The latter includes the staff of her current employer: Mad Thinker, an android named Awesome Andy, her roommate Augustus "Pug" Pugliese, and the time-displaced western hero, the Two-Gun Kid.

SPIDER-MAN

Affiliations	Solo **8**	Buddy **10**	Team **6**

Distinctions

FRIENDLY NEIGHBORHOOD HERO?
WISECRACKER
WITH GREAT POWER COMES GREAT RESPONSIBILITY

4 or **8**
+1 PP

Power Sets

SPIDER-POWERS

ENHANCED SENSES **8**	ENHANCED STAMINA **8**
SUPERHUMAN REFLEXES **10**	SUPERHUMAN STRENGTH **10**
SWINGLINE **8**	WEAPON **8**
WALL-CRAWLING **6**	

SFX: *Grapple.* When inflicting a web-related complication on a target, add D6 and step up your effect die.

SFX: *Spider-Sense.* Spend 1 PP to add ENHANCED SENSES (or step up if already in your pool) and reroll all dice on a reaction.

SFX: *Second Wind.* Before you make an action including a SPIDER-POWERS power, you may move your physical stress die to the doom pool and step up the SPIDER-POWERS power for this action.

SFX: *Spider-Tracer.* Spend 1 PP or use an effect die to create a TRACED complication for a target. You may track that target anywhere until the complication is removed or ENHANCED SENSES is shutdown.

SFX: *Web Constructs.* When creating web-related assets, add D6 and step up your effect die.

Limit: *Exhausted.* Shutdown any SPIDER-POWERS power to gain 1 PP. Activate an opportunity to recover or during a Transition Scene.

IRON SPIDER ARMOR

CYBERNETIC SENSES **6**	SUPERHUMAN DURABILITY **10**
FLIGHT **6**	

SFX: *Immunity.* Spend 1 PP to ignore stress, trauma, or complications from toxins, radiation, or lack of breathable air.

SFX: *Waldoes.* If your pool includes both ENHANCED SENSES and CYBERNETIC SENSES, step up your effect dice.

Limit: *Stark Override.* Change one, two, or all three IRON SPIDER ARMOR powers into complications to gain 1 PP for each. Take an action vs. the doom pool using a TECH Specialty to recover the power or shutdown IRON SPIDER ARMOR.

Specialties

ACROBATIC MASTER **10**	COMBAT EXPERT **8**
COVERT EXPERT **8**	PSYCH EXPERT **8**
SCIENCE EXPERT **8**	TECH EXPERT **8**

[You may convert Expert D8 to 2D6, or Master D10 to 2D8 or 3D6]

Milestones

COPING WITH HUMOR

1 XP when you crack a joke while inflicting stress on an opponent.

3 XP when you point out how absurd a situation has become.

10 XP when you either stop joking and declare a situation deadly serious or vow to retire the mantle of Spider-Man forever.

TEAM PLAYER

1 XP when you give support to another hero not already on your team.

3 XP when you confront a team member about your place on the team.

10 XP when you either walk away from your team or join it at a cost to your family.

PP

STRESS / TRAUMA

P △4 6 8 10 12
M △4 6 8 10 12
E △4 6 8 10 12

XP

History

Raised by his Uncle Ben and Aunt May, science prodigy Peter Parker grew up shy and bookish. He had trouble making friends and was something of a social outsider in his school. When he was fifteen years old, Peter went on a school field trip, during which an irradiated spider bit him. The radioactive venom somehow caused a series of mutations that gave the boy superhuman abilities.

Attempting to earn money to help his financially struggling family, Parker donned a costume and tried his hand as a small-time television celebrity. Thinking himself too important because of his newfound fame, Peter ignored the chance to stop a thief escaping the studio one day, only to return home later to find that a burglar had murdered Uncle Ben. Hunting the burglar down, Parker discovered the killer was the man he had chosen to ignore earlier. Consumed by guilt, and having his future celebrity career curtailed by a set of critical editorials published by J. Jonah Jameson's *Daily Bugle*, Peter began a checkered career as the costumed vigilante Spider-Man. He eventually put Jameson's animosity to good use by making a living as a news photographer selling to the *Bugle* and specializing in photos of his alter ego.

Peter eventually graduated college and developed a strong relationship with girlfriend Mary Jane Watson, a romance that evolved into a happy, if problematic, marriage. Leaving his work with Jameson behind him, Parker used his science credentials to become a teacher, and more recently personal assistant to Tony Stark AKA Iron Man. As Spider-Man he is now a member of the Avengers, a life-changing event for him and his family.

Personality

Peter Parker is a courageous and good-hearted man driven by crushing guilt and an unshakeable moral core. The death of Uncle Ben taught him that with great power comes great responsibility. He is the everyman—mortal, fallible, and often subject to the cruel whims of fortune—who nevertheless gives his all to fight and bleed for his conscience. Spider-Man hides his fears and uncertainty in battle under an incessant torrent of wisecracks and taunts.

Abilities & Resources

Spider-Man possesses superhuman strength, agility, and reflexes, as well as a sixth sense attuned to danger. An attraction field based around his palms and the soles of his feet enables him to cling to most surfaces and even climb them. A recent "rebirth" has granted him additional spider-related powers, including organic webshooters and stingers that he can extend from his palms.

Despite having extraordinary powers, Peter frequently has to rely on his exceptional scientific acumen. Before his new powers manifested, he had designed, constructed, and used mechanical "web shooters" and various other gadgets. Tony Stark created a new suit of red and gold armor that complements his own abilities, in addition to extending his already considerable senses.

Spider-Man benefits from the resources and mentorship of Tony Stark, which also shoulders him with significant professional responsibility. Parker has a small circle of contacts through the Daily Bugle (such as reporter Phil Urich), as well as the emotional support of his wife Mary Jane and his Aunt May. Other than his powers and intellect, though, Parker normally has little else to rely on besides pure gumption and blind luck; if he were to end his relationship with Stark, he would be sacrificing the security of both himself and his loved ones.

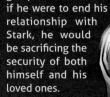

SPIDER-WOMAN

Affiliations

SOLO **8**   BUDDY **6**   TEAM **10**

Distinctions

ALLURING
PRIVATE INVESTIGATOR
TRIPLE AGENT

4 +1 PP   or   **8**

Power Sets

BIO-ELECTRIC METABOLISM

FLIGHT **6**   SUPERHUMAN STAMINA **10**

VENOM BLAST **8**

SFX: *Immunity.* Spend 1 PP to ignore stress, trauma, or complications from toxins, radiation, or disease.

SFX: *Pheromones.* When using any powers to inflict mental stress, add a D8 and step up your effect die.

Limit: *Uncontrollable.* Change any BIO-ELECTRIC METABOLISM power into a complication to gain 1 PP. Activate an opportunity or remove the complication to recover the power.

SPIDER-POWERS

ENHANCED SENSES **8**   SUPERHUMAN REFLEXES **10**

SUPERHUMAN STRENGTH **10**   WALL-CRAWLING **6**

SFX: *Second Chance.* If your pool includes a SPIDER-POWERS power, spend 1 PP to reroll.

Limit: *Exhausted.* Shutdown any SPIDER-POWERS power to gain 1 PP. Activate an opportunity to recover or during a Transition Scene.

Specialties

ACROBATIC EXPERT **8**   COMBAT EXPERT **8**

COVERT MASTER **10**   MENACE EXPERT **8**

MYSTIC EXPERT **8**   PSYCH EXPERT **8**

[You may convert Expert D8 to 2D6, or Master D10 to 2D8 or 3D6]

Milestones

DOUBLE-DOUBLE CROSS

1 XP when you talk to Hydra agents as if they are allies.

3 XP when you give orders to S.H.I.E.L.D. agents in the heat of battle.

10 XP when you either cripple a Hydra operation or betray an ally in order to venture deeper into Hydra, leaving your team behind.

VIPER'S DAUGHTER

1 XP when you argue with an ally because you perceive them as mistrusting you.

3 XP when you take emotional stress from an ally.

10 XP when you either become true friends with an ally, trusting them with your life and your secrets, or betray an ally to an enemy.

History

To save his daughter's life, Jonathan Drew transformed her. He conducted experiments that super-charged young Jessica Drew's metabolism, giving her a variety of superhuman powers. Jessica grew up on Wundagore Mountain among the High Evolutionary's New Men, until Hydra recruited and brainwashed her to be a living weapon and assassin codenamed Arachne. Hydra sent her to attack S.H.I.E.L.D. and its director, Nick Fury. Fury managed to break Jessica's conditioning and turn the confused young woman against her villainous masters. Seeking redemption and her own destiny, Jessica became the sensational Spider-Woman.

As Spider-Woman, Jessica has had many strange adventures, highs, and lows. She has encountered monsters, murderous madmen, and magicians. She has worked with everyone from Captain America to the Thing. A run-in with the sorceress Morgan Le Fay resulted in Jessica's apparent death, but her spirit and body were later reunited. After her resurrection, her powers became erratic and unreliable, and she gave up her costumed identity, instead working with her friend Lindsay McCabe as a private investigator. During this time, various others took up the mantle of Spider-Woman, but Jessica eventually regained her abilities and took up her heroic identity once again.

Since then, Spider-Woman has struggled to find a place, both in her normal life and in the superhuman community. She recently rejoined S.H.I.E.L.D. She also rejoined Hydra, who actually restored her powers, and is now working as a personal double agent for S.H.I.E.L.D.'s spymaster, Nick Fury. On top of all of this, she's a full-time Avenger.

Personality

Spider-Woman is a mix of strength and confusion. Her willpower, intellect, and compassion make her a good teammate and companion. However, complications with her powers and her unusual history make it hard for her to get close to others and form meaningful attachments. She is particularly guarded when first meeting people, concerned that any strong feelings are the result of her pheromone-based powers. This makes Spider-Woman seem mysterious and unapproachable, but those who gain her trust and friendship quickly find a devoted hero and loyal friend.

Abilities & Resources

Spider-Woman possesses superhuman strength, agility, and stamina. Her enhanced metabolism makes her immune to poisons and disease, as well as giving her the ability to build up and generate bio-electric "venom blasts" and cling to walls. These powers also super-charge her pheromones, making reactions to her—positive and negative—much more intense than usual. Spider-Woman is a skilled covert operative, investigator, and hand-to-hand combatant, having received training from both S.H.I.E.L.D. and Hydra. Her costume and enhanced physique allow her to glide on air currents.

Spider-Woman has an eclectic mix of allies. She has worked closely with the Shroud, Tigra, Werewolf by Night, and several heroes with ties to the espionage community like Ms. Marvel, Wolverine, and Nick Fury. Her friend and ex-partner, Lindsay McCabe, is one of the few relatively normal people she knows. As a S.H.I.E.L.D. agent she has access to the resources of that organization, subject to authorization from her superiors.

SUB-MARINER

Affiliations

SOLO 10	BUDDY 6	TEAM 8

Distinctions

HUMAN-ATLANTEAN HYBRID
IMPERIOUS REX!
LONG & COLORFUL HISTORY

 4 +1 PP or 8

Power Sets

AQUATIC MUTANT

ENHANCED REFLEXES 8	FLIGHT 6
GODLIKE STRENGTH 12	SUPERHUMAN DURABILITY 10
SUPERHUMAN STAMINA 10	SWIMMING 8

SFX: *Berserk.* Add a doom die to your next attack action. After your action, step up the doom die and return it to the doom pool.

SFX: *Foul-Tempered.* Step up or double any AQUATIC MUTANT power for one action. If the action fails, add a die to the doom pool equal to the normal rating of your power die.

SFX: *In His Element.* Before you take an action including an AQUATIC MUTANT power while underwater, you may move your physical stress die to the doom pool and step up the AQUATIC MUTANT die for this action.

SFX: *Mighty Fortitude.* Spend 1 PP to ignore stress, trauma, or complications caused by aging, disease, poison, radiation, or vacuum.

Limit: *Mutant.* When affected by mutant-specific complications and tech, earn 1 PP.

Limit: *Need...Water...Now.* Step back your GODLIKE STRENGTH power to gain 1 PP. Immerse yourself in water to recover the power.

Specialties

| BUSINESS EXPERT 8 | COMBAT EXPERT 8 |
| MENACE MASTER 10 | PSYCH EXPERT 8 |

[You may convert Expert D8 to 2D6, or Master D10 to 2D8 or 3D6]

Milestones

IT'S ONLY ARROGANCE IF IT'S NOT TRUE

1 XP when you explain to a surface-dweller exactly what you think of their stupidity.

3 XP when you engage in a conflict with other heroes in order to prove your superior qualities.

10 XP when you either sacrifice an important personal goal to validate a point of ego, reputation, or pride or you swallow your pride and admit to your own error.

POWER IS THE ULTIMATE APHRODISIAC

1 XP when you tell a powerful woman how majestic her power is to behold.

3 XP when you explain to a powerful woman's suitor or spouse why they are not worthy of her love.

10 XP when you either ask a powerful woman to be your queen or declare her unworthy and seek another match.

History

Son of human sea captain Leonard McKenzie, and Fen, an Atlantean princess, Namor is a creature of two worlds and has never comfortably fit in either. Violent in defense of his undersea kingdom, he has also protected humanity from terrible enemies. Attacking New York City in response to surface-dweller incursions, he later joined forces with the Allies against the Axis forces, working alongside Captain America and the original Human Torch as one of the Invaders.

Mentally attacked and afflicted with amnesia, Namor wandered the surface for decades before being recognized and returned to lucidity by Johnny Storm. Believing his people destroyed by the surface world, the Sub-Mariner spent years as its enemy, allying himself with such figures as Doctor Doom or Magneto in one scheme after another against the Fantastic Four and the Avengers. As his memories slowly returned and he discovered his people still alive and in need of his guidance, Namor stabilized somewhat. He has fought alongside and as a member of the Avengers, made uneasy peace with the Fantastic Four, and is a founding member of the Defenders. As a member of Iron Man's Illuminati, Namor has been involved in a number of critical turning points in recent superhuman history.

Personality

Where others see arrogance, Namor simply sees truth and birthright. He is royalty, immensely powerful and charismatic. He stands second to none—just ask him. Modesty is for lesser creatures. He's also brave to a fault, passionate in his convictions, and aggravatingly honorable. His belief in *noblesse oblige* may be unshakeable, but his imperious manner tends to undermine any intended beneficence. His epic ego can overshadow any of these traits, though, and his temper is equally legendary. Namor doesn't feel bound by the "base" morality of "hypocritical" surface-dwellers, making him more a force of nature with pointed ears and scaly shorts than just another hero or villain.

Namor makes no secret of his affections, especially his love for Sue Richards. He's gone to great lengths to woo her and made his intentions very clear to her husband, Reed, as well.

Abilities & Resources

The Sub-Mariner is immensely strong and superhumanly resilient, far beyond other Atlanteans, and he has fought toe-to-toe against the likes of the Thing and Hercules. Naturally amphibious, he must be careful of how long he spends both below and above the water, as prolonged imbalances can make his behavior erratic. He can fly, a result of a mutation beyond even his unusual parentage. Out of water, Namor weakens over time. Though approaching a century in years, he looks and acts like a man still in the prime of his life.

Namor, a sovereign with access to sunken treasure around the globe, is wealthy beyond measure. As King of Atlantis, he commands a military with advanced technology and superhuman warriors and he benefits from diplomatic rank and government connections. He has a reputation as dangerous and sometimes erratic, one earned over decades, and he knows how to turn that to his advantage. Having fought both for and against humanity, as well as alongside and against many of its champions, Namor has allies on both sides of the hero/villain divide and no qualms about using any of them, when he sees fit.

THING

Affiliations	Solo **6**	Buddy **10**	Team **8**

Distinctions

I'm a Monster!
It's Clobberin' Time!
Wotta Revoltin' Development

4 +1 PP   or   **8**

Power Sets

ROCKY ORANGE HIDE

Godlike Durability **12**	Godlike Strength **12**

Enhanced Stamina **8**

SFX: *Area Attack.* Against multiple targets, for every additional target add a D6 and keep an additional effect die.

SFX: *Collateral Damage.* Instead of spending 1 PP, add a D6 to the doom pool to create a ROCKY ORANGE HIDE stunt.

SFX: *Haymaker.* Double GODLIKE STRENGTH for an action, then add the second-highest rolling die from that action to the doom pool.

SFX: *Invulnerable.* Spend 1 PP to ignore physical stress or trauma results unless caused by mystical attacks.

Limit: *Moody.* Step up emotional stress caused by doubt, guilt, or self-worth to gain 1 PP.

Specialties

Combat Expert **8**	Cosmic Expert **8**
Psych Expert **8**	Vehicles Master **10**

[You may convert Expert D8 to 2D6, or Master D10 to 2D8 or 3D6]

Milestones

BLUE-EYED BOY FROM YANCY STREET

1 XP when you spend a Transition Scene either enjoying simple pleasures with the Richards family or going on a romantic date.

3 XP when a bystander who is close to you is embroiled in danger because of your relationship with them.

10 XP when you either welcome someone into your life, trusting that they can handle the dangers of your fantastic lifestyle or push your loved ones away so that they never get hurt because of you.

WHAT TIME IS IT?

1 XP when you lead a charge into a dangerous battle, yelling your battle cry.

3 XP when you take stress from standing toe-to-toe with a villain who possesses a D12 in one of their power sets.

10 XP when you either apologize to an opponent for clobbering them or deal trauma to a global threat, rending it defeated.

PP

STRESS / TRAUMA

P △4 6 8 10 12
M △4 6 8 10 12
E △4 6 8 10 12
XP

History

A street tough turned ace pilot, Ben served as pilot on the famous space flight that bombarded its crew with cosmic rays and created the super team known as the Fantastic Four. The most physically altered by the accident, Ben became a being of orange rocky skin and amazing might. Calling himself "The Thing," Ben became one of the world's most recognizable super heroes.

Ben has been "cured" of his inhuman appearance before, but he always reverts back to it out of necessity or some twist of fate. He's traveled the cosmos, worked with numerous heroes, and even found love a few times. He's left the Fantastic Four periodically, only to return to a team he sees as his true family. The Thing's brawls with various villains and powerful menaces are legendary. He's gone toe-to-toe with everyone from the Hulk to the Champion of the Universe. In the latter matchup, the Thing's dogged determination and refusal to quit saved the whole planet from destruction. The hero's battle cry of "It's Clobberin' Time!" is welcomed by allies, feared by enemies, and no one ever forgets Ben Grimm, the ever-lovin' blue-eyed Thing.

Personality

Underneath the Thing's rocky orange hide and gruff attitude is a hero's heart and adventurer's spirit. He's loyal, brave, and refuses to quit even in the face of impossible odds. Despite his inherent goodness, the Thing's own disgust at his inhuman appearance is his key weakness. On some level he cannot bring himself to believe he isn't the monster he appears to be. This makes him try even harder to be a good and decent person, but it often makes him angry and deeply wounded by any rejection, real or imagined.

Abilities & Resources

The Thing's orange rocky skin is incredibly durable. He is capable of withstanding amazing punishment, such as being knocked through several buildings by a devastating blow, only to emerge slightly woozy and very annoyed. He's one of the stronger heroes in the Marvel Universe, capable of lifting great weights and slugging it out with giant monsters and other menaces.

The Thing is an experienced brawler and pilot. He can fly nearly anything and is at home in the middle of a scrap. No scientist, he has nevertheless become familiar with many alien races and strange phenomena from his adventures with the Fantastic Four.

The Fantastic Four aren't just the Thing's friends—they're his family. The Thing has teamed up with nearly every hero on Earth—and beyond—at some time or another. He's worked closely with the likes of Spider-Man, Ms. Marvel, Captain America, and also with little-known heroes such as the Aquarian and Skull the Slayer. His good reputation means he can even call upon resources from organizations like S.H.I.E.L.D. occasionally. He has a longstanding and sometimes troubled romance with blind sculptor Alicia Masters, whom he loves dearly. The Thing is surprisingly wealthy, having gained a share of the Fantastic Four's patents over the years, but done little with the wealth.

TIGRA

Affiliations

Solo (8) **Buddy** (6) **Team** (10)

Distinctions

ADVENTUROUS WERE-CAT
BORDERLINE FERAL
MYSTICAL LEGEND

(4) +1 PP **or** (8)

Power Sets

CHOSEN CHAMPION OF THE CAT PEOPLE

ENHANCED SPEED (8) **ENHANCED STRENGTH** (8)

PSYCHIC RESISTANCE (8) **SUPERHUMAN REFLEXES** (10)

SUPERHUMAN SENSES (10) **SUPERHUMAN STAMINA** (10)

SFX: *Claws & Fangs.* Step back the highest die in your attack action pool to add D6 and step up physical stress inflicted.

SFX: *Immunity.* Spend 1 PP to ignore stress from disease, poison, or psychic attack.

SFX: *Multipower.* Add more than one CHOSEN CHAMPION OF CAT PEOPLE power to your pool. Step back each CHOSEN CHAMPION OF CAT PEOPLE die in your pool once for each die beyond the first.

SFX: *Pounce.* On a succesful reaction against a physical attack, inflict physical stress with your effect die at no PP cost. Spend 1 PP to step it up.

Limit: *Human Form.* Shutdown CHOSEN CHAMPION OF CAT PEOPLE power set to assume human form. Recover CHOSEN CHAMPION OF CAT PEOPLE power set to revert to feline form.

Specialties

ACROBATICS MASTER (10) **COMBAT EXPERT** (8)

COSMIC EXPERT (8) **COVERT EXPERT** (8)

CRIME EXPERT (8) **MYSTIC EXPERT** (8)

VEHICLES EXPERT (8)

[You may convert Expert D8 to 2D6, or Master D10 to 2D8 or 3D6]

Milestones

EVERY CAT HAS ITS CLAWS

1 XP when you flirt with another hero.

3 XP when you either accept or rebuff the advances of another hero.

10 XP when you either break off a relationship to maintain your independence or commit deeply to a monogamous relationship.

FELINE HERITAGE

1 XP when you engage in innocent catlike behavior in everyday life.

3 XP when you admit to a friend that you engage in feral catlike behavior that sometimes makes you feel out of control and uncomfortable.

10 XP when you attempt to abandon one of your souls in favor of the other or find a balance and peace between your feline and human souls.

History

Still grieving over the shooting death of her husband, Bill, Greer Grant Nelson needed work and found it with her old professor, Joanne Tumulo, who was working on human augmentation. As Dr. Tumulo's test subject, Greer gained feline-like powers. Donning a gold and blue costume and calling herself the Cat, the young woman fought various costumed villains.

Shortly afterwards, Dr. Tumulo revealed her true nature as one of a race of humanoids evolved from felines. The Cat People used science and sorcery to protect themselves and keep their existence secret. After Greer was mortally injured while operating as the Cat, Tumulo used her people's science and magic to save her friend by transforming her into "the Tigra," the chosen champion and protector of the Cat People.

As Tigra, Greer joined the Avengers, traveled the cosmos, and had numerous solo adventures. At times her feline nature has caused her problems, making her unpredictable or feral. She has also lost her powers temporarily, usually by rejecting the "tiger soul" that fuels her powers. She even joined the Chicago police department for a time, following in the footsteps of her murdered husband. These days, Tigra is an active solo hero, eager to aid her friends and allies.

Personality

Greer is a mix of feline and human instincts and urges. She loves attention and affection, but it's tempered with reason and a desire to maintain her independence. She is a loyal friend, generally pleasant and fun-loving, though she can be vindictive if hurt. In her darker moments, Tigra often seems conflicted and even a bit lonely, not quite fitting in with either the Cat People or humanity. This can lead to her being overly secretive, and sometimes she tries to handle things by herself when she should instead seek aid.

Abilities & Resources

Tigra's physical transformation gives her a number of superhuman abilities. She's strong, tough, fast, incredibly agile, and possesses senses keener than a cat's. She sports the claws and orange and black-striped fur of a cat, and her twin souls, human and feline, make her highly resistant to psychic attacks. She is a trained detective and pilot. Her abilities, combined with extensive training, make Tigra a skilled combatant and amazing acrobat. In addition to these abilities, Greer has an affinity with magic, a talent that remains largely undeveloped.

Although Tigra possess an amulet that allows her to resume human form, she rarely uses it, viewing her feline-human hybrid form as her true self. She has a diverse group of allies, including Werewolf by Night, Moon Knight, Wonder Man, and many of her fellow Avengers. She befriended Spider-Woman (Jessica Drew), back when the hero was without powers, and maintains a friendly, flirtatious, and occasionally romantic relationship with Yellowjacket (Hank Pym). The Cat People see Tigra as their champion and emissary and have aided her many times in the past with their sorcery and advanced science.

She has spent a long time traveling the galaxy with former Avenger Starfox, and has worked with the mysterious psychic Moondragon as well.

WASP

Affiliations   SOLO **6**   BUDDY **8**   TEAM **10**

PP ☐

Distinctions
FASHIONISTA
FOUNDING AVENGER
HEROIC SOCIALITE

△ **4** +1 PP   or   **8**

STRESS / TRAUMA

Power Sets

ALTERED CELLULAR STRUCTURE

ENHANCED REFLEXES **8**   ENHANCED STRENGTH **8**

GROWTH **10**   SHRINKING **10**

SFX: *Giant Strength.* Shutdown SHRINKING to step up ENHANCED STRENGTH. Recover SHRINKING by stepping back ENHANCED STRENGTH.

SFX: *Multipower.* Add more than one ALTERED CELLULAR STRUCTURE power to your dice pool. Step back each ALTERED CELLULAR STRUCTURE die in your pool once for each die beyond the first.

Limit: *Exhausted.* Shutdown any ALTERED CELLULAR STRUCTURE power to gain 1 PP. Activate an opportunity to recover or during a Transition Scene.

Limit: *Size Matters.* Add a complication equal to GROWTH or SHRINKING to an opposing dice pool to gain 1 PP.

INSECT POWERS

BIO-ELECTRIC BLAST **8**   ENHANCED FLIGHT **6**

INSECT CONTROL **6**

SFX: *Wasp's Sting.* Spend 1 PP to step up BIO-ELECTRIC BLAST to D10. Step back to 2D6 for subsequent actions. Activate an opportunity to recover.

SFX: *Sting Barrage.* Step up or double BIO-ELECTRIC BLAST for your next action. Remove highest rolling die and use three dice for your total.

Limit: *Exclusive.* Shutdown INSECT POWERS to activate GROWTH. Shutdown GROWTH to recover INSECT POWERS.

Specialties

BUSINESS EXPERT **8**   COMBAT EXPERT **8**

COSMIC EXPERT **8**   PSYCH MASTER **10**

[You may convert Expert D8 to 2D6, or Master D10 to 2D8 or 3D6]

P △4 6 8 10 12

M △4 6 8 10 12

E △4 6 8 10 12

Milestones

HEART OF THE TEAM

1 XP when you aid another character in combat or in recovering mental or emotional stress.

3 XP when you discover the source of a teammate's emotional or mental problems and attempt to help through a support action.

10 XP when you help teammates recover from a long-term emotional or mental problem or kick them off the team so they can find the solution to their problem on their own.

OVER IT

1 XP when you flirt with other heroes or reject their advances.

3 XP when you help out a romantic partner despite significant personal risk—mental, emotional, or physical.

10 XP when you reconcile with an old flame or move on by starting a new relationship.

XP ☐

History

When an extra-dimensional creature killed Janet Van Dyne's scientist father, she convinced her father's associate, Dr. Henry "Hank" Pym, to help her fight it. The young socialite became the costumed hero known as the Wasp, with Pym taking on the identity of Ant-Man. Janet was attracted to costumed heroics, as well as the handsome, if somewhat socially obtuse, Pym. The pair worked alone for a time, but soon allied with fellow heroes Iron Man, Thor, and the Hulk to form the Avengers. Janet also became a successful fashion designer and remains well known for the wide variety of costumes she sports in her heroic identity.

Janet has been a key member of the Avengers for most of her heroic career, eventually leading the group as chairperson. She took periodic leaves of absence, but always returned to the action, camaraderie, and adventure of being an Avenger. After an up-and-down courtship, she and Hank eventually married, but this ended badly after he suffered a series of severe mental breakdowns. She has had other relationships since, including several attempts to reconcile with Hank, but nothing has stuck.

Recently, Wasp accidentally reminded a disturbed Scarlet Witch of traumatic events involving the fellow Avenger's children. This triggered events that led to the breakup of the Avengers for a time, as well as the apparent deaths of several members. Injured during these events, she and Hank attempted another go at leaving the team and being together, but they've since decided to just be friends.

Personality

While originally somewhat flighty and even spoiled, the Wasp has become one of the most experienced and cagey Avengers in history. She is in many ways the heart of the team, providing her fellow members with support, understanding, and the occasional shocking wake-up call. She's a romantic who does truly love her former husband, but she's also a pragmatist who realizes they have had their chance. She is confident, courageous, and while not the strongest or most powerful Avenger, she is among the most loyal and steadfast.

Abilities & Resources

Altered by "Pym particles," Wasp's genetic structure allows her to shrink down to mere inches or grow to several stories tall. When shrunk she can fly and channel bio-electric energy into potent "stinger blasts," and has a limited ability to communicate with and control insects. When grown she is superhumanly strong and durable, but she's more comfortable at smaller sizes.

In addition to her powers, Janet is very capable and talented. Trained in combat by Captain America, she is also a skilled businesswoman, designer, strategist, and leader. Her adventures with the Avengers have given her an impressive array of experiences to draw on, and her intuition and social skills make her a natural confidant. She's also very wealthy, having used her inheritance and skills to become even more financially successful.

As a founding Avenger and one of the premier heroes on Earth, Wasp has numerous allies and friends. Her former husband Hank, currently using the identity of Yellowjacket, still cares for her deeply. She is close to most heroes who served on the Avengers during her numerous and lengthy stints on the team, including She-Hulk, Ms. Marvel, Black Knight, Goliath, Hawkeye, and others. She also maintains decent relationships with numerous old flames, including Iron Man and the super-mercenary Paladin. Her status as a famous designer, heiress, and celebrity hero also affords her numerous contacts in the media.

WOLVERINE

Affiliations	Solo 10	Buddy 6	Team 8

Distinctions

CENTURY-LONG LIFETIME
I'M THE BEST THERE IS AT WHAT I DO
MASTERLESS SAMURAI

4 +1 PP **or** 8

Power Sets

FERAL MUTANT

ENHANCED REFLEXES	8	ENHANCED STRENGTH	8
GODLIKE STAMINA	12	SUPERHUMAN SENSES	10

SFX: *Berserk.* Add a doom die to your next attack action. After your action, step up the doom die and return it to the doom pool.

SFX: *Focus.* If your pool includes a FERAL MUTANT die, you may replace two dice of equal size with one stepped-up die.

SFX: *Healing Factor.* Spend 1 PP to recover your physical stress and step back your physical trauma.

Limit: *Mutant.* When affected by mutant-specific complications or tech, earn 1 PP.

WEAPON X PROGRAM

ADAMANTIUM CLAWS	10	PSYCHIC RESISTANCE	10

SFX: *Adamantium Skeleton.* On a successful reaction against edged or blunt attack action, either convert opponent's effect die into a WEAPON X PROGRAM stunt or step back your effect die and inflict it as physical stress. If your opponent's action succeeds, spend 1 PP to use this SFX.

SFX: *Fearsome.* When using WEAPON X PROGRAM powers to inflict emotional stress, add a D6 and step up your effect die.

SFX: *Immunity.* Spend 1 PP to ignore telepathy or mind control.

Limit: *Heavy Metal.* On a magnetic attack or while swimming, change any WEAPON X PROGRAM power into a complication to gain 1 PP. Activate an opportunity or remove the complication to recover the power.

Limit: *Toxic Metal.* If GODLIKE STAMINA is shutdown, take D10 physical stress at the beginning and end of every action scene.

Specialties

COMBAT MASTER	10	COVERT MASTER	10
CRIME EXPERT	8	MENACE MASTER	10
VEHICLE EXPERT	8		

[You may convert Expert D8 to 2D6, or Master D10 to 2D8 or 3D6]

Milestones

...AND WHAT I DO ISN'T VERY NICE

1 XP when you first choose to inflict physical stress in a scene.

3 XP when another hero rebukes you for your violence or you threaten another hero with violence.

10 XP when you kill someone in front of innocents or recover from your berserker rage in front of innocents without having inflicted trauma on anyone.

"NOW IT'S MY TURN!"

1 XP when you separate from your allies, accepting no help, so that you can hunt an enemy down alone.

3 XP when you inflict trauma on a villain due to an asset created by an ally.

10 XP when you either admit that you needed an ally's help, declaring that they are good to have around in a scrap or explain to an ally why they are a danger to themselves and any team they serve on.

PP

STRESS / TRAUMA

P
4 6 8 10 12

M
4 6 8 10 12

E
4 6 8 10 12

XP

CIVIL WAR

History

James Howlett was born sickly to wealthy parents in late 19th Century Canada. Abuse, betrayal, lost love, murder, and the manifestation of his mutant abilities lead young James to flee his ruined home with his first love, a girl named Rose. Eventually he lost Rose as well and fled into the wilderness to live with a pack of wolves.

Leaving the forest after a time, James spent decades having a series of strange and half-remembered adventures. Under the name Logan, he fought in World War II, met Captain America, and worked for various intelligence services. Later he came to the attention of the Weapon X program, which was attempting to make the perfect assassin and killing machine. The program bonded Adamantium to Logan's skeleton and bone claws, making them unbreakable. The process also broke Logan's mind, causing his memories to fragment and reverting him to an animal state. He wandered the Canadian wilderness until Heather and James MacDonald Hudson found him. The couple helped restore his sanity and recruited him for Canada's Department H.

As Department H's operative, Logan took the name Wolverine. He fought the Hulk, worked with Alpha Flight, and went on various missions until Charles Xavier recruited him for the X-Men. Wolverine stayed with the X-Men for years, leaving periodically in attempts to find peace or put together the fractured memories of his past. When the Scarlet Witch altered reality to create a world where mutants were no longer hated and feared, she also restored all of Logan's memories, which remained when reality resumed. He is currently with both the X-Men and the Avengers, splitting his time between both teams, while finding time to deal with his recovered memories.

Personality

Wolverine is gruff, blunt, but extremely loyal and passionate. He combines the code of a samurai warrior with the instincts and impulses of a predator. Wolverine is often protective of younger, less experienced heroes and teammates, but he never coddles them, preferring to help them grow and advance through "tough love." Wolverine isn't proud of his berserker rages and past activities as an assassin and killer, but he isn't drowning in shame either. Instead, he accepts what he is, expects others to do the same, and tries to use those skills and experiences for good.

Abilities & Resources

Wolverine possesses uncanny stamina and recuperative abilities. This healing factor allows him to recover from terrible wounds, rendering him functionally immune to poisons and diseases, and greatly retarding his aging. His skeleton and natural bone claws are bonded with Adamantium, making them unbreakable and the claws hyper-sharp, capable of cutting through nearly anything. Wolverine also has enhanced physical abilities and heightened senses.

In addition to his powers, Wolverine has several lifetimes of training and experience. He speak multiple languages, is a trained spy, soldier, and assassin. He has mastered various forms of combat, particularly unarmed ones and those using bladed weapons. He is an expert woodsman and tracker, skills augmented by his mutant senses.

Wolverine has been there and done that. There are few superhumans in the Marvel Universe he hasn't fought with or against—often both. In particular, he has worked closely with Spider-Man, Nick Fury, Captain America, and Spider-Woman. He is surprisingly close to fellow X-Man Shadowcat and spent years in love with teammate Jean Grey and rivals with her longtime beau, Cyclops. He has numerous contacts in the intelligence community and extensive criminal contacts centered around the Southeast Asian island of Madripoor, many of whom he had forgotten about until recently.

WONDER MAN

Affiliations	Solo 6	Buddy 10	Team 8

Distinctions

Been Dead Before
Hollywood Hero
Ionic Powerhouse

4 +1 PP or **8**

Power Sets

ENERGY-AUGMENTED FORM

ENHANCED REFLEXES	8	ENHANCED SENSES	8
GODLIKE DURABILITY	12	GODLIKE STAMINA	12
GODLIKE STRENGTH	12	SUBSONIC FLIGHT	8

SFX: *Immunity.* Spend 1 PP to ignore stress, trauma, or complications caused by aging, disease, poison, radiation, or vacuum.

SFX: *Multipower.* Add more than one ENERGY-AUGMENTED FORM power to your dice pool. Step back each ENERGY-AUGMENTED FORM die in your pool once for each die beyond the first.

SFX: *My Fists Hit Like Thor's Hammer!* Double GODLIKE STRENGTH for an action, then add the second-highest rolling die from that action to the doom pool.

Limit: *Flirting with Instability.* Step up a mental or emotional stress die being used against you to gain 1 PP. Step back the stress to the previous rating afterwards.

Specialties

BUSINESS EXPERT	8	COMBAT EXPERT	8
PSYCH EXPERT	8	TECH EXPERT	8

[You may convert Expert D8 to 2D6, or Master D10 to 2D8 or 3D6]

Milestones

AVENGER WHO HAS SEEN IT ALL

1 XP when you talk about crazy things you have seen as an Avenger.

3 XP when you call out an old enemy and deal them stress.

10 XP when you decide this life is not for you and leave the Avengers or take over leadership and decide the team needs a radically new direction.

MEDIA DARLING

1 XP when you give an interview about your work as a super hero.

3 XP when you attack an enemy, causing emotional or mental stress, by using the media.

10 XP when you either lead a high profile team that has its own camera crew or decide that you need to shun the media.

PP

STRESS / TRAUMA

P 4 6 8 10 12

M 4 6 8 10 12

E 4 6 8 10 12

XP

History

Industrialist Sanford Williams had two sons, Simon and Eric, and one company, Williams Innovations. The elder, Eric, wanted nothing to do with his father's business and secretly became quite an accomplished career criminal, working with the Maggia crime syndicate. The younger, Simon, therefore inherited his father's business at the tender age of 22. Despite his studious bent and technical acumen, the younger Williams sibling proved woefully unsuited to managing a corporation. Competition from the likes of Stark Industries was crushing Williams Innovations; in desperation, Simon approached his brother for help. Following Eric's advice, Simon embezzled from his own company then unwisely invested in Maggia businesses. When his board of directors discovered his crimes, Williams found himself ousted, indicted, and then convicted.

"Rescued" from his prison sentence by Baron Zemo and the Masters of Evil, Simon joined the Masters to strike directly at Stark, who Williams was led to believe was the reason his life had come crashing down. Zemo used ionic ray technology to transform Williams into "Wonder Man," a powerhouse that infiltrated the Avengers as a new hero. Although Williams believed Zemo's story that he needed continuous treatments for his new form to survive, his conscience ultimately wouldn't let him betray his new teammates, and he turned against Zemo. Seeming to die from the side effects of his ionic enhancement, Simon instead fell into a coma-like state while his body continued to change. Through a complicated set of circumstances, Simon eventually revived.

He fought alongside the Avengers for many years, leaving for short periods to pursue a Hollywood career and work with the West Coast Avengers and Force Works teams. While fighting with Force Works against the Kree, Simon again appeared to die. His ionic energies dispersed, only to be resurrected later by the Scarlet Witch's hex-magics.

Personality

At heart, Simon Williams is a good man, but one burdened by considerable guilt and feelings of inadequacy. Under pressure, he responds impulsively. He finds himself alienated by the nature of his powers. He now knows he's effectively immortal, and that realization is proving difficult for him on an emotional level. Although he loves the Scarlet Witch, he feels unworthy of her, conflicted by his complicated psychological relationship with her ex-husband, the synthezoid Vision. Sadly, his experiences may drive him toward the idea that he and his fellow superhumans ultimately do more harm than good, regardless of their intentions.

Abilities & Resources

As Wonder Man, Simon Williams is no longer really human in any physical sense. Essentially ionic energy bound in organic form with Simon's consciousness, he is on par with Thor in terms of strength and is, for all practical purposes, indestructible. Even when an attack of sufficient magnitude disperses his physical form, he simply reforms some time later, though he sometimes requires external help. Williams doesn't tire or get sick, ignores temperature and pressure extremes, and doesn't even bleed. In his current form, he can channel ionic energy for flight, and his senses perceive beyond the human range.

Simon has a background in engineering and electronics, and he's smarter than he conveys in the company of people like Stark and Pym. He's a decent actor with stuntman training, and tutelage at the hands of Captain America and S.H.I.E.L.D. experts has made him a respectable unarmed combatant.

YELLOWJACKET

Affiliations   **SOLO** `6`   **BUDDY** `10`   **TEAM** `8`

Distinctions

EPIC GUILT COMPLEX
NEED TO PROVE MYSELF
TOWERING INTELLECT

`4 +1 PP` or `8`

Power Sets

SIZE OF AN ANT

ENHANCED REFLEXES `8`   **FLIGHT** `6`

INSECT CONTROL `6`   **SHRINKING** `10`

SFX: *Miniaturized Arsenal.* When using SIZE OF AN ANT to create tech-related assets, add a D6 and step up your effect die.

Limit: *Gear.* Shutdown INSECT CONTROL or FLIGHT or both to gain 1 PP. Take an action vs. the doom pool to recover.

Limit: *I'm Tiny!* Change SHRINKING into a complication to gain 1 PP. Activate an opportunity or remove the complication to recover the power.

SIZE OF A BUILDING

ENHANCED STAMINA `8`   **GROWTH** `10`

SUPERHUMAN DURABILITY `10`   **SUPERHUMAN STRENGTH** `10`

SFX: *Area Attack.* Against multiple targets, for every additional target add a D6 and keep an additional effect die.

SFX: *Gargantuan.* Step up or double any SIZE OF A BUILDING power for one action. If the action fails, add a die to the doom pool equal to the normal rating of your power die.

Limit: *Too Big!* Change GROWTH into a complication to gain 1 PP. Activate an opportunity or remove the complication to recover the power.

Limit: *Mutually Exclusive.* Shutdown SIZE OF A BUILDING to activate SIZE OF AN ANT. Shutdown SIZE OF AN ANT to recover SIZE OF A BUILDING.

Specialties

COMBAT EXPERT `8`   **COSMIC EXPERT** `8`

SCIENCE MASTER `10`   **TECH MASTER** `10`

[You may convert Expert D8 to 2D6, or Master D10 to 2D8 or 3D6]

Milestones

MAKER

1 XP when you use your TECH Specialty to create a new resource in the form of a robot, artificial intelligence, or computer.

3 XP when you get into a conflict with your creation.

10 XP when you help your creation find its place in the world, or inflict trauma on it and deny responsibility for its existence.

OWN WORST ENEMY

1 XP when you try to make yourself feel better by pointing out the shortcoming of a loved one.

3 XP when you do something really nice to make up for having wronged someone you love.

10 XP when you either take responsibility for your cycle of abuse and seek outside help to end it, or break off your current romantic relationship, blaming the problems on someone else.

PP

STRESS / TRAUMA

P   4 6 8 10 12

M   4 6 8 10 12

E   4 6 8 10 12

XP

History

Emotionally traumatized by the murder of his first wife, Henry "Hank" Pym dedicated himself to helping humanity in order to find some peace or purpose in her death. His research yielded a number of discoveries, the most prominent of which were the size-changing Pym Particles and a cybernetic helmet he could use to communicate with insects. He used these inventions to become the costumed hero Ant-Man, the first of many heroic personas.

Pym met his future wife when he defeated an alien invader who had killed her father. Janet Van Dyne convinced Hank to use his research to transform her into the Wasp. Pym and Van Dyne founded the Avengers, but Pym himself went through a number of heroic personas such as Giant-Man and Goliath before driving himself to a nervous breakdown. Under the persona and separate personality of Yellowjacket, Hank married Janet, who wasn't fooled by the new identity. Despite the happy wedding, the following years saw Pym's expulsion from the Avengers for recklessness and brutal behavior, the disintegration of his marriage, and even his framing and imprisonment for treason. It took some time for Pym to redeem himself, first in his own eyes and then in the eyes of his former friends and teammates. He had finally returned to duty with the Avengers when the madness of the Scarlet Witch tore the team apart. In the aftermath, Hank and Janet both left heroics to give their relationship another chance, but they have since gone their separate ways.

Personality

Henry Pym is a brilliant man who often proves to be his own worst enemy, never living up to his impossible standards. His need for validation has driven him to nervous breakdowns, and his sometimes questionable emotional stability has cost him his marriage and the respect of his peers. While Stark and Richards appreciate Pym's technical acumen, they hold his judgment suspect and find it difficult to accept his conclusions or actions, especially if they think he's having an emotional "episode." Despite his great accomplishments in many different fields, Pym focuses more on his failures than his successes. He carries the guilt of having created Ultron, a genocidal monster of the first order, who Pym knows was programmed partially from copies of his own personality engrams.

Abilities & Resources

A genius in multiple disciplines, Pym has created cybernetic means to communicate with insects and true artificial intelligence in the form of the Ultron entity, but he is perhaps best known for his discovery of the exotic Pym Particles. Able to add or subtract mass and size from physical objects, these particles allow users to become as small as insects or grow to giant size. Over time, exposure to these particles has resulted in Pym (and ex-wife Janet Van Dyne) being able to make these size changes by themselves. In addition to changing his own size, Pym normally carries weapons, vehicles, and other equipment shrunk and safely stored about his person. He can return pieces of this technological arsenal to normal size in seconds and is rarely caught without gear handy.

Applying his great intellect to combat applications, Pym has mastered the use of his various sizes as tools in a fight, changing size at the most opportune moment to throw enemies off-balance or to hit targets from vulnerable angles.

GLOSSARY OF GAME TERMS

Act: A chunk of time involving multiple Scenes, all of it leading up to some pivotal point or moment.

Action: Rolling dice to achieve a desired outcome. Opposed by a reaction.

Action order: The order in which the characters act, determined by the situation and then by the players.

Activate an opportunity: Spending a PP or a doom die to gain a benefit from an opponent's opportunity (roll of 1 on the dice).

Attack action: An action taken to inflict stress or a complication on a target character or trait.

Affiliations: Three traits—SOLO, BUDDY, and TEAM—that embody a hero's comfort level, capability, and confidence with others or alone.

Asset: A beneficial effect die that can be added to a hero's dice pool.

Complication: A problematic effect die that is added to an opposing dice pool.

Datafile: Sheet with everything you need to know about your hero and the traits—powers, significant backgrounds, abilities, and so on—that you can use in the game.

Dice pool: A collection of dice from various traits on your hero's datafile that support or help to achieve a goal.

Distinction: A trait that represents defining backgrounds, personality traits, or catchphrases that summarize important facets of the hero's outlook and approach to life.

Doom dice: Dice in the doom pool.

Doom pool: The pool of dice the Watcher uses in place of PP to add to the heroes' opposition and activate additional threats, challenges, and situations.

Effect die: A die from your roll not included in your total, and used to create an asset, complication, or stress.

Event: A single, over-arching storyline, incorporating several Acts and many Scenes.

Experience Points (XP): Earned by hitting triggers in Milestones and used to unlock datafile updates, gain new traits and resources, or trigger interesting developments in the story.

Extraordinary success: When your action total is 5 or more points higher than your opponent's reaction total.

Framing a Scene: Establishing who is present in a Scene and where they are.

Hitting the trigger: Completing the requirements on a Milestone to get an XP award.

Limit: Restriction on a Power Set that helps the player generate PP.

Major character: Usually an antagonist of the player heroes, created using the same rules hero datafiles are created with.

Milestone: A guide to the sorts of decisions the hero should make or seek out during play.

Minor character: Usually a secondary villain or hero in the current Event, with limited datafiles.

Mob: Anywhere from two to a dozen or more individual Watcher characters that act and behave as a unit.

Opportunity: Any die that comes up a 1 in a roll.

Panel: A moment in the Scene, usually encompassing a single character's action or effort to do something.

Plot Point (PP): The currency of play; earned by investing in the story or taking risks; spent to enhance your hero's actions, activate opportunities rolled by the Watcher, and more.

Power Set: A thematic collection of super-powers, special effects (SFX), and Limits on those powers.

Power trait: A trait in a Power Set that represents a standard super-power.

Push: Adding a D6 to your dice pool.

Reaction: Rolling a dice pool in response to an action.

Recovery action: Rolling dice to attempt to recover from stress or trauma more quickly.

Resource: A stunt linked to a Specialty representing contacts, knowledge, or tools.

Scene: A period of time centered on a single conflict or situation.

Scene Distinction: Traits put on a Scene by the Watcher; they may help or hinder the heroes.

Shutdown: When you can't use a power trait or Power Set until the recovery condition is met.

Specialty: A trait that represents skills, contacts, knowledge, and training beyond the level of an average person. Each Specialty is rated at either Expert or Master.

Specialty character: Sometimes referred to as a mook, thug, or minion, very often nameless and without much more than a handful of traits.

Special effects (SFX): Personalized tricks that individualize Power Sets to suit a hero.

Step: The difference between consecutive sized dice, such as the difference between a D4 and D6. The difference between a D4 and a D8 is two steps, and so on.

Step back: Switch out a die for one with fewer sides.

Step up: Switch out a die for one with more sides.

Stress: Negative traits gained as a result of conflict; can be emotional, mental, or physical.

Stress out: When a kind of stress (emotional, mental, or physical) exceeds D12; the character can't take any actions until stress is recovered.

Stunt: A D8 push die that's thematically linked to a hero's Power Set or Specialty.

Support action: Using your action to try to help another hero, usually by creating an asset.

Total: A measure of how much effort your hero has put forward, usually the sum of two dice in your dice pool.

Traits: Powers, significant backgrounds, abilities, and so on.

Transition Scene: A Scene that represents a break in the action, when the heroes can plan, establish resources, and recover from stress and trauma.

Trauma: Persistent negative traits that result from being stressed out.

Trigger: A specific element of a Milestone that earns you XP for meeting the conditions it sets.

Watcher: Player responsible for maintaining the coherent universe around the super heroes through knowledge of the rules and the Event and by playing Watcher characters.

Watcher characters: The super villains, helpful allies, innocent bystanders, and others that inhabit the game and which are played by the Watcher.

DATAFILE INDEX

CIVIL WAR BIBLIOGRAPHY

Marvel's CIVIL WAR event touched almost every active title at the time, and has been collected in both trade paperback and hardback collections since. You can pick up the collections at your local comic book store, or read and purchase individual issues from Marvel.com. This MARVEL HEROIC ROLEPLAYING EVENT BOOK and its supplements can't possibly cover all of the individual storylines and characters from the crossover, so you may find many more ideas for Scenes, Milestones, Unlockables, and datafiles by reading the collections listed below.

KEY COMIC ISSUES

Civil War #1-7, Civil War: Front Line #1-11

TIE-IN COMIC ISSUES

Amazing Spider-Man #529-538, New Avengers: Illuminati #1, Fantastic Four #536-543, Black Panther #18 & 23-25, Blade #5, Cable & Deadpool #30-32, Captain America #22-25, Civil War: Battle Damage Report, Civil War: Choosing Sides, Civil War: The Return #1, Civil War: War Crimes #1, Civil War: X-Men #1-4, Civil War: Young Avengers & Runaways #1-4, Civil War Files, Daily Bugle: Civil War Edition, Fantastic Four #538-543, Ghost Rider #8-9, Heroes For Hire #1-3, Iron Man #13-14, Iron Man/Captain America, Moon Knight #7-9, Ms. Marvel #6-8, New Avengers #21-25, Punisher War Journal #1-3, She-Hulk #8, Thunderbolts #103-105, Winter Soldier: Winter Kills #1, Wolverine #42-48, X-Factor #8-9

COLLECTED IN TRADE PAPERBACK

Civil War: Road to Civil War *ISBN 978-0785119746* Amazing Spider-Man #529-531; Fantastic Four #536-537; New Avengers: Illuminati
Civil War *ISBN 978-0785121787* Civil War #1-7
Civil War: Black Panther *ISBN 978-0785122357* Black Panther #19-25
Civil War: Captain America *ISBN 978-0785127987* Captain America #22-24; Winter Soldier: Winter Kills
Civil War Companion *ISBN 978-0785125761* Civil War Files; Civil War: Battle Damage Report; Marvel Spotlight: Mark Millar/Steve McNiven; Marvel Spotlight: Civil War Aftermath; Daily Bugle: Civil War Special Edition
Civil War: Fantastic Four *ISBN 978-0785122272* Fantastic Four #538-543
Civil War: Frontline, Vol. 1 *ISBN 978-0785123125* Civil War: Frontline #1-6
Civil War: Frontline, Vol. 2 *ISBN 978-0785124696* Civil War: Frontline #7-11
Civil War: Heroes for Hire *ISBN 978-0785141808* Heroes for Hire #1-5
Civil War: Iron Man *ISBN 978-0785123149* Iron Man #13-14; Casualties of War; The Confession
Civil War: Marvel Universe *ISBN 978-0785124702* Choosing Sides; The Return; The Initiative; She-Hulk #8
Civil War: Ms. Marvel *ISBN 978-0785123057* Ms. Marvel #6-10; Ms. Marvel Special
Civil War: New Avengers *ISBN 978-0785124467* New Avengers #21-25
Civil War: Peter Parker, Spider-Man *ISBN 978-0785121893* Sensational Spider-Man #28-34
Civil War: Punisher War Journal *ISBN 978-0785123156* Punisher War Journal #1-4
Civil War: The Amazing Spider-Man *ISBN 978-0785122371* The Amazing Spider-Man #532-538
Civil War: Thunderbolts *ISBN 978-0785119470* Thunderbolts #101-105
Civil War: War Crimes *ISBN 978-0785126522* Civil War: War Crimes; Underworld #1-5
Civil War: Wolverine *ISBN 978-0785119807* Wolverine #42-48
Civil War: X-Men *ISBN 978-0785123132* Civil War: X-Men #1-4
Civil War: X-Men Universe *ISBN 978-0785122432* X-Factor #8-9; Cable & Deadpool #30-32
Civil War: Young Avengers & Runaways *ISBN 978-0785123170* Civil War: Young Avengers & Runaways #1-4
Civil War: Script Book *ISBN 978-0785127949* Scripts to Civil War #1-7

Collected in Hardcover

Civil War *ISBN 978-0785121787*
Civil War: Avengers *ISBN 978-0785148807*
Civil War: Fantastic Four *ISBN 978-0785148814*
Civil War: Front Line *ISBN 978-0785149491*
Civil War: Spider-Man *ISBN 978-0785148821*
Civil War: The Underside *ISBN 978-0785148838*
Civil War: X-Men *ISBN 978-0785148845*